THE
ANCIENT WORLD
An Historical Perspective

THE
ANCIENT WORLD:
An Historical Perspective
Second Edition

Henry C. Boren
University of North Carolina

Prentice-Hall, Inc., Englewood Cliffs, New Jersey 07632

Library of Congress Cataloging in Publication Data

Boren, Henry C. (Henry Charles),
    The ancient world.

    Bibliography: p.
    Includes index.
    1. Civilization, Ancient.   I. Title.
CB311.B65 1986   930   84–26404
ISBN 0-13-036450-9

Editorial/production supervisiion and
    interior design: Dee Amir Josephson
Cover design: Lundgren Graphics Ltd.
Manufacturing buyer: Barbara Kelly Kittle

Printed in the United States of America

10 9 8 7

ISBN 0-13-036450-9   01

To My Wife, Martha

CONTENTS

LIST OF CHARTS AND MAPS

CHARTS

MAPS

PREFACE

During the several years that I worked on this revision, I strove toward the following goals: To make the information presented here as accurate and up-to-date as possible; to make the text more readable; and to restructure the material so as to make the book a better tool for teaching and study.

Many changes were made in response to comments of friends (and strangers)who used the first edition, and I have had the help of professional reviewers.

The themes have been pointed up a bit (see the Introduction). Reorganization has placed the cultural discussions closer to the relevant chronological/ political narrative core. A considerable amount of new material has been added throughout; there is one entirely new chapter that takes the narrative to about 500 A.D. A small amount of material has been deleted—in particular, that dealing with the Far East in the bronze age (most respondents said they did not use these sections). The language has been made sex-neutral, and more material has been added on women in the appropriate chapters.

The charts have been improved and cast into a more readable format. There are more illustrations and new maps; moreover, some of the first edition's maps have been improved. The expanded index has more topical entries; when used with the revised and lengthened lists of books for further reading at the end of each chapter, these will help students to find additional reading on topics of interest or to get started on a research paper.

Henry C. Boren

INTRODUCTION

A. HISTORY: ITS NATURE

In one sense history is all that ever happened to mankind. In another, the term applies to the survivals of the human past, in whatever form: documents mostly, but also buildings, tools, and the like. History is in another sense a discipline which includes both the techniques for recovering and evaluating materials (again, primarily, written documents) and also the process of writing it in logical and readable form for the use of others. Finally, the word history sometimes means the finished product of the historian.

Because history (in the sense of discipline and finished product) can never be altogether scientific, and because the world changes, so that what is important in one age seems less so in another, history must constantly be rewritten. This necessity is interestingly illustrated in the case of three great historians of antiquity, of succeeding generations. When Eduard Meyer wrote the obituary of the great historian of ancient Rome, Theodor Mommsen, he said, "Many have regretted that the man whom they looked upon with deep reverence identified himself so completely with a view which to them seemed to belong to the past and no longer to provide an adequate standard for judging the present and its great tasks." When Meyer's own obituary was written years later, by Victor Ehrenberg, the same words were quoted as being equally applicable to him.[1]

[1] See Ehrenberg, *Aspects of the Ancient World* (New York, 1946), p. 231.

History also has to be rewritten, of course, because of the recovery of new materials out of the past. In a sense, because of this, ancient history is not ancient at all, but most modern. Advances have been most spectacular in the Near East, for there huge quantities of written documents have come to light, best known of which are the Dead Sea Scrolls.

B. HISTORY: ITS ROLE

"Know Thyself," the ancient Greeks wisely said. The dictum is as important for groups as for individuals. Here, of course, is the chief role of history. It does not predict the future nor does it give easy solutions for present problems. As each generation of historians tries to illuminate the past in terms of the pressing concerns of the present history is made continuously relevant, helpful to present understanding and to wise planning for the future.

Professional historians for the most part disavow any intention of producing work that can adequately serve either as a standard of judgment for the present or as a guide for the future. But they do think that those who are aware of the past are better equipped to face present and future decisions.

C. HISTORY: ITS CONCERNS

History lies in change, in process, consequently in chronology. Historians usually investigate dynamic societies, not static ones. They seek development—which may or may not be progress. Also, they emphasize those dynamics of the past which point to the present, which inspire our own traditions, culture, outlook, direction. Western civilization is still the most dynamic element in the modern world; its history therefore speaks to every educated man. The tap roots of our civilization are firmly grounded in the ancient world. Thus the study of the present should begin with antiquity.

Historians ordinarily concentrate on human institutions more than on individuals. Single persons are considered as they influence the group. This is inevitable, for the actions and policies of the group expressed through its leaders—heads of state, for example—impinge upon the lives and well-being of every person.

This volume traces the development of human institutions from the prehistoric family to the sprawling Roman Empire. In the first section, the Ancient Near East, the emphasis is often placed on early, pioneering archaeology rather than upon recent refinements. This is deliberate. The history of the recovery of the past is important in itself, and quite interesting as well. Moreover, the greatest strides, the most significant discoveries, often were the earlier ones. More recent developments have not, of course, been neglected where they suggest important revision of accepted views. Somewhat greater space is devoted to religion than in most textbooks.

Two themes, though not endlessly reiterated, help give unity to this work. These are, first, that much of human history—and prehistory—revolves about the antithetical struggle between group security and individual freedom, and secondly, that in the world of mind, religion, especially in the Hebrew tradition, and Greco-Roman rationalism are the principal strands that have controlled the nature and direction of western civilization.

The Greeks provide us the best examples of states that permitted the greatest individual freedom; however, they were often unstable and warlike: the city-state of Athens illustrates this best. The state that achieved the greatest degree of security for its members was the Roman Empire. Better than any previous state, Rome developed the institutions of government and law to establish justice for its huge population; yet Rome also tended to stifle dynamic individuals and to relegate large populations in the provinces to a secondary role in public affairs, at best.

This volume is a scant summary, the merest introduction. The author's purpose has been to produce a book that is long enough to serve as an orderly core for either a semester's or a year's study, and yet is brief enough to permit assignment of significant amounts of collateral reading. Major segments of the book deal with the Ancient Near East, Greece, and Rome. The size and organization of this volume will allow teachers to vary the emphasis of the material through omissions of sections or whole chapters and through assignment of additional readings, either from collections of source documents or from the lists of Books for Further Reading appended to each chapter.

Chart 1 Prehistory

PERIOD	AREA	PEOPLE	CULTURE
Lower Paleolithic c. 5,000,000 to c. 125,000 years ago	East Africa: Kenya, Tanzania Java, China	Australopithecus Homo erectus	Pebble tools Rough, chipped tools Family unit
Middle Paleolithic c. 125,000 to c. 35,000 years ago	Europe, North Africa, Near East	Neanderthaloids (homosapiens?)	Mousterian: flaked tools; shafted tools Ceremonial burials Use of fire
Upper Paleolithic c. 35,000 to c. 9,000 B.C.	Europe	Cro-Magnon (and other) homo sapiens	Magdalenian (and other): Cave art forms; sophisticated stone tools, bone tools (harpoons, etc.); bow and arrow, spear thrower Extended family unit
Mesolithic (transitional) c. 9,000 B.C. to c. 7,000 B.C.	Near East: sites such as Beidha and Cayönü		More sophisticated food gathering; beginnings, domestication of animals; invention of sickles; extensive use of microliths
Neolithic c. 7,000 B.C. to c. 4,000 B.C.	Near East: important sites, Zawi Chemi Shanidar, Jericho, Catal Hüyük		Production of food; domestication of animals; agriculture; ground and polished stone tools; pottery; weaving Village life; tribal organization
Chalcolithic c. 4,000 B.C. to c. 3,000 B.C.	Near East		Use of copper, primarily for ornaments; beginnings of writing; wheel used for pottery and carts Larger villages; division of labor (craftsmen)

PART I Prehistory and the Ancient Near East

1

BEFORE HISTORY

History is written primarily from documents. The age of history, therefore, must necessarily be defined as that period which follows the invention of writing and the production of documents, only some of which endure. That date—with respect to the ancient Near East and Western civilization—is about 3000 B.C. The emphasis on this date is to some degree a convention, for no documents exist for the history of most peoples even long after that date. Important civilizations must often be studied chiefly from the unwritten materials dug up by archaeologists. The date is convenient, however, for other reasons: Bronze, though it may have been invented a millennium or more before this date in Anatolia or the Balkans, began to come into general use about this time, signaling the age of metals, and in addition, the agricultural towns of Mesopotamia began developing what may properly be called the first real civilization. But some attention must first be directed to the long, long ages before this comparatively brief period that we call "history."

A. PHASES OF HUMAN DEVELOPMENT IN PREHISTORY

No character out of prehistory can come alive except through the imagination. We can know little of the aspirations, hopes, and dreams of early people. Even so, archaeologists have provided an astonishing amount of information on prehistoric ways of life. They have sifted through ancient garbage heaps and the ashes of centuries of campfires. Caves and graves have been made to yield those durable objects that endlessly endure, usually bones and tools fashioned of bone and stone. Careful study of all these objects makes it possible to detail the physical conditions of prehistoric life and something of the social conditions as well. The written accounts of these conditions tend to be either technical, almost devoid of the human warmth and color that can enliven the pages of "history," or semifictional, going far beyond what may be inferred from the facts. Historians cannot, however, permit themselves to indulge in fancy.

Classification by Stone Age Tools

It was natural for the early students of prehistory, a century or so ago, to arrange their findings through classification of surviving tools. They invented descriptive terminology: the Paleolithic or early Stone Age, the Mesolithic or middle Stone Age, and the Neolithic or new Stone Age. Paleolithic tools were made from frangible stone, mostly flint. Many Neolithic tools were fashioned by a new process, grinding and polishing. Dense stones such as granite could then be used to produce better axes and adzes, new types of tools needed for a settled life. These ages cannot be assigned specific time periods, for they describe levels of accomplishment. Thus Columbus found a Neolithic technology when he arrived in the New World, and indeed some cultures today are still Neolithic—and a few, Paleolithic, as that of the tiny group called Tasaday in the Philippines.

In some ways the old terms, *Paleolithic* and *Neolithic,* are now seen to be inadequate because the types of tools used in those periods do not accurately indicate cultural development. At the Koster archaeological site in western Illinois, for example, we have learned that the American Indians developed ground stone tools as early as 6500 B.C., several thousand years before they developed agriculture. The same discrepancy is noted at some sites in the ancient Near East, though the ground stone tools there do not precede agriculture by so many years. Evidence has shown, too, that tools such as sickles and querns for grinding grain came into use during intensive phases of food gathering rather than with the subsequent age of agriculture. Even the usefully descriptive terms, *food gathering* and *food producing,* often imply, quite improperly, a sudden transformation from one to the other. We have learned that the change was gradual and uneven. The terms *Paleolithic* and *Neolithic,* however, have become so entrenched in the language of both the specialist and the general public that it seems best to continue to use them as tags indicative of relative human development.

Classification by Human Remains

Obviously, people existed before tools. Another approach to learning about humankind before history, therefore, is to study their bones. Some anthropologists and biologists or paleontologists are primarily concerned with the physical development of humans as biological creatures. The historian, even in a survey, must give some space to their findings.

A century ago Darwin's theories of the descent of humankind produced furious opposition from religious leaders, the echoes of which are still heard. His general ideas, with modifications, are now accepted by virtually all biologists, and only a few religious leaders see them as a threat to religion; most believe that nothing in the factual basis of the theory of evolution rules it out as an instrument of divine creation. One might note, similarly, that although historians are necessarily preoccupied with human causation—the motives and actions of individuals—it does not mean that all historians would eliminate the possibility of divine intervention in history. This is not the kind of thing on which historians attempt to make a final judgment.

Human remains before history may be classified in terms of cultures. A culture in this sense means the total way of life of a particular group of people as shown by the things they made and the ways in which they made them, the ways in which they gathered or produced their food, buried their dead, and so on. A culture is usually named after the site where it is first identified. When a culture becomes complex and involves protourban centers, writing, and specialized craftspeople, we call it a civilization.

New scientific techniques have aided greatly in establishing dates in the prehistoric as well as historic periods. The geologist dates the rocks of the earth's surface by determining what percentage of the uranium in some of them has turned to lead. Bones and other organic objects can also be dated by various methods because they too involve the gradual decay of one element as it is transformed into another. Most useful in this analysis is the carbon 14 method, despite recent discoveries that demonstrate previously unsuspected variables. Every organic or living thing absorbs this radioactive isotope, which begins to deteriorate at a regular rate on the death of the organism. A careful measurement by a skilled technician of an uncontaminated sample of, say, bone, leather, or charcoal can yield a fairly reliable date within a relatively narrow range. Since the half-life of carbon 14 is a bit over 5,700 years, it is most useful over a range of about 25,000 years. Scientists are developing a new C-14 system, however, in which they count the C-14 atoms instead of the beta rays of decaying atoms; much smaller samples can be used, and it is hoped that the new system will be more accurate and useful over a wider range, perhaps 100,000 years. A potassium-argon technique has been used to date several lava deposits in East Africa in which some of the most significant and oldest fossil remains of hominids—humanlike creatures—have been found. A recently developed technique, involving measurement of *thermoluminescence*, permits the dating, within limits, of ceramic objects. Thermoluminescence is an atomic "glow" that takes place when the object is heated, as displaced atomic particles move back into a regular pattern. Obviously, this process is useless for any period before the invention of pottery. However, within the period of history—at least in connection with major civilizations—the ordinary, comparative methods used by historians are usually more precise and accurate for determining dates.

B. PALEOLITHIC MAN

Early Human Remains

Bones such as those discovered in Java in 1890 and again in 1937 to 1940 (Java man, *Pithecanthropus erectus*) and in the 1920s, 1930s, and again since the 1960s near Peking (Peking man, *Sinanthropus erectus*) and dated to about 500,000 years ago were once thought to be those of the earliest "man" (*Homo erectus*). But subsequent discoveries, especially by the late L. S. B. Leakey and his wife, Mary, at Olduvai Gorge in Tanzania and more recently by their son, Richard, and others in Kenya, have forced revisions of older views. Homo erectus may date back one million years. And creatures approaching the biological features of modern humankind are now thought to have lived millions of years ago.

The Leakeys found remains of a type of *Australopithecus* (southern ape-man; they called it *Zinjanthropus*) among lava deposits that date back nearly two million years. This hominid may have used pebble tools. Richard Leakey in 1972 found a skull of a relatively advanced type in Kenya, along with hundreds of stone tools, which he dates to nearly three million years ago. And a Harvard expedition to Kenya in 1971 reported bone fragments of a hominid dated to five and a half million years ago. It now seems apparent that several different types of hominids lived contemporaneously in that East African region, some of which have simply disappeared in a biological dead end.

New discoveries often raise more problems than they solve. Scholars who have studied this sparse but significant new material from East Africa do not agree on what it all means. Moreover, remains of many other types of early hominids have been unearthed all over the world. Even an anthropology textbook could do no more than outline the major finds and the work done in connection with them. Our sketch is intended merely to provide some perspective.

A rather widespread type of early human who lived chiefly in Europe and adjacent areas during the middle Paleolithic age (from about 125,000 to 35,000 years ago) is called *Neanderthal*, after the valley in Germany where the remains were first identified. Neanderthal bones have been discovered not only in Europe but also in the entire Mediterranean area and as far east as Iran. Neanderthaloid types ranged still farther. The disappearance of the Neanderthalers at the beginning of the Upper Paleolithic age, about 35,000 years ago, is something of a mystery. In Asia it appears that they may have interbred with other types, but in Europe it seems more likely that they were annihilated by more advanced humans such as the Cro-Magnon, who flourished in the Upper Paleolithic. The Cro-Magnon, named after a rock shelter in France where the skeletal remains were first discovered, or more likely some earlier relative, was perhaps the first true *Homo sapiens*, though some so describe the Neanderthalers. The latter were short and heavy. Their skulls had a capacity at least as large as ours, with heavy browridges and sloping foreheads. Cro-Magnon people had high foreheads and were taller.

Life in the Paleolithic Age

Paleolithic people were predators and scavengers; they survived, doggedly, by their wits and skill in the use of simple weapons and tools. Food gatherers, they were extraordinarily dependent on the environment for the nature and quality of what they ate and how they dressed. If the herds they hunted migrated, they had to move with them; if crustaceans and fish were scarce at a seaside habitation, they changed location and perhaps eating habits as well.

The search for security in Paleolithic times was, then, primarily the struggle for food and for protection from the elements. The savagery of the age has been overemphasized, but the people did struggle with beasts and perhaps with each other. To survive, Paleolithic humans had to spend most of their time hunting and fishing, manufacturing weapons, and preparing skins for clothing. The social unit was the extended family, not a large community, for no environment could support a dense population of food gatherers. Many a modern city has more inhabitants than the entire globe supported in the Paleolithic age.

Much, if not most, of our information about Paleolithic people has come from caves, primarily because other habitation sites have disappeared. Evidence has survived, in other words, only in protected places. It should be assumed that Paleolithic people learned to construct rude shelters and then huts, perhaps partially buried in the ground for warmth, in the manner common in later ages. They learned to use fire, a most important achievement, probably, of the Lower Paleolithic, though means of kindling it may not have been invented until the Upper Paleolithic.

Paleolithic Tools

In the Lower Paleolithic era tools were quite simple. The earliest of these now known, found in an East African gully in 1977, are believed by the excavators to be two and a half million years old. A very early tool was the crude hand axe, formed from a pebble that had only to be chipped on one side to make a useful implement. Scrapers and borers, needed to prepare skins for human use, also were devised rather early. For thousands of years, however, only a few new tools and new methods of manufacture were developed. Then came hafted tools, a brilliant accomplishment, and the invention of the spear, which greatly eased the task of the hunter. Meanwhile, skilled toolmakers devised new ways of flaking and chipping stone and some of them became real artists. Delicately chipped knives, axes, and spearheads became things of beauty to be treasured.

In the Upper Paleolithic age (from about 35,000 to 9000 B.C. in Europe) people invented important new tools and weapons. The spearthrower had greater

Examples of early stone tools. Core tools on the left, flake tools on the right. (Courtesy, American Museum of Natural History)

range and penetrative ability, though probably at the expense of accuracy. The bow and arrow was perhaps the first tool with the capacity to store up energy for sudden release, and it greatly increased the productivity of the hunter. A similar device was soon used for making fire and for boring or drilling holes, the bowstring looped around a straight stick. Fishermen now fashioned bone harpoons and, eventually, fishhooks. Bone needles were invented as well as bone whistles, which were probably used to control hunting parties.

Paleolithic Cultures: Mousterian, Magdalenian

A typical culture of the middle Paleolithic age was the Mousterian, named after the site where it was first found, Le Moustier in France, and associated with the Neanderthal people. Remains have been found over a remarkable range, extending from western Europe and North Africa to central Asia. Mousterian tools were of several types, mostly made from rather thick flakes; some points seem to have been used for spears, and other tools also may have been hafted. The family seems already to have been a strong unit; graves were carefully prepared and there are indications of funeral feasts. One individual found in the Shanidar cave in the Kurdish region of Iraq, though born with a withered arm, lived to be about forty years old. His relatives must have helped him during his whole, rather long, life. The burials indicate not only care for the dead but also belief in life beyond death; food and sometimes other objects were interred along with the corpse. Possibly the Neanderthalers only thought that the individuals might revive and need their possessions. However, more complex beliefs are implied by a variety of other finds, such as the use of red ocher paint on the bodies in France and the enclosure of the body of a child by a ring of horns at a site in Soviet Uzbekistan. A burial at Shanidar included a bouquet of flowers, judging by pollen analysis.

The best-known culture of the Upper Paleolithic age is the Magdalenian, associated with Cro-Magnons. The major new tools of the period have already been mentioned. The Magdalenians made particular use of reindeer bone, which was plentiful for these hunting groups. Their society was somewhat more complex than that of the previous ages, most likely because the newer weapons, including the harpoon, spear thrower, and bow and arrow, made possible a somewhat denser population. The clan organization typical in later ages probably developed in this culture, and society may have been matrilineal, with descent reckoned through the female line.

Ice Age Art

The most startling and impressive development of Cro-Magnon and other Upper Paleolithic types in southwestern Europe was in art, samples of which were discovered only in the last century. When a Spanish nobleman, Don Marcelino de Sautuola, accidentally discovered realistic, perfectly preserved paintings of long extinct animals in a cave on his property at Altamira, his announcement was ridiculed even by scholars. But later discoveries by archaeological expeditions excavating caves blocked for centuries by debris proved the astonishing truth: These Ice Age people could paint. The style developed over thousands of years, through crude beginnings to fine realism and a sort of impressionism. Various techniques and methods were used, including finger painting, "crayons," and blowing powdered pigments onto a fat-covered surface. Preliminary sketches were sometimes made. Engraved and half-relief figures have also been found in the cave rock.

Much of the painting was hidden, with some difficulty, in remote recesses of caves. It appears, therefore, that its purpose was magical: to assist hunters in finding game. Pregnant animals occasionally appear, and one fertility scene portrays human beings. These paintings were probably intended to assure plentiful game and to make women fertile. Nonetheless, some of the work was surely done for pleasure alone—art for art's sake.

Small statuettes from this period, often of pregnant women or of phallic symbols, were also found in the late nineteenth century. Again, the intention was probably magical—or perhaps it should be called "religious." For here we may have the earliest evidence for worship of a great mother goddess, so familiar in later human history.

Magdalenian culture disappeared with the end of the last Ice Age, about 10,000 years ago. It is difficult to account for the decline and disappearance of this rather highly developed culture. One is tempted to speculate that a much greater use of shelters outside of caves—houses of poles covered with skins are known to have existed in the Upper Paleolithic age—may simply have caused what is really just a gap in our evidence. But this hypothesis cannot be a complete explanation.

Bison, prehistoric cave drawing, Altamira, Spain. (Les Editions Braun et Cie, Paris)

Paleolithic People in the Western Hemisphere

Homo sapiens made an entry into America during the Upper Paleolithic age, crossing over the land bridge that then existed at what is now the Bering Strait. Certain animals—mammoths, elephants, bison—went along at the same time, during one of the thaws of the last Ice Age (called the Wisconsin in America), it has usually been thought. Eskimos seem to have taken the same route at a somewhat later time.

Spear points have been found among the bones of mammoths and elephants at several sites in the southwest and Great Plains regions of the United States, graphic evidence that these early people were efficient big-game hunters. Charcoal from one occupation site in southern California has been dated back as much as 100,000 years, and other occupation sites have been attributed to even earlier times, though most scholars are skeptical of such early dates.

The fine spear points, the Sandia, Clovis, and Folsom among others, usually considered to be 10,000 to 12,000 years old, indicate a culture comparable with that of contemporary western Europe, though they have some distinctive features. Clovis and Folsom points, for example, are fluted for better hafting and more effective penetration. At a site in Utah dated to the end of the Paleolithic or the beginning of the Mesolithic age, there is evidence of the art of basket weaving— earlier than anywhere else known. The question of the development of agriculture in the Western Hemisphere is much argued. It probably evolved independently of the Old World cultures—and much later.

The Mesolithic: Transition Toward Food Production

The term *Mesolithic* describes a period that saw the transition from the food-gathering Paleolithic to the food-producing Neolithic. In response to changing environment in some areas (as in a period of desiccation such as that which occurred in the Near East after about 10,000 B.C.) or to pressures of increasing population, people developed more intensive food-gathering practices that led, eventually, to the domestication of animals and plants. The development was gradual; thus, for example, "herding"—exercise of some control over and protection of wild herds or flocks—was a learning stage that slowly led to domestication.

The dating of the first domestication of animals is continually being revised. The dog (or wolf), it now seems definite, was domesticated even in the Upper Paleolithic age. The information comes from several places, including a Magdalenian site in France and another location in Utah. A Massachusetts anthropologist claims a date of about 13,000 B.C. for domesticated cattle in East Africa. The earliest solid evidence for domestication of animals other than the dog has been uncovered at Zawi Chemi Shanidar and the Shanidar cave (the same one where Neanderthal bones and Mousterian materials of an earlier period were found) in northern Iraq. Sheep seem to have been domesticated there by about 9000 B.C., according to C-14 dates.

Intermediate steps, varying from place to place, also mark the progress toward true agriculture. A combination of local invention and dissemination from advanced areas—probably more of concepts than of exactly repeated techniques— brought a slow and uneven movement involving an intensified use of plants and their seeds as the primary means of subsistence, practices that laid the basis for a fully agricultural economy. The new practices were often entered upon reluctantly, out of necessity, for people had to work harder for the larger and surer return, and they lost a degree of freedom.

It may well have been the women, whose husbands, the great hunters, were not doing so well of late, who mostly learned to protect the best stands of wild grains, to improve the crop through weeding and eventually through digging and then seeding. The earliest dating for the domestication of cereals also is often revised. A site recently excavated in southern Egypt yielded some barley grains that may have been domesticated; the date claimed by the excavators is 15,000 B.C. The usual date in the Near East is about 8000 B.C.

Some tools associated with agriculture and once thought to belong to the Neolithic era were in fact developed in this transitional time. Some genius invented the sickle, for example, using small chips of sharp-edged flint or obsidian set in a split stick or a bone. The weighted digging stick, precursor of the hoe, was invented, along with tools for preparing grain, especially the saddle quern on which grain was ground by rubbing with a hand-shaped stone.

Several small villages of the Near East that existed during this period of mesolithic transition have been carefully excavated. Among these are Beidha in southern Jordan and Cayönü in Turkey. Set in an area that is now desert, Beidha some 10,000 years ago was surrounded by forests of oak, juniper, and pistachio. The one hundred or so persons who then lived there built houses that were mostly round and partially dug into the ground. They hunted, of course, but they knew how to grind stone to make querns and mortars for preparing the wild barley that they harvested in quantity. By 7000 B.C. or soon after, they probably had domesticated this barley. Among their various bone and chipped tools of stone were some made of obsidian, which was imported all the way from Anatolia several hundred miles to the north.

Cayönü was located in southern Anatolia near the Taurus mountains and may have been a bit larger than Beidha. Its inhabitants also hunted and gathered wild wheat and legumes. One building had a ground stone, terrazzolike floor. These people of Cayönü not only had bone and obsidian tools but also made some use of copper, hammered to form pins and beads. It is curious that these copper objects appear in the early but not the later levels of the village. By the end of the Mesolithic era they had domesticated sheep, goats, and pigs, as well as some plants.

C. A QUICKENING PACE: THE NEOLITHIC "REVOLUTION"

Only twice in human history has a series of technological advances triggered a transformation in human affairs so massive as to deserve to be called revolution: The first was the food-producing transformation of the Neolithic era; the second was the Industrial Revolution of the last two or three centuries. Food production, especially agriculture but also domestication of animals, enabled people at least in greater measure to control their environment. Its impact on human affairs still continues through improvement in methods and in varieties of plants, and since the Industrial Revolution, through the use of fossil fuels in mechanization of agricultural production.

Some may well question the use of the term *revolution* to describe a process that stretched over a couple of thousand years in its formative stages and in a real sense still continues. Yet if *revolution* means drastic and significant change, the introduction of agriculture certainly qualifies; moreover, as compared with the Paleolithic years preceding, the Neolithic period brought about a tremendous acceleration in the rate of change in the lifestyles of the peoples of the earth. Controlling the environment in order to increase food production made humans—in contrast to those in earlier ages—creators of wealth in storable forms. Although the exploitation of animals and the land had—and continues to have—its unlovely aspects, it was this concept that impelled people to seek a continually increasing excess production, which meant an accumulation of wealth and all that derived from it.

Food production made possible a denser, more settled population; it led to the division of labor and specialized craftspeople; it structured society into classes, including an upper class that could support art, architecture, and literature; in its wake came urbanization and new governmental and legal forms. In our own times we are acutely aware that not all the changes have been good: Much greater upper-class domination of the lower classes (and areas) became possible; land was exposed to erosion or to creeping sterility through overcropping or salinization—as in ancient Mesopotamia and the Indus River Valley—because of inadequate irrigation and drainage; and many species of animals and birds were either drastically reduced or actually made extinct.

The production of food by means of flocks and herds does not demand an altogether settled existence; Neolithic shepherds in the Near East were forced to move from one area to another as the seasons changed or as forage was consumed. Such shepherds were not rootless nomads, however; they moved about within certain areas and built wells and cisterns, which they jealously guarded. They usually lived in tents, suited to their roving existence, and thus could migrate with relative ease when necessary. Neolithic farmers, on the other hand, had to stay in one place for at least a season, preferably longer, and they needed homes near their fields so they could protect their crops from animals and thieves. Storage space for the crops and some facilities to care for a few domestic animals also had to be provided.

It will never be possible to identify with certainty the area where agriculture first began. Interestingly, the suggestion has been made that the development occurred at somewhat different times in four separate places, by peoples of four different racial groups and involving mostly different plant species. The four groups are the Caucasoid peoples in the Near East (primitive wheats and barley, mostly), the Mongoloid peoples in Southeast Asia (various cereal grasses), the Negroid peoples of western Africa (mostly the millets, yams, sorghum), and the Indian peoples of middle America (squashes and maize). Probably the real situation was more complex, and other areas, as in East and Northeast Africa and in Europe, may have seen similar development.

Wherever agriculture may first have been practiced, it is certain that the best evidence now available for the earliest agricultural towns of considerable size is from the ancient Near East. Zawi Chemi Shanidar, already mentioned as a site for evidence of the early domestication of sheep, developed agriculture quite early also and was probably a small Neolithic town in the fullest sense by perhaps 8000 B.C.

Jericho, just above the Dead Sea in Palestine, is one of the oldest known agricultural villages. Carbon 14 dates confirm that an agricultural community existed there by about 8000 B.C. also. It was for this site that archaeologist Kathleen Kenyon coined the term "pre-pottery Neolithic" to describe the period before the invention of pottery. By about 7000 B.C., the town encompassed several acres and was surrounded by a stone wall several feet thick, with a large tower. Houses were made of sun-dried brick with compacted clay floors and domed roofs not unlike some still seen in the region. Agriculture was possible only through irrigation from the large spring that still gives life to the spot. One may infer a certain level, not only of technical accomplishment, but also of complex social and political institutions. Evidence of religious practices include cult statues, some apparently of a mother goddess, with small shrines. Perhaps the people worshiped ancestors: Skulls of the dead were sometimes plastered (as in other contemporary sites) and fitted with artificial eyes to make them into something like portrait busts.

Not as old as Jericho but astonishing for its size and notable for its contributions to knowledge is Catal Hüyük on the southern Anatolian plateau in Turkey. At its height, this town covered about thirty-two acres and contained about a thousand homes for its several thousand inhabitants. Archaeologists have identified a dozen or more products of cultivation, including three types of wheat plus fruit and nuts. More than fifty types of tools were used, some made of imported stone. Excellent pottery was produced by 5900 B.C., and the inhabitants wove several kinds of fibers into cloth. As for art and religion at this exceptional site, not only statuettes but also wall paintings have been found. Catal Hüyük was continuously inhabited from about 6700 B.C. to about 5700 B.C., after which it mysteriously declined, though a village across the river continued to exist for some centuries. The reasons for the town's decline and fall are unexplained.

Though it had a large population, Catal Hüyük is not called a city, for it lacked the complex governmental and social structures that characterize an urban community. Still, such towns necessarily brought with them massive changes. Before the Neolithic era, even in the permanently settled villages, most close relationships were within a kinship pattern: The family, the extended family, or perhaps the clan provided the framework within which rules and relationships were governed. In the larger villages, however, groups with no such ties of kinship had to learn how to relate to each other; that is, people had to develop new structures that could accommodate such diverse groups. The egalitarianism of the simpler society of an earlier age began to break down; leaders became both wealthier and more powerful as new class structures emerged. Specialization in pottery, in toolmaking, or in trade produced a division of labor. The village's pastures and woodlots might be used in common, but tilled plots and one-family houses brought with them new concepts of private property, creating problems that had to be worked out. The process would eventually lead to systems of law. Architecture naturally evolved also, as people devised suitable housing near the land they cultivated. Although it is possible—even usual—for agricultural villages to stagnate, changing little for hundreds of years, it is nevertheless clear that at the beginning they brought dynamic change.

The most profitable land, Neolithic people learned, was in the river valleys; in the flood plains of the Near East, only minimal crops could be raised without irrigation. But to irrigate the rich alluvial soil was no simple task. It was not enough for one man to dip water out of the river for his own tiny crop; communal irrigation systems had to be devised, canals built and maintained. To collect consistent supplies of water, reservoirs were constructed. Natural lagoons formed at high water were probably dammed to create the first such reservoirs. Such irrigation complexes fostered the growth of villages into towns and ultimately, in the Bronze age, into cities.

Technological advances largely determined the physical conditions of human existence in the Neolithic age. Denser populations required greater cooperative action. People were forced to find new ways still of living together with some degree of security. One notable new construction technique was the use of sundried bricks, which made possible better homes and public buildings, and after a few centuries, town walls as well.

Invention of Pottery and Weaving

Early Neolithic people learned to make pottery from clay. Metals were mostly unknown, so the development of pottery was vastly important for storage and cookery. Another achievement was the making of thread from animal and vegetable fibers and the weaving of thread into cloth. Weaving and pottery manufacture were both the result of long processes of experimentation that we can scarcely appreciate.

The invention of pottery has proved to be the greatest possible boon to the archaeologist. A pot was easily broken, of course, and scarcely ever mended, but the discarded sherds are virtually indestructible. Careful study of developmental sequences in the techniques and styles employed in the manufacture of pottery has made it possible for archaeologists to date sites and strata quite accurately, within relatively narrow limits, by potsherds alone. Different methods in manufacture, different sizes and types, changing decorative patterns—incised or painted—and the composition of the clay itself, all have their story to tell. Occasionally, to the delight of the excavators, sherds are found inscribed with the name of a maker or client or with correspondence, written in ink. These *ostraka* (the Greek word for potsherds is used in this restricted sense by archaeologists) have preserved written documents that would have decayed centuries ago had they been written on paper.

Division of Labor: The Craftsperson

The developing crafts (tool making, pottery making, weaving, and a host of others) soon produced craftspersons—specialists in one or another of these manufactures. In the Paleolithic age there may have been craftspersons who worked full-time making flint tools, but artisans as a class arrived only in the late Neolithic age. They fashioned finer tools than most individuals could, and in turn, through barter, obtained more food and other necessary things than they themselves could have grown or made.

The end of the Neolithic age saw the invention of writing and the wheel. This period, in the Near East about 4000 to 3000 B.C., is sometimes called the *Chalcolithic* (copper-stone) age because copper came into general use, first as decorative beads, and later, when it was learned that hammering hardened and compacted the metal, for somewhat satisfactory tools. The wheel was used initially in making pottery, perhaps, but was soon adapted to crude transport. Sailing vessels now plied the rivers, aiding the development of extensive trade. In Mesopotamia, where the soil was rich, raw materials—even stone—had to be brought from a distance.

Most important, at the end of the age, systems of writing slowly evolved from pictures and then pictographs and logographs (symbols for words). Writing allowed efficiency in the expanding world of business and trade; more important, the accumulation of knowledge in reliable and systematic form—which continues in the present at an accelerating rate—could now begin.

D. BRONZE AGE CIVILIZATIONS

Civilization: Social and Political Change

Civilization may be described as a complex, literate, urban-centered culture. When a town became something more than the focal point of an agricultural operation, it became a city, a political and social center, with a population more diversified than that of an agricultural village. These Bronze Age cities contained craftspeople, administrators, and priests. In some cities there were full-time warriors; in others, there were also merchants and traders. The surplus food produced by the cities' adjacent irrigated land allowed their upper classes to enjoy leisure time; they could engage in cultural pursuits or patronize artists and writers.

Bronze Age cities required new social structures. The old relationships based on kinship that had endured through the Paleolithic age, and with modifications through the Neolithic age as well, gave way to new structures based on occupation and position. Kinship was still a factor, but its importance receded. Artisans such as potters, builders, and weavers formed guilds of sorts. Administrators, priests, and warriors also joined forces to support common goals; together, they tended to form an upper class or nobility. Below them were free persons, whether artisans, farmers, or traders, and still lower, serfs and slaves.

In a primitive world, the natural variation in individual abilities may have meant the difference between the great hunter and the poor one, the warrior-leader and the second-rate follower. But when technology extends the power and potential of certain people who can use it, the inevitable result is that individual differences will be accentuated. If the whole group does not somehow prevent it, the relative distance between the rich and the poor, the strong and the weak, will become greater. In the modern world, of course, this tendency is even more pronounced, though modern governments do intervene massively to rectify the balance.

The various groups within the growing new cities of the Bronze Age, and the competition among cities, created conditions that demanded new political institutions. The new class structure and the new political structure developed simultaneously. The most crucial single factor to cause political change was probably warfare, for it was necessary to protect both the irrigation system and the increasing wealth within the city's walls. There were also, to be sure, wars of expansion, which no political leader of the ancient world ever thought it necessary to justify. Successful warfare in all ages necessitates the efficient organization of both manpower and resources and an unambiguous command structure as well. The wars between emergent Bronze Age cities certainly helped to produce the characteristic political unit that then evolved: the city-state.

The City-State

The city-state embraced an area no larger than an average county in one of the United States. The city was the center—political, economic, and religious. The leader of the city-state was often the leader of the army. Whatever his title, he was a sort of warrior-king, and sometimes the chief priest as well. And whatever his actions, he and his people recognized that the outcome of their struggle to protect themselves from neighbors or outlanders was in the hands of the gods. The priest, who could propitiate the gods and interpret their will, thus ranked as a very important person. Not surprisingly, the priests, who administered the property of the gods, were often wealthy.

The emphasis in religion long before the Bronze Age had shifted from Paleolithic magic and the worship of a great mother to a Neolithic worship of a great sky-father god and earth-mother goddess, to correspond with the rise of agriculture. Numberless local deities also entered the pantheon, but gods playing the role of great mother remained important, as religion tends to combine new and old. In the Bronze Age the focus of worship was on a patron deity of the city. Growing observation of the heavens also meant that celestial deities were stressed, sometimes in abstract, conceptual terms. In Babylon, for example, Shamash, the sun god, came to be also the god of law or justice; in Egypt a similar role was attributed to Horus and a daughter of Re, both also associated with the sun.

Riverine Civilizations

Civilizations arose in the great river valleys for reasons, as we have seen, that were economic. All civilizations must have an economic basis. It has also always been true that only when agriculture produces a surplus, so that not all people have to work at food production, can some be free to work at tasks that enrich human existence. In the modern world, mineral wealth and industrial production are vital—though an agricultural surplus is still absolutely basic to progress in other spheres. In the Bronze Age, metals began to form a new source of wealth, but throughout the ancient period, even in the Iron Age, good land was fundamental.

The earliest civilization probably arose in the great river valley formed by the Tigris and Euphrates, in an area called by the Greeks *Mesopotamia*—"between the rivers." Almost as early was the civilization of the great Nile valley. Not much later came those civilizations developed in the Indus River valley to the east, in the valleys of the Yellow and Yangtze Rivers in China, as well as in others bordering Mesopotamia on the east and south. Southeast Asia also produced early civilization, though some of the reported dates are suspect and continual disorders in recent years have made careful archaeological exploration all but impossible.

Aerial photograph taken from a Gemini space capsule shows the area from eastern Egypt to the Persian Gulf (extreme upper right corner). (National Aeronautics and Space Administration)

In the next chapters we shall consider those civilizations that are distinctly in the Western tradition.

BOOKS FOR FURTHER READING

BURKITT, M. *The Old Stone Age,* New York, 1963.

BURNEY, C. *The Ancient Near East,* Ithaca, N.Y., 1977.

CHILDE, V. *What Happened in History,* Baltimore, 1954.

CLARK, G. *World History in New Perspective,* 3rd. ed., Cambridge, 1977.

COHEN, M. N. *The Food Crisis in Prehistory: Overpopulation and the Origins of Agriculture,* New Haven, 1977.

DEETZ, J. *Invitation to Archaeology,* New York, 1967.

GABEL, C. *Man Before History,* Englewood Cliffs, N.J., 1964.

HAWKES, J. and L. WOOLLEY. *Prehistory and the Beginnings of Civilization,* New York, 1963.

LEAKEY, L. *Adam's Ancestors: The Evolution of Man and His Culture,* New York, 1960.

LEAKEY, R. *The Making of Mankind,* London, 1981.

MELLAART, J. *Catal Hüyük,* New York, 1967.

MELLAART, J. *The Neolithic of the Near East,* New York, 1975.

REDMAN, C. *The Rise of Civilization,* San Francisco, 1978.

VLAKOS, O. *New World Beginnings,* New York, 1970.

Chart 2 Period of Early History, 3000–300 B.C.

	MESOPOTAMIA	EGYPT	OTHER AREAS
Early Bronze Age c. 3000 B.C. to c. 2100 B.C.	Protoliterate, predynastic age. Growth of cities. Early dynastic age. Gilgamesh king of Uruk. Sargon's empire.	Archaic period. Thinite period (unification): First and Second Dynasties. Old Kingdom, pyramids; Third and Fourth Dynasties.	Rise of civilization in Aegean, Indus areas, probably in China. Syrian cities important, especially Ebla.
Middle Bronze Age c. 2100 B.C. to c. 1600 B.C.	Third Dynasty of Ur; Ur-Nammu, first known law code. Kingdoms of Babylon (Hammurabi), Mari, Assyria.	First Intermediate period; Seventh through Eleventh Dynasties. Middle Kingdom; Twelfth Dynasty. Second Intermediate period: Thirteenth through Seventeenth Dynasties. Hyksos. Expulsion of Hyksos.	Height of Knossos, other Aegean centers. Shang Dynasty, China. Mycenaean Age. Decline of Knossos, other Cretan sites. Hittite Old Kingdom.
Late Bronze Age c. 1600 B.C. to c. 1200 B.C.	Kassites. Assyria strong.	Empire; Eighteenth through Twentieth Dynasties. Hatshepsut. Thutmoses III. Akhnaton. Ramses II.	Destruction of Indus civilization. Kingdom of Mitanni. Hittite Empire. Suppiluliumas. Israelite entry into Palestine.
Iron Age 1200 B.C. 1000 B.C.		Ramses III repels invasion of the Sea peoples. End of Egyptian Empire. Twenty-first Dynasty. Twenty-second Dynasty.	Sea peoples destroy Hittite Empire, cities of Syria, Byblos, and so forth. Period of Judges in Israel, then Kingdom. Phoenician cities flourish. Kings Saul, David, Solomon, then Divided Monarchy: Israel, Judah.
900 B.C.	Assyrian Empire expands under Shalmaneser III.		Ahab King of Israel; Jezebel.
800 B.C.	Tiglath-pileser III. Shalmaneser V.	Twenty-third Dynasty. Twenty-fourth Dynasty. Twenty-fifth Dynasty.	Phoenicians colonize Carthage, other sites. Fall of Kingdom of Israel to Assyria; Judah subjected.

700 B.C.	Sargon II. Sennacherib. Assurbanipal.	Twenty-sixth Dynasty. Necho II.	Phoenicians sent by Egyptian king Necho around Africa. Rise of Empire of Medes and Persians. Destruction of Jerusalem; Babylonian captivity.
600 B.C.	Fall of Assyria; Neo-Babylonian or Chaldean Empire. Nebuchadnezzar, Nabonidus.		

PERSIAN EMPIRE

	Fall of Babylon to Persia under Cyrus.	Twenty-seventh Dynasty, Persian, established by Cambyses.	Asia Minor conquered by Cyrus. First Jewish exiles permitted to return. Thrace taken by Persia; Scythians repel Persians.
500 B.C.	Darius III, the Great. Xerxes I.		Greeks defeat Persians at Marathon. Greeks defeat Persians at Salamis, Plataea. Athenians lead Greeks, establish empire. Peloponnesian War; victory of Sparta, allies.
	Artaxerxes I, Darius II. Artaxerxes II.	Egyptians encouraged by Athens to revolt against Persia.	March of the 10,000 against Persia. Persia involved in Greek wars.
400 B.C.	Artaxerxes III. Darius III, defeated by Alexander.		
330 B.C.	Alexander the Great destroys the Persian Empire.		

2

THE ANCIENT NEAR EAST
IN THE BRONZE AGE

Whole millennia of ancient Near Eastern history are now known that were never dreamed of little more than a century ago. To a Judeo-Christian world predisposed to great interest in the area because of its biblical associations, some of the discoveries of archaeologists have at times taken on an aura of romance. In December 1872 George Smith of the British Museum reported to the British Society of Biblical Archaeology that among the museum's clay tablets excavated decades before at Nineveh, he had found a Chaldean account of the Flood. At the expense of a London newspaper and with considerable fanfare, Smith made an expedition to Nineveh on the Tigris in modern Iraq to seek a missing fragment from one of the tablets. Astonishingly, he quickly found it. The tablet was part of the Gilgamesh epic, discussed later in this chapter.

Earlier excavators had offered notice that extraordinary discoveries in the Mesopotamian region could be made. Austen Henry Layard, a British diplomat-scholar, had found the remarkable library of Assurbanipal; the publication in 1852 of his fascinating account of the Nineveh excavation had been widely read. Other extensive if superficial excavations had also yielded significant materials. Another British scholar-soldier-diplomat of the period was Henry (later Sir Henry) Rawlinson. Using the trilingual inscription of King Darius the Great of Persia that had been carved on a rocky bluff near Behistun on the fringe of northern Mesopotamia, Rawlinson did much to decipher cuneiform writing; he published his work in 1847—and the study of "Assyriology" was well under way. More, and more careful, excavations of the great "tells"—flat-topped eminences that contain, in layer upon layer, the remains of ancient cities—have produced information about a far earlier civilization than that of the Assyrians so well known from the Bible.

A. CITY-STATES OF THE TIGRIS-EUPHRATES BASIN

An amazing amount of early history was made in the Asian Near East within the bounds of a region called "the Fertile Crescent." This semicircular band of land stretches from Palestine and Syria on the west up, over, and down through Mesopotamia on the east. (Syria should not be confused with Assyria, located farther to the east on the upper Tigris River.) It is bounded by the Mediterranean Sea on the west, by the mountains of eastern Anatolia and Armenia on the north, and by the Zagros Mountains on the east. Within the crescent's two horns and to the south lies the Arabian Desert. There are many easy avenues of access into the Fertile Crescent, and throughout history immigrants and invaders on occasion have swarmed into the region. The earliest true civilization, it seems, developed in the eastern horn of the crescent—above the Persian Gulf in lower Mesopotamia.

Mesopotamia: Climate, Geography

Mesopotamia is the rather large area between and along the two great rivers of the Near East, the Euphrates and the Tigris. Both arise in the Armenian mountains to the north, and at one point near their sources they are rather close together. The Tigris flows mostly south; the Euphrates swings west, then south and southeast. In far antiquity they debouched separately into the Persian Gulf, but today they join together a few miles north of the gulf.

Lower Mesopotamia is conventionally subdivided into two parts: Sumer and Akkad. Sumer, the lower section, was unsuitable for permanent settlement until a few centuries before 4000 B.C. because it was until then a marsh. A long-held view that the waters of the Persian Gulf once extended far north of the present coastline has been challenged by geologists. Perhaps the Euphrates formed a lagoon near the city of Ur that connected with the gulf. The rivers have built up the land during their characteristic annual flooding, but the basin has subsided as the soil accumulated. The soil is thus alluvial and quite deep.

The climate of Mesopotamia is hot and humid, and because the winter rains are not substantial, only the most primitive agriculture is possible without irrigation. The Tigris and Euphrates often overflow in spring, from rains and melting snows to the north. These floods are irregular and can be terrifyingly destructive, as is known from both modern and ancient experience. They also gave rise to the story of the Flood in the book of Genesis and in earlier Semitic and Sumerian accounts as well. Successful irrigation on any scale has always required careful organization.

The land was rich, though under intensive irrigation it tended to become gradually less productive through salinization. The staple crop, barley, however,

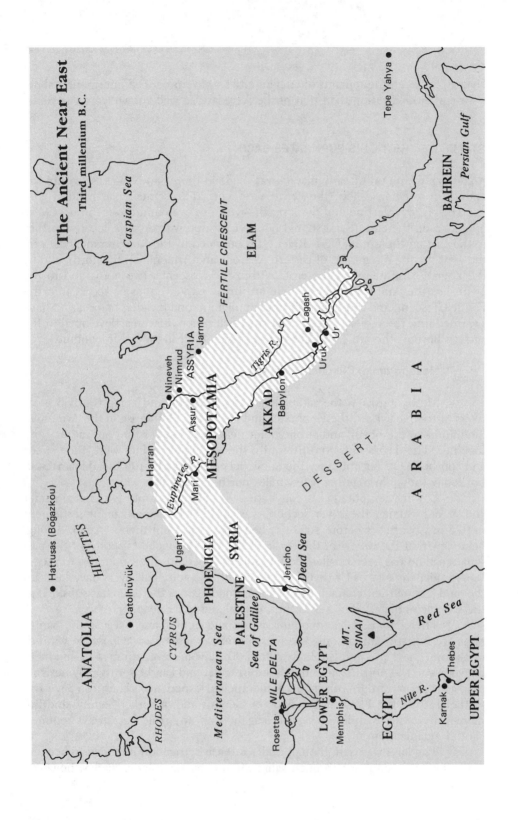

The Ancient Near East

Third millenium B.C.

tolerated salt somewhat better than wheat. Beer was made early, both from dates and from barley. And though minerals and fuel were scarce, there were palm trees that were marvelously useful—fruit, trunk, and leaves. Even the outer layers of bark were useful, as fiber for rope.

The Sumerians

Who were the Sumerians? There is as yet no exact answer to that question. Some of their pottery and certain of their practices, especially the building of ziggurats imitative of mountains, upon which they built temples, suggest that they came from mountainous country to the east. Some of their traditions, however, suggest that they lived near the sea long before the historic period, and the archaeology shows long habitation of the area by the same people. Perhaps they were indigenous to lower Mesopotamia. Probably the people who created the earliest civilization there were already a racially mixed group. In any event, the term *Sumerian* is more a linguistic than a racial one.

A surprising degree of trade—even sea trade—was developed by these inhabitants of lower Mesopotamia in the immediate prehistoric period. Scholars have been aware for several decades that the Ubaid culture, named after a site near Ur, was widespread, extending into upper Mesopotamia. In the last few years, however, numerous potsherds from Tell al' Ubiad, Ur, Eridu, and other places have been found widely disseminated in the Persian Gulf area, in Qatar, Bahrain, and eastern Saudi Arabia. This and other information is leading to a reevaluation of Ubaid society, which must have been more complex and more advanced than was previously thought.

The Early Dynastic Age

It is a Sumerian tradition that their oldest town was Eridu, and indeed, archaeologists have uncovered a remarkable series of temple structures there: Beneath a ziggurat dating to about 2000 B.C. they found a sequence of sixteen temples (each earlier and smaller than the one immediately above, of course), spanning a period of almost 4,000 years. By the middle of the third millennium B.C., several other cities stood out, including Ur, Uruk, Lagash, and Umma. In Akkad to the north, the cities of Nippur (the most important religious center) and Kish were prominent. To the east of lower Mesopotamia, in the area called Elam in antiquity, sites such as Susa had shown early growth, paralleling that of the Mesopotamian towns. By the middle third millennium, however, when the Sumerian sites had become cities ruled by dynasts, Susa had ceased to develop, and the archaeology suggests at least cultural dominance from the west. At Tepe Yahya, 600 miles farther southeast, Mesopotamian influence can also be seen in some of the pottery, seals, and the like, but a different sort of writing (proto-Elamite) had developed. To the northwest, in Syria, the same cultural penetration from Mesopotamia is seen, but here city-states, notably Ebla, rivaled in importance the contemporary Sumerian states.

These Sumerian cities were ruled by successive dynasties of kings or priest-kings. Hence the early Bronze Age, down to about 2400 B.C., is called the *early dynastic age*. Writers of a later period preserved the remembrance of these various dynasties in lists of kings which, in the lengths of reigns indicated, are in many instances totally unbelievable. The kings are divided into two groups, those who reigned before the Flood and those who reigned after. One list contains eight antediluvian kings who ruled a total of 241,200 years! The list remarks that "kingship was sent down from heaven," a comment repeated after the Flood. We may infer that the Sumerian rulers claimed a divine origin for the kingship—at least in the later period when the king lists were compiled.

Some of the lists of later kings assign more believable reigns. When the British archaeologist Sir Leonard Woolley was excavating at al-Ubaid near Ur, he found a temple dedication inscription that proved the existence of the first king of the first dynasty of Ur, Mesannepadda, who ruled in approximately 2500 B.C. On the same site, deeper down, Woolley uncovered evidence of a great flood—the one he thought was so firmly implanted in the memory of all the peoples of the region. It has not been possible, however, to identify a single flood as *the* Flood, and to place all the postdiluvial dynasties immediately after it. All attempts to collate evidence relating either to the Flood or to the king lists are inconclusive.

The ziggurat at Ur, much restored. (Courtesy of T. Edward Franklin)

Tomb Excavations at Ur

The riches of the kings of the early dynastic age were also demonstrated in the excavations of Woolley in a cemetery near Ur. These royal tombs yielded rich helmets, vessels, harps, and pots; sixteen of them contained the remains of human beings who had been slain and buried with the kings and queens to serve them beyond the grave. The "Great Death Pit" held seventy-four skeletons. Mrs. Woolley's sculptured bust of one queen, Shub-Ad (Pu-Abi), adorned in wig and hair jewelry, has made this wife of King Akalamdug a familiar face in textbooks. Buried at different times, the king and queen had with them dancing girls, musicians, personal attendants, a sledge-chariot drawn by a yoke of asses, and two ox-drawn carts. One magnificent harp was decorated with a bull's head in gold and lapis lazuli. A kind of "standard" with ivory carved panels set in bitumen is important for what it shows of the life and achievements of the king. These objects are among the most prized possessions of the British Museum. Other fine objects from Ur may be seen in the University of Pennsylvania museum.

Cities of the Early Dynastic Period

Almost all construction in these cities was of sun-dried bricks. At first the cities were not walled, but as they grew rich they required protection. The most notable feature of each was the temple to the patron god, which was erected atop a ziggurat large enough to raise it well above the walls. These ziggurats were usually built up in layers, growing with the town. Some, as that at Ur, where the best-preserved one is to be found, were irrigated on the top levels. To the approaching traveler, its greenery must have seemed to float in the sky, especially in the dry season when the plain, the walls, and the buildings, all of clay, were a scorched dun color.

The ziggurat was not only the religious center of town, it was the social, political, and economic focal point as well. The temple staff tended to be quite large and included slaves, serfs, and various craftsmen. The serfs worked the "land belonging to the god" for the priests. Farmers were liable for services such as maintaining the irrigation canals, a never-ending, vital chore. The revenues of the temple, usually collected in kind (a portion of the crops or animals), supported not only the priests but also the other officials. Wages were calculated largely in bread and beer, made from the primary crop, barley. Other land within the city-state's irrigated complex was held by individuals or families. Presumably such persons paid the equivalent of taxes, owed labor on canals and roads, and served in the army. In this age, armies were small, probably only a few hundred men. Commanders rode in chariots—if one may use that term to describe the heavy, four-wheeled carts that onagers (wild asses) laboriously pulled along. Infantry soldiers wore helmets and carried shields, spears, and battleaxes.

In some Sumerian cities the ruler was the *en* or *ensi* (Semitic *ishakku*), probably originally a priest; later the term meant approximately "governor," a man subordinate to the *lugal,* or king, who may initially have been a military leader. In the city of Kish, one ruler was a woman named Ku-Baba, by origin a tavern keeper, who had a long reign. She may have been worshiped later, as Gilgamesh of Uruk was. At any rate, a goddess of that name is heard of later, in northern Mesopotamia and in Anatolia. In each of these cities a sort of council of city notables and an assembly made up of the army—presumably all male, able-bodied full citizens— tended to develop.

As far as possible the Sumerians made do with the materials at hand. They used clay for sun-dried and baked bricks (though fuel was expensive); they even used clay, baked until vitrified, for such objects as sickles; these broke easily, no doubt, but they must have been fairly satisfactory. Stone, both for building and for making tools, had to be imported. Copper was available at no great distance. Tin, however—which makes up about 10 percent of bronze, the other element being copper—had to be brought in from a distance, perhaps from Elam, in modern Iran.

B. THE FIRST EMPIRES

Conflict and Consolidation

In human terms it seems inevitable that the new city-states, once just small villages with their irrigation complexes, should have become embroiled in wars. The political texts and the art of the period are quite preoccupied with petty wars over boundary disputes and water rights along canals. King Agga of Kish may have been one of the earliest monarchs whose imperialistic expansion brought other rulers under his sway, possibly including the renowned Gilgamesh of Uruk (biblical Erech), who will be mentioned later. A "stele of vultures," now in the Louvre, celebrated a victory of Lagash over Umma. Ur probably controlled a rather large area at one point. At last, however, Lugalzaggisi, king of Umma, conquered Lagash and Ur and came to dominate all Sumer, with Uruk as his new capital. There is evidence that he mounted one military expedition that penetrated northwest to the Mediterranean. It was perhaps the timber of the Amanus region that drew his attention.

Sargon of Agade: A Semitic Empire

Lugalzaggisi's empire soon fell in turn to a storied king, Sargon (Shar-rumkin) of Agade in Akkad, about 2350 B.C. Sargon reputedly reigned for fifty-six years. Our sources have it that his empire extended through all of Mesopotamia and westward over the Fertile Crescent to the Mediterranean, possibly on to Cyprus and up into Anatolia. Here, too, it was timber, plus minerals—especially silver—that fueled Sargon's imperialism.

Third in succession after Sargon was his grandson, Naram-Sin. This vigorous king pushed into the lands bordering the Persian Gulf as far south as Oman. He was a prosperous monarch. Literary and archaeological evidence indicates that he was paid an extensive tribute and that his trade extended as far east as distant India. Naram-Sin called himself "King of the Four World Regions," and for centuries every monarch in Mesopotamia with imperialistic ambitions would assume that grandiloquent title. He also referred to himself as "the god," apparently a new claim for Mesopotamian rulers. Omen texts tell of internal disorders and of invasions that ultimately weakened the empire in the latter days of Naram-Sin, and soon after his death it fell to pieces. Most likely, the Akkadian kings had simply overreached themselves: Their communications system especially must have been inadequate to control so large an empire.

Depredations of the semibarbarous Guti from regions to the east had blunted the power of the Agade dynasty. Akkadian weakness permitted the Gutians to gain control of the Akkadian portion of the empire and parts of Sumer as well. The confusion of the period is despairingly echoed on the king list: "Who was king? Who was not king?" Some of the Sumerian cities held back the tide, however—principally Lagash, whose king, Gudea, is well known through the several statuettes of him that have been found. Gudea undertook only defensive wars and gave his attention to building temples and canals.

Ur III: A Sumerian Empire

The famed Third Dynasty of Ur (or simply Ur III), founded by Ur-Nammu about 2111 B.C., finally stabilized the whole area of lower Mesopotamia. In the brilliant and prosperous period that followed, a late flowering of Sumerian culture occurred. The ziggurat at Ur, the capital, was built to magnificent proportions, and temples were constructed or restored in several other cities. The canals so important to the irrigation complexes were renewed, and an extensive trade developed. The literature, which along with Ur-Nammu's law code will be discussed later, centered on legendary earlier figures, such as Gilgamesh, and was probably compiled chiefly in this age.

The empire of Ur III fell shortly before 2000 B.C., partly because of Elamite revolts in the east and partly because of attacks by a new incursion of Semites called Amorites, who moved into Mesopotamia from their homeland in Syria or Arabia. These Amorites had been immigrating for some decades. The successor states to Ur, all kingdoms of some antiquity already, included Isin in Akkad, Larsa in Sumer, Mari on the middle Euphrates 300 miles upstream, and Assyria on the upper Tigris. The final end of Ur under Elamite attack shocked its people. A poignant poem, "Lamentation Over the Destruction of Ur," suggests that the fall was by divine decree; Ur's patron deity could not thwart the decree of Enlil, leader of the gods.

New Discoveries at Ebla

A dig at Tell Mardikh in Syria has produced what has been described as the most important archaeological find since the Dead Sea Scrolls came to light in the 1940s. A team of archaeologists headed by Paolo Matthiae of the University of Rome, in excavations that still continue, has recovered materials, including an archive, that will do much to illuminate the history of the whole Fertile Crescent during the third millennium B.C. Several thousand clay tablets found in 1974 through 1976 firmly identified the site as ancient Ebla, long known through numerous references in inscriptions, especially from the time of Sargon and his grandson Naram-Sin, as an important state in the region of Syria. The evidence demonstrates that Ebla flourished about 2600 B.C. to 2250 B.C. (with a secondary period about 1800–1600 B.C.) and controlled a large area from the Amanus Mountains, with their valuable timber and minerals, to Mari, 200 miles southeast on the Euphrates River.

Both Sargon (around 2350 B.C.) and Naram-Sin a century later claimed to have taken Ebla; the city was indeed temporarily destroyed in the period, but at this writing the archaeologists do not agree which date best fits the evidence. The excavations have been marked by heated exchanges among members of the original team concerning the proper interpretation of the finds. Also, unfortunately, the whole controversy has taken on political overtones that have delayed the publication of these significant materials.

The kingdom of Ebla—it is doubtful whether one should call it an empire—was more important than had been suspected, politically, economically, and culturally. Most important to the scholar is certainly the archive, comprising almost 20,000 clay tablets and fragments, mostly written in Eblaite, as the city's Semitic language has been termed, which employed the Sumerian cuneiform system. This is the earliest large archive found anywhere, though some earlier Sumerian tablets have been found in small numbers in sites of ancient Sumer. The new tablets will do much to aid in the further, more accurate decipherment and translation of Sumerian, and they will also, of course, cast light on related Semitic languages such as Akkadian, Phoenician, and Hebrew.

Many geographic names are included in the archive, as well as names of kings and other persons. Much of the very undignified controversy concerns some of these names and efforts to identify them with names from the Bible. Some of the claims are doubtless premature; some of the signs can be read in different ways and may mean different things. One such discussion centers on the question of whether the tablets contain the name YA, a shortened form of the name used later for the god of the Hebrews, *Yahweh*. Another involves the question of whether Sodom and Gomorrah and the other "cities of the plain" are mentioned on the tablets. Since the archive belongs to a short period of only a century or so in the middle of the third millennium, any implications for the time of the patriarchs mentioned in the Bible will be only by way of general background; for if these biblical figures are historical, they surely belong to a considerably later period.

At any rate, this immensely important dig will add immeasurably to our knowledge of almost everything in the whole area. The tablets—which include the earliest known bilingual dictionaries or word lists—are most important. Some of the things learned, to be sure, are minor; for example, the city had its own brand of beer, named *Ebla* after the city.

Hammurabi and the Amorite Empire of Babylon

Ur III, which may also have encompassed Ebla, was the last predominantly Sumerian empire. As new waves of Semites swept into Mesopotamia, its population became increasingly Semitic. It was the Amorite dynasty established at Babylon in Akkad that next achieved dominion over the whole region—the feat of the sixth king of the dynasty, the famous Hammurabi (c. 1792–1750 B.C., or 1728–1686 by a late chronology).

Hammurabi is best known for his body of laws, discovered in 1901 in ancient Elam. Excavations at Mari, chiefly in the 1930s, have turned up clay tablet

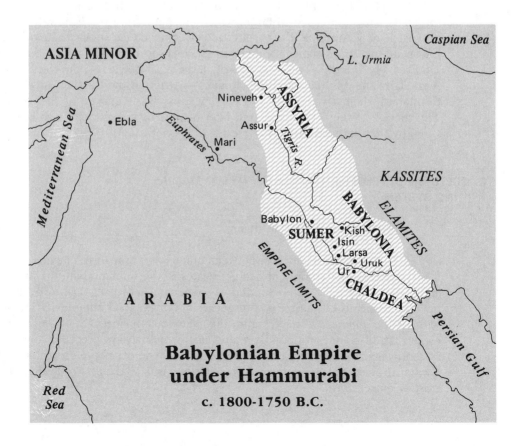

Babylonian Empire under Hammurabi

c. 1800–1750 B.C.

archives of great benefit in understanding the diplomatic history of the time. We learn how the wily Hammurabi played off one enemy against the other to conquer his opponents one by one. He took Larsa in about his thirtieth year and Mari a few years later. Hammurabi administered his dominions vigorously, giving attention to the welfare of his subjects, as the introduction to law text claims. Hammurabi's son and successor, Samsuiluna, and the following kings to the end of this Babylonian dynasty had long reigns but were less successful. Although they held on to the land along the Euphrates in the west, southern Mesopotamia broke away from the empire, and a raid of the Hittites from Asia Minor about 1595 B.C. caused devastation all the way to Babylon itself. Soon after, a semibarbarous people from the mountainous country to the northeast—the Kassites—overran Akkad and established themselves as rulers of what remained. Indo-European names appear among the gods of the Kassites, though they seem not to have been an Indo-European people. The Kassites assimilated the older culture, and their rulers governed a Babylon that began to produce a new, creative literature and again to become an educational center. We know that the city provided the scribes Assyria needed for its government departments in the twelfth century B.C.

Other invaders of the upper Euphrates and of the lands north of Assyria were the Hurrians (biblical Horites), who later, led by Indo-European elements, founded a kingdom called Mitanni, which extended from the Euphrates to parts of what is now Armenia. Recent archaeological evidence shows that some Indo-European-speaking peoples had been in the area south of the Caspian Sea a thousand years before this. The weakness of all the great powers—from the Hittites in Anatolia to the Assyrians and Babylonians—permitted the Kassites and Hurrians to establish themselves firmly and begin to absorb the culture of their captives. The success of these invaders—and later of the Hittites as well—was in part assured by their intensive use of horse-drawn chariots.

C. CULTURAL DEVELOPMENT OF EARLY MESOPOTAMIA: WRITING SYSTEM

Evolution of Writing Systems

One marked distinction between animal and human intelligence (though it may be a distinction only of degree) relates to the human ability to symbolize, an ability most clearly demonstrated in connection with language. Most animals have some means of audible communication, but no great complexity is possible without the ability to conceive and understand symbolically. Such development came first, of course, with spoken language, which always precedes any written system. This sequence must be kept in mind, for the development of writing has always involved the problem of conveying by visual symbols words that already exist in spoken form.

Writing systems seem always to have developed along a pattern in which pictures came first, perhaps in the form of tags (heads of animals, for example) used to keep inventories. Then followed pictographs, in which the picture symbolized something other than what was actually pictured. Thus, a foot meant not merely a foot but also to walk or to go. In an ideogram the symbol stands for an abstraction. In the Sumerian system, for example, the sign for a star came to symbolize heaven; it could also allude to a god. Moreover, combinations of symbols could be utilized for a new meaning. Again illustrating from the Sumerian, the symbol for bowl—meaning food—when combined with the symbol for mouth meant "to eat." Philologists now often use the term *logogram* to replace the narrower term *ideogram*; a logogram is any written sign that stands for a whole word.

Obviously, during the development of a language, a very large number of quite complicated characters existed that for the most part still retained their pictographic qualities. Further steps were required to simplify the symbols or characters and to reduce their number. For the Sumerians, simplification meant the slow elimination of the pictographic nature of the characters. Students had then to recognize characters, not pictures. The solution to the need to pare down the vast numbers of characters lay in phonetics. Characters could be made to represent phonetically—that is, by sound rather than by visual representation—all the aural nuances of spoken language. Thus the Sumerians used the symbol for water (the original pictograph looked somewhat like a stream) to mean "in" because the word for "water" and the word for "in" sounded alike. This phonetic principle made possible the representation of words for which no pictograph or ideograph could easily be invented, and when widely applied—it could even be applied to new languages with a totally new vocabulary—led to a gradually simplified system using basic sets of symbols. During the transition period there would still be thousands of symbols, some used phonetically and some not—doubtless a difficult time for students of the art of writing.

The protracted changes in the symbols for simpler and faster writing, and the cutback in their number, can be traced, often in detail, in the Sumerian system. A totally phonetic system at length emerged with a limited number of symbols, each standing for a syllable (syllabary). Finally, after more centuries of development, the idea of individual symbols for each separate sound led to a true alphabet. Improvement often came in the application of the writing system to a new language, when old traditions no longer exercised a restraining influence. Real alphabets developed somewhat later than the Sumerian period under consideration here.

Sumerian Writing: Cuneiform

The Sumerians probably produced the first writing system. A separate one, little known and undeciphered, was developed only a little later in Elam, and those created in the Nile and Indus River Valleys—the last not yet deciphered—were

Original pictograph	Pictograph in position of later cuneiform	Early Babylonian	Assyrian	Original or derived meaning
				bird
				fish
				donkey
				ox
				sun day
				grain
				orchard
				to plow to till
				boomerang to throw to throw down
				to stand to go

The origin and development of a few cuneiform characters. (New York Public Library)

almost as early. We call the Sumerian system *cuneiform,* from Latin words meaning "wedge-shaped," because the symbols were impressed on damp clay tablets with a square-cut, triangular-shaped reed. To the untrained eye, the result looks like chicken tracks. Numerous tablets designed for teaching the writing system in schools have been found. Valuable to modern scholars as well, some, as those from Ebla, are much like dictionaries; others are lists of synonyms involving different languages.

The fact that the Sumerians chose to write on clay—as did, for many centuries, most peoples who lived in and about the Fertile Crescent—has been supremely fortunate for modern scholars. Once baked, these clay tablets are almost as indestructible as potsherds. Even if only sun-dried, they can with care be excavated intact from the damp Mesopotamian soil and redried or baked, if it seems desirable. Perhaps 250,000 of these tablets have been discovered, preserving for today's scholars invaluable information that otherwise would have been irretrievably lost.

The cuneiform writing system endured for an astonishingly long period. It was used almost exclusively throughout the Fertile Crescent and surrounding area at least until the middle of the second millennium B.C., and in diminishing degree until about the beginning of the Christian era. The most used language, however, was not Sumerian but Akkadian and related tongues.

D. EARLY MESOPOTAMIAN LITERATURE

Many of the greatest works of ancient Mesopotamian literature have Sumerian antecedents, but the popular and enduring forms are Semitic. Gilgamesh, the mythical-legendary king of Uruk, was a sort of semidivine hero of the Sumerians, but the tablets that preserved the finished poem, and which were dug up at Nippur and Nineveh, give the story in Akkadian; it is a distinctly semitic version.

An Early Great Epic Poem: Gilgamesh

This Akkadian work is one of the world's earliest great epics. Gilgamesh is portrayed as a swashbuckling monarch somewhat resented by the citizens of his city, Uruk, who begged the gods for relief. They sent him a competitor, a primitive, hairy savage, Enkidu. But Gilgamesh employed a prostitute who civilized him a bit—a "modern" theme that is clearly as old as literature. After a ferocious fight, Gilgamesh and Enkidu became great companions and performed heroic tasks, among them the slaying of the terrible monster of the cedar forest, Huwawa. The love goddess Ishtar (Sumerian Inanna) herself fell in love with Gilgamesh, but to little avail. In rejecting her, Gilgamesh pointed out how most of her former lovers had come to grief. In reprisal Ishtar persuaded Anu, the great sky god and her father, to send a terrible "bull of heaven" to kill Gilgamesh and Enkidu. The two, however, succeeded in killing the bull. But then a council of gods decreed that one of them must die. Enlil, god of the air, caused the decision to go against Enkidu, who fell sick and expired. Gilgamesh, now brought up short and forced to confront human mortality, set out to seek immortality, one of humanity's great quests.

Gilgamesh learned of a man who had found immortality, one Utnapishtim (Sumerian Ziusudra), and went to find him. A friendly and philosophical (and semidivine) bar girl tried to persuade him to accept man's fate, and to eat, drink, and be merry. But Gilgamesh continued his search and at length found Utnapishtim—the Babylonian Noah who had survived the Flood. (It was this account that George Smith found on a tablet in the British Museum and presented to the world.) Utnapishtim's story is told in language strikingly similar to that of the book of Genesis, though without the moral background or the monotheistic form. Warned by a god of the coming deluge, Utnapishtim built a huge square vessel as instructed and loaded it with people and all living things. Then,

> With the first glow of dawn,
> A black cloud rose up from the horizon.
> Inside it Adad thunders, . . .
> Who turned to blackness all that had been light.
> The wide land was shattered like a pot! . . . .
> No one can see his fellow,
> Nor can the people be recognized from heaven.

The gods were frightened by the deluge,
And, shrinking back, they ascended to the heaven of Anu . . .
The gods, all humbled, sit and weep, ...
Six days and six nights
Blows the flood wind, as the south-storm sweeps the land.
When the seventh day arrived, ...
The sea grew quiet, the tempest was still, the flood ceased.
I looked at the weather: stillness had set in,
And all of mankind had returned to clay.
The landscape was as level as a flat roof.[1]

The "ark" landed on a mountain called Nisir. Utnapishtim sent out, at intervals, a dove, a swallow, and a raven. When the raven did not return, he left the vessel and poured out a libation to the gods. The gods, feeling rather sorry about what they had done, gave Utnapishtim immortal life by way of compensation. The secret of rejuvenation he now gave to Gilgamesh: He was to dive to the bottom of the river and find a specific plant. This he did, but before he could eat it, a snake stole it away. As for Gilgamesh, he went the way of all the world, but humans later deified him.

Other Babylonian Literary Works

Fragments of many other pieces of Mesopotamian literature are known to us. Surviving copies belong to the time of Assyrian greatness but derive from early history of Mesopotamia. One Semitic myth tells how the great Marduk, patron god of Babylon, after a fierce battle with the great mother goddess, the dragon Tiamat, created the world from her body, slicing her in half to form the heavens and the earth. Humans he created from her evil consort, Kingu. Another tale, this one Sumerian, offers an etiological explanation of the seasons. Inanna (Semitic Ishtar) made a journey to the nether world, perhaps seeking Dumuzi (Tammuz), her dead lover, and was held there, lifeless and hanging on a nail. But because Inanna—the goddess of love—was a fertility deity, the earth dried up and yielded no fruit. The wise god Enki eventually persuaded the rulers of the underworld to give up Inanna; she was sprinkled with the water of life and, of course, the world again became fruitful. Various forms of this myth persisted to Greco-Roman times. Other well-known Greek myths, as for example those preserved in Hesiod's *Theogony*, probably have their origins in Mesopotamian literature.

E. EARLY MESOPOTAMIAN LAW AND SOCIETY

The Earliest Collection of Laws

The black diorite stele which contains the Hammurabic laws almost intact, one of the prizes of the Louvre Museum, was discovered in 1901 on the site of ancient Susa. Earlier texts are now known. The Sumerian laws of a king of Isin,

[1]From J. B. Pritchard, ed., *The Ancient Near East: An Anthology of Texts and Pictures* (Princeton, 1958), p. 68.

The Stele of Hammurabi. Hammurabi stands before the sun god, the "Lord of Justice and Lawgiver." (Cliché des Musées Nationaux)

Lipit-Ishtar, dates nearly 150 years earlier than those of Hammurabi. And one king, Bilalama, a Semite, promulgated the "Laws of Eshnunna" some 70 years before that. Earlier still are the laws of Ur-Nammu, founder of the Third Dynasty of Ur. Fragmentary as these last texts are, they all nonetheless show clearly a direct line of development that came down to—and continued past—Hammurabi. Through a 1,500-year period, the laws grew more strict and severe.

A certain king of Lagash named Urukagina issued a series of laws around 2400 B.C. that already shows a degree of comprehensiveness and organization, designed to bring about social reforms. These laws illustrate the way in which collections of the edicts of a king formed a sort of transitional stage that led to the more ordered and more extensive compilations that came later and that may properly be termed "codes." Urukagina wished to protect his people from the depredations of official bureaucrats and priests and from the domineering upper classes. He reduced taxes and fees, which were exorbitant even for burial of the dead. A wealthy man could no longer force a poorer and less powerful man to sell his property if he did not wish to do so. Unfortunately, neither Urukagina nor Lagash seems to have been very strong, for the city was soon conquered.

The social, political, and economic implications of these laws are notable, though a word of warning concerning the nature and degree of their significance is in order. Written laws do not necessarily indicate the real situation. Was Urukagina, for example, able to control his own bureaucracy and his rapacious nobles? Modern experience with similar situations would tend to suggest a skeptical answer. His laws may reflect only one monarch's good intentions. What is law, really? One pragmatic reply is that it is what the magistrates and courts actually enforce. As historical evidence, then, laws and law codes must be evaluated with great care. Incidental information in them about social classes or areas of social and economic activity is more dependable than is the information about morals and standards.

The Law Codes and the Social Classes

Three social classes are mentioned in the Hammurabic laws. The upper class was a rather broad group (at least in law), and to call them nobles is somewhat misleading. They were full citizens and included officials, priests, and warriors. The second class, that of freemen ("middle class" would also be misleading), included artisans, professional people, merchants and traders, and some farmers. At the bottom were slaves (or serfs), some of whom had certain rights: They could own property, for instance.

To commit an offense against one in the upper class called for a more severe penalty than to commit the same offense against one in the lower classes. On the other hand, for certain offenses upper-class felons were punished more severely because they were expected to behave as one of the elite. The principle of revenge—an eye for an eye, a tooth for a tooth (*jus talionis*)—was applied, but not for all situations. In particular, when the offense was against the lower classes, a money payment could be made. When fines were permitted as alternatives to physical punishment, the rich were obviously in a favored position. Of course, money compensation could mean more than vengeance to an aggrieved poor person.

The very complexity and sophistication of the sections of the Hammurabic laws dealing with such matters as marriage and the family, property, inheritance, and slander and other crimes show long development and wide experience in all sorts of situations. For example, if a man in the upper class was captured in war, what of his spouse? If she was well fixed financially, she was expected to stay at home and take care of family matters for her absent husband. If, however, she could not maintain herself, she could remarry. If the first husband came home, the decision was his whether she should come back to him. If she had children by both husbands, each father took his own. Women could engage in business; they seem often to have run beer halls, frequently of questionable character.

Other sections of the text fixed prices for commodities of all sorts, as well as for physicians and builders. The laws also set penalties for malpractice and also for shoddy construction. Inheritance and dowry were closely controlled; a man could not capriciously disinherit his son, for example. Commerce and exchange were carefully regulated as well. Records had to be kept if recourse to the law was to be taken. In general, strict justice was the ideal, with no room for mercy. Surprisingly, the laws are silent about many sorts of crimes. It is assumed that these were dealt with in traditional, well-known ways—as, perhaps, through the family.

F. EARLY MESOPOTAMIAN RELIGION

Religion is extremely important in history—as it still is today—and it deserves much more space than it is usually given in a work of this kind. At its historical best, religion is a unifying, integrating force, providing the basic value structure that holds the society together. At its historical worst, it is, as Marxists have charged, a ruler's instrument for oppression of the masses. In the nations of the West today, the role of religion seems of little consequence, though this may be an illusion. Even when religion plays a passive rather than a dynamic role in societal affairs it is still a salient factor in history, for religious beliefs and the religious organizations reflect the nature of a society almost as well as does its government, if with different emphases.

To define religion in terms that most persons would accept is not easy. It involves a person's relationship with—perhaps even a means of confrontation with—assumed supernatural powers. Through it one seeks to ward off the evil and attach to oneself the good and the strong among these powers. Both aspects may be involved in connection with a single deity if it is seen as somewhat capricious, capable of both hurtful and helpful acts. Mesopotamians believed in numerous frightful demons and attempted to ward them off through rite, incantation, and magic (mechanical manipulation of both the natural and supernatural by one who has knowledge). The more beneficent powers they attempted to bind to themselves by magic also, but primarily through rite (including festivals and religious drama), offerings, construction of images, shrines, and temples. Very early, religion also came to involve the ultimate concerns which thinking persons in every age must confront: the origins and destiny of humanity and all that exists, the causes of good and evil, the meaning of the physical and spiritual sides of human beings. Another and also somewhat inadequate definition of religion is that it is a means through which one attempts to know the unknowable. It follows that in those times people sought through religion answers to many questions that today we would seek to answer through science or philosophy.

Mesopotamian Gods

The early Mesopotamian religion contained a strand developed in the earlier peasant culture—the Inanna-Dumuzi (Akkadian Ishtar-Tammuz) story has already been mentioned, for example—and some elements from more primitive times. It adapted structurally to civilization and city-state organization primarily through its emphasis on both a single patron deity for each city and local religious festivals as well as through its development of bodies of priests and priestesses with high social and sometimes political standing. Personal and family religion, perhaps, continued to center on the older deities related to nature or to agriculture. Kings, however, wanted a religion that bolstered their own authority and gods that nurtured and protected the state. An excellent example of the trend is seen in Babylon in the days of Hammurabi, where Marduk, the patron deity, was conceived as the creator god, indeed, but also primarily as the warrior-leader.

The Mesopotamians arrayed the gods in hierarchical order: The big three of the Babylonian gods were Anu, the sky god; Enlil, the god of air or wind; and Enki (Akkadian Ea), the god of earth with its subsoil water. Other important deities were associated with the heavenly bodies: Inanna (Ishtar), goddess of love and fertility, was identified with the planet Venus; Utu (Shamash), god of justice, with the sun; Nanna (Sin), with the moon. Also of great importance were Adad, the storm god, and Marduk. Enlil, patron deity of Nippur, by 2500 B.C. was considered the general ruler of the rest of the gods.

Religion in Life and Afterlife

Some of the early dynastic kings, as we have noted from their tombs, evidently hoped for a pleasant life after death and took along with them servants, dancers, and harpists. In general, however, there was no great emphasis on an afterlife. The emphasis was rather on life on earth. Of greatest importance in religion was the necessity to placate the gods, to learn what life had in store, and to find an explanation for the apparent illogic of a world in which the good sometimes suffer and the evil prosper. To placate the gods was largely a matter of supporting the temples and priests and offering sacrifices as they demanded. The contradictions of an otherwise orderly universe were partially explained by positing the existence both of benevolent deities and of demons, often conceived as composite monsters; one, for example, had the features of a lion, a snake, and an eagle. The spirits of the dead were sometimes thought to be malevolent also. The ancient Mesopotamian, then, saw religion as a way to attempt to control the conditions of life and destiny. Failure to accomplish this was no doubt attributed to ignorance of the will of the gods.

Practitioners of the Religious Arts

A host of religionists and conjurers helped to exorcise the demons, to rid the body of its ills (a connection with medicine is obvious), and above all, to foretell the future. "Omen texts" have been discovered in large numbers. The Mesopotamian practitioners forecast the future through astrology, the pseudoscience of the stars, through the inspection of livers or of all the entrails of sacrificed animals, through the observation of smoke from burning incense and the spreading of oil dropped in water, or through the interpretation of dreams. Clearly, religion entered intimately into every facet of human life.

G. OTHER MESOPOTAMIAN ACHIEVEMENTS

Art and Architecture

Art in ancient Mesopotamia was highly developed. At one time the most valued treasures might be pottery or cylinder seals; at another, jewelry or statuary. Sculpture became important in the middle third millennium: The "standard of Ur," for example, illustrates well the skill in bas-relief in the early dynastic period. Gudea, ruler of Lagash, left several statues, and Naram-Sin and Hammurabi were portrayed on famous reliefs.

Much of the architecture might seem unattractively monotonous today. But many of the greater structures, mostly temples, with typically low rectangular lines and crenellated wall surfaces that catch the interesting interplay of light and shadow, seem quite modern. Uruk, which had an enclosure wall six miles long, has been called a "cathedral center" because of its temples, the greatest of them dedicated to the goddess of love and fertility, Inanna. The "white temple" there, with its imported limestone facing, horizontal and vertical lines, and interior columns made of clay decorated with ceramic cones set in geometric patterns, illustrates well the abilities of early Sumerian architects and artists. The use of baked and ceramic bricks partly offset the lack of stone in the area, though fuel for baking was limited, and most structures were made of sun-baked bricks. The Mesopotamians even knew how to form the true arch and dome, as Woolley found in the graves near Ur. They did not apply these architectural feats, however, to structures of any size.

Numbers: Weights and Measures

Any agricultural society must work out a system of weights and measures. In the early barter economy, barley was a common medium of exchange, with the value of a lamb or of an ox as a standard unit. With the development of cities, silver became the medium of exchange—though traded by weight. True coinage was an invention of a much later period. The system that evolved was based on a *talent* of about sixty-seven pounds; one-sixtieth of a talent was a *mina,* and one-sixtieth of the mina was a *shekel.* This system was widely used throughout the ancient world; the Greeks used it, with variations, as did the Romans.

The numbers system was based on a combination of sixes and tens. Sixty was thus a much used number; our inheritance from the system in measuring time and degrees in angles is plain. For practical arithmetic, the system was easier to use than our decimal system. As an example, the number 360 (the number of degrees in a circle) can be divided by 10, 9, 8, 6, 5, 4, 3, and 2. Our typical number

100 can be divided only by 10, 5, 4, and 2. Sixty was considered a kind of complete number (it was the basis for expressing fractions), and it was assigned to the god Anu. Enlil, who originally was second in importance, was assigned the number 50, and so on down the ranks. A fairly well-developed system of geometry was necessary in an agricultural society—particularly in the river valleys with their irrigation complexes and flood problems. Some indications of the development of what we would call algebra and some logarithmic tables have also been found.

These scanty paragraphs can do no more than hint at the astonishing accomplishments of the people who inhabited that great cradle of civilization, Mesopotamia.

BOOKS FOR FURTHER READING

BERMANT, C., and M. WEITZMAN. *Ebla: A Revelation in Archaeology*, New York, 1979.

BOTTERO, J., E. CASSIN, and J. VERCOUTTER, eds. *The Near East: The Early Civilizations*, New York, 1967.

BURNEY, C. *The Ancient Near East*, Oxford, 1977.

BURNEY, C. *From Village to Empire: An Introduction to Near Eastern Archaeology*, Oxford, 1977.

CHIERA, E. *They Wrote on Clay*, Chicago, 1938.

CONTENAU, G. *Everyday Life in Babylon and Assyria*, New York, 1966.

JACOBSEN, T. *The Treasures of Darkness: A History of Mesopotamian Religion*, New Haven, 1976.

KRAMER, S. N. *From the Tablets of Sumer*, Indian Hills, Colo., 1956.

KRAMER, S. N. *The Sumerians*, Chicago, 1963.

LLOYD, S. *The Archaeology of Mesopotamia*, London, 1978.

MALLOWAN, M. *Early Mesopotamia and Iran*, New York, 1965.

MORREY, P. *Ur 'of the Chaldees'—A Revised and Updated Edition of Sir Leonard Woolley's Excavations at Ur*, Ithaca, N.Y., 1982.

MOSCATI, S. *Ancient Semitic Civilizations*, London, 1957.

MOSCATI, S. *Face of the Ancient Orient*, Chicago, 1960.

OPPENHEIM, A. L. *Ancient Mesopotamia*, Chicago, 1964.

PRITCHARD, J. B. *Ancient Near Eastern Texts*, Princeton, 1954.

PRITCHARD, J. B. *The Ancient Near East: Supplementary Texts*, Princeton, 1969.

ROUX, G. *Ancient Iraq*, 2nd ed., London, 1980.

3

ANCIENT EGYPT

Ancient Egypt has never faded from human memory. The great cities of ancient Mesopotamia moldered into tells marking sites whose very names were forgotten, but the monuments of ancient Egypt, built of enduring stone, have given mute testimony for century after century of the magnificence of its antique civilization. Lively literary accounts, moreover, especially by Herodotus, the Greek historian of the fifth century B.C., kept alive additional information about early Egypt. Herodotus wrote not only of the well-known Giza pyramids but also other works that later disappeared, such as the labyrinthine buildings and hydraulic works in the Fayum region. He estimated that these works exceeded in cubic volume all the masonry of all types built by the Greeks up to his own time. Remains of this "labyrinth" have been discovered in recent years.

In spite of the eminent visibility of the Egyptian monuments, the country was not well known to the West during the Middle Ages and early modern period. It was a military expedition that revived interest in the area: Napoleon's invasion of Egypt in 1798. Perhaps consciously imitating Alexander the Great—for Napoleon knew Plutarch well—he took along with him on the expedition some 150 *savants*. These scholars traveled from Lower to Upper Egypt and copied monuments that exceeded in size and grandeur anything they had expected. The results were published in the popular multivolume *Description de l'Egypte*. Ultimately more important, in digging a trench the French soldiers in 1799 found the famous Rosetta stone. Because the British were the ultimate victors in the Egyptian campaign, the Rosetta stone is in the British Museum. Copies were made, however, and widely circulated.

From the inscription on the Rosetta stone, Jean Champollion was able by 1822 to announce the decipherment of hieroglyphics. By mid-century, Egypt, like Mesopotamia, was being ransacked for portable antiquities for Western museums. A Frenchman, Auguste Mariette, was able to persuade the Khedive of Egypt to start a museum, with Mariette himself as director, and to control somewhat the sale and export of antiquities. He and his successor, Gaston Maspero, partially curtailed clandestine digging and saved some of the finest objects for display in the Cairo museum. A truly scientific survey and excavation, however, came only when an Englishman, Flinders Petrie, began a careful measurement of the pyramids at Giza in 1881. Petrie also pioneered in the analysis of potsherds in sequence-dating (see p. 13).

Probably the most publicized archaeological find ever made was Howard Carter's discovery of the almost intact tomb of Pharaoh Tutankhamon in 1922. The incredible variety and richness of the finds of that tomb still dazzle visitors to the Cairo museum, as some of the objects bedazzled the thousands of Americans who saw them when they were on tour in the United States in 1978 and 1979. Yet Tutankhamon was one of the least important of the pharaohs.

A. THE LAND AND THE PEOPLE

Only in the sixth millennium B.C. was Egypt thickly settled. Most of the populace was typically Mediterranean, though there were frequent admixtures of Nubian and Ethiopian immigrants from the south all during antiquity, especially in periods of governmental weakness. What first brought people to the Nile Valley was the desiccation that followed the last Ice Age, which gradually reduced a great mass of land to desert or semiaridity. The African Sahara, as large as the United States, was only a part of a vast arid belt that stretched from the Atlantic Ocean to the Arabic peninsula and from there through Iraq and Iran to modern Pakistan, where the monsoon rains finally contained the dryness.

The Nile

From far antiquity it was remarked that Egypt was the gift of the Nile. The inhabitants recognized their dependence on the river and gave it reverence. The Nile flows out of Lakes Victoria and Albert in East Africa, nearly 4,000 winding miles from the Mediterranean. For about the last half of the ninety-day journey to the sea, the Nile waters course through an almost rainless desert. The annual miracle of the Nile's astonishingly high and predictable flood cannot be explained by anything observable downstream. The floods result from rains in the watersheds of the White Nile and two major tributaries, the Blue Nile and the Atbara. Before construction of modern dams, the flood reached an average depth of about 45 feet

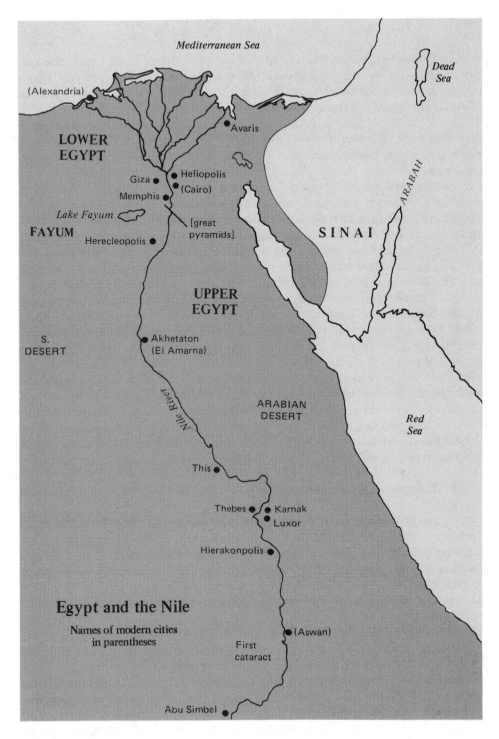

Egypt and the Nile

Names of modern cities
in parentheses

Ancient Egypt.

at Elephantine on the southern border of Egypt, some 600 miles from the sea. The water normally begins to rise in July, reaches a peak in September, slacks a bit, and then reaches a still higher level in October. Thereafter the river ebbs to a low from about April through June.

Water for a parched land was not the only gift of the Nile. The silt it deposited each year also renewed the soil. Egypt's farmers, therefore, could not exhaust the land, nor was it subject to salinization, as in Mesopotamia. One ancient name for Egypt was the Black Land. Photographs made by some of the first U.S. astronauts dramatically show the contrast between that long, narrow strip of dark and productive soil and the flanking desert sands, scorched and sterile. No agriculture above primitive levels was possible in ancient Egypt without irrigation, and there, as in Mesopotamia, impelling necessity demanded human cooperation to water the land. Because irrigation was easier in Egypt, because there was less trade, and because the habitable portion of the country was a serpentine, narrow strip hundreds of miles long, Egypt remained more rural than Mesopotamia.

The Nile furnished food, too—fish and fowl. It was, in addition, an easy transportation route. People could drift down the river, of course, and since the wind blows upriver to the south most of the year, they could easily sail back upstream. The delta region is called *Lower Egypt*, and the land to its south is *Upper Egypt*. Sometimes the term *Middle Egypt* is used to designate the area around Memphis near modern Cairo and the Fayum west of the river, a basin below sea level where a lake would form when the Nile overflowed. Temperatures are high but the air is less humid in Egypt than in Mesopotamia, and the climate is healthful. The land provided stone of fine quality and variety; gold could be mined in the eastern desert and copper in the Sinai across the Red Sea. Most other metals and timber were imported.

Topographical Isolation

Egypt was protected from outsiders by the topography. To the east lay desert, low mountains, and the Red Sea. To the north was the Mediterranean. To the west sprawled the great and inhospitable Sahara. To the south along the Nile, cataracts (rapids rather than falls) and the narrowness of the river's gorge made defense easy. Access to the country along the coasts to the west and to the northeast could easily be cut off. For centuries Egypt controlled its own destinies without serious external threat.

The regularity with which the Nile bestowed its blessings and the protection of topography gave to Egypt's people a sense of security, of optimism and confidence. With this went also a feeling of changelessness, of almost no sense of history. One year was much like every other; from generation to generation all was the same. Egypt's very security, however, meant that less pressure was exerted to make improvements. For example, Egypt used only copper and almost no bronze down to about 2000 B.C., and as we shall see, the arrival of the Iron Age meant decline. Still, Egypt's accomplishments in the third and second millennia B.C. were tremendous.

B. EARLIEST EGYPT

From the predynastic (and prehistoric) age, which ends about 3000 B.C., through the era of Egyptian greatness, Egypt can be divided into historical segments. These segments are known as the Archaic, or Thinite period; the Old Kingdom; the Middle Kingdom; and the New Kingdom, or Empire. Sandwiched between the last three are two intermediate stages.

The Dynastic King Lists

Egyptian history is discussed in terms of dynasties, following the ancient king lists. Several such lists have been preserved: Two were inscribed in stone on temple walls, one has survived on a famous papyrus roll, and fragments of the third century B.C. historian Manetho give us further information. The papyrus (Turin papyrus) adds the names of gods who ruled before men. Some of the lists—Manetho is most important here—supply lengths of reigns as well. It would seem, then, that modern historians could compile a chronologically accurate history from the earliest period. But there are always complications. Some of the dynasts ruled only a part of Egypt, so that there is some overlapping of dynasties. Also, the names vary. In fact, each king had several names, and those listed are not always the names used on monuments or tombs. Further, the earliest of the lists mentioned was compiled about 1,500 years after the founding of the First Dynasty—which naturally left ample room for error. Manetho seems to have used an older list for the first two dynasties, one that we have only in fragments. The largest piece of this early inscription is called the Palermo stone, because it is located in a museum at Palermo. Predictably, modern scholars also disagree on the date for the founding of the First Dynasty. Most would place it within a 400-year period, from about 3200 B.C. to about 2800 B.C. The chronology becomes more exactly determinable in later periods, and after the founding of the Middle Kingdom it is probably accurate to within a margin of error of ten or fifteen years.

Early Mesopotamian Influences

Egypt was unified far earlier than Mesopotamia. Political unification, however, is not the all-important criterion of civilization, and in some very significant ways Mesopotamia seems to have been more advanced. Writing, for example, developed earlier in Mesopotamia. In concept, Egyptian hieroglyphics are much like Mesopotamian cuneiform. The inventory tags and protoliterate tablets, steps that illustrate the development of a writing system, are found in Mesopotamia but not in Egypt. Therefore, it is usually thought that the Egyptians got the idea of a writing system from the Sumerians. In other ways also, Egyptians seem to have learned from Asians. Both in materials and in form, major architectural monuments of the Archaic period, especially the tombs called *mastabas*, bear a close resemblance to Mesopotamian models. These were constructed of mud brick, like the temples of Sumer, although later ones were built of brick-sized stones. Only later did the Egyptians go to the larger stones, which required more labor to install but much less labor to prepare. Cylinder seals were imported into Egypt, and stylized artistic motifs appear in Egypt that are characteristic of Mesopotamia. Evidence of this sort seems sufficient to establish a chronological priority for Mesopotamia. However, it does not establish any argument for qualitative priority in achievement. In some ways Egyptian achievements are more impressive. Early sculpture in Egypt, for instance, is much superior to that of contemporary Mesopotamia. And Egypt's influence endured. When a new cycle of ancient civilization began with the ancient Greeks, the Egyptian influence was immediate and profound.

C. UNIFICATION: THE THINITE PERIOD (c. 3100–2700 B.C.)

In the prehistoric age, Egypt's progress toward unification followed the usual pattern of development from smaller to larger states until finally, along with a sudden flowering of civilization, two kingdoms were formed corresponding to the geography of the country, Lower Egypt and Upper Egypt. By about 3100 B.C., the two kingdoms were combined into one.

Just who was the first pharaoh of all Egypt is difficult to determine. Manetho's list and two others say Menes. Archaeological evidence indicates it was a man with the Horus name Aha. A mace head from Hierakonpolis shows a man wearing the crown of Upper Egypt and calls him Scorpion (at least his name is written with that sign); he seems also to be celebrating a victory over Lower Egypt. A famous palette shows on one side a ruler called Narmer, wearing the crown of Upper Egypt, conquering his enemies of Lower (or Northern) Egypt; the other side shows him wearing the crown of Lower Egypt. It is possible though not probable that all these names refer to one and the same pharaoh. Possibly Scorpion began the unification, which was completed by Narmer-Menes, the first king of the First Dynasty. Aha, possibly the same as Teti on the king lists, may be the second monarch of the First Dynasty.

Other matters relating to the Thinite period are equally difficult. The capital was apparently at This. However, a tradition preserved in Egyptian literature has it that Memphis was built by Menes and became the first capital. Archaeology does not solve this contradiction. Memphis certainly became important quite early. Perhaps the future will bring new evidence regarding the "Union of the Two Lands." What is certain is that the unification of Egypt was crucial for its people:

Central authority was urgently needed, for any disruption usually meant famine shortly thereafter. The irrigation system, above all, required order.

D. THE OLD KINGDOM (c. 2700–2200 B.C.)

The God-King

The Third through the Sixth Dynasties, about 2700 to about 2200 B.C., constitute the Old Kingdom. Its capital was at Memphis, and its kings, as in the Archaic period, were god-kings. In Mesopotamia, as we have seen, even those rulers who were not priest-kings claimed their kingship was divinely ordained. But in Egypt the king was god; at the same time he was also the son of a god who at death took his place between Re, the sun god, and Horus, a falcon deity also identified with the sun, sometimes with the son of Re. The implications of this god-king doctrine for the theory of government can be easily deduced. All authority and power went back to the pharaoh, a title meaning literally "great house." In practice, however, the pharaoh was not so absolute, because an old nobility, whose members retained high status and position, helped to set limits on the pharaoh's power. Chief officials included a vizier, a chief architect, and a chief judge—all "seal-bearers" and all supposed to look out for the interests of the "Lord of the Two Lands." A number of provinces, or Nomes, were each under a governor, whose hellenized title is Nomarch.

The very position of the pharaohs was so lofty that they left little evidence concerning personal feelings or views. We can know little of the essential character of the great kings who constructed the massive works that have endured for so many centuries.

The Pyramid Age

In many ways the Old Kingdom was the most brilliant age of ancient Egypt. An early king of the Third Dynasty, Zoser or Djoser, left a most impressive monument in the first of the great pyramids, the Step Pyramid at Sakkara. The pyramid began as a mastaba tomb of traditional type, but it was enlarged in stages into a huge structure enclosed within a walled area containing subsidiary monuments. The architect, Imhotep, was renowned also for his wisdom. Sometime after his death he was accorded divine honors, and centuries later he was still worshiped at numerous shrines. Scale model reconstructions of the Step Pyramid and its enclosure, with a thirty-foot high white wall, regularly recessed, make it clear enough to the appreciative modern eye why Egyptians revered Imhotep.

The true pyramid with the typical complex—causeway to the Nile with a valley temple, a mortuary temple near the pyramid itself, and a boat pit, all within an enclosure—came with the Fourth Dynasty, about 2600 B.C. The first king of that dynasty, Sneferu, actually built three pyramids, the largest called the Bent Pyramid, located at Dashur. It was about 620 feet square at the base and 336 feet high. It is "bent" because the angle changes about halfway up; perhaps the original height was reduced because the great weight of rock was threatening to collapse the tomb chamber. All the great pyramids were flanked by smaller tombs for relatives and high nobles.

The Great Pyramid

The pyramids at Giza are, of course, the largest and best known. The Great Pyramid there was built by Khufu, successor of Sneferu. The other two were constructed by later kings of the dynasty, Khafre and Menkaure. Probably it was Khafre who built the nearby Sphinx. Everything about the Great Pyramid is impressive. No more massive structure existed until the completion of the Grand Coulee Dam in the state of Washington. With a base of 756 feet, the pyramid was originally a little more than 480 feet high. Its mass of more than 2 million stone blocks, averaging about 2½ tons each, covers about 13 acres. One red granite slab

Temple and pyramid of Khafre, Egypt. (V-DIA/SCALA)

in the "king's chamber"—one of three at the end of long passageways—weighs 50 tons. The core of the pyramid is of local limestone; the outer covering, now gone, was of higher quality Tura limestone brought from across the Nile and upstream. The granite came hundreds of miles down the river from Upper Egypt. Careful analysis shows at least three changes of plan during construction.

It is likely that most of the work was done during those months when the Nile was in flood—there being little else for the peasants to do. These huge structures were built with long ramps and immense manpower but without the use of wheel or pulley. Herodotus reported an Egyptian tradition that the Great Pyramid required the labor of 100,000 men for twenty years. It is instructive to remember, however, that he, writing in the fifth century B.C., was farther in time from the date of construction of this pyramid than we are from the birth of Christ. Yet engineers today estimate that Herodotus's report was not far off the mark. The historian also says that the Egyptians remembered Khufu and his son as oppressors.

Certainly the pyramids give mute testimony of the great political power and the financial resources of the pharaohs who built them, and of long periods of peace. One may also note the obvious skills in quarrying and transporting the huge stones and in architectural planning and execution. It is easy to infer much else, from astronomical knowledge (the structures are oriented almost perfectly in north-south and east-west directions) to religious beliefs and practices. The latter are seen in the form itself, which was sacred to the sun, and in inscriptions and contents. Both the objects and the pictures are a rich source of information about everyday life.

The pyramids were tombs of the god-king. But they were more. It is not difficult to imagine the thrill that passed through the heart of many an Egyptian when the earliest rays of the never-veiled divine sun touched with brightness the white tips of these graceful structures, heralding another new day.

E. RELIGION IN THE OLD KINGDOM

Deities of the Nile and the Sun

Herodotus wrote that the Egyptians were the most religious of all people, and it is true that almost everything that remains, from pyramids to literature, seems suffused with religion. Their religion shows all the expected marks of a long evolution. Deities were associated with the heavenly bodies and with animals and insects—from bulls and crocodiles to scorpions and beetles. In a country of a beneficent, never-failing sun and an equally beneficent river and land (along the river), it was natural that two groups of gods should have been emphasized, solar and riverine, or land. The Egyptians made some attempts to reconcile these and other religious strands, but clearly Egyptian priests did not think it necessary to rationalize completely their religious ideas—or it could be, of course, that what seemed rational to them does not to us.

The gods—who were given anthropomorphic characteristics—were often grouped by twos or threes: husband-wife or husband-wife-child—so Geb and Nut, earth and sky, or the riverine deities Osiris and Isis with their child Horus, who was associated both with the Nile and with the sun. Political unification tended to produce national gods through identification of similar deities. Thus at Heliopolis, Aton, Horus, and other solar deities were somehow equated with Re. Early pharaohs of this period associated themselves with Horus and later ones with both Horus and Re; those of the New Kingdom or Empire identified with Amon-Re, Horus, and sometimes Aton. Amon was originally an air god of Thebes. Other major gods included Ptah, crafts god of Memphis; Apis, the Memphis bull god; Hathor, the cow goddess (a mother goddess); and Thoth, the Word of Ptah. There were a host of others. Since Memphis was the capital city in this period, its gods naturally were seen as important, even predominant—at least by its residents. In an Old Kingdom document named the *Memphite Theology,* the city is seen as symbolic of the unity of the country and is called the "hinge" of Egypt. Ptah is presented not only as the creator of the gods and all that is but also as symbolic of that unity. The Temple of Ptah reflected the same theme, for it had one door that opened to the south, toward Upper Egypt, and one to the north, toward Lower Egypt.

Emphasis on an Afterlife

Because archaeologists work mostly with tombs, they have learned much about the Egyptians' views of an afterlife. The mastabas, the pyramids, many of their temples, the offerings made to the dead by Egyptians of all ranks, all testify to the belief in and search for a happy afterlife. The smooth rhythms of the seasons in Egypt, with the regular Nile and the dependable sun, made it easy for the Egyptians to be optimistic and confident about both this life and an afterlife—in contrast to the Mesopotamians, whose less secure land and terrifying floods produced thoughts of demons and an afterlife to be dreaded, not sought. Despite the idea that the deceased might go to a place of the dead, Egyptians thought that a part of the personality, the Ka, the "double" or "vital force," remained in or near the tomb, and consequently, must be provided for. It was necessary to keep the body intact and to provide tomb offerings. Those who could afford it were therefore mummified; the tomb was made secure; food offerings were provided both at burial and later if possible; pictures of the deceased inspecting fields, harvest, and so on were painted on the walls of the tomb or shown by scale models. Such pictures, images, and even words, it was thought, could substitute for real objects. For the journey to the solar heaven, the dead person was sometimes provided with a model boat and crew—or even, as in the case of Khufu and the pyramid builders, with full-size ships. From tomb paintings and models, then, we learn much of Egyptian everyday life.

Model of fishing boat and crew taken from Egyptian tomb; it comes from a later period.
(The Metropolitan Museum of Art, Museum Excavations, 1919–20; Rogers Fund,
supplemented by contribution of Edward S. Harkness)

Egyptians eventually conceived a pleasant "heaven" in the skies and a sort of "hades" of fire and crocodiles under the Nile. The god Osiris became the judge of the dead. The heart of the deceased, as we may see graphically in several remaining judgment scenes, was weighed against Ma'at, goddess of justice and order, whose symbol was a feather. (Some of these beliefs evolved after the Old Kingdom.)

Osiris symbolized the resurrection and became judge of the dead because he, too, died and was brought back to life. A famous myth tells of the struggle between Osiris and his brother, Set, who killed his brother. But Isis found the dead Osiris and breathed new life into him. Their son, Horus, avenged Osiris, losing an eye in the fight with Set. There may be an echo of history in this story. Set was from Upper Egypt, Osiris from Lower Egypt. One version of the tale proclaims the risen Osiris as ruler of all. Perhaps the real struggle, ascribed to the gods in the myth, was that for political unity in the Archaic period. The story of Osiris is one of the earliest of the numerous accounts of the dying and reborn god who became a benefactor of humanity. It seems, however, that in early Egypt the hope of an afterlife was reserved for the upper classes. The poor person, in this period, had little to hope for in the afterworld.

The fact that the dead were judged, and that there were separate places for the good dead and the wicked dead, presupposes the development of moral concepts. And, indeed, the Egyptians did come to associate morality with religion—by no means a usual thing in human history. The deceased were required to show that they had done no evil. Here, for example, is a much-abridged statement of a monarch of the Old Kingdom:

> I gave bread to all the hungry . . .
> I clothed him who was naked . . .
> I never oppressed anyone . . .
> I speak no lie.[1]

Despite these views, so familiar in later religions, Egyptians came to rely as much on magical formulas as on good deeds for their hope in the afterworld. This may be seen as early as the *Pyramid Texts*, which belong to the last centuries of the Old Kingdom, and especially in the Book of the Dead, dating to the period of the New Kingdom. It remained important to them to make as solid an arrangement as possible for continuing food offerings for the dead. Still, in their emphasis on morality and religion, and in their well-worked-out views of an afterlife, the Egyptians contributed much to the development of more-advanced religious concepts.

F. LANGUAGE, LITERATURE, AND ART IN THE OLD KINGDOM

Hieroglyphics

It was the Greeks, near the end of the Ancient period, who gave to the Egyptian system of picture writing the name *hieroglyphics,* which means "priest-carvings," or "sacred writings." By that time hieroglyphs were used almost solely by priests, and usually the picture-signs were sculptured in low relief on stone. For writing on papyrus—the very durable paper made by Egyptians from the papyrus reed that grew in abundance along the Nile—the Egyptians developed two simplified scripts derived from hieroglyphics: hieratic and demotic. In the hieroglyphic system, a complicated combination of pictographs, ideographs, and phonetic symbols was used. It was not easy for men like Champollion to decipher the writing, even after the discovery of the Rosetta stone, an inscription of 196 B.C. in hieroglyphics, demotic, and Greek.

The writing system included twenty-four phonetic symbols, each of which stood for a single consonant—an embryonic true alphabet. Yet the Egyptians never

---

[1] J. H. Breasted, *Ancient Records of Egypt,* 5 vols. (Chicago, 1905–1907), 1:240.

did anything to simplify the system. In fact, the addition of determinatives, though making the meaning clearer, increased the number of sign combinations. Perhaps the Egyptians did not change their system because for them the visual system itself had become a real art form. The phonetic symbols made it easier for neighboring peoples to use the Egyptian symbols for their own language, and to go on to develop a system basically alphabetic. At the same time, the alphabet was also developing from Mesopotamian usages.

Literature of the Old Kingdom

Time has erased most of the inscriptions and papyri that date to the Old Kingdom. One famous papyrus originally of this period is called *The Instructions of Ptah-Hotep,* a wise old vizier of the Fifth Dynasty. Ptah-Hotep advised young men, with a touch of irony,

> Let not thy heart be puffed up because of thy knowledge;
> Be not confident because thou art a wise man.

For officials, he advised,

> If thou art one to whom petition is made, be calm as thou listenest to the petitioner's speech. Do not rebuff him before he has swept out his body or before he has said that for which he came. A petitioner likes attention to his words better than the fulfilling of that for which he came. . . . It is not (necessary) that everything about which he has petitioned should come to pass, [but] a good hearing is a soothing of the heart.[2]

The establishment speaking!

Other papyri that seem to have originated in the Old Kingdom include a long one relating to medicine and another to mathematics. Both show a knowledge advanced for the age. In his time Herodotus noted that Egyptian physicians tended to be specialists rather than general practitioners. This specialization went back to the earliest times. Surgery, too, was advanced.

Art, Sculpture

Enough has already been said of Egyptian architecture in connection with the pyramids to demonstrate the great achievement in the construction of buildings. But Egyptian sculpture and painting are equally impressive. Both became highly stylized. To many, the stiffness of shoulders and legs in sculpture and the unrealistic means used to portray humans in profile in painting and relief demonstrate a lack of ability on the part of the artists. But such a reaction is a mistake.

[2]J. P. Pritchard, *Ancient Near Eastern Texts* (Princeton, N.J., 1955), p. 412. (Translation by J. A. Wilson.)

The Egyptians very early developed certain features of style, and these they canonized and for the most part retained for three thousand years. Their best work shows clearly their superior ability to represent what they wished. Words cannot really prove this point, nor can textbook illustrations. Only a visit to one of the great museums of the world can begin to produce a proper impression of the marvelous achievements of the ancient Egyptian artists.

G. THE DECLINE OF THE OLD KINGDOM; THE FIRST INTERMEDIATE PERIOD

Collapse of an Ordered World

We do not know all the causes of the decline of the Old Kingdom. Probably the later dynasts were personally less effective than their predecessors. One major factor, however, was the tendency of the key governmental offices to become hereditary within an aristocratic family. The various nomes tended to become almost independent little feudal monarchies. The decrease in building perhaps evidences a general economic slump. Eventually, the Union of the Two Lands broke up.

With the erosion of authority and economic well-being, some areas plunged into complete disorder. The so-called prophet Nefer-Rohu gives us some idea of the situation and mentions low Nile floods that meant crop failures.

> This land . . . there is no one who is concerned with it, no one who speaks, no eye that weeps. . . . The sun disc is covered over. It will not shine. . . . The rivers of Egypt are empty, the water is crossed on foot. . . . Everything good is disappeared, and the land is prostrate because of woes. . . .
>   This land is helter-skelter. . . . I show thee the land topsy-turvy. That which never happened has happened.[3]

Other texts tell of robbery and pillage, even of pharaonic pyramids. It is true that these accounts were written during a later period of stability, to contrast that time with the earlier disorder, but the picture is probably accurate enough nevertheless. The old optimism and confidence evaporated. One long, sophisticated poem from this age elaborates a cynical theme and even a longing for death.

Centers of Order Amid Chaos

In a few centers, however, during this First Intermediate Period, order prevailed. Separate dynasties ruled at the same time over portions of the divided country. One such dynasty was located at Heracleopolis in Middle Egypt, though

---

[3] J. B. Pritchard, *The Ancient Near East: An Anthology of Texts and Pictures* (Princeton, N.J., 1958), pp. 254–255.

there, too, dangerous factions tended to arise. The *Instructions for King Meri-Ka-Re*, written by a pharaoh for his son during this intermediate period, warns that if an official is popular, excitable, and an excellent speaker, he should be eliminated forthwith. On the other hand, another famous work from Heracleopolis in the same age shows that Ma'at (the goddess of justice) still ruled. This work, *Protests of an Eloquent Peasant*, tells of a peasant who was mistreated by a minor official. Perhaps only because of his exceptional eloquence, he was able in a series of speeches to take his story all the way to the king. Ultimately, the offending official was fired and the peasant given his job. Even if this story was fiction, the warning was clear.

The kings of Heracleopolis were apparently the most powerful in Egypt for a time during this period. It was the kings of Thebes in Upper Egypt, however, who reunited the land.

H. THE MIDDLE KINGDOM (c. 2060–1785 B.C.)

Kings of Thebes Achieve Reunification

The reunification of all Egypt was accomplished by a king named Mentuhotep II of the Theban Eleventh Dynasty, who became king about 2060 B.C. and within a couple of decades defeated the ruler of Heracleopolis. He and a successor of the same name ruled for about sixty years. The Middle Kingdom, though, is virtually identical with the Twelfth Dynasty, which was founded by Amenemhet I after a period of disorder. Amenemhet had been vizier of the last Eleventh Dynasty king before he became pharaoh, most likely in 1991 B.C. Amenemhet transferred his capital to a fortified site not far from Memphis in order to maintain more effective control over the two lands.

Eleventh Dynasty kings had been sons of Re in the usual fashion; but Twelfth Dynasty monarchs usually were sons of Amon, Thebes' patron deity. He was identified with other solar deities and indeed was often called Amon-Re. The Middle Kingdom monarchs still were god-kings, but they had lost something of majesty since Khufu. Perhaps the spectacle of a vizier becoming a divine monarch tarnished the image. Moreover, the feudal, decentralized power and society that had developed from the last century of the Old Kingdom stubbornly resisted any change.

The Twelfth Dynasty, nonetheless, brought peace, and along with that blessing, a greater social consciousness on the part of officials of all ranks seems to have manifested itself. Words purported to be those of Amenemhet set the tone; he was said to have boasted that "none was hungry in my years, none thirsted then; men dwelled in peace." In instructions to his son and successor, Sesostris I, Amenemhet stressed his care for the poor and the orphaned. But he warned his son not to trust subordinates, and he made it clear that he had not been able to gain the loyalty of all. Attempts on his life had soured his outlook. Indeed, it seems that Amenemhet was assassinated.

The greatest domestic blessing of the dynasty was the curbing of the power of the provincial, landed nobility. The archaeology shows the consequent rise in prosperity of artisans and small farmers. Sesostris III conquered Nubia and added it to his dominions. To get his ships upstream for the expedition, he cut a channel through the Aswan rapids, an impressive engineering feat.

Prosperity: Trade, Building Construction

Egypt's power and prosperity under the Middle Kingdom were displayed in various ways. Military expeditions, though few, penetrated south as far as Cush and possibly to the northeast as far as Syria; trading expeditions were again sent to far-off Punt; and copper mines in Sinai and gold mines in Nubia yielded their treasures for Egyptian coffers. Much building activity within Egypt gives testimony also to good government with prosperity. The emphasis was not on tombs but on temples and projects useful to Egyptian agriculture. The great temple complexes near Thebes, so closely associated later with the New Kingdom, were begun in this period. Most useful probably was a vast irrigation project at the Fayum in Middle Egypt.

The Fayum Basin, well below sea level, received the waters of the Nile when the river was in flood; when the Nile subsided, however, the water flowed from Fayum Lake (the Greek historians called it Lake Moeris). Amenemhet III (c. 1842–1797 B.C.) undertook huge works that had a double purpose: to reclaim land around the lake for farm production by controlling more precisely the level of the lake, and also to make better and more efficient use of the lake's waters for irrigation during the three months or so when the Nile was low. One single wall that he constructed was twenty-seven miles long. Altogether, more than 17,000 acres of land were made available for farmers and other thousands were better irrigated.

Middle Kingdom Literature

The literature of the period was of course varied, but it may be illustrated by an interesting work that reads much like a novelette, *The Story of Sinuhe*. Its immense popularity may be gauged by the numerous complete or partial copies that have survived. Sinuhe was a noble who for some obscure reason fled Egypt at the accession of Sesostris I. He took refuge with sheiks of the desert to the east and in Palestine. One of them, Retenu, took a dislike to him and challenged him to personal combat. Sinuhe evaded Retenu's missiles and his great war axe and shot him through the throat with his arrow. Thereafter he despoiled Retenu's property (as the latter had intended to do to him) and became wealthy. His sons grew up and became tribal leaders. When Sinuhe grew old and feeble, however, nostalgia for his own country overwhelmed him and somehow he got permission to return. The reader can almost feel Sinuhe's relief when he finally returned home and was bathed and shaved and dressed in fine linen. Then he slept on a bed instead of the floor of a tent. A pyramid was constructed for him; he would not, after all, have to be buried in a sheepskin in the sand.

Middle Kingdom Religion

The somewhat less lofty position of the pharaoh and of the nobility during the Middle Kingdom had interesting religious repercussions. A sort of "democratization" of religion, as it has sometimes been called, took place. People of the middle and lower classes—to judge by the contents of their tombs—began to hope for the afterlife once aspired to only by the upper classes. Yearly rites in the sanctuaries of Osiris, which reenacted the myth of his death and resurrection, now involved pilgrimages of great crowds of persons. Osiris by now was considered the chief god of the afterworld. Magical incantations, written on wooden coffins used by these classes, called *Coffin Texts*, were designed to ensure safe passage to the world beyond.

The last important king of the Middle Kingdom was Amenemhet III. The Thirteenth Dynasty kings somehow could not cope: A period of decline led to a second breakup of the unified land and produced the Second Intermediate Period.

I. THE SECOND INTERMEDIATE PERIOD (c. 1785-1575 B.C.); THE HYKSOS

As the authority of the Thirteenth Dynasty kings waned—and they certainly ruled all Egypt for a time—an increasing number of Asiatics established themselves in the eastern delta region. Manetho preserves a tradition of an invasion of the Hyksos, a violent irruption from the northeast that swept over all the land. The remains do not seem to bear out his story, however. Probably the Asiatics first managed to set up an administrative segment of northern Egypt as a virtually independent state; then, with help from others from the Phoenicia–Palestine area, they managed to enlarge their territory, expanding as far as Memphis. The Hyksos capital was at Avaris in the eastern part of the Nile Delta. Eventually they put all Egypt under tribute as kings of the Fifteenth and Sixteenth Dynasties. The term *Hyksos* means "highland rulers"; literary tradition makes it "shepherd kings," but this is wrong. Perhaps "foreign kings" would be more accurate terminology. The Hyksos used weapons that were perhaps new to the Egyptians, including the horse-drawn war chariot and the compound bow. Probably through syncretic identification, the Hyksos worshiped Set (identified with their own god, Baal) as their chief god.

A period of weakness and warfare naturally afflicted the people, and once again, as in the First Intermediate Period, literary remains lament destruction and disorder, though as before, the writers possibly exaggerated. Not only did Asiatics dominate much of the land from the delta, but Nubians moved in from the south and controlled portions of Upper Egypt. Domination by these Asiatics rankled the Egyptian conscience and banished the usual confidence and optimism. The Egyptians learned to hate, and they whetted their fighting abilities. The lasting impression made by the Hyksos did much to establish the essential character of the restored kingdom that followed.

J. THE NEW KINGDOM OR EMPIRE (c. 1575–1086 B.C.)

Expulsion of the Hyksos

The honor of smashing the Hyksos and of driving them out of Egypt belongs to two sons of Sekenenre, a king of the Theban Seventeenth Dynasty, Kamose and Ahmose. Apophis, the Hyksos ruler in their capital, Avaris, apparently heard that Sekenenre was plotting rebellion, for he sent an absurd message to the Theban king; he declared that the hippopotamuses in the pool beside Sekenenre's palace bellowed so loudly at night that he could not sleep. Since the two cities were several hundred miles apart, it must have been clear that there was an underlying symbolism. Sekenenre's mummy survives—and it has three holes in its skull. Perhaps Apophis made good his threat.

Kamose, however, took up the cause. An indication both of his problem and of his determination is evident in this hieratic document discovered early in this century (it is copied from a hieroglyphic stele discovered in 1954):

> I should like to know what serves this strength of mine, when a chieftain is in Avaris and another in Cush, and I sit united with an Asiatic and a Nubian, each man in possession of his slice of this Egypt, and I cannot pass by him as far as Memphis. . . . I will grapple with him and slit open his belly. My desire is to deliver Egypt and to smite the Asiatics.[4]

Against Kamose, Apophis attempted to make alliance with the Nubians to the south, but his message was intercepted. Kamose defeated the Hyksos and began a four-year siege of Avaris. After a time he either died or was killed, and Ahmose, his brother, succeeded. It was he who finally cleared the land of foreign rule and reigned over a reunited Egypt. Despite his relationship to the last rulers of the Seventeenth Dynasty, Ahmose is accounted the founder of the greatest dynasty of the New Kingdom or Empire, the Eighteenth. According to an inscription found at Karnak, the mother of these two kings, Queen Ahhotep, at one critical point— perhaps at the sudden death of Kamose—rallied the kingdom, preserving it for her other son; she may have been coregent with him for a time. The powerful position called "God's wife of Amon," held by other important queens in later years, may first have been created for her.

---

[4]Paraphrased by Sir A. Gardiner, *Egypt of the Pharaohs* (Oxford, 1961), p. 166.

The New Kingdom was militaristic, imperialistic, absolutist; in consider-able degree these characteristics were a reaction to the Hyksos' domination. A century after the foreigners were driven out, the Egyptian pharaohs, campaigning in Palestine and Syria, still called their invasions crusades against the Hyksos. A larger and more professional army was now maintained. The two viziers to the king were usually generals, their posts primarily military commands. Egypt's kings ruled from Cyrene on the west to Syria and beyond to the northeast and far into Nubia to the south (see map, p. 61). Government officials, including nomarchs, were appointed by the king and controlled by him. Imperial Egypt became the most powerful state in the Near East.

Hatshepsut: First Great Queen

One of the most remarkable rulers of the New Kingdom was the great Queen Hatshepsut (c. 1504–1482 B.C.). Her predecessors after Ahmose, Amenhotep

Model of the Temple of Queen Hatshepsut at Deir-el-Bahri. Note the remarkably modern-looking lines. (The Metropolitan Museum of Art)

I and Thutmose I, had stabilized the frontiers far beyond the bounds of Egypt proper. Thutmose had campaigned even to the Euphrates River east of Syria. There he no doubt had collided with the Hurrian kingdom of Mitanni (or Hanigalbat). He also pushed imperial frontiers deep into the Sudan. Hatshepsut was a daughter of this great king, who had no sons by his royal wife; a son by a secondary wife, however, married Hatshepsut, his half-sister, and became pharaoh (Thutmose II). He was short-lived, however, and his young son—again by a concubine and not by Hatshepsut—Thutmose III, remained in the background for more than twenty years as his stepmother ruled, first as regent and then as pharaoh.

Since the very concept "pharaoh" was masculine, together with all symbols and appurtenances of the office, artists and scribes were a little confused in portraying the queen and in cutting inscriptions. They sculptured her as a man, complete with beard, and referred to her in typical fashion as "son" of Amon-Re. To legitimize her position, Hatshepsut claimed to be literally the child of Amon and to have been crowned by Thutmose I himself.

Hatshepsut gave most attention to peaceful pursuits: Internal building and external trade were given priority. However, there were some military campaigns during her reign and she herself led one of them. She also had one of the most beautiful temples ever constructed carved into the side of a rocky bluff at Deir el-Bahri near Thebes. Featuring long colonnades on three terraces, the total effect is enormously pleasing to the modern eye. Reliefs show that the terraces were landscaped with myrrh trees imported from far away, with roots encased in balls of earth. At Karnak, near Thebes, she also added to the complex of temples to the god Amon, patron deity of the capital city.

Return to Imperialism: Thutmose III

Thutmose III hated Hatshepsut. When he finally succeeded to the throne he tried to obliterate the queen's name from the land. The hieroglyphic cartouches that spelled her name were chiseled out of her monuments and replaced with his own. Thutmose was much more imperialistic than his stepmother, partly because by this time the frontiers required attention. He made nineteen campaigns into the Palestine-Syria region alone and subdued the Hurrians, who had gained control of northeastern Syria. He was responsible, too, for beginning a tremendous building program at Karnak—to Amon, of course. Obelisks erected by Thutmose now stand in New York, London, Rome, and Istanbul. He reigned in his own right from about 1482 to 1450 B.C.

The New Kingdom reached its apogee with the reign of Amenhotep III (c. 1412–1375 B.C.), great grandson of Thutmose III. His power was great and his land was prosperous. Though all the agricultural land belonged to him—through most of history the *fellahin* have been tenants—probably the masses were better housed and better fed than their modern counterparts have often been. As is fitting for a grand monarch, Amenhotep erected huge buildings, pylons, and temples;

Egyptian Empire
18th Dynasty c. 1500 B.C.
◉ Capitals
■ Battle areas

some were at the twin temple centers of Karnak and Luxor, and some were along the magnificent way he constructed between the centers. Statues of himself seventy feet high, which the Greeks called the "Colossi of Memnon," stood in front of his funerary temple on the west bank of the Nile. He also built a huge new palace near Thebes.

Perhaps Amenhotep became too accustomed to peace, or perhaps the age became decadent. His new palace, called "The House of Rejoicing," seems somehow symbolic. Late representations of Amenhotep show him fat and somnolent, and we have solid evidence that the empire was in the same condition. This evidence comes from a site downriver from Thebes, called Tell el 'Amarna. Here, in 1887, a peasant woman found several clay tablets, which eventually, along with others to the number of about 350, found their way into the hands of dealers and collectors for the world's great museums. The tablets were official correspondence, mostly written to Amenhotep and to his son, Amenhotep IV, from the Palestine-Syria region. They tell of a breakdown in Egyptian control in that area and of Hittite kings and local sheiks moving in. The Egyptian rulers, however, did little about it.

Golden throne of Tutankhamen; the Pharaoh and his wife. (Photograph by Harry Burton, The Metropolitan Museum of Art)

The Religious Revolution of Akhnaton

Amarna was in that time Akhetaton, a new capital built mostly by Amen-hotep IV (Akhnaton). The names tell the story: Amenhotep, "Amon is satisfied," was dropped in favor of Akhnaton, "beneficial to Aton." Akhetaton means "horizon of Aton." The new city, some distance north of Thebes, was dedicated to the Aton, god of the sun disc. Akhnaton promoted religious revolution, making Atonism the state religion. He dissolved old priesthoods and closed the temples of the other gods. Amon-Re, hitherto the chief deity of the Empire, was a particular target of suppression. In a famous "psalm" to Aton, attributed perhaps correctly to Akhnaton, the writer declares,

> Thou appearest beautifully on the horizon of heaven,
> Thou living Aton, the beginning of life!
> .   .   .   .   .
> How manifold it is, what thou hast made!
> They are hidden from the face [of man].
> O sole god, like whom there is no other!
> Thou didst create the world according to thy desire,
> Whilst thou wert alone. . . .[5]

This hymn is much like earlier ones dedicated to Amon-Re—also a "universal" deity. And it also demonstrates that imperialism tends to produce a universal religion. The gods of the conquerors are always thought to be more powerful than those of the conquered. Thus the chief deity of Thebes tended to be accepted throughout the empire and to some degree beyond. Akhnaton's hymn, however, stresses prominently that Aton was "sole god." It seems to suggest monotheism, though on other grounds Atonism appears to have been something less than that. The Aton, earlier portrayed with a hawk-headed human form, was now pictured as the sun disc, and rays from the disc, like streamers, bless the devotees below.

The priests of Amon had become powerful and rich. To them went official portions of both spoils and tribute. It is therefore suggested that Akhnaton's motives in making Atonism the state religion were to curtail that priestly power—or, alternatively, that they were personal, perhaps in reaction to a family quarrel. Still, the lengths to which Akhnaton went in the interest of Aton suggest sincerity. Moreover, new forms of art and architecture broke strikingly with the past. The concept Ma'at (here it must mean Truth) brought realism. The most famous work of the Amarna age, the bust of Akhnaton's beautiful wife, Nofretete, is hardly typical. Akhnaton himself is presented as rather ugly, misshapen, effeminate. Some reliefs show a remarkably casual air. Also illustrative of the period are the finds of the tomb of Tutankhamon, son-in-law and successor of Akhnaton. Magnificent and rich they certainly are, but cloying, too, and sometimes overdone.

Tutankhamen—once Tutankhaton—was forced to return to Thebes and abjure the religious revolution of his father-in-law. Amarna, abandoned, became an accursed ghost city, and Akhnaton and all his family were branded "heretics" and "enemies." Tutankhamen, only a child when he came to the throne, died at eighteen. Except for the accident of the discovery of his intact tomb in 1922, he would not deserve mention. His widow, Ankhesenamon, the daughter of Akhnaton, tried to obtain another husband from the great Hittite king Suppiluliumas, but the Hittite scion was killed before he reached Egypt. The Eighteenth Dynasty staggered to a close. A general, Harmhab, who had served under Akhnaton but

[5]Pritchard, *ANE Anthology*, pp. 227–229.

Akhnaton and Nofretete. A model in relief from the workshop at Akhetaton (Amarna).
(Courtesy of the Brooklyn Museum, Charles Edwin Wilson Fund)

who had not been a convert to Atonism, at length took charge of the empire. He restored order internally and also recovered some lost territory on the frontiers. Apparently Harmhab had a long and somewhat successful reign, but he had no heir. His successor, short-lived Ramses I, founded a new dynasty in about 1303 B.C.

Restoration Under the Nineteenth Dynasty

The best-known pharaoh of the Nineteenth Dynasty is Ramses II (c. 1290–1223 B.C.). Campaigning vigorously in Syria to restore the old frontiers, he met with some success. We have his boastful account of a desperate battle with the Hittites, who ambushed him at Kadesh on the Orontes River. Only the king's personal courage, he claimed, snatched victory from the jaws of defeat. The frontier was stabilized at that location, however. A few years later he and the Hittite king, Hattusilis III, drew up a remarkable peace treaty that included such "modern" features as a nonaggression clause, provisions for conditional mutual aid, and an extradition agreement. Both kingdoms were weakened, however, by their long and hard-fought rivalry.

Ramses was perhaps the greatest builder of all the pharaohs. Best known are the huge Hypostyle Hall in the temple of Amon-Re at Karnak and the temple at Abu Simbel. The latter has been sawed into blocks in recent years and raised to a new site at tremendous expense in order to rescue it from the rising waters of the Aswan lake behind the Russian-built dam.

Invasions of the "Sea Peoples" and Decline

A series of foreign invasions undermined Egypt's strength beyond recovery at the end of the Nineteenth and during the Twentieth Dynasties (c. 1195–1086 B.C.). The invaders came from west and north, by land and by sea, and they included the Danu (perhaps Greeks?), the Peleset (Philistines), and others, some of whose names mean nothing today, such as the Sheklesh and the Weshesh. Ramses III (c. 1192–1160 B.C.) met the invaders and won, but at a terrible cost. Still, he managed to build extensively. His great temple at Medinet Habu is one of the best preserved major structures from ancient Egypt. Despite Ramses' supreme efforts, however, internal affairs were in disorder at the end of his reign.

The eight pharaohs of the Twentieth Dynasty following Ramses III—all also named Ramses—presided over a declining empire. Yet this was not at all a "dark age" as far as documentation is concerned, for much is known of life in Egypt during the period. Two of the longest scrolls of papyri preserved from antiquity, along with a mass of other evidence, illuminate the age and cast light on earlier times as well. The Harris papyrus, detailing Ramses III's building activities, and the equally important Wilbour papyrus, dealing with taxation and other matters, make it possible for scholars to estimate that as much as a third of the cultivable land of Egypt was then controlled by the temple priests, mostly those of Amon-Re at Thebes. Obviously, Akhnaton's efforts had not permanently reduced the financial power of this group. Much of the rest of the land—as was usually the case—belonged to the pharaoh. The first known organized workers' strikes date from the reign of Ramses III. There were numerous strikes in later years, usually because of a shortage of the food that was a part of their wages.

The end of the Twentieth Dynasty signals the end of the New Kingdom or Empire (1086 B.C.). There were later dynasties, naturally, and some of the pharaohs ruled a united Egypt. However, the age of the Twenty-first Dynasty and several others in antiquity remain generally obscure; often the pharaoh controlled only a fragment of historical Egypt. Sheshonk I of the Twenty-second Dynasty was rather strong, as we learn from the Hebrew Bible. The Twenty-fifth Dynasty was Ethiopian; the Twenty-sixth, ruling from Saïs, brought a brief renaissance in the seventh and sixth centuries B.C.; and the Twenty-seventh was Persian. After the Thirty-first Dynasty, Alexander the Great established Macedonian rule (the

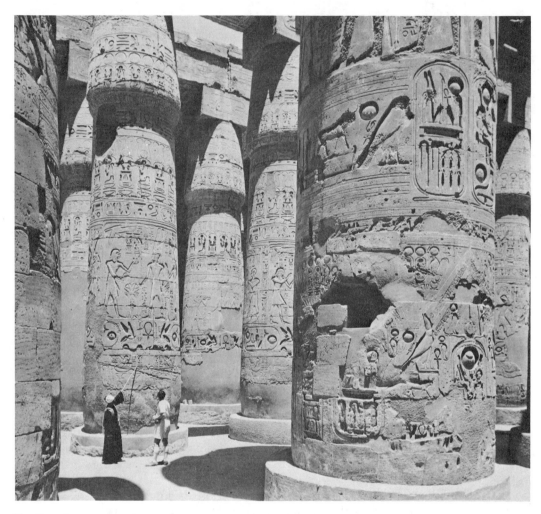

The pillars of the Hypostyle Hall. New Kingdom. (Through the courtesy of TWA Transworld Airlines, Inc.)

Ptolemies, ending with Cleopatra). Then, from 30 B.C. to the end of antiquity, the Romans held Egypt in their tight grasp.

Other Bronze Age Civilizations

The accomplishments of the earliest civilizations gradually diffused throughout the world. Ideas more than material objects spread, took root, and produced, not imitations of the original, but distinctive new growths. Thus it appears that the idea of writing spread from Mesopotamia, not the actual cuneiform system. The idea, carried afar, produced Egyptian hieroglyphics, a different hieroglyphic in Crete, and still different writing systems in both the Indus Valley (modern Pakistan) and China. And once the concept from Mesopotamia was introduced, the new system in each instance appeared suddenly, without long development. The later techniques for the smelting of copper and the production of bronze seem either to have spread swiftly from their Near East birthplace or to have been invented elsewhere independently—for not all of the great achievements of civilization were disseminated through diffusion. Archaeology and history know of many instances of separate development, often contemporaneous. Copper smelting and casting and pottery making, for example, seem now to have developed independently in Europe and thus were not imported from the Near East.

BOOKS FOR FURTHER READING

ALDRED, C. *Akhenaten and Nefertiti*, New York, 1973.

ALDRED, C. *Egypt to the End of the Old Kingdom*, London, 1965.

DESROCHES-NOBLECOURT, C. *Tutankhamen: Life and Death of a Pharaoh*, Boston, 1963.

EDWARDS, I. *The Pyramids of Egypt*, London, 1961.

EDWARDS, I. *Treasures of Tutankhamun*, London, 1963.

EMERY, W. *Archaic Egypt*, Baltimore, 1961.

FAGAN, B. *The Rape of the Nile: Tomb Robbers, Tourists, and Archaeologists in Egypt*, London, 1977.

FRANKFORT, H. *Ancient Egyptian Religion*, New York, 1948.

GARDINER, A. *Egypt of the Pharaohs*, Oxford, 1961.

LICHTHEIM, M. *Ancient Egyptian Literature*, 2 vols., Berkeley, 1975–1976.

MERTZ, B. *Red Land, Black Land*, New York, 1966.

MERTZ, B. *Temples, Tombs, and Hieroglyphs*, New York, 1964.

MORENZ, S. *Egyptian Religion*, London, 1973.

REDFORD, D. *Akhenaten; the Heretic King*, Princeton, 1984.

RUFFLE, J. *The Egyptians: An Introduction to Egyptian Archaeology*, Ithaca, N.Y., 1977.

SANDARS, N. *The Sea Peoples: Warriors of the Ancient Mediterranean, 1250–1150 B.C.*, London, 1978.

STEINDORF, G., and K. SEELE. *When Egypt Ruled the East*, Chicago, 1957.

VAN SETERS, J. *The Hyksos*, New Haven, 1966.

WHITE, J. *Everyday Life in Ancient Egypt*, London, 1963.

WILSON, J. *The Culture of Ancient Egypt*, Chicago, 1951.

4

HITTITES, PHOENICIANS, HEBREWS

A century ago no student of ancient history guessed that the Hittites once ruled a great empire comprising most of Asia Minor, Syria, and the region of the upper Euphrates. Evidence brought up by the spade has now proved that they did. Information on the Hittites once derived mostly from the Hebrew Bible. There the Hittites appear as a minor tribal group, listed along with the Hivites, Jebusites, Girgashites, and others as competitors with the Hebrews for the control of Palestine. Yet one mention of them in II Kings 7, dated to the last half of the ninth century B.C., suggests that the Hittite kings were men of some power: Israel's Syrian opponents fled because they thought the Hebrews "had hired the kings of the Hittites" against them. We now know that these "kings" were local chieftains who presided over the last remnants of the Hittite Empire, which flourished several centuries earlier.

In the late nineteenth century, Oxford professor A. H. Sayce collated scraps of information that had been accumulating and suggested that they indicated a Hittite dominion of considerable size. He noted especially certain art forms and finds of an unknown type of hieroglyphic. Serious and marvelously successful excavations began in 1906 with a German expedition led by Hugo Winckler. He chose to dig at Bogazköy, a promising site within the semicircular orbit of the Halys River, about ninety miles east of Ankara in modern Turkey. The ruins were of the ancient Hittite capital Hattusas. Winckler quickly began to find clay tablets by the thousands, the actual archives of the ancient empire.

Unfortunately, Winckler became so excited over his discoveries that he did not adequately superintend the excavations. The clay tablets, lying in orderly rows, were chucked out helter-skelter by workers who kept no record of their order. One reason for Winckler's excitement was that on the tablets he could read—those written in Babylonian cuneiform (Akkadian)—he found diplomatic correspondence that strikingly corroborated and supplemented information already in the historical record. He was especially elated by the discovery of a copy of the treaty made between Ramses II of Egypt and the Hittite king, Hattusilis (see p. 65), the text of which he had already seen in hieroglyphics on the walls of Ramses' temple in Egypt. These discoveries by Winckler and others, continuing and multiplying to the present, have made it possible to learn something of both the history and the culture of the Hittites.

A. THE HITTITES: A HISTORICAL SKETCH

Origins; The Old Kingdom

Apparently, the Hittites moved into the Anatolian plateau region around the beginning of the second millennium B.C. The name itself offers no clue to their origins, for *Hittite* derives from the name *Hatti*, given to the region of central Anatolia where they settled. One Hittite religious myth tells of their sun god coming up out of the water, which perhaps implies a previous location west of a large body of water—the Black Sea or, more likely, the Caspian? The invaders spoke an Indo-European language, which means that they were linguistically related to Greeks and Italians, among others, some of whom were also on the move at about that time.

The Hittites as a ruling elite set up a monarchy called the Old Kingdom; it was organized politically and socially along tribal and feudal lines. In some ways they were conquered by the conquered: Much of their culture was the product of assimilation. In the late seventeenth century B.C., Hittite kings began to expand south out of Asia Minor into Syria and adjacent areas. About 1600 B.C. a king named Mursilis carried out a raid as far south as Babylon, helping to put an end to what remained of the empire over which Hammurabi had ruled earlier. But then attacks from within Anatolia and disputes among the aristocracy over succession to the throne contributed to the empire's decline.

New Kingdom or Empire, c. 1450–c. 1200 B.C.

Renewed Hittite power at the end of the fifteenth century B.C. and during the fourteenth came after a reorganization of the kingship, which was strengthened at the expense of the nobles. Resurgent Egyptian thrusts up into Syria under the kings of the Eighteenth Dynasty helped spark the Hittite revival because the Egyptians weakened the Hurrians in upper Syria. Later, Egypt made an alliance with the Hurrian kingdom, Mitanni, which was centered on the upper Euphrates

Black Sea

• Hattusas
(Boghaz-koui)

Halys R.

TARUS MTS.

Sarus R.

Pyramus R.

Carchemish •

Euphrates R.

Orontes R.

Ugarit •

SYRIA

CYPRUS

SYRIAN

DESERT

Mediterranean

Kadesh

Byblos •

Sea

Sidon •

• Damascus

PHOENICIA

Tyre •

Sea of
Galilee

14th Century B.C.

Jerusalem

Ascalon •

Gaza •

Hebron

*Dead
Sea*

Hittite Empire
Kingdom of Mitanni
Egyptian Empire

River and dominated Assyria to the east and much of Syria to the west as well. In the days of Akhnaton, however, the Egyptians, occupied with their religious struggle at home, gave little support to their Mitannian ally, and Syria was open to penetration by the Hittites.

The imperialist Hittite king who skillfully seized the opportunity to expand at the expense of Egypt and its ally Mittani bore the alliterative name Suppiluliumas (c. 1380–1340 B.C.). In several campaigns he blunted the power of Mitanni and then destroyed it; next he conquered Syria. His sons became kings of some areas, and the rulers of other states became his vassals. A smaller Mitanni was reconstituted as a buffer state with Assyria farther east. The widow of Tutankhamen, it will be recalled, appealed to Suppiluliumas for a husband who, she said, would become king of Egypt. Suppiluliumas' correspondence shows that he hesitated, unbelieving. "Such a thing has never happened to me in my whole life," he wrote. He ordered an investigation. But then it was too late; the son who might have become Ankhesenamon's husband was killed at the borders of Egypt. If he had become king of Egypt, the history of the Near East might read much differently.

Another son of Suppiluliumas, Mursilis II (c. 1339–1306 B.C.), fought hard to hold the empire together. A vassal kingdom of Arzawa in western Asia Minor gave the Hittites continual trouble, and there were incursions from the northeast. Mursilis' son and successor, Muwatallis (c. 1306–1282 B.C.), had revolt on his hands in Syria, where the power of Egypt penetrated once again under the kings of the Nineteenth Dynasty. In a tremendous battle at Kadesh, which Ramses II claimed he won (see p. 64), Muwatallis fought the Egyptian armies to a draw. After a few years' standoff, Hattusilis III (1275–1250 B.C.), brother of Muwatallis, made the permanent treaty with Ramses already mentioned and stabilized the frontier for some years.

The succeeding Hittite kings also faced revolts, however, especially in Asia Minor from Arzawa, now under a vigorous new dynasty, and from Ahhiyawa, which seems to have been an island-based sea power (Rhodes?). The latter had once been on good terms with the Hittites, even sending royal sons for military training at Hattusas. Possibly the Ahhiyawans were as some think, Greek: Achaeans. In any event, the Ahhiyawans joined in the great campaigns of the "sea peoples" who struck inland and then south all the way to Egypt. They destroyed the Hittite Empire and all the cities along the Phoenician coast. Egypt, as we have seen, managed to beat off the invaders. Petty kings, usually called Hittite, continued to rule remnants of the empire in northern Syria. But the great days of Hittite power ended by about 1190 B.C.

B. HITTITE CULTURE

The mixed character of the Hittite culture is symbolized in the writing systems discovered by Winckler at Hattusas. There were two systems, borrowed from Mesopotamia and Egypt. There were also several languages: Hittite, from the conquered population, and Babylonian (Akkadian). In language, literature, art, religion, law, and government, the Hittites were borrowers and assimilators. Nevertheless there was, always, an element of originality. Even an untrained eye can quickly

Hittite relief from Carchemish. The composite figure presumably represents some deity.
Archaeological Museum, Ankara (New York Public Library Picture Collection)

learn to recognize the distinctive characteristics of Hittite sculpture, done mostly in low but sometimes in high relief. It is a sort of hybridized collation of Egyptian and Mesopotamian styles.

Technical and Military Innovations

In general terms, one of the most important achievements of the Hittites—at least of peoples ruled by the Hittites—was the advance made in the process of smelting iron. Their smelting process, at first localized in Cilicia late in the period of the empire, introduces the Iron Age. The new techniques, however, came too late to benefit the Hittite armies. Iron weapons could not be made cheaply, and at first they were probably no better than good bronze. Not until the rise of the Assyrians were whole armies equipped with iron weapons.

The Hittites did introduce important military innovations, although they learned a few things from the Hurrians, too. In chariotry and in siege tactics, their equipment was the best in the world. They had bigger horses, which could draw large, three-man chariots. And as for siege tactics, it astonished the world when Suppululiumas was able to take the strongly fortified city of Carchemish in Mitanni in just eight days. They also improved city defenses; gates were redesigned, and the idea of secret exits in walls for counterattacking a besieging enemy was also probably theirs.

Government and Law

In government, the king, though less powerful in the earlier period, was a strong figure in the Hittite Empire. He was not a god, not even the chief priest of the patron deity in the capital, but in state ceremonies he did function at times as a priest and he did become a god at death. Like all Indo-European peoples, however, the Hittites venerated their ancestors, so the fact that the king became a god at death probably does not mean much. The nobles held the key offices, with the most sensitive reserved for men connected with the king. The older feudal system of control of both local government and military procurement was gradually displaced during the empire by a more centralized system.

Mesopotamian influence was especially great not only in language but also in economics. Some cities located on trade routes within the empire were predominantly Babylonian. The law code, discovered in fragmentary form at Hattusas, demonstrates the commercial influence of Mesopotamia. The earliest laws of the Hittites were most concerned with rural problems; later additions to the code provided greater protection for commerce and movable property. Hittite law was somewhat less severe than that of the Semites of Mesopotamia; there was, for example, less use of the death penalty. That Hittite law was less harsh illustrates a principal difference in point of view between the Hittites and the earlier peoples of the Mesopotamian region. The Mesopotamians tried to propound what they thought was the law of the gods. The Hittites considered the law to be a man-made matter.

Religion and Literature

The religion and literature of the Hittites manifest the same combination of inner inspiration and foreign influence. Even Aryan deities from Mitanni were included in the official pantheon. Mesopotamian names for gods—Anu and Ishtar, for instance—turn up frequently. To some degree, it is possible to distinguish groups of gods that correspond to the various population groups of Anatolia. The chief deities of the Hittites were the sun goddess of Arinna, Wuru-semu; the weather god, or lord of the storm, Teshub; and Telepinus, a fertility deity. Teshub was a Hurrian god, and the religion and other elements of Hittite culture are sometimes termed Hurro-Hittite. The mythical story explaining the seasonal cycle was accepted, but with variation. Telepinus simply wanders away and goes to sleep, whereupon life on earth grinds to a halt. It is the lowly bee who eventually finds him and stings him to wakefulness and to a resumption of his duties. Other Hittite literature, except for the diplomatic correspondence already mentioned, includes few documents that are basically historical. In two or three accounts that have been found, however, the reigning king does justify his acts or his accession to power.

Recently, scholars have been stressing the Hittites' role as transmitters of culture. It is possible to see through them the various influences of Mesopotamia in later Western culture. In literature—especially the fertility myths—as in mathematics and astronomy, connections can be seen with later Mediterranean civilization, sometimes specifically, sometimes only generally. In view of the rather close relationship between the Hittites and the Greeks in Asia Minor, it is not unlikely that the role of the Hittites in the sweep of civilization westward was great. Both Homer and Hesiod seem to have used themes that must have been transmitted to the Greeks by the Hittites from the epic of Gilgamesh, translations of which, in three languages, were found at Bogazköy.

C. THE PHOENICIANS

Civilization and urban life came early to the eastern Mediterranean littoral, almost as early as to Mesopotamia and Egypt. An ancient tradition in the Phoenician city of Byblos, twenty miles north of present-day Beirut, claimed that it was the oldest city in the world, and indeed some of the cities in the area show evidence of a continuous history of 7,000 years or so. Certain inland cities, such as Damascus and Aleppo, also have a long history, and as we have seen (p. 28), Ebla had an advanced culture and powerful government in the middle of the third millennium B.C. The peoples of this area developed a civilization most closely approximating that of the Mesopotamians. They, too, were mostly Semitic, as was their language; naturally, the people also adopted the cuneiform system of writing that had evolved in Mesopotamia.

At the beginning of the Old Kingdom in Egypt, Phoenicians were already shipping their famous cedar lumber for use in the palaces and tombs of the Egyptian pharaohs and aristocrats. In turn, Egyptian products were sent to Phoenicia. Byblos became the chief center for distribution of Egyptian papyrus outside the country of origin, and in fact the word for book, *biblos* (thus *Bible*), derives from the name of that city. Phoenicians also became early distributors of bronze and other metal products. In recent decades, underwater archaeologists have recovered large chunks of bronze in the shape of bull hides, as well as finished bronze pans and implements, from ancient Phoenician shipwrecks of the middle second millennium B.C.

The Homeland

The location of their great cities, of course, helped to make the Phoenicians what they were. Their chief cities, Byblos, Tyre, and Sidon, were not only harbors on the eastern Mediterranean but also trading centers on the western curve of the Fertile Crescent. Such a city as Ugarit, farther north in modern Syria, was also a cosmopolitan center, a meeting place for crosscurrents from Egypt, Mesopotamia, and Hittite Anatolia. Connections with the Aramaic cities like Damascus, a few miles inland, also gave the Phoenicians access to important land routes. Their seamen, understandably enough, carried a distillation of culture with them on their journeys west.

The homeland produced certain products that were much in demand. Lumber from the Lebanon mountains, which paralleled the coast in two ranges separated by an interior valley, was widely exported. Metal products have already been mentioned. A superior and very expensive dye, which the Greeks simply called *purple*, was laboriously extracted from a species of shellfish.

Navigation, Exploration, Colonization

The Phoenicians sought always to improve the physical conditions of trade: better ships, better navigation, permanent trading stations, or full-fledged colonies. And they courageously explored uncharted and far-off regions. In antiquity exploration was desultory at best. The Romans at their height, for example, supported it but little. Here the Phoenicians pioneered.

It was probably the Phoenicians who built the first decked ships, the better to withstand the pounding of the Mediterranean's sudden storms. Most shipping, nevertheless, hugged the coasts. Phoenician navigators compiled logs that described the coastline minutely for their sailors; good anchorages (or, rather, protected beaches; ordinarily, boats were drawn up on the beach at night) and harbors were marked, hazards carefully noted, as were sources of fresh water and supplies.

In exploring and trading, the Phoenicians cruised not only the length of the Mediterranean but also probably north along the Atlantic shoreline as far as Britain and south along the west of Africa as far as Nigeria. There is some evidence of their having visited the Azores. One celebrated expedition in the service of Pharaoh Necho II of Egypt in the sixth century B.C. completely circumnavigated Africa from the Red Sea south and back via the Atlantic. The Greeks refused to believe the story brought back of the sun's movement across the sky on the right hand instead of the left. Our modern conclusion is that the story tends to prove the Phoenicians' claim; it shows that they passed to the south of the equator. The trip reportedly took three years. Other stories of Phoenician expeditions along the western coast of Africa, however, are described so vaguely by the Greeks that one suspects the wily Phoenicians deliberately misled the people who had become their chief competitors at sea.

The rivalry with the Greeks in western waters involved, of course, the products of trade—chiefly precious and semiprecious metals. Agricultural products could not possibly be profitable over a long haul. In exchange for the metals the traders gave manufactured items of high unit value.

Phoenicians and Greeks also competed in actual colonization of the western Mediterranean. The Phoenicians settled harbor sites and adjacent agricultural land along the North African coast, especially from Tunisia westward. Carthage became their most important North African colony. They were also predominant in southern Spain, western Sicily, and Sardinia. We now know that the earliest Phoenician colonization in the western Mediterranean occurred in the tenth century B.C., possibly in Sardinia; there is similar evidence for early settlement in Spain. The Greeks, who came west somewhat later, were concentrated in southern Italy, eastern Sicily, southern France, and to a lesser degree, eastern Spain.

The political independence that helped make the Phoenician achievement possible was the chance byproduct of the decline of great empires, primarily as the result of the destructive migrations of the sea peoples. These destroyed the major Phoenician cities as well, but they were rebuilt early in the twelfth century and within a matter of decades were again flourishing centers.

The Phoenicians had no unified political federation that spurred them on. The homeland was divided into city-states that sometimes cooperated and sometimes fought with one another in alliance with nearby states. Nor was there really a western empire. Phoenician tended to support Phoenician in the West, as Greek tended to support Greek. But neither of these great peoples ever managed to unite themselves politically. In their homeland the Phoenicians fought redoubtably against the Assyrians and Babylonians as each created an empire, but they finally yielded to both. In the later Persian Empire their ships furnished the fleets that in the fifth century B.C. brought oriental armies into Greece. The high period for Phoenician independent action and influence belongs to the six centuries between about 1200 and 600 B.C.

Disseminators of Culture

Culturally, Phoenicians were carriers more than originators. Their religion is now much more completely known than it was a few decades ago when scholars depended primarily on information from their Hebrew neighbors. Phoenicians, Hebrews, and other Canaanites had a similar background. The Phoenicians ultimately developed lofty concepts comparable to those of the Greeks, among others, and they frequently centered these concepts around one of the Baals, as Baal Shamin, the Lord of Heaven. And as in other ancient religions, each city had its patron deity. At Tyre, Melkart was the chief god; his consort, Astarte, was worshiped later as Tanit at Carthage, the colony of Tyre. The Greeks equated Melkart with Hercules. The Phoenicians put great stress on ethical values, but they also practiced temple prostitution and human sacrifice, at least in times of great danger. Recent archaeological finds at Carthage confirm what their enemies, the Romans, claimed: that Phoenician children were immolated down to at least 300 B.C. and probably later.

The form of written letters used by the Greeks, later by the Romans, and thereafter by all the Western world, came from Phoenicia. Whether this means that the Phoenicians should be credited with inventing the alphabet, however, is doubtful—and partly a matter of terminology. Forms of alphabets certainly were developed in the area, long before the high period of the Phoenicians, both from cuneiform and from hieroglyphics. But exactly who adapted these systems into the earliest alphabets is not yet precisely known. Archaeologists have found a cuneiform alphabetic system at Ras Shamra (ancient Ugarit) north of Phoenicia and date it to a period soon after 2000 B.C. At that time the Egyptian hieroglyphic was being similarly modified into an alphabet in the Sinai peninsula farther to the south.

There is also the matter of how an alphabet should be defined. The Semites generally did not write the vowel sounds but supplied them in the pronunciation. If, as some eminent linguists hold, there is no true alphabet until vowel sounds are written, then the credit for inventing one must go to the Greeks. Even so, here as elsewhere, the Phoenicians certainly played their characteristic role: They were the transmitters of all sorts of remarkable Near Eastern legacies to the West.

D. THE HEBREWS

If space in this volume were apportioned solely in relation to the political importance of successive kingdoms and empires, the Hebrews would deserve little more than a sentence in this chapter. On the other hand, if space were allotted in accordance with persistent influence in the modern world, the Hebrews would deserve many more pages than the few that follow. Three of the world's great religions derive from that of the Hebrews: Judaism, Christianity, and Islam. In general, the strongest forces operating in Western civilization today go back to Israel and Greece.

Since the Middle Ages, organized religion and church officers have played a gradually lessening role in politics, society, and the economy of all the great Western countries. The Hebrew approach to life, however—in the West the Judeo-Christian outlook—is still an underlying and integrating force for both individuals and states. People of the twentieth century have often attempted to combine the Judeo-Christian view of life with the rationalist-intellectual view that derives primarily from the thought and method of the great scientists and philosophers of ancient Greece.

To blend a scientific-rationalist approach to human knowledge with any sort of deep religious conviction is not easy. In individuals and in whole societies the effort continues to be made nonetheless—sometimes unwittingly, sometimes deliberately. Results have been erratic. The United States, for example, has at times seemed afflicted with a sort of spiritual schizophrenia as these forces pull in opposite directions.

E. HEBREW HISTORY

Origins

The later Hebrews by tradition traced their origins back to the patriarch Abraham. The Bible itself shows that not all the Hebrews of history, even in a very early period, were descendants of this single patriarch. Nevertheless, it is appropriate to begin with these traditional progenitors. Abraham was said to have come from Ur, which would place him in Sumer—if indeed his city was that Ur rather than another Ur in the vicinity of Haran on the upper Euphrates (which the Ebla tablets apparently mention), where his family and near relatives are said to have lived. Abraham next migrated to Palestine. He and his nephew Lot are pictured as well-to-do nomads whose wealth was in flocks and herds. Their travels and the manner of life indicated in the Bible fit in well with what is known from history and archaeology of the movements of Semitic peoples in this period. This does not mean precisely, as is sometimes claimed, that the finds of archaeology confirm the Hebrew tradition; the details of the biblical narrative are impossible to confirm—or to deny. The narrative is, however, basically plausible, even though it was written down at a much later time.

The greatest events of early Hebrew history in the Bible are these: the migration into Egypt of the descendants of Abraham, their fall into slavery, the Exodus from Egypt under the leadership of Moses, and the entrance into Palestine under Joshua after forty years of wandering. It is easy to dismiss the whole narrative as unhistorical because of the supernatural events described as part of the story. Yet again, the account can be made to fit—with some difficulty—into the framework of secular history, even though for the first three of these events there is no evidence outside the Bible.

Exodus

The biblical account places the length of captivity in Egypt at 400 or 430 years. Exact dating was not a fetish in antiquity, and this figure may simply mean ten or eleven generations (the Hebrews tended to take forty years as a generation). The earliest inscriptional evidence of a people Israel may be the stele of Pharaoh Merneptah found in Palestine and dated about 1220 B.C. The stele seems to mention Israel in connection with an Egyptian campaign there. For this and other reasons the first half of the thirteenth century B.C., in the reign of Ramses II, seems the most likely date for the Exodus; the wandering and entrance into Palestine come before 1220. If the entry into Egypt had occurred some 400 years before the Exodus, that would place the migration in the period of the Hyksos occupation of Egypt. Further, if the Hebrews were a part of that mixed group called the Hyksos, it can easily be seen how one of their number, Joseph, might rise to a position of importance in the government. The rise of a pharaoh who "knew not Joseph" would refer to the period after the expulsion of the Hyksos and would explain the fall of the Hebrews into servitude.

Excavation of the sites that marked the invasion of Palestine by Israel yields disappointingly little information regarding the chronology. At Jericho not much remains that is recent enough to provide information. The site called Ai in the Bible—said to have been destroyed by the Israelites—was in ruins long before the late Bronze Age and not rebuilt. But nearby Bethel was destroyed in the thirteenth century. Perhaps a confusion of names? Some other sites mentioned in the Bible as destroyed by Israel were indeed razed in the thirteenth century. The most important of these was Hazor, an impressively strong city in northern Palestine. It was more than two centuries before the Hebrews controlled the best, most productive portions of the land.

The Israelites, loosely organized by tribes, at first controlled only the Jordan valley and the high ground west of it. Leaders called "judges" arose as occasional champions against their enemies, especially the Philistines, who established themselves in the coastal area to the west. A judge like Samson could only provoke the warlike Philistines. At length the Israelites demanded a king of their own. Samuel, the last of the judges and a prophet as well, picked Saul, who was acclaimed by the tribes of Israel as their first king. The date was about 1020 B.C.

F. THE UNITED MONARCHY (c. 1020-921 B.C.)

Saul

Saul enjoyed some successes against the Philistines and others. But he was no grand monarch. His capital and his residence were unpretentious, and he had only a few hundred retainers. Efforts to increase his power met opposition even from Samuel; military levies were half-heartedly supported at best. When Saul began to suffer from fits of depression and when his military successes ended, his popularity vanished. Finally, about 1000 B.C., he and his sons were killed in battle by the Philistines at Mount Gilboa on the great plain called Jezreel or Esdraelon in north-central Palestine.

David

In the later years of Saul's reign, David had been the focus of opposition to the old king. And, indeed, the prophet Samuel declared that God's favor had been transferred from Saul to the young warrior. David was a charismatic leader whose reputation in war stood high, and he was the logical successor. The new king won a victory over the Philistines and captured the ancient Canaanite city of Jerusalem, which now became the capital of the united kingdom. Besides all of Palestine, David came to control the Negev and Sinai desert region to the south. He took tribute from the Philistines and from the people of Moab, Edom, and Ammon, all of whom lived east of the line of the Jordan, the Dead Sea, and the dry Arabah Valley that connects the sea with the Gulf of Aqabah. Other Transjordanian lands and southern Syria were also under his aegis. Considering the times, Israel had become a major power.

Solomon

The apex of the kingdom of Israel came in the brilliant and prosperous reign of Solomon, son of David (c. 961–922 B.C.). Solomon was later renowned for his wisdom, though to some it might seem unwise for a king to have a harem of

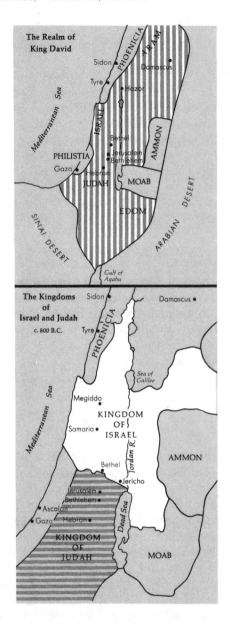

The Realm of King David

The Kingdoms of Israel and Judah c. 800 B.C.

300 wives and 700 concubines. His reputation for wisdom came perhaps from the fact that he started a collection of wise sayings, the Proverbs. The wives, many of them, were the result of diplomatic alliances; the most important probably was the daughter of a pharaoh of Egypt.

Solomon emphasized trade and commerce. He dominated the principal routes into Arabia and sat astride the roads from Mesopotamia to Egypt. He smelted copper in many places as an object of trade. The once-publicized mines at Ezion-geber in the Negev now appear not to have been worked in this age, though the mine shafts discovered in 1974 not far distant may have been worked by Solomon. Sometimes in conjunction with Hiram of Tyre, Solomon sent out shipping fleets to East Africa, Cyprus, Cilicia, and perhaps as far west as Spain. The story of the Queen of Sheba (in Yemen) coming to visit Solomon with sample goods is not at all unlikely.

Solomon was also a great builder. With timber from Phoenicia, he built a huge palace, called "The Forest" because of the amount of cedar used in its construction. More than a residence, it housed state offices. Much smaller, but significant both politically and religiously, was the Temple to Yahweh that he constructed at Jerusalem. Since the time of David, Jerusalem had become the religious center of the Hebrews as well as a political capital. Phoenician workers poured the great bronze pillars that stood before the temple and they aided in the artwork. Solomon also erected strategic forts, though he undertook few military campaigns. Hazor, Megiddo, and Gezer are three of the more important installations from which he held sway over his own territory and made it secure from attack. His expensive military establishment was organized about a core of chariotry. Horses came from Cilicia; the chariots, from Egypt.

Solomon's standing army, his building projects, his political establishment, his wives—all were expensive. Despite a bustling trade and successful commercial ventures, there was never enough money. And the measures that centralized his authority tended to loosen the old tribal ties. Even the priests, though supported by the king, were displeased with the degree of control he exercised—and with the various pagan influences that emanated from his harem. At his death the seeds of revolt lay ready to sprout.

G. THE DIVIDED MONARCHY (c. 921 B.C.): ISRAEL AND JUDAH

The Northern Kingdom: Ahab and Jehu

Under Solomon's son and successor, Rehoboam, the northern part of the kingdom seceded, and Rehoboam found himself unable to do anything about it. From that time until its destruction, the northern kingdom, called Israel (or the kingdom of Samaria after that became its capital), was separate from Judah (the kingdom of Jerusalem). The two sister states cooperated closely at times, but they also battled each other, too.

The northern kingdom, Israel, was more populous and more prosperous because within it lay the productive plain of Jezreel and a nearby market in the cities of Tyre and Sidon. Israel was often condemned by the Yahwist religious leaders. Its Phoenician connections and the larger Canaanite element in its population brought religious lapses in the view of the southern priests and prophets.

Their harsh judgments, however, have sometimes been mitigated by the different standards of historians.

The best-known king of Israel was Ahab (869–850 B.C.), son of Omri and husband of Jezebel, a Tyrian princess. Jezebel naturally supported the Baals of her Phoenician homeland and incurred the hatred of the Yahwists, whom she persecuted. Ahab is pictured by the Yahwists as weak and unscrupulous. But by chance, Assyrian records give a different account of Ahab's ability. He led an alliance of Israel, Tyre, and Damascus so powerful that for a time it halted the advance of expanding Assyria. Ahab's effort, however, and his military campaigns in Transjordan (for example, against Moab) bore heavily on the populace. Economic decline was soon followed by a struggle for the throne after Ahab's death.

Jehu (842–815 B.C.) finally seized the throne, killed all the blood relatives of Ahab, and restored the Yahwist religion. Israel, however, was never again as strong as it was under Ahab. Jehu paid tribute to Assyria. Some of his successors were prosperous enough, but in 722–721 B.C., after a coalition of Israel and Damascus was crushed by Assyria, Shalmaneser V and Sargon II destroyed Israel and razed its cities, including Samaria, the capital. Deporting the Hebrews from Israel and replacing them with men from elsewhere in the empire, the Assyrians changed the demographic character of the region and permanently weakened whatever bonds still held the two groups of Hebrews together. The Jews of later history derive mostly from the southern kingdom.

The Southern Kingdom: Hezekiah and Josiah

The kingdom of Judah endured until 587 B.C. as a more or less independent entity. At the time of the fall of Israel, Judah was allied with Assyria, and the Assyrians considered the little state part of their empire. A few years after the destruction of Israel, Judah, under King Hezekiah (715–687 B.C.), revolted. The Judeans were encouraged by a resurgent Egypt (then under an Ethiopian dynasty, the Twenty-fifth), by rebellion elsewhere in the Assyrian Empire, and by Hebrew reformers hoping to escape the religious influences fostered by the Assyrians. Besieged by Sennacherib, Hezekiah was forced to return to the fold and pay heavy tribute, but Jerusalem itself was not taken. A later king, Josiah (640–609 B.C.), was also a religious reformer. Lauded in the Hebrew Bible for his efforts, Josiah was able to effect reforms chiefly because the Assyrian Empire was disintegrating. Hebrews rejoiced when the Assyrian capital Nineveh fell to the Babylonians and Medes in 612 B.C. But Josiah was killed when he tried to stop an Egyptian force from coming to the aid of the remnants of the Assyrian Empire.

The Babylonian Captivity

The victory of Babylon over Assyrians and Egyptians in 605 did not, however, bring freedom to Judah. On the contrary, Jerusalem was soon taken by the Babylonians, and a revolt brought violent repression in 597 B.C. and again in 587

B.C. On both occasions large numbers of Jews of the upper classes were carried off to Babylonia. In 587 the last king, Zedekiah, was forced to watch the execution of his sons; he was then blinded and also sent captive to Babylon. Jerusalem was destroyed and looted. Palace, temple, and walls were razed to the ground. The poignant and bitter feelings of the captive Jews are vividly expressed in Psalm 137 (RSV):

> By the waters of Babylon, there we sat down and wept, when we remembered
>   Zion. . . .
>
> If I forget you, O Jerusalem, let my right hand wither!
> Let my tongue cleave to the roof of my mouth, . . .
>
> O daughter of Babylon, you devastator . . .
> Happy shall he be who takes your little ones and
>   Dashes them against the rock!

In Babylon most Jews managed to retain their identity and their religion. As we know from a Babylonian document, Zedekiah was apparently well treated. Yet, understandably, the Hebrews were pleased when Cyrus, king of Persia, defeated and took Babylon in 539 B.C. Cyrus and later Persian monarchs allowed the Hebrews to return to Jerusalem and to rebuild it, but Judah remained part of the empire of Persia and was not independent. When in 332 B.C. Alexander the Great of Macedonia took over Palestine in the process of conquering the Persian Empire, Judah came under his control. After his death Palestine was ruled by Macedonian dynasts who were the successors of Alexander; first the Ptolemies of Egypt, and after 200 B.C., the Seleucids of Syria.

H. THE DEVELOPMENT OF THE HEBREW RELIGION

Religion and History

One of the great strengths of Judaism, as well as of Christianity and Islam, is that it is a religion rooted in history rather than in myth. Yet it should not be assumed that great developments can always be explained by a study of surrounding events, in some way analogous to ecological studies in science. One does not "explain" Moses, Jesus, Mohammed, or for that matter, Socrates and Plato by scrutinizing the society that produced them. Nonetheless, by examining their society one does understand them better.

In a very early period, the religion of the progenitors of the people of Israel was the polytheism of other west Semites. When they migrated, however, they tended to accept the religion of the new land. Thus the Israelites were doubtless affected, religiously, by their stay in Egypt. One naturally looks, for example, for some indication of influence of Akhnaton's religious views on Israel. But the differences are greater than the similarities—for example, once the Hebrew leaders had settled on a single god, they did not at all identify him with the sun—and most scholars think there was little direct influence.

Moses and Monotheism

The Hebrew Bible underscores the leadership of Moses in the wilderness of Sinai during the catalytic events that made Israel a people and at the same time established the exclusive worship of one god, Yahweh.[1] It was said that through Moses God made a convenant with the tribes of Israel. In return for their loyalty and worship of him alone he would be to them a special deity and bless them in various ways. Such a contract relationship between a people and God has been compared with the amphictyonies of the Greeks, such as the Delphic Amphictyony to the god Apollo. The comparison may be useful, but it is certainly not exact. The idea of a covenant relationship with God for each Hebrew and for the nation as well is one of the most emphasized concepts of the Bible.

Whether the religion of the Mosaic period should be called monotheism is doubtful. Perhaps a few leaders were monotheist; certainly most Hebrews even long after the Exodus were not. Some scholars describe the religion of Israel at that time as a species of monolatry, or henotheism; that is, the Hebrews worshiped one god only but did not deny the existence of others.

The Reforming Prophets

A great period in the development of the Judaism of history came with the age of the reforming prophets—after the middle of the eighth century B.C. Amos was perhaps the first. Isaiah came a little later. In the time of the Babylonian conquests and captivity, Jeremiah, Ezekiel, and "Second Isaiah" were also leading prophets. There had been "prophets" at least as far back as Samuel. Samuel had a group of followers, apparently more or less apprentices, who with their successors were called "sons of prophets." They "prophesied" mostly ecstatically. Amos, curiously, declared that he was neither a prophet nor the son of a prophet, though he said he spoke in the name of God.

The reforming prophets were very much involved in politics, simply because the religion was also. Israel was a kind of theocratic state; political and religious leaders supposedly cooperated together in the name of God to guide the people. Amos predicted the fall of Israel to Assyria—which did not make him popular in high places. When some twenty years later Isaiah, with the Assyrians at

---

[1]In Hebrew, the name is written with four consonants, YHWH. The name was considered too sacred to pronounce, and since the vowel sounds were never written, the knowledge of them was lost. In early English translations of the Bible, vowels were supplied by using those from the word *Adonai* ("Lord"; this word was regularly substituted for YHWH wherever it appeared) and the name then spelled *Jehovah*. Modern scholars ordinarily use the spelling *Yahweh* as probably more accurate.

the gates of Jerusalem, argued that Judah could not possibly win, he was considered bad for morale, to say the least; some said he was being treasonous. Jeremiah predicted Jerusalem's fall to the Babylonians during the last siege; he was imprisoned and otherwise mistreated.

These prophets made God preeminently a god of history—or, perhaps more to the point, a god *in* history. Israel fell, they declared, because as a group its people broke the covenant with God. The Assyrians were thus not merely the conquerers of Israel, they were actually the "rod of God's wrath" (Isaiah 10:5). The deliverance of the city of Jerusalem in the time of Hezekiah reinforced these views. It caused some Jews to believe that their faith in God made the city impregnable to any foe, including the Babylonians. But the prophets saw Judah's corruption, her paganism, her spiritual prostitution. These, they said, would eventually bring on her the wrath of God by the hand of the Babylonians.

The Religious Influences of Exile and Restoration

Once in exile, however, the prophets preached the forgiveness of God upon repentance and the hope of a future restoration and golden age. Somehow the actuality of restoration, however, never measured up to their magnificent phraseology, especially that of the "Second Isaiah" as the latter chapters of the Hebrew book are often called. In consequence, many Hebrews felt that the real restoration was still to come. And it was to be accompanied with the restoration of the House of David, with religious revival, and with the outpouring of God's blessings on his favored people. Later sects, the Essenes and the Pharisees, placed particular emphasis on the leadership of the Anointed One, the Messiah, in effecting this restoration.

The great reforming prophets concentrated on an ethical transformation. Mere sacrifice and ritual could not please God, they maintained. Only ethics in action could do that. God for them was truly the sole god. He was the god of the Assyrians and the Babylonians also, whether or not they realized it—though not in the special sense that he was god of Israel. In these several ways, then, the developed religion of Israel was distinctive: it combined a strict monotheism with lofty ethics; in it God was ruler of the destinies of *all* people. This meant that in some usually explicable fashion, God was the guiding force behind human history.

The period after the Babylonian exile brought the restoration of the Yahwist religion in Judah. The temple was rebuilt and the liturgy restored. The stress laid on racial-religious purity tended to place the Jews in religious and cultural isolation. Still, they had been influenced by the religious crosscurrents encountered in exile. Dualistic concepts (Satan as well as God), the idea of a cosmic struggle between the forces of light and darkness with ultimate victory for the forces of order, and the teaching regarding a resurrection—much of which is evident in the Dead Sea Scrolls—are all usually taken as evidence of Persian-Zoroastrian influence.

I. THE HEBREW BIBLE AS LITERATURE

Organization

Quite aside from religion, the Hebrew Bible contains what is by far the most remarkable collection of history, poetry, philosophy, and romance to come out of the ancient Near East. The collection of books in the Hebrew Bible is divided into three main sections: the Torah (Law), the Prophets, and the Scriptures, or Writings. The Torah consists of the Pentateuch, five books attributed to Moses but in the present form put together at a later period and from several more or less parallel accounts. The Prophets are subdivided into the Former and the Latter. The Former Prophets are the historical books, Joshua, Judges, Kings, and Chronicles (some of which also show strands of composite authorship); the Latter Prophets are again subdivided into Major and Minor groups. The Writings include books compiled over a long period of time (Psalms, Proverbs) and the later works. Thus, for example, Daniel is listed with Scripture rather than with the Minor Prophets.

Law

The law code, or the Torah, has some unique features. Many of its provisions show Babylonian influences; some sections, for instance, are worded in a fashion closely similar to the code of Hammurabi. But there is a greater humanitarianism evident than in earlier law codes. Special sections provide for the welfare of widows, orphans, and even slaves. Lending money at interest (to fellow Jews) was prohibited; the taking of collateral was permitted but limited. In contrast with earlier codes, no distinction was made between classes. Of course, any student even of recent history knows that when some individuals are powerful and others are weak there is likely to be a broad gap between theory and practice in the application of law.

Philosophy

The Book of Job deserves a special comment because it deals essentially with a question that has always troubled the religious person. Why does evil exist? The date of Job is disputed; the picture of life it presents could easily belong to a very early period, but its position in the Bible and its theology and sophistication argue for a later date. It has been called a drama without action. As the consequence of encounters between God and Satan, God permits the Devil to afflict Job in order to test his faith. Job loses children, wealth, and health. The reasons for Job's suffering become the chief subject of discussion between Job and friends who come to visit him. They expound learnedly the view that Job is being punished for his sins and advise him to repent. Job denies that he has sinned, and in the process eventually becomes almost the accuser of God—who finally enters the controversy and rebukes them all. God emphasizes the unknowable wonders of

The Dead Sea Scrolls in the Shrine of the Book. (Israeli Government Tourist Office)

creation and man's comparatively insignificant knowledge. Ultimately Job is restored to health, wealth, and children. The question of the existence of evil in a world controlled by a beneficent god is answered in this way: God does not cause evil but permits it for his own inscrutable purposes, one of which is to improve individuals.

The Book of Ecclesiastes is a remarkable volume of literature also. Written by one Koheleth (or "the Preacher," traditionally thought to be Solomon though the book is late for his authorship), this work astonishes readers by its mechanism, its determinism, and its pessimism. Man's purpose is to endure; what he thinks is pleasure is transitory and vain. As for the possibility of life after death, the writer is profoundly pessimistic.

> There is no man that lives always, or that hopes for this:
> A living dog is better than a dead lion.

> For the living know that they shall die,
>   but the dead know nothing more
> Neither have they a reward any more:
>   for the memory of them is forgotten.

It is possible, perhaps, to find a bit of optimism in the last verses. At death, the spirit does "return to God, who gave it."

The Septuagint

A Greek translation of the Hebrew Bible, made in Egypt between about 300 B.C. and 100 B.C., has been extremely influential. Called the *Septuaginta*—abbreviated *LXX*—because seventy scholars are supposed to have participated in the translation, this version includes books omitted from the Hebrew canon. Some of the extra books are important historically: The two Books of the Maccabees, for example, tell of the Jewish struggles for independence from Seleucid control in the second century B.C. Jerome, translator of the Latin Vulgate, the official Bible of the Roman Catholic church, used the canon of the Septuagint; Protestant Bibles now usually follow the Hebrew canon and omit the extra books.

BOOKS FOR FURTHER READING

AHARONI, Y.   *The Archaeology of the Land of Israel,* Eng. lang. ed., Philadelphia, 1982.

AHARONI, Y.   *The Land of the Bible: A Historical Geography,* rev. ed., Philadelphia, 1979.

ALBRIGHT, W.   *From the Stone Age to Christianity,* New York, 1957.

ALBRIGHT, W.   *The Biblical Period from Abraham to Ezra,* New York, 1963.

BRIGHT, J.   *A History of Israel,* 3rd. ed., Philadelphia, 1981.

DE VAUX, R.   *Ancient Israel,* 2 vols., New York, 1965.

GURNEY, O.   *The Hittites,* rev. ed., Baltimore, 1964.

HARDEN, D.   *The Phoenicians,* New York, 1962.

LLOYD, S.   *Early Anatolia,* New York, 1967.

MACQUEEN, J.   *The Hittites and Their Contemporaries in Asia Minor,* Boulder, Colo., 1975.

MELLAART, J.   *The Archaeology of Ancient Turkey,* London, 1978.

MOOREY, P.   *Biblical Lands,* London, 1975.

VAN SETERS, J.   *Abraham in History and Tradition,* New Haven, 1975.

WRIGHT, G.   *Archaeology and the Bible,* rev. ed., Philadelphia, 1962.

5

LATER ORIENTAL EMPIRES:

assyrians, chaldeans, persians

In the last millennium before the present era, successive large empires dominated the Near East. Persia, the last of these before Alexander, was the largest. In human history the largest political units have been most successful in establishing peace, order, and prosperity. Ideally, then, it might be thought that up to the limits of effective exercise of control, the larger the empire the better. But as our study of the Greeks will show, certain other aspirations of the human soul are apparently best served when governmental units are small—even if their smallness results in wars, privation, and insecurity.

As conquerors, the Assyrians, Chaldeans, and Persians—and perhaps all others who ever attempted to govern an empire—found their most difficult task to be that of maintaining control over local government. The Assyrians tried stern coercion and deliberate and calculated terror. Leaders of revolts were impaled on stakes, skinned alive, or tortured in other indelicate ways, all of them publicized by the Assyrians. Assyrian kings supposed that such punishment would deter other would-be rebels. But what it reaped was a harvest of hate that became too great a burden. Finally, revolts in the subject monarchies revealed that Assyria was only a shell, that widespread loyal support no longer existed, not even in Assyria itself. When that occurred, the empire fell.

Chaldea in many ways followed the Assyrian imperial system. The Babylonians centralized authority and punished rebels repressively. But to little avail. The Chaldean Empire, too, though compact and blessed with good communications, crumbled with surprising ease.

The Persian Empire made notable political innovations. Satraps (governors) were put in charge of satrapies (provinces), replacing local kings or potentates. In an enormous undertaking, roads were built or improved. A post system enabled royal messengers to move swiftly over long distances. Because the Persian Empire stretched more than 3,000 miles on an east-west axis, communications were vital. Perhaps more important, Persian rulers were religiously tolerant and economically liberal. Yet this empire also weakened and fell through decay from within followed by invasion from without. Perhaps it was simply too large, for it tottered to its end more from dead weight than from the blows of the relatively small army of Alexander the Great.

Modern archaeology has added significantly to our knowledge of these three empires, but in main outline their history was already known through the Bible and through Greek sources, especially Herodotus' *Persian Wars*.

A. The Assyrian Empire (c. 858–612 B.C.)

The Setting

Assyria's location on the upper Tigris River meant that it was intimately involved in everything Mesopotamian, from culture to politics. Assyrians were Semites, closely related to the Babylonian Akkadians. The empire of Sargon of Akkad embraced Assyria around 2300 B.C. Somewhat later, kings of the Third Dynasty of Ur dominated the land. Shamshi-Adad (c. 1815–1782 B.C.), an Amorite like Hammurabi, seized control of Assyria and made it a leading kingdom, expanding its influence into the middle and upper Euphrates regions. After him, the Babylonian Hammurabi claimed control of the kingdom. Still later, the Hurrian rulers of the Kingdom of Mitanni dominated Assyria. When Suppiluliumas and the Hittites defeated Mitanni, Assyria, now free, once again rose to prominence. The cyclical pattern continued, however: The kingdom was strong in the fourteenth century, weak in the thirteenth, strong again in the twelfth.

Early Expansion

Tiglath-Pileser I (c. 1115–1077 B.C.), an energetic and fierce conqueror, became the prototype of the typical Assyrian ruler. His own records testify that he devised deliberate and brutal terror as a fixed policy. But he also, like some of the later Assyrian kings, stood between civilization and chaos. He crushed a semi-barbarous invasion from the northwest and extended his dominions as far west as Phoenicia, some of whose cities paid him tribute. But the empire then lost its strength, as did all of Mesopotamia, for reasons not well known.

In the ninth century, under Shalmaneser III (858–824 B.C.), Assyria once again waxed strong, driving west toward the Mediterranean and south to Babylon. As we saw in the sections on Hebrew history, Shalmaneser found himself checked

Winged Lion: guardian of the palace gate from the Palace of Ashur nasir pal II at Nimrud (Calah). (The Metropolitan Museum of Art, Gift of John D. Rockefeller, Jr., 1932)

by the alliance of Israel, Damascus, and Tyre. The check was temporary, however. He severely punished Damascus and soon brought Syria and Israel, too, under tribute.

Assyria's long, exhausting efforts to retain control of Babylon, then under Chaldean kings, was probably a mistake. Assyria's greatest military effort should have gone against its chief enemy in the north, Urartu, a kingdom centered about Lake Van. When Assyrian kings were preoccupied with the struggle against Babylon, the kings of Urartu bit off large chunks of Assyrian-dominated territory. For a time Assyria was able to maintain a valiant effort on all fronts. Under Tiglath-Pileser III (746–727 B.C.), Shalmaneser V (727–721 B.C.), and Sargon II (721–705 B.C.), Urartu was reduced in part, rebellious Babylon rewon, and troublesome Syria and Israel again subdued.

Imperial Heights

Assyria reached its height under Sennacherib (705–681 B.C.) and his son Esarhaddon (681–669 B.C.). Babylon again rebelled and was callously sacked, and Elam, east and south of ancient Sumer, submitted. Esarhaddon briefly occupied Egypt after routing the army of its Ethiopian rulers. At that point the Assyrian Empire included all the Fertile Crescent plus Egypt, Elam, Media, and territories in Armenia and Asia Minor west to Cilicia.

When the son of Esarhaddon came to the throne, Assyria seemed almost invincible. This son, Assurbanipal (669–626 B.C.), proved competent and intelligent, but though he strove mightily, and usually with success, he could not hand down intact to his successors the empire he had inherited. Egypt was the first loss: A vigorous new dynasty asserted Egyptian independence. A great and costly campaign barely kept Elam under control. Babylon continually raised rebellion and was virtually independent at Assurbanipal's death.

Finally two vassal kings, Nabopolassar of Babylon and Cyaxares of Media, headed up a conspiracy that besieged and destroyed Nineveh in 612 B.C., a date that marks the end of Assyria as a power. What remnants of it remained were obliterated despite Egyptian support in a battle at Carchemish on the upper Euphrates, in 605 B.C., by Nebuchadnezzar of Babylon.

B. ASSYRIAN CULTURE

Relief Sculpture

In art, architecture, literature, religion, and law, Assyrian culture was part and parcel of that of the general Mesopotamian region. Yet somehow the Assyrian achievement is often distinctive, demonstrating a freshness and originality even though within accepted patterns. These striking qualities are best seen in art, more particularly in the relief sculpture, of which an astonishing amount remains. The

Assyrian Empire

At its Height, about 665 B.C.

◉ Capitals
■ Battle

Assyrian ideal, brutal and masculine, stands out in the portrayals of both men and animals. Disciplined ranks of soldiers courageously attack walled cities; hunted lions charge to certain death. Assyrians, the Spartans of the Near East, admired strength, toughness, discipline, endurance, and loyalty.

The sculpture portrays more than brutality, however. Something magnificent is symbolized in the dying lioness, hindquarters paralyzed by cruel arrows, that still faces her enemies and snarls defiance. This element of pathos comes through even more touchingly in the scene of the hunted wild ass that, at the risk of her life, drops out of the fleeing herd as she looks back anxiously toward her colt, which is unable to keep up. Yet the hard ruthlessness is nearly always there. In one relief, Assurbanipal and his wife eat peacefully in a vineyard, but close by on a tree hangs the head of the Elamite king who tried to revolt.

The best relief sculptures were dug up at Nineveh, last of four capitals of Assyria (the others: Assur, Calah, Dur Sharrukin). Several of the later kings lavished their resources on Nineveh, especially Sennacherib and Assurbanipal. Many of the sculptures the latter commissioned are among the finest pieces in the British Museum. It has been estimated that if the bas-reliefs recovered from Nineveh were placed in a line they would stretch for nearly two miles. There were twenty-seven gates, all strongly fortified, guarded by massive composite creatures in stone. It was at Nineveh also that Assurbanipal collected his library, again demonstrating that Assyrians were more than hunters and warriors. We shudder when we see the sculptured panels showing men tied asprawl to four stakes, being flayed alive. Such savagery is the dark side of the Assyrian character. But it had virtues as well. The picture of Assyria as a parasitic kingdom living off crushed and cowed subjects is inaccurate and unfair. The Assyrians were probably no more brutal than most others in their time. Darius the Great of Persia, who has no particularly evil reputation, nevertheless once impaled 3,000 Babylonian leaders when he put down a revolt. But because the Assyrians publicized their brutality, their repute is low.

Religion

Assyrian religion was typically Semitic, much like that of the earlier Akkadians. The chief god was Assur, rather than Marduk as in Babylon. Ishtar was venerated in Assyria, as throughout Mesopotamia. When Assurbanipal campaigned in Elam, he discovered a statue of Ishtar that had been carried away from the city of Uruk about 1,500 years earlier; piously, he restored it to the ancient Sumerian site. It was to Ishtar as well as to Assur that Assurbanipal prayed for vengeance on the Greek ruler of Lydia, Gyges. Gyges had been allied with Assyria against the barbarous Cimmerians, but he had broken the treaty; when Gyges was killed in battle, the Assyrian king gave due thanks to his gods.

Architecture

In architecture, Assyrians introduced no outstanding new elements. Yet restorations of their walls, gates, and buildings are always impressive. Their use of stone must have given them a feeling of permanence that was lacking in areas where the building material was chiefly mud brick. This readily available limestone made possible the reliefs that adorned buildings and walls. The massive, human-headed winged lion and bullgod sculptures that stood sentinel at the gates of Assyrian cities must have helped any onlooker to feel, not merely to be aware of, the might that was Assyria.

Assyrians were excellent administrators who kept careful records, and modern historians are among the beneficiaries. Surviving annals give a clear though one-sided picture of military campaigns and territorial acquisitions. The basis for Near Eastern chronology through several centuries derives from Assyrian *limmu* lists of important magistrates, including the kings in their first regnal year. In recent years, for example, Hammurabi has been more accurately dated through a collation of Assyrian and other records.

Assyria's Lasting Reputation for Violence

The world will probably continue to view Assyria through eyes like those of the Hebrew prophet Nahum, who called Nineveh that "bloody city." He—understandably enough—exulted at the news of its destruction.

> Nineveh is laid waste
> Who shall bemoan thee?

Byron vividly echoes the same attitude. His lines,

> The Assyrian came down like a wolf on the fold,
> And his cohorts were gleaming in purple and gold,

describe Sennacherib's descent on Jerusalem. No imperial power in any age can expect to be loved by its victims. Even so, quite aside from ideals, can small nationalities ever be free? If the Assyrians had not dominated Judah the more barbarous Cimmerians might have. Moreover, the destruction of Nineveh did not mean freedom for Judah. Kings like Assurbanipal deserve to be remembered for more than their military exploits. And Nineveh was much more than a "bloody city."

C. CHALDEA OR NEO-BABYLONIA (626–539 B.C.)

The Magnificent City

Chaldean Babylonia calls to mind, usually, either Nebuchadnezzar's armies carrying away captive Jews of ravaged Jerusalem or the grand city, Babylon, described by a bedazzled Herodotus, sprawling in magnificence alongside the Euphrates. The Greek historian exaggerated a bit the extent of the city. When its chief excavator, Robert Koldewey, led a German expedition at the site several years before World War I, he found nothing quite so extensive as the fifteen-mile-square city that the ancient traveler described. What does remain is impressive enough. The Ishtar Gate, decorated with griffins and other figures in brightly colored glazed tiles, is truly remarkable—sufficiently remarkable for Koldewey to carry it off to Berlin, where it stands, reconstructed, in a special huge room of the Berlin Museum.

Nabopolassar (625–605 B.C.), as we have seen, aided in the siege of Nineveh. He lived long enough to learn that his son and successor, Nebuchadnezzar (605–562 B.C.), had crushed the last remnants of Assyrian power at Carchemish. All the Syria-Palestine region was swiftly brought under Babylonian control; even the island fort-city Tyre submitted. Babylon maintained its alliance with Media,

**Chaldean Empire
at the Time of
Nebuchadnezzar**
About 570 B.C.

⊙ Capitals
★ Ruins

and Nebuchadnezzar married a Median princess. Babylon was rich. The best agricultural land and the most important trade routes of the Fertile Crescent lay in
her dominions. Certain Babylonian industries, principally textiles and metals,
flourished. Nebuchadnezzar could and did play the role of the grand monarch.

Nabonidus: Last Great King of Babylon

The last king of the Chaldean Empire was Nabonidus (555–539 B.C.). For
some reason it seems he encouraged Cyrus, king of Persia, to rebel against the
dominant Medes—a ploy that proved to be a mistake. Persia soon grew stronger
than Media and turned on Babylon. When Cyrus' armies appeared before Babylon
in 539 B.C., the great city fell without a fight. Perhaps most Babylonians preferred
Cyrus over Nabonidus as their king.

Possibly the Jews in Babylon were also pro-Persian. The author of the late
chapters of Isaiah names Cyrus as chosen by God. One of Cyrus' first acts was to
pass an edict to permit Jews to return to their homeland. Without question, the
Jews hated the Chaldeans, as the anti-Babylonian emotion displayed in the Book
of Daniel testifies (though the book as now compiled is of later date). Belshazzar,
crown prince of Babylonia, arrogantly and impiously made sacrilegious use of the
vessels from the temple even as the enemy surrounded the seemingly impregnable

Detail of the Ishtar Gate at Babylon, Nebuchadnezzar's day (restored).
(Staatsbibliothek preussischer Kulturbesirz, Berlin)

city. Then appeared the handwriting on the wall, which, interpreted by Daniel, prophesied impending doom.

The Babylonians' disaffection with Nabonidus seems to have been connected with his religious policy. The king apparently tried to make Sin, the moon god, the chief god of the empire, displacing Marduk, patron deity of Babylon. Nabonidus' mother was high priestess of Sin at Haran on the upper Euphrates, and the king made his daughter chief priestess to the same god at Ur and at the same time spent a huge sum restoring Ur's ziggurat and temple. He also announced plans to rebuild the temple at Haran on a magnificent scale, though he was never able to effect them because of opposition in Babylon. Nabonidus, moved by some deep conviction, not only attended to Sin; he neglected Marduk. Our evidence includes complaints against him in Babylon that for years he had failed to conduct the new year's celebrations to Marduk.

Nabonidus' motivation and intent cannot be known. He may have felt that the empire was too Babylon-centered, that Marduk was not a universal enough deity to serve as chief god for the whole empire. Sin, on the other hand—or at least a god identified with the moon—was worshiped everywhere. Curiously, Nabonidus withdrew from Babylon and for ten years lived in the Arabian desert, leaving his son Belshazzar to act for him. But Nabonidus was not, as he is sometimes pictured, in scholarly retirement or semimonastic retreat. He was planting colonies in Arabia along important trade routes. The Persian threat in 539 B.C. brought him back to Babylon, but he was unable to rally the people. It is even speculated that he himself opened the gates of the city to Cyrus. However it happened, Cyrus was welcomed as a liberator by the Babylonian citizens. Cyrus took care to be properly installed as king of Babylonia by Marduk, and he meticulously and promptly celebrated the new year's festivals.

The Art and Architecture
of Nebuchadnezzar's Babylon

Nebuchadnezzar embellished Babylon and made it a showplace of the age. He built the Hanging Gardens, one of the Seven Wonders of the ancient world, it was said, to please his Median wife; languishing in the flat, hot Babylonian plain, she was unhappy away from her homeland of hills and mountains. Basically the gardens were an artificial plateau irrigated on top by a continous-chain-type pump. The structure, part of a large palace, was faced with stone, a rarity in Babylon, rich as the city was. Probably the gardens were said to be "hanging" because at a distance from the city the greenery on top seemed to float in the air, unsupported. Important too was the ziggurat, with its temple of Marduk, lofty enough even centuries earlier to give rise to the story of the Tower of Babel. The citadel, also faced with stone, loomed above one corner of the city. The Ishtar Gate opened to a Triumphal Way leading to the precincts of Marduk; the gate and the walls flanking the avenue were decorated with colorful griffins and other creatures on a blue background, all in enameled brick. The city walls, more massive than those at Nineveh and about the same length—eight miles—were girded with a moat filled with water from the connecting Euphrates River. The river even ran under a portion of the wall. One story of the city's fall had Cyrus divert the entire river into an irrigation reservoir so that his army could march under the wall. With the fall of the city in 539 B.C., the empire collapsed—swallowed up in the huge and ever-expanding Persian Empire.

D. EMPIRE OF THE MEDES AND PERSIANS (612–330 B.C.)

Most people today remember the Medes and the Persians from either the visions of the Four Empires in the Book of Daniel or, more likely, from the Greek accounts of the great battles with the Persian invaders at Marathon, Salamis, and Plataea. The wars with Greece were important enough to the Medes and Persians, but hardly so crucial as they were to the Greeks. From the viewpoint of the Persians, most of our textbooks have overemphasized these wars. Yet for Western civilization the conflicts acquire great significance because the Greeks themselves became the intellectual leaders of the civilized world. The Greco-Persian collision is often described in detail for another quite simple reason: We know more about this portion of Persian history because the Greek historians wrote about it. In this chapter we shall attempt a balanced sketch. Persia's wars with the Greeks will be given greater emphasis in the section on Greek history.

The Medes and the Persians lived in a plateau region ringed by mountains, the Medes south of the Caspian Sea, the Persians farther south, east of Elam. The Elburz Mountains just below the Caspian rise as high as 18,000 feet; to the west, overlooking the Mesopotamian plain, is the considerably lower Zagros range. Most of the land of the Medes and Persians was (and is) semiarid—suitable more for pasture than for agriculture, though in some areas enough water was found to irrigate crops. The Medes raised the best horses in the Near East; everywhere flocks and herds were their standards of wealth. As might be expected of a people made up mostly of nomads, the clan or tribe was the chief social and political unit in an early period. Both Medes and Persians spoke an Indo-European language. Though the areas they dominated were racially mixed, their ruling class seems to have been Aryan, related to the invaders who destroyed the Indus River civilization around 1500 B.C. and to the Hittites and some Mitannians.

E. POLITICAL HISTORY OF THE MEDES AND PERSIANS

Rise of Media

Media was probably unified as a kingdom under the impact of both barbarian invasions and Assyrian raids. The Assyrians valued the horses of the Medes, and after the middle eighth century B.C. they dominated much of the region and established a kind of typical vassal kingdom. The Median monarchs in their turn gained ascendancy over the Persians to the south—who were also ruled by a king but now vassal to the Median rulers. Both Medes and Persians were thus loosely subject to Assyria.

Cyaxares (c. 633–585 B.C.) transformed Media into a real power. As we have seen, he joined with Nabopolassar of Babylon to destroy Assyria in 612 B.C. While Babylon consolidated its hold on the Fertile Crescent, Cyaxares seized the former Assyrian dominions to the east of the upper Tigris and to the north from Lake Van westward into Anatolia. He also controlled some new territory to the east of Media, but how much is uncertain. Median expansion into Anatolia brought war with the king of Lydia, who also was attempting to take advantage of the Assyrian demise. A celebrated eclipse of the sun in 585 B.C.—later claimed to have been predicted by Thales, a Milesian Greek—caused the opposing armies to halt at this sign of displeasure from the gods and a peace was negotiated that set the common boundary between Lydia and Media on the western sweep of the Halys River.

Media Subordinated; The Persian Empire and Cyrus

In 550 B.C. Astyages (585–550 B.C.), the son of Cyaxares and a comparatively weak ruler, was deposed by the Persian king, Cyrus the Great. Cyrus was king of Persia from 559 B.C. and of the whole empire from 550 to 529 B.C. The Medo-Persian Empire thus suddenly became the Persian Empire. This dynasty of Persian kings is termed *Achaemenid* because it was founded—several generations earlier—by a king called Achaemenes.

We have little beyond unreliable Greek sources to explain why Cyrus turned on Astyages. The Persian is presented as the noble hero; Astyages, as the cruel scoundrel. But ambition is as likely an explanation as any. Though Cyrus used force to assert his hegemony over the whole empire, apparently no major war took place between Persians and Medes; the army of Astyages, it seems, simply deserted to the Persian.

Greek historians, especially Xenophon in his *Cyropaedia (Education of Cyrus)*, presented Cyrus as the enlightened paragon. What we know from his deeds confirms a degree of tolerance and enlightenment, but mostly he was a warrior. His first acquisition was the kingdom of Lydia. Its king was the legendary Croesus. Reportedly encouraged by the Delphic Oracle in Greece, Croesus tried to expand east across the Halys River on hearing of the disorder within Medo-Persia. But Cyrus moved west with his army, defeated Croesus, who soon died or was killed, and then took over all of western Asia Minor (548–546 B.C.). Many Greeks in this region thus became Persian subjects. In subsequent years Cyrus conquered huge chunks of territory in Iran eastward to the edge of the Indus valley. And, as we have seen, at last he took over Babylon and the Fertile Crescent in 539. Cyrus was killed while campaigning northward in an effort to add Armenia to the empire.

Cambyses

Cambyses, son of Cyrus (529–522 B.C.), wished to perpetuate the image of the king as conqueror. He therefore invaded and annexed Egypt and received as well the submission of Cyrene on the Mediterranean west of Egypt. Herodotus gives Cambyses an especially bad image, portraying him as cruel, alcoholic, and disrespectful of the Egyptian gods. In some details this picture is demonstrably false, though there may have been defects in his character. The king died or was killed while hastening home to put down a revolt.

In our sources (p. 20), the revolt was the work of a Magian priest, Gaumata, who claimed to be Bardiya (or Smerdis), the brother of Cambyses. Cambyses, however, reportedly had already killed Bardiya. Several noblemen eligible for the throne, including Darius, joined together to defeat the false Bardiya. Herodotus tells a delightful and no doubt fanciful story of what followed. The noblemen agreed to ride their horses to a certain field at dawn and that man would be king whose horse neighed first. The cunning groom of Darius took the nobleman's stallion to the field the preceding night and introduced him to a willing mare. When the horse therefore arrived at the field the next morning his romantic memories caused him to neigh wildly. Whereupon Darius was acclaimed king. One learns more about Herodotus than about Persian history from this tale.

We have Darius' own account of the revolt and his accession, on the famous cuneiform Behistun inscription mentioned in Chapter 2. Darius claimed that Gaumata seized the throne in the absence of Cambyses, that the latter died naturally, and that he alone, with the aid of the god Ahura Mazda and a few other Persians, was able to slay the false Bardiya and keep the kingship in the family. (Darius was from a parallel branch of the Achaemenid family.) There are skeptics who suspect that the Bardiya Darius killed was the real son of Cyrus, and that Cambyses had not killed his brother at all.

Darius the Great

Darius (521–486 B.C.) felt that he, too, must be the warrior-king. He therefore expanded into the Indus region on the east and into Europe on the west. The Greek historians told how the Persian king's army crossed the Bosporus over a bridge of ships in 513 B.C. Much of Thrace and Macedonia, with their valuable gold and silver mines, was annexed, but a move north of the Danube River to subdue the Scythians nearly resulted in disaster. Overall, however, Darius could report a successful campaign. Aside from this particular campaign, Darius and earlier Persians must have been more successful against the Scythians than the Greeks knew. Recent archaeological digs in the Soviet Union, in the Crimea, and around the Sea of Azov have shown that Persian influence, if not control, of the area was extensive.

Darius the Great's imbroglio with the Greeks began in 499 B.C. with a revolt of the Ionians—Greek inhabitants of the western shore of Asia Minor. Causes for the revolt surely related to social, political, and economic changes then affecting all the Greek cities. Some support came to the Ionians from the Greek mainland; Athenians helped the Milesians to burn Sardis, for example, the Persian administrative center in Asia Minor. As a consequence, Darius decided to punish the mainland Greeks, Athens in particular. His first expedition, moving along the north Aegean by land and sea, was aborted because of the terrible storms that battered his supply fleet. The second expedition, in 490 B.C., came to grief at Mar-

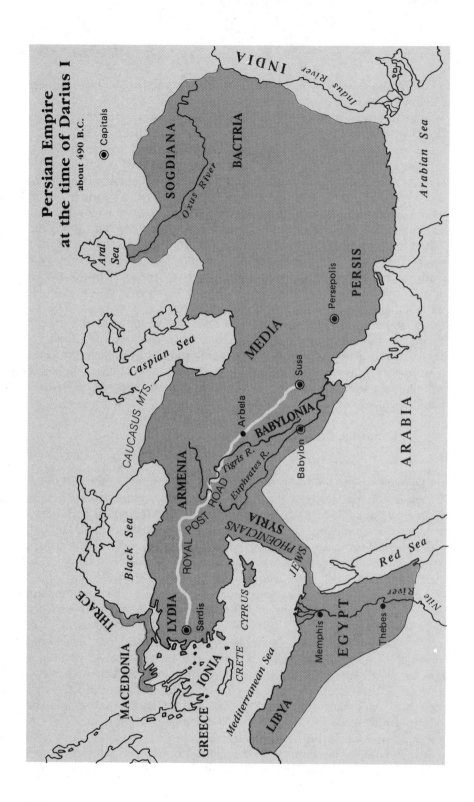

Persian Empire
at the time of Darius I
about 490 B.C.

◉ Capitals

athon. The Persians captured several islands that had been trouble spots, however, so for Darius the Greek campaign was no ignominious failure. Still, the setback called for future action—which Darius never lived to undertake.

Administrative Organization

Darius gave much attention to administration, and it was he who set up the provinces called satrapies, governed by appointed satraps. Civil authority was in their hands, but not military; the military districts did not correspond to the boundaries of the satrapies. Darius was a cautious, suspicious man. In his time, also, communications were vastly improved. The most famous route was the Royal Road that led 1,500 miles from Sardis in Asia Minor to Susa, the capital. He set up posts along all the major roads at intervals of a day's journey, thereby making feasible a rapid relay of messages or the swift movement of imperial officials. Because the empire was about the size of the forty-eight continental United States, only such measures made it possible to hold it together. The Greek historians wrote about imperial spies, the "eyes and ears of the king." They seem, however, to have misunderstood terms that applied to two government departments, though Darius did, of course, take pains to keep himself well informed.

A new capital, Persepolis, located east of the old one and at a higher elevation, was also the work of Darius. Susa was too hot during much of the year. Ecbatana, the old Median capital north toward the Caspian Sea, was also an administrative center, but Darius wanted something new and grand. The remains show both Assyrian and Greek influence though there are distinctive features. Curiously, not many foreigners visited the site. Before Alexander no Greek to our knowledge had seen Persepolis. Yet it had the main treasury and it was surely too extensive to have been only a residential palace.

Xerxes and the Later Kings

Xerxes (485–465 B.C.) first occupied himself with putting down a revolt in Egypt that had broken out before Darius' death. After that success he was ready for vengeance on the Greeks for their defiance of his father. The great invasion of 480 B.C. probably mustered the largest land army yet assembled by any king, though the Greeks' estimates running into the millions were wildly exaggerated. The defeats of 480 and 479 in Greece, and even more, the later defeats on the Asia Minor littoral at the hands of Greek amphibious forces, were serious. Indeed, the Asia Minor littoral became for the Persians a kind of running sore. Babylon also revolted against Xerxes but was successfully reduced. Unfortunately, Xerxes compounded his problems by deciding that his predecessors had been too considerate of local mores. His efforts to change that made the Persian kings far less acceptable in a number of quarters.

Among the later kings to the end of the empire were Artaxerxes I (465–424 B.C.), whose chief worry was another revolt in Egypt, abetted by Athens; Artaxerxes II (404–359 B.C.), who was nearly deposed by his brother Cyrus, with the help of more than 10,000 Greeks; and Darius III (336–330 B.C.), defeated and displaced by Alexander the Great. Darius III was in some ways the most pitiable of all. In fact, the quality of kingship from Darius the Great onward seems to have deteriorated with each accession. Major causes for decline, besides bureaucratic dead weight, incompetence, and the normal difficulties of holding together so disparate and widespread a mass of people as those living in imperial Persia, seem to have been mostly economic. Too much was spent on palaces and harems. Above all, too great a percentage of the precious metal taken in taxes was simply melted into bullion and stored in the king's treasure houses. The consequent shortage of hard currency had a depressing effect.

F. PERSIAN RELIGION AND CULTURE

In terms of their later impact, two Persian contributions to civilization were primary. The first was the idea of one world, of the unification of all "civilized" people; the second was Zoroastrianism. The Greeks caught the vision of one world but did not successfully implement it. The idea was again dominant in the days of Rome; the poet Vergil, for example, expressed it eloquently. It may also be seen in the works of the Christian apostle Paul. In the medieval age it was the spirit of the so-called Holy Roman Empire. And in the early modern period it remained a potent concept, influencing the actions of many a king.

Zoroastrianism

The Zoroastrian religion was immensely influential, also. Zoroaster (Persian Zarathustra) himself remains a shadowy figure. Many scholars have decided to accept the first half of the sixth centurey B.C. as the time in which he flourished, but there is some evidence that would place him earlier. The chief source of information about this Persian religion is the sacred book of the later Zoroastrians, the Zend Avesta. A proper understanding of it, however, requires at least as great a scholarly effort as has been put into the study of the Hebrew Bible. The language itself is not well understood, many words are obscure in meaning, and even the order of the book is a matter of dispute.

The Sacred Books

The Zend Avesta was written down only in the Sassanian period, in the third century A.D. The earliest part is the Yasna, in which are found seventeen Gathas or hymns. These are usually thought to be the writings of Zoroaster himself. Unless interpreted allegorically, they imply a certain naiveté and a rather rural life for the prophet. The work indicates that the prophet endured a period of persecution, but was finally given protection by a ruler named Vishtaspa.

The ruins of the entrance to the Palace of Darius at Persepolis. (Iran Information and Tourism Center)

In many ways Zoroaster's role in Persia is analogous to that of the reforming prophets in Palestine. Like them he preached social justice and taught theology. Like them he claimed inspiration from his god, Ahura Mazda. Zoroaster spoke of a cosmic dualism, of a struggle between the forces of good, centered in Ahura Mazda, and those of evil, headed by Ahriman. Ahura Mazda was god of light, order, righteousness, and truth. Ahriman stood for darkness, chaos, injustice, and the lie. So great is the focus on Ahura Mazda, however, that some see Zoroaster as virtually a monotheist, though the developed religion in Achaemenid times remained basically polytheistic. In a later time, Ahura Mazda was no more than chief of the gods of light. The later religion also acquired priests: the Magi, who took over the religion. In Zoroaster's lifetime, they probably opposed his views.

Humankind in the Cosmos

Humanity's role in the cosmic struggle assumed great significance. Each person was to choose sides in the struggle; naturally the prophet taught that one should fight on the side of Ahura Mazda.

> Contemplate with clear mind the two ways
> Between which every man must choose for himself; . . .
> Now in the beginning the two spirits which are as it were twins
> Are the one good, the other evil,
> In thought, word, and deed. And between these two
> The wise make a good choice, but not the foolish.[1]

Zoroaster and his followers wove strands of existing religious beliefs into a new theological fabric, but many of the old elements remained. Worship of fire and earth and of certain of the older gods continued. Mithra, for example, son of the sun, became a chief helper of Ahura Mazda. Still later he was the focus of a related but separate religion, Mithraism. Zoroaster seems to have taught of a final judgment, the "bridge of separation," and spoke of saviors—who may only have been right-thinking rulers. His later followers, however, came up with a more precise set of eschatological beliefs based on millennia. The world was to last 12,000 years arranged in quarters of 3,000 years each. The first period was a golden age. The second saw the outbreak of warfare between the dual gods. At the beginning of the third came Zoroaster, to help tilt the balance in favor of the Good. The last was to be a new golden age.

Zoroaster influenced not only Persians and other orientals but also Hebrews and Christians, among others. One of Plato's pupils refers to him, and it is possible that the great philosopher himself received some of his celebrated ideas from the prophet's view of the nature of man.

This example of the influence of an eastern religious leader on the greatest mind of the Greeks serves to reemphasize the extensive and continuing impact of the ideas and ways of ancient Near Eastern civilization on Western civilization.

---

[1]*Yasna 30*; from A. C. Bouquet, *Sacred Books of the World* (Baltimore, Md.: Penguin Books, 1954), p. 117.

BOOKS FOR FURTHER READING

AHARONI, Y.   *The Archaeology of the Land of Israel,* Eng. lang. ed., Philadelphia, 1982.

BRIGHT, J.   *A History of Israel,* 3rd. ed., Philadelphia, 1981.

CONTENAU, G.   *Everyday Life in Babylon and Assyria,* New York, 1966.

COOK, J.   *The Persian Empire,* New York, 1983.

CULICAN, W.   *The Medes and the Persians,* New York, 1965.

FRYE, R.   *The Heritage of Persia,* Cleveland, 1963.

GRANT, M.   *The History of Ancient Israel,* New York, 1984.

GRAYSON, A.   *Assyrian and Babylonian Chronicles,* New York, 1975.

MOSCATI, S.   *Ancient Semitic Civilizations,* New York, 1957.

OATES, J.   *Babylon,* London, 1979.

OLMSTEAD, A.   *History of the Persian Empire,* Chicago, 1948.

POSTGATE, N.   *The First Empires,* Oxford, 1977.

ROUX, G.   *Ancient Iraq,* 2nd. ed., New York, 1980.

SAGGS, H.   *The Greatness That Was Babylon,* New York, 1962.

Chart 3 The Mycenaean and Hellenic Periods

PERIOD	THE MYCENAEAN AGE (LATE HELLADIC PHASE OF AEGEAN CIVILIZATION)
c. 1600–1100 B.C. Late Bronze Age	Flourishing period for Mycenae, Tiryns, Pylos, other royal cities both on the mainland and the islands. Eruption of volcano on Santorini (Thera); decline in nearby cities including those on Crete. Over a period of time, destruction of Mycenae, other Aegean cities.

EARLY IRON OR "DARK" AGE

PERIOD	
c. 1100–800 B.C.	Petty kingdoms, agricultural states, dominated by aristocrats; tribal organization; the military dominated by the cavalry. Many Greeks migrate to the west coast of Asia Minor.
800–600 B.C. Period of Renascence	Extensive colonization to the North Aegean, Black Sea regions, and to North Africa, south Italy, Sicily, south France, east Spain; competition with Phoenicians in the western Mediterranean. Development of trade, rise of trading and artisan classes.
600 B.C.	Rise of the polis. Development of the heavy infantry phalanx. Sparta a relatively advanced state; Messenian wars; gradual transformation into a militarized society. First tyrants; Gyges in Lydia; Cypselus and Periander in Corinth.

	ATHENS	SPARTA	OTHER
600 B.C.	Cylon attempts tyranny. Draco's law code. Solon's reforms. Peisistratus.	Military aristocracy. Further expansion in Peloponnese.	Corinth, other Greek cities also strong trading centers. Thales, Pythagoras.
500 B.C.	Cleisthenes; democracy. Persians defeated at Marathon.	Formation of Peloponnesian League.	Ionian revolt against Persia. Persian invasions of Greece.

	Persians defeated at Salamis. Aeschylus	Leader of alliance against Persia; defeat Persians at Plataea. Period of Spartan isolation.	Heracleitus, Parmenides. Many Greek states join Persians, others in Greek alliance.
	Athenian leadership of Greeks; Delian League founded.	Leadership against Athens.	Most states in either Athenian or Spartan alliance.
	Period of Pericles' leadership. Sophocles, Euripides, Herodotus. Building of Parthenon. Anaxagoras, the Sophists.		

PELOPONNESIAN WAR (431–404 B.C.)

400 B.C.	Aristophanes, Thucydides.	Period of dominance of Greece.	Corinth, other Spartan allies disaffected; Persia supports alliance against Sparta. King's Peace. Ionian Greeks under Persia.
	Defeat, end of empire, 30 tyrants. Restored democracy; death of Socrates. New Confederacy. Plato, the Academy.		
	Rebellion; end of second federation. Isocrates.	Defeats by Thebans: Leuctra, Mantinea.	Period of Theban dominance of Greece. Epaminondas.

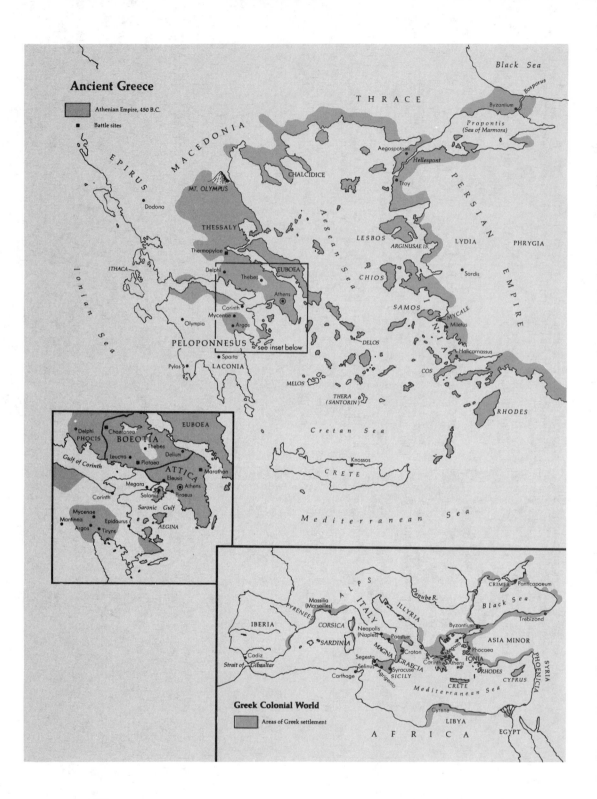

Ancient Greece

Athenian Empire, 450 B.C.

■ Battle sites

Black Sea

THRACE

Bosporus

Byzantium

Propontis
(Sea of Marmora)

EPIRUS

MACEDONIA

Aegospotami

Hellespont

PERSIAN

MT. OLYMPUS

CHALCIDICE

Troy

Dodona

THESSALY

LESBOS

LYDIA

PHRYGIA

Thermopylae

ARGINUSAE IS.

Aegean

ITHACA

Delphi

EUBOEA

Sea

CHIOS

Sardis

Thebes

Athens

SAMOS

EMPIRE

Corinth

MYCALE

Mycenae

Miletus

Olympia

Argos

N

Sparta

PELOPONNESUS

see inset below

DELOS

Halicarnassus

Pylos

LACONIA

COS

MELOS

RHODES

THERA
(SANTORIN)

Cretan Sea

Knossos

CRETE

Mediterranean   Sea

Inset (Boeotia/Attica)

Delphi

EUBOEA

PHOCIS

Chaeronea

BOEOTIA

Gulf of Corinth

Thebes

Leuctra

Delium

Plataea

ATTICA

Marathon

Megara

Eleusis

Athens

Salamis

Piraeus

Corinth

Saronic Gulf

Mycenae

AEGINA

Mantinea

Epidaurus

Argos

Tiryns

Greek Colonial World

Areas of Greek settlement

ALPS

CRIMEA

Panticapaeum

Massilia
(Marseilles)

PYRENEES

ITALY

ILLYRIA

Danube R.

Black Sea

IBERIA

CORSICA

Neapolis
(Naples)

Byzantium

Trebizond

Cadiz

SARDINIA

Paestum

ASIA MINOR

MAGNA

Croton

Neapolis

Phocaea

Strait of Gibraltar

Segesta

GRAECIA

Corinth

Athens

IONIA

Selinus

Syracuse

RHODES

SYRIA

Carthage

Agrigento

SICILY

CRETE

CYPRUS

PHOENICIA

Mediterranean Sea

Cyrene

AFRICA

LIBYA

EGYPT

PART II Greece: The Hellenic and Hellenistic Periods

6

THE EARLIEST HISTORY OF ANCIENT GREECE

A. AEGEAN CIVILIZATION

In the middle of the nineteenth century, when George Grote published his justly famed, multivolume *History of Greece*, archaeology had not yet revealed the existence of Mycenaean Greece nor of Aegean civilization of an even earlier period. For Grote, the historic period began with the first Olympic games in 776 B.C. He was well aware of the extensive gap in his information, but earlier centuries, he remarked, could not be described "upon anything like decent evidence." The three centuries before the first Olympiad remain rather shadowy—as indeed the two centuries following—but since Grote's day a series of archaeological digs, some not only exciting but also romantic, has added immensely to our knowledge; and the stream of important discoveries continues. Almost two millennia of history previously unknown—not all Greek but all relating to Greece—have been more or less illuminated by these excavations.

We use the term Aegean to describe the civilization of the period about 3000 to 1100 B.C. in the entire area about the Aegean Sea—on Crete (where the term Minoan is also used), on the islands (Sporadic, Cycladic), on the western coast of Asia Minor, and on the Greek mainland (Helladic). The late phase of Aegean or Helladic civilization on the mainland is usually termed Mycenaean, from its major site.

Schliemann: Pioneer in Classical Rediscovery

One of the more romantic figures among the archaeologists who have revolutionized the state of our knowledge about the third and second millennia B.C. in the eastern Mediterranean was Heinrich Schliemann, best known for his digs at ancient Troy and Mycenae, the former in northwest Asia Minor and the latter in the northeast Peloponnese. Schliemann was a German of a poor family who had little formal education. Self-taught, however, he became an excellent linguist and a successful businessman in the Low Countries and in Russia. He went to California to see to the affairs of his brother who had died during the Gold Rush, and by reason of his residence there when the territory entered the Union, claimed that he was an American citizen.

Schliemann had dreamed from childhood of seeing ancient Troy and the other sites familiar to him from Homer's *Iliad*. Contemporary scholarship tended to dismiss Troy and the Trojan War as fiction, but Schliemann had faith in Homer somewhat like a fundamentalist preacher's confidence in the literal truth of the Bible. In retirement in his forties, a world-traveled multimillionaire, Schliemann decided to pursue his dream. He studied philology for a time at the Sorbonne in Paris, terminated an unsuccessful marriage to a Russian woman, and for a second wife chose a seventeen-year-old Greek beauty by whom he had two children, Agamemnon and Andromache. Sophia proved to be a great help to Heinrich in his work.

After an inspection of likely sites in the area of northwestern Asia Minor (Turkey) near the Dardanelles, where ancient Troy was commonly supposed to have been, Schliemann decided that the mounds at a place called Hissarlik probably hid the remains of the fabled city. Excavation at the site began in 1870, and the rich discoveries, including numerous objects of gold, quickly captured the attention of the world. Schliemann soon convinced all but the most skeptical that he had indeed found Troy—though few were as sure as he that he had proved the literal truth of the Homeric story. It is ironic that Schliemann dug right through the city he sought. The richest level, which he thought was the Troy of Homer, 1200 B.C., is now dated back to about 2000 B.C. It was a part of Aegean civilization. Schliemann also excavated the Greek mainland sites Mycenae and Tiryns and again turned up marvelous objects such as a king's gold mask (for Schliemann "the mask of Agamemnon") and a gold cup (naturally, "the cup of Nestor"). We now know that these objects were older than Homer's date for the Trojan War, and like Troy, that they too belong to the Aegean civilization. Even before Schliemann's death it was realized that his and other related finds pointed to a new and great age, a kind of ancient age of ancient Greece, the knowledge of which had been lost. But it was left to a young Englishman to work out the form of this civilization through the study of Schliemann's work and through his own excavations. This was Arthur Evans.

Sir Arthur Evans: The Excavations at Knossos

The startling finds made by Evans on Crete beginning in 1900 revealed perhaps the single most important center of Aegean civilization, the ancient city of Knossos, near modern Heracleion. Older than Troy II and a great city a thousand years before Mycenae, Knossos yielded up marvel after marvel. Evans found a palace that covered more than five acres, with hundreds of rooms arranged, originally, on four floors. The architecture, rich color, tapered columns, and terra-cotta drains for flush toilets impress every visitor who sees the remains—and Evans' restorations—at Knossos. Pottery found at the site and other art forms, especially frescoes, compare favorably with contemporary work anywhere. The total effect created by the frescoes is of life enjoyed to the full, of relative ease and prosperity. Evans also found three systems of writing, a kind of hieroglyphic and two scripts, which he called Linear A and Linear B.

Knossos was apparently the center of a considerable empire, at least a commercial empire, for the palace had a tremendous number of storerooms for oil and other products. Yet the site was not heavily fortified, and little attention seems to have been given to military matters. Because the culture centered at Knossos was found to be widespread throughout the Aegean, and because a tradition preserved from antiquity tells of a Cretan "thalassocracy," or sea empire, it has been postulated that the kings of Knossos ruled extensive naval dominions. Other sites of some size have also been unearthed on Crete, with palace complexes similar to that of Knossos. The rulers of Knossos, therefore, do not seem to have controlled the whole island, at least not over a long period. Perhaps Knossos' chief importance lay in its maritime commerce, and its security depended on a strong navy. Evans named the civilization after King Minos of Knossos in later Greek legend, dividing it into early Minoan (c. 3000–c. 2100 B.C.), middle Minoan (c. 2100–c. 1550 B.C.), and late Minoan (c. 1550–c. 1100 B.C.).

The Aegean: An Advanced Civilization

The Aegean civilization lagged very little behind those in the Tigris–Euphrates and Nile valleys. The Bronze Age came two or three centuries later, perhaps, but in some ways the culture was as advanced as the others. To the modern taste Kamares ware, for example, a fine, brilliant, polychrome pottery of the early middle period, seems superior to Egyptian or Mesopotamian ware of the same age. A seagoing people naturally visited both the eastern Mediterranean littoral and Egypt, with cultural interchange the natural result. The idea for the hieroglyphic writing probably came from Egypt, and it has been claimed that Linear A is basically a Semitic language. Cretan imports have been discovered in Egypt, especially of the Middle Kingdom and Empire periods, and Egyptian manufactures have been dug up on Crete.

The high period for Knossos, Crete, and the Aegean civilization in general came during the middle Minoan period, from about 2000 B.C. to about 1550 B.C. The decipherment of Minoan Linear B two decades ago forced a rethinking of the probable "history" of this civilization. The problems posed, incidentally, illustrate well the difficulty—one might say the impossibility—of writing history solely from archaeological data. To the surprise of scholars, the script turned out to be Greek. In recent years many tablets written in Linear B have been dug up on the Greek mainland, especially at Pylos in the southwest Peloponnese. The current view is that the Achaeans (Greeks) adopted the superior Aegean culture, conquered Knossos about 1550, and in the late Minoan period ruled all or part of Crete. The late phase of Aegean culture on Greece itself is called Mycenaean, as we have seen.

Battered by both earthquakes and invasions over a period of several centuries, Knossos and Crete declined, and by 1100 B.C. the island had lapsed into obscurity. Cataclysmic volcanic activity on the Aegean island of Thera probably affected the whole of the eastern Mediterranean. Knossos was shattered by an earthquake about 1570 B.C. and burned about 1400, probably the result of another earthquake. The final invasions of Crete were probably made by the "sea peoples" who destroyed the Hittite Empire and certain Phoenician cities, and who were stopped only at great cost by the Twentieth Dynasty Egyptian pharaohs.

Sites on Thera have been under excavation for some years, and have produced some remarkable remains, including numerous frescoes. Because the island has been rather romantically connected with the lost Atlantis of the myth propounded by Plato, the archaeological work has received much publicity in the press. A great deal is yet possible at the site, where vestiges of the ancient civilization are buried under many feet of pumice stone and ash. Thera has been called the Minoan Pompeii.

B. THE MYCENAEANS

Mycenae: Aegean Civilization on the Mainland

An ancient tradition regarding fabled Mycenae, "rich in gold," has been essentially substantiated by modern excavators, beginning with Schliemann in 1876. The National Museum in Athens prominently displays the gold masks, cups, jewelry, and other objects he found in a circle of shaft-graves within the ancient city walls. Schliemann at first thought he had found the grave of Agamemnon, but we know now that the objects date from about 1500 B.C., or three centuries before the time of that Homeric hero. Subsequent excavators found, among other things, a second grave circle outside the walls, also rich in content and belonging to a period about a century earlier. No more impressive finds have been made elsewhere of this mainland-centered civilization, although similarly rich but little-noticed items have been found at a tomb at Peristeria in western Messenia. Thus it seems not inappropriate that Mycenae has given its name to this period. The Mycenaean age, again, is the late Helladic phase of Aegean culture in the area of Greece proper.

The mature phase of Mycenaean culture occurred during the two centuries before 1200 B.C. and is characterized by heavily fortified palace-centers. Some sites contain Linear B records, and most yield up the remains of fine pottery and frescoes plus equally fine weapons and equipment—all evidence that this was a flourishing period. Mycenae did not, however, rule the entire area; apparently a number of kingdoms existed there. Mycenaean power was minor in a world dominated by such empires as those of the Egyptians and the Hittites.

Centers of Mycenaean Culture

Mycenae, Tiryns, Pylos, and other Mycenaean sites were not cities in the true sense; they were chiefly royal residences and citadels. The fortification walls at Tiryns are up to forty feet thick, and the lintel of the famous Lion Gate at Mycenae is estimated to weigh twenty tons. It is rather puzzling that so high a level of culture could be reached with so little in the way of urban life. A partial explanation is that the culture was adopted, imported along with artists and architects from other centers of Aegean civilization. Some of the tombs are impressive. Called *tholos* tombs, the finest of them are built up of overhanging tiers of rock into corbeled "beehive" domes. Largest is the so-called Treasury of Atreus at Mycenae, which has a dome about forty-five feet high and almost as wide.

The remains of the Mycenaean cities testify to a rather strong, centralized government; the kings must have been relatively rich. It is difficult to account for the wealth indicated by the finds. It may result in part from local manufactures, perhaps begun with immigrant artisans brought in from Crete, and in part from trade, but most likely the riches came from plundering expeditions to the east and south.

The Linear B tablets tell us the king's title: *wanax*. The later term for king, *basileus*, describes a subordinate in charge of one of the lesser towns. The army commander was perhaps second only to the king. Priests were important, as were the heads of the various bureaus of government, and indeed there seems to have been a quite complex bureaucracy. An amazing variety of artisans is attested to in the tablets—doubtless, along with peasants and soldiers, comprising an extensive class of free citizens. At the bottom of the social order, as usual, were serfs and slaves. Mycenaean frescoes, in contrast to those of the earlier period on Crete and the Cyclades, emphasize hunting and military rather than natural scenes. Clearly the Mycenaeans preferred the more vigorous life. The techniques are quite comparable to those in the islands, even if a bit coarser.

About 1400 B.C., as we have seen, many of the island centers of Aegean civilization were destroyed, apparently by a terrific volcanic eruption at Thera.

Knossos was devastated by fire, possibly related to earthquake, but recovered quickly. Several other major sites on Crete were destroyed and were not reconstructed. The presence of Linear B tablets at Knossos in this period and other evidence have led some scholars to postulate a Mycenaean conquest of that city and the use of it as a center from which to dominate the island. Others feel, however, that the evidence is not strong enough to support this hypothesis.

Mycenaean influence, at any rate, now reached new heights and penetrated to new areas. Most of the Aegean islands apparently came under Mycenaean control, to judge solely by the archaeology. And Mycenaean influence extended much farther. Byblos in Syria, for example, has yielded large quantities of Mycenaean ware. Mycenaean pottery has turned up also at Tell el Amarna, the site of Akhnaton's capital far up the Nile in Egypt. Mycenaean traders exchanged their wares even in the western Mediterranean. Mycenaean objects have been found in southern Italy and Sicily, as well as in adjacent islands. It has even been suggested that Taranto, in southern Italy, might have been a Mycenaean colony.

The Decline of the Mycenaean Age

During the late thirteenth century B.C. Mycenaean civilization declined, and after 1200 B.C., there was a period of general collapse. Part of the city of Mycenae outside the walls was destroyed, and later, two more disasters struck inside the citadel itself. Pylos, Thebes, and other palatial centers met with similar destruction. Yet Athens and some other sites escaped the violence—or perhaps they perpetrated the destruction. All the area gradually relapsed into a state of near barbarism in a rather mystifying way. Mycenae burned about 1125 B.C., and Knossos was finally destroyed about 1100 B.C.

The cause of this general decline has usually been ascribed to the Dorian invasion told of in the literature. Speaking a dialect of Greek, but less civilized than their Achaean predecessors, the Dorians, it was thought, destroyed the major cultural centers, especially in the Peloponnese, where they settled. This blow or series of blows was believed to have brought down Mycenaean civilization. It may be, however, that the Dorians did not play such a role at all and that they came in as immigrants later than has usually been thought. Mycenaean decline may have resulted from a long drought caused by a small shift in the trade winds that bring Greece her rainless summers. The land may have been partly depopulated, and the Dorians may simply have repopulated the land when the rains returned. The few sites known to have been destroyed, such as Pylos, probably suffered at the hands of starving marauders. The great drought also could have caused the decline of the Hittite Empire and the displacement of peoples who about 1200 B.C. ravaged the eastern Mediterranean cities and attacked Egypt (the sea peoples).

The drought theory is plausible; moreover, it is true that the archaeological evidence from the Peloponnese does not specifically support an invasion. Still, it is hard to see how the drought—which did not affect the country as a whole but only parts of it—could have brought about so complete a cultural breakdown. People even forgot how to write. Perhaps the most satisfactory reconstruction of events will combine both drought and Dorian invasion: A country weakened internally by the desiccation of the land was struck by Dorian invaders, who probably lived on the fringe of the more civilized area and took advantage of the situation. Because there is some evidence of the use of the Dorian language in the Peloponnese before the period of destruction, some have concluded that the Dorians might have been subject peoples who turned on their masters in a time of drought or of general warfare.

C. GEOGRAPHY OF GREECE

General: Topography and Its Influence

Greece is tiny. The entire area dominated by Greeks during the period of their highest achievements, including the islands and the coastland of Asia Minor but excluding overseas colonies founded after 800 B.C., would equal no more than the land area of one of the moderate-to-small U.S. states.

The Greeks live intimately with both the mountains and the sea. The valleys, though relatively small, are quite fertile; when well watered, their deep soil is very productive. But most of the land is mountainous, and probably no more than 10 percent is easily cultivable; another similar segment can be terraced for cultivation or used for pasturage. The rest included, in an early period, some forested uplands that later became bare and eroded.

The mountains reach a height of almost 10,000 feet at Mount Olympus in Thessaly and more than 8,000 feet for Mount Parnassus at Delphi. Generally they are disposed in ranges running northwest to southeast. South of the great rift forming the Gulf of Corinth they form a backbone for the Peloponnese. From there, to the east and south, they sink into the Aegean, where their peaks form the Cyclades Islands. Beyond the Cyclades are the Sporades—Rhodes is the largest of this group—so that in calm summer weather the island-strewn sea provides easy access to the mainland of Asia Minor.

Curiously, therefore, geography tended to isolate the Greeks, on the one hand, and force them out into the sea and so to far places, on the other. The system of rugged mountains and interior valleys cut up their land into compartments suitable for the development of small states, jealous of their independence. But proximity to the sea, good harbors, and the island steppingstones led to intercourse with the outside world. These diverse tendencies affected the growth of Greek civilization in diverse ways.

Specific: The Compartmented Regions

Now we will look at the major land areas of Greece. South of the Gulf of Corinth lies the Peloponnese; connected with the rest of Greece only by the isth-

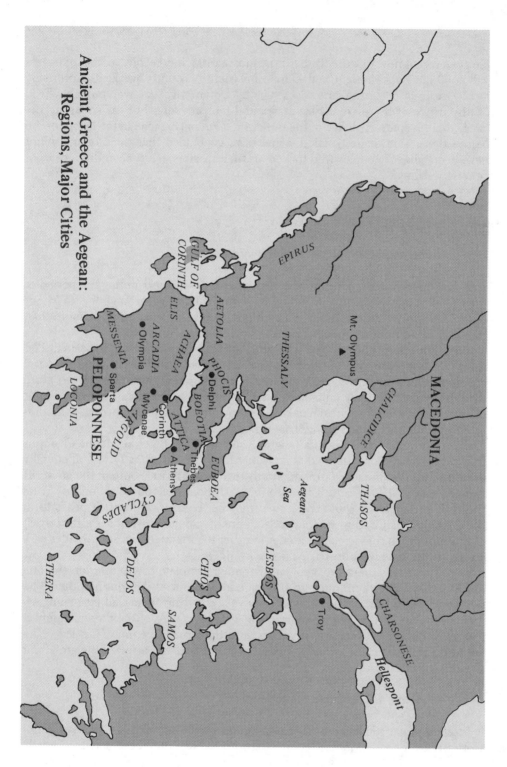

Ancient Greece and the Aegean:
Regions, Major Cities

GULF OF CORINTH

EPIRUS

ELIS

AETOLIA

MESSENIA

ARCADIA

● Olympia

ACHAEA

PHOCIS

● Delphi

THESSALY

Mt. Olympus ▶

MACEDONIA

CHALCIDICE

PELOPONNESE

LACONIA

● Sparta

ARGOLID

● Mycenae

● Corinth

ATTICA

BOEOTIA

Thebes ●

● Athens

EUBOEA

THASOS

CYCLADES

DELOS

THERA

Aegean Sea

LESBOS

CHIOS

SAMOS

● Troy

CHARSONESE

Hellespont

Ancient Greece. (New York Public Library)

118

mus in the northeast, this large landmass is almost an island. The narrow entrance into the Peloponnese was controlled by the city of Corinth with its lofty citadel, the Acrocorinth. To the south lay Argos, the chief city of the Argolid, with its fruitful plain controlled in Mycenaean times by Tiryns and Mycenae. In the southeast Peloponnese was Laconia, the territory of ancient Sparta. This city, on the river Eurotas, sprawled below the snowcapped peaks of the Taygetus range. In the southwest Peloponnese was Messenia, with a rich plain coveted by the Spartans. Pylos in the extreme southwest was important only during the Mycenaean age. In the northwest, Olympia, in the rather rugged territory called Elis, was known for its Olympic games and its Temple of Zeus. Achaea along the gulf on the north and Arcadia in the center complete the survey of the Peloponnesian peninsula. Both these areas are composed predominantly of hills and mountains, with small valleys.

Traversing the isthmus to the north, one first entered the territory of Megara, which controlled the northern exit from the isthmus and the Peloponnese. Around the Saronic Gulf to the east lay Attica, a not-too-well-watered plain surrounded on the landward sides by mountains. Eleusis, home of the mysteries of Demeter, and Athens occupied prime sites. Nearby, in the bay, lay the island of Salamis, and farther out in the Saronic Gulf was Aegina. Northwest of Athens, across Mount Cithaeron, Thebes with its productive plain was the chief city of Boeotia. Just off the coast to the northeast was the large island of Euboea. To the west a road led through the territory of Phocis to the oracle of Apollo at Delphi, magnificently situated on the flank of Mount Parnassus, slightly inland from the Gulf of Corinth. Farther west, extending to the Ionian Sea, lay Aetolia. Northward along the west coast was Epirus, where an oracle of Zeus was located at Dodona. The Ionian Islands opposite Aetolia and Epirus included Ithaca, reputed home of Odysseus, and Corcyra (modern Corfu). Except for Thebes, these are all rugged areas as well.

North of Delphi is Thessaly, but the road led northwest from Thebes, around Mount Parnassus and through the narrow coastal pass at Thermopylae. Thessaly had the largest plains in Greece, which produced the greatest quantity of cereal grains. Horse breeding was also important here. Farther north toward Macedonia the road passed through the beautiful Vale of Tempe, just beyond storied Mount Olympus. The three fingers of the Chalcidice probe out into the north Aegean just beyond Thessalonica. Farther east lay Thrace and the straits separating Europe from Asia Minor. Along the tongue of land called the Chersonese (modern Gallipoli Peninsula), the straits were called by Greeks the Hellespont; the channel leading into the Black Sea was the Bosporus. After the Greeks settled the coast of western Asia Minor (1000 B.C. and after), the areas along the eastern Aegean littoral were named after the local dialects: Aeolis, east of the important island of Lesbos; Ionia farther south, with the islands of Chios and Samos offshore; and Caria in the southwest. The island of Rhodes is just south of here.

Greece, then, was small but tremendously varied. Greeks lived in compartmented districts, yet were thrown inevitably into common endeavors because of similar problems and the proximity of the sea. They found themselves challenged, but not overwhelmed, by a sometimes tough environment. Geography did not in any primary way determine the course of Greek history, but its role was nonetheless great.

D. THE DARK AGE (c. 1100–800 B.C.)

The eclipse of Mycenaean civilization was succeeded by centuries of darkness. Archaeology can show no important new construction for this period, and there is little evidence of economic activity, nor any of intellectual activity. The Mycenaean territories lapsed into cultural isolation. There is one positive aspect of the cultural isolation of the "Dark Age," however: It brought about eventual cultural unification.

Out of the Shadows

After about 1000 B.C. there was a slight quickening in cultural pace. A new form of pottery appeared called *protogeometric*—later, *geometric*. This pottery appears to have originated in Attica; archaeologists have found it in numerous places scattered over much of the eastern Mediterranean and even in the west. The traders who carried the pottery were not necessarily Athenians, for Athens was both small and not active in this early trade. The wide dissemination of geometric pottery and later of Corinthian ware obviously implies a return to the sea by some Greeks, and also a degree of economic activity even in essentially rural Athens. Full recovery, however, was to require centuries.

Another fact of the period was the Ionian migration, a movement of Greeks across the Aegean to the eastern islands and the western shores of Asia Minor. This colonization of Ionia by Athenians is reported by the later historian Thucydides. Ionia is the central area of the coast: To the north, Aeolian Greeks (the terms are linguistic) established themselves, and Dorian Greeks settled on the southwestern coasts. Western Asia Minor thus became permanently Greek in population, and its inhabitants often shared the history and accomplishments of the mainland Greeks. All Greece, as well as the Aegean littoral and islands, became racially and culturally homogeneous.

This movement demonstrates that even in isolation, Greece was never completely cut off from the Orient. Two other major cultural developments underline this observation. First, the Iron Age came to Greece, and doubtless this knowledge of ironworking derived from Asia Minor or Syria; as we know, the Hittites first produced the metal in quantity. Second, near the end of this epoch, the Greeks adopted the Phoenician alphabet. The need for a system of writing perhaps made itself felt first on the commercial level.

Literary Lamps

Between the Greece of Herodotus and Thucydides and the earlier, Mycenaean civilization, then, there lay a cataclysmic break, bridged only by folk memory and, in a few places, the eloquent testimony of massive ruins, as at Mycenae and Tiryns. The break was in many ways complete. A new system of writing and other cultural equipage had to be developed. In a direct way the Greece of Pericles seems to owe little to Greece before Homer; yet it is clear that the influence of the past was pervasive, even if it was almost subliminal and expressed in myth rather than in history. Such stories as those of Perseus, the reputed founder of Mycenae, Bellerophon (Argos), and Heracles (one of whose labors involved a Cretan bull) illustrate how the memories of the past survived in fabulous, unhistorical ways. Such Greek myths are preserved by various writers; many of these surely go back to this or an even earlier age. Since some of these myths have been shown to contain elements of fact, it is sometimes assumed that judicious analysis of almost all the myths can yield historical data; however, this is a fallacious assumption. Archaeology or reliable history must first lay a foundation before any building blocks drawn from myth can be used. Some myths, even those that seem based on historical event, may be purely imaginative invention.

A second sort of literature that casts some dim light on this dark period is the Greek epics of Homer, the *Iliad* and *Odyssey*. The problems involving date, composition, authorship, validity of content for use as historical data, and the like are tremendously complex, as shown by the voluminous modern literature relating to these matters.

In general, Homer's descriptions seem best to fit the time of composition (c. 800–700 B.C.), though he has some accurate information of the earlier time—as when he describes a long shield used then but not in his own age; and the Catalog of Ships shows some accurate knowledge of sites no longer important when the poems were written. He tells of a society dominated by a warrior aristocracy whose kings were first among equals. These kingdoms seem petty and poor compared with Mycenae, their economy being almost altogether agricultural. The chief gods were already the Olympian twelve. Perhaps Homer was more important as a maker of history than as a source of historical information. The *Iliad* and *Odyssey* became the great schoolbook of Greece for centuries. Alexander the Great carried copies of them with him on his prolonged campaigns. These poems are still judged the greatest epics of all time.

Indirect Illumination

Another way of learning more about the Dark Age is to study the conditions of society and the state at the end of the period and to infer from them what changes had occurred not long before. In this way, one perceives that somehow the petty monarchies gave way to aristocratic oligarchy and that the old warfare involving individual combat between warrior-leaders was superseded by an aristocratic cavalry as the chief fighting force. A tradition in Athens suggests that one of their kings, when unable to lead the army at a critical time, was given a general as his assistant. Soon the kingship in that state became elective—at first for ten years, then annually. By this time the real power in Athens was in the hands of an administrative officer, called the *archon*, and the commanding general, or *polemarch*. The king, or *basileus*, was no longer very important. The influence of the aristocratic families was exercised especially through the tribes, whose power (since much of the land was held by them) was economic as well as political and judicial.

E. CURRENTS OF CHANGE (800–600 B.C.)

At a gradual but ever-quickening pace, the Greek world was transformed after 800 B.C. In internal development, aristocratic oligarchies sometimes lost their holds on governmental structures, as new groups in the towns made common cause with the smaller, nonaristocratic farmers. Foreign influence came through the contact of the Ionian Greeks on the shores of Asia Minor with the older civilizations of the Near East and through a gradually developing trade. No doubt some memory remained of the extensive trade of Mycenaean days—as the *Odyssey*, in a distorted way, may indicate—and the revived commerce followed the older routes, mostly to the west. Still, many decades of experience were needed to establish routes and marketing arrangements and to design and build improved ships. By the beginning of the sixth century B.C., several Greek states had coinage systems and soon would have money economies.

The traders, their suppliers, the shipbuilders, and the other town-based artisans, when supported by the small landholders, put considerable stress on the traditional fabric of society and government. Toward the end of the period, military change that brought larger armies also created tension in the old structures. But for many Greeks in those years, emigration, especially to Italy and Sicily, provided a sort of safety valve.

Colonization and Emigration

Hesiod, a Boeotian poet of the eighth century B.C., may perhaps help us understand the impulse toward emigration and settlement in far countries that arose at this time. Hesiod was a farmer—by no means among the poorest of them—but his poem, "Works and Days," presents a rather grim picture of unremitting labor for little gain. It may have been largely poverty and overpopulation, then, that drove Greeks of his time to the sea, though human oppression, a yen for adventure, and land hunger must have been important also. Trade surely was important as well. It is often denied in contemporary scholarship that trade provided motivation; and it is true that the largest and eventually the most important colonies were established in places where good land was available. However, there is much archaeological evidence of trade at some sites before they were colonized, as at Cumae near Naples in southern Italy; moreover, several of the earlier colonies were carefully situated at commercially strategic sites controlling trade routes. At the very least, traders provided information for would-be colonizers. Both trade and the need for land (because of overpopulation) arose in part because of the same facts: Basic raw materials and foodstuffs were in short supply. The mountains had already been denuded of their forests, so that even lumber was needed; grain, wool, and hides often had to be brought into the land also.

Two sorts of colonies were established: Some were basically trading stations, which collected goods for shipment to the homeland; others were larger-scale settlements, usually located on good agricultural land. The latter type developed into independent city-states much like those at home. Most of the colonies were founded by individuals, though sometimes a whole city of mainland Greece or elsewhere joined in the effort and became a "mother city" (*metropolis*). However founded, the overseas colonies were not controlled from Greece; no empire resulted from this substantial emigration. Ties were maintained with the mother cities, but these were commercial and religious, not political.

The areas colonized, both from Greece and the Greek areas of western Asia Minor, included sites on the Ionian and Adriatic seas; south Italy; eastern Sicily; southern France; eastern Spain; the area of Cyrene, west of Egypt in North Africa; the north Aegean; and nearly all the shores round the Black Sea. By far the largest number of colonists went to the west, which became a kind of frontier region for Greeks. In southern Italy, which the Romans called Magna Graecia (Great Greece), the cities of Tarentum, Croton, Sybaris, Rhegium, Cumae, and Naples, as well as Syracuse in eastern Sicily, grew until they were among the most important Greek cities anywhere.

Colonization in the north Aegean area, begun by Euboeans in the eighth century B.C., was in large part simply the result of a desire for agricultural land. The area also supplied timber—especially the Thracian lands toward the east—which was much needed by the Greeks at home. Gold and silver mines in the region, so important to Greeks and Macedonians later, were discovered only at the end of the seventh century B.C. and after. Thracians fought fiercely against Greek encroachment, and indeed, they never were really displaced.

Trade and colonization into the Black Sea and its coastlands came still later. No doubt the Greek sailors were deterred by the fast-moving currents that flow west through the Bosphorus and the Hellespont, and they found the climate less hospitable; fishing, however, was better than in the Aegean. Apparently Greeks first settled on the northern shore of Asia Minor, at Sinope and Trapezus. Actual settlement of what is now south Russia must have been resisted by the Scythian inhabitants, about whom Greeks—the historian Herodotus in particular—told many fabulous tales. Scythians, like Thracians, were fierce warriors who had driven out the Cimmerians and pursued them even into Asia Minor. They had many barbarous customs: Herodotus claimed that they blinded all their captives. He added that their climate was really barbarous; it rained in summer instead of in winter, and as for the cold weather, it lasted eight months of the year. To make mud in cold weather, one had to build a fire, not just add water. An extensive trade developed with the Scythians. From the Crimea and adjacent areas Greeks brought home grain, wool, hides, and furs.

Trade must be two-way: If basic materials are to be imported, something must be exported. As we have seen, the Greek states developed pottery for export—the best pottery in the world—plus wine, olive oil, and other products. The new emphasis on produce and manufactured goods for export caused changes in the economy and society that were of the greatest importance; this will be discussed later in this chapter.

Greeks, perhaps mostly from Asia Minor, visited Egypt during the seventh and sixth centuries B.C., not only for a growing trade relationship but also to serve as mercenaries in Egyptian armies. The twenty-sixth Dynasty Pharaoh Psamtik (Greek Psammetichos) and his son Necho II are known to have used Greek *hoplites* (heavily armed foot soldiers) extensively.

The Rise of the Polis

Of the concomitant changes marking the period 800 B.C. to 600 B.C., one of the more important was the rise of a new sort of state, the *polis*. The city-state—as the term is usually but inadequately translated—was the most typical Greek institution. Centered about a single city (usually), the polis was a genuine community, where the focal city gave its citizenship to all in the area and was itself the political, economic, social, cultural, and religious hub of the state. The poleis of the historical period were, of course, the result of a period of consolidation or conquest. Attica, for example, at one time had twelve poleis; according to Athenian tradition, the twelve cities, through a process of consolidation (*synoikismos*), became one polis—Athens—in the days of the legendary hero Theseus.

The restricted size of the polis brought a broad participation in the affairs of state and thus made possible an emphasis on the individual, which in turn led to the progress associated with significant human achievement. In a state of this scale, everyone could know almost everyone else (certainly, that is, those worth knowing). But the polis fostered the intense particularism, rivalry, and internecine warfare that also, unfortunately, were typically Greek. Nevertheless, the great thinkers Plato and Aristotle could envision no more satisfactory kind of state in which to create an optimum balance between order and freedom and yet make possible a high degree of human fulfillment.

Military Changes

Citizens of the United States often tend to forget that all power in a state ultimately depends on the military or its civilian equivalent, the police. Citizens of Latin America are rarely allowed to forget it. To put it another way, the military establishment of a state usually reflects the society in some important fashion.

Occasionally, however, some technical change in the military compels a change in the armed forces, which leads inexorably to changes in the state itself. That is, the army then tends to change society to reflect military reality. In this age such a military change did involve political and social changes.

Warfare in this period came to be dominated by the *hoplite*, or infantry-man, fighting in phalanx formation. In the age of the Trojan War, individual combat between heroes had predominated; then came a period in which aristocratic cavalry formed the core of a state's armed forces. Now, however, the battle ranks of the phalanx required large numbers of men armed with shield (*hoplon*), helmet, breastplate, greaves, and thrusting spear. It became necessary to use every man who could afford this equipment and, ultimately, to enfranchise all such men, for the dominant concept of the full citizen was that of a person who was capable of bearing arms for the state. In some states, this change produced a broadened oligarchy, but hardly a democracy, for not many men could buy such expensive arms. Yet this military change tended to reduce the power of the old aristocratic families and was in some places a step along the road toward democracy.

A good example of the results of the change may be seen in Sparta, where, indeed, the idea of the hoplite formation may have developed. The Messenian wars of the late eighth and the mid-seventh centuries B.C. made it imperative to modernize the army—which meant increasing its size to include every possible hoplite. Soon after, all hoplites were enfranchised. At that point, Sparta was surely one of the most liberal states in Greece, in several ways. But here the Spartans froze the military-political development (perhaps *fossilized* would be a better term). The state became a rather rigid oligarchy, which we shall consider later in greater detail.

In the seventh century B.C., some of the most deadly fighting and, in consequence, military innovation took place in the major Greek city-states of Asia Minor. These included Magnesia, Smyrna, Ephesus, and Miletus. When they were not struggling against the Lydians to the north (who eventually destroyed old Smyrna), they were forced to defend themselves against invading Cimmerians or (Thracian) Treres; in between times, they fought with each other. Improved defenses such as the massive walls and gates at Smyrna, as well as better battle formations, meant survival. The chief cities of Ionia as early as perhaps 800 B.C. formed a league that must have helped them to endure—or even expand—and also must have provided some pattern for the later and better-known leagues of the mainland Greek states.

Changes in Class Structure

The wealth and power of the older aristocracy lay in the land. Society was basically rural, and many social, political, and juridical matters were dealt with through the tribes, which were dominated by the great families. When the poleis developed, based on town centers, the aristocrats mostly moved into those centers. One result was that the tribes—or anything connected with kinship—became less important. Land, once allocated by the tribes, it seems, and controlled by the families, came to be held in private ownership. Aristocrats often favored such changes, for they wished to plant olive groves and vineyards, which brought greater return, especially in a developing export market, but also required more capital investment and long-term ownership or control of land.

The free peasants or small landowners, who remained in the rural areas, to a degree lost touch with their natural leaders, the landed aristocrats. The two groups no longer had a community of interests. Location, rather than the older tribal ties, tended to determine one's pursuits. Further impetus toward change was the rise, over a long period, of colonization and trade, with its export-import emphasis. Pottery, oil, wine, and other products were exchanged for foodstuffs, raw materials such as wool, and luxury items. Gradually shipbuilding, pottery, and other industries grew, along with the port cities, some of them centers of poleis. Such activity brought with it also the beginnings of a development of both a middle class and a class of artisans or urban workers.

The revival of general economic activity in the Aegean is to some extent reflected in the poem of about 700 B.C. mentioned previously, Hesiod's "Works and Days." Though hardly optimistic in tone, the poem yet assumes a general desire to gain wealth that is totally uncharacteristic of a static society. And in the centuries following, Greek society and the economy were to become more dynamic still.

The evolving new groups did not fit into the existing sociopolitical structure and had no part in it. Their needs were different. The merchants, for example, required protection at sea from piracy, laws relating to contracts, and the like. Similarly, the lower-class laborers who worked in pottery shops or shipyards found that the old order paid little attention to their needs. These groups therefore were an unstable element in aristocratic states and tended to support any new structure that would weaken the old system—if the change ministered to their own problems, that is. When the rural peasants made common cause with these new groups against the aristocrats, often under a wealthy, middle-class leader, or when for various reasons an aristocratic leader became opposed to the majority of his class, the consequence was drastic political change in many of the states.

The Rise of Tyranny

During the seventh and sixth centuries B.C., leaders called *tyrants* arose and brought about significant political, economic, and social changes. The term *tyrant*, which in Lydia may have meant only "king," was applied to a variety of rulers whose common denominator was that they came to power in some extra-constitutional fashion and their rule represented some fundamental break with tradition. Some tyrants were aristocrats. The ancient writers imply an association with wealth, which may indicate simply that these leaders sought the wealth that accompanies power; however, it is more likely that most of them represented men of wealth—nonaristocratic landowners, merchants, and traders—against the entrenched power of the hereditary nobility. Some tyrants did not hold formal office but ruled through control of a political organization, somewhat like a big-city boss in modern times. Most tyrannies were short-lived, but almost all were significant, especially in weakening the power of the aristocratic oligarchies.

The first man to be called *tyrant* by the Greek historians was Gyges of Lydia, who overthrew the previous Lydian king in the mid-seventh century B.C. In fact, he only established a new line of kings. In Greece proper, Pheidon of Argos and Cleisthenes of Sicyon were among the earliest tyrants. In Corinth tyranny lasted longer than in most states: Cypselus, the first tyrant, overthrew the aristocratic Bacchiadae and ruled for three decades; his son Periander also had a long reign. In the mid-sixth century B.C., as we shall see, Peisistratus rose to become tyrant at Athens through use of mercenary soldiers and ruled for most of three decades.

Some tyrants got support from and in turn supported the nonaristocratic, smaller landowners; Peisistratus is a good example. However, it appears that most of them drew their chief support from city people, most important of whom were surely the merchants and traders. This is indicated not only in the literature but also by the fact that tyrants generally encouraged trade, sent out colonies, established systems of weights and measures as well as coinage (beginning about 625 B.C.), issued new laws, and sometimes made constitutional changes favoring these classes. At Corinth, for example, Cypselus and Periander maintained trade contacts—confirmed by archaeology primarily through finds of Corinthian pottery—as far afield as Egypt, Asia Minor, the northern Aegean (where the Corinthians established the colony of Potidaea), and the Black Sea areas, as well as various locations to the west, both in Greece and in the islands, where again several colonies were founded. Corinthian exports besides pottery included manufactured bronze goods and art objects of gold, silver, and ivory. In fairness to the Bacchiad aristocrats expelled by Cypselus, it should be said that the era of trade expansion began with them.

The word *tyrant* originally did not carry a negative connotation, and probably in most states only the aristocrats initially disapproved of the tyrants' work. But inevitably, some of them abused their great power, and soon the word began to acquire its present meaning.

The tyrants played the role of destroyers of the old oligarchies, but they also made possible further political development. Once the tyrants were in turn thrown out, many Greek states elected to proceed toward democracy. There were sporadic returns to aristocratic rule, as at Corinth; but, no longer bound to the land, the aristocrats there generally looked after the interests of all classes better than most other oligarchs.

Typically, then, from Homeric times to the fifth century B.C., political development in Greece proceeded from monarchy to aristocracy to tyranny to some form of democracy. It should be stressed, though, that scarcely any state in Greece was ever really "typical."

F. CULTURAL QUICKENING IN THE SEVENTH CENTURY B.C.

The impetus for the cultural awakening later in the period under discussion came in considerable part from the Orient. The evidence is obvious and pervasive: The alphabet which the Greeks adopted and adapted came from the Phoenicians, as (probably) did most of their new knowledge of metalworking and improvements in ship design; Greek pottery everywhere took on oriental aspects, as did bronze objects such as fine caldrons. The same orientalizing tendency is seen also in western areas and in Etruscan centers in Italy. Oriental influence can be seen also in art, architecture, and sculpture, as in science, mathematics, and beginnings of philosophy (to be discussed in the next chapter).

Protoscientists of Greek Asia Minor

The Eastern influence naturally is first seen among Greeks in Asia Minor because of their more intimate association with the older, oriental cultures. Egypt especially influenced these early Greeks. Those who visited that country were enormously impressed with its antiquity and surprised by the skepticism of Egyptians to whom they related Greek myths and legends. According to the historian Herodotus (fifth century B.C.), Hecataeus of Miletus, a sixth-century B.C. geographer and travel lecturer, told some Egyptian priests that he was descended from the gods sixteen generations back. They, in turn, showed him 345 statues of priests, each of whom, they claimed, was the son of his predecessor—which would mean a time period of 10,000 years or so—and remarked that during all that time no one had observed any gods on earth, though before that their rulers had been gods. Obviously they exaggerated, but at any rate, the reply was shocking and perhaps enlightening to Hecataeus. Early sculpture in western Asia Minor shows distinct Egyptian influence, and some architectural innovations may also owe something to Egyptian temples and monuments. Egyptians or Babylonians must have furnished Greek scholars of the region the astronomical information they later used in their studies of the physical world.

Earliest Greek Literature

Any survey of early Greek literature must of course begin with the poet Homer, probably of the eighth century B.C., and the two epics attributed to him, the *Iliad* and the *Odyssey*. Composed and long preserved orally until definitive written versions were produced in the sixth century B.C., these works emphasized the heroic, aristocratic virtues and helped to mold Greek character for centuries. In the high period of Greek history they were standard school texts. Quite a different poem is the "Works and Days" of Hesiod, the Boeotian poet of about 700 B.C.—who, like Homer, has been mentioned earlier. In some ways Hesiod appears to have put himself deliberately in opposition to the values and themes of Homer. Hesiod's views are not those of the aristocracy, nor did he really approve of sea trade; his was a middle-class rural orientation. He did, however, give advice to those who would go to sea: The weather is not safe in the spring for the seafarer until the fig's leaves at the top of the tree are larger than a crow's foot. Hesiod chose to emphasize justice, peace, and hard work rather than pride, war, and vengeance—all Homeric themes.

The seventh century B.C. produced several important lyric poets, whose works have survived only in fragments. Archilochus of Paros (later of Thasos) was popular all through antiquity, and it is surprising that we have only a few lines of his many works. Some of them have the quality of the epigram[1]:

> Overdo neither sorrow nor joy:
> A measured motion governs man.
> * * *
> Truth is born as lightning strikes.
> * * *
> It's not your enemies
> But your friends
> You've got to watch.

Archilochus became a professional soldier, and his most famous lines are those in which he rather carelessly said he'd thrown away his shield as he was retreating from some fierce Thracians. He added that he knew where he could buy another one just like it. For this and other reasons Archilochus became *persona non grata* at Sparta, which was just developing its strongly militaristic society. But he deserved better. Of army service he wrote,

> Shield against shield,
> Keep the shield-wall tight,
> And the gift of death they bring,
> Let no man take.

Perhaps this also was of army service:

> And I, alone in the dark,
> I was promised the light.

The greatest woman poet of antiquity and one of the greatest lyric poets of all time was Sappho of Mytilene on the island of Lesbos, where she held a kind of school for young women, teaching both poetry and music. She loved some of her pupils dearly:

> Anaktoria so far away, remember me,
> Remember me, who had rather

---

[1] All quotations of both Archilochus and Sappho are from G. Davenport, *Archilochos, Sappho, Alkman: Three Lyric Poets of the Late Greek Bronze Age* (Berkeley, Calif., 1980).

> Hear the melody of your talking
> And see the torch-flare of your smile
> Than the long battle line of Lydia's charioteers,
> Round shields and helmets.

Just as those lines also reflect the military glory of Lydia in western Asia Minor, so do the following reflect the growing trade of that region:

> They come in ships on the ocean.
> Far gifts they bring, wrist-chains of gold,
> And purple coats and silver jars,
> And carved toys incredibly strange,
> And things made of ivory.

Sappho, too, remained popular for many centuries. Catullus, a Roman lyric poet of the first century B.C., wrote a charming love poem in what was almost a translation of some lines of Sappho.

Other poets of the time include Alcman and Tyrtaeus, both of whom lived in Sparta, at least for a time, and wrote there; what remains of the former's works are lines to be sung by choruses of Spartan girls at religious festivals; Tyrtaeus, however, is remembered for the martial poems that inspired Spartan youth in the difficult days of the Second Messenian War.

A later and quite important poet was Pindar of Thebes (518–438 B.C.), who will be mentioned here even though he belongs to a later century. Pindar's values were aristocratic, and he seems to fit in with this earlier age. He sang the glories of the victors at the great athletic festivals, the Olympic, Isthmian, Nemean, and Pythian games (the last at Delphi). His eulogies were not so much intended to applaud the individual winners as to praise dedication, courage, and agonizing effort. His poems were much treasured by many Greeks, among them Alexander the Great.

BOOKS FOR FURTHER READING

ANDREWES, A. *The Greek Tyrants*, New York, 1963.
BOARDMAN, J. *The Greeks Overseas*, Baltimore, 1964.
BURN, A. *The Lyric Age of Greece*, London, 1960.
DAVENPORT, G. *Archilochos, Sappho, Alkman: Three Lyric Poets of the Late Greek Bronze Age*, Berkeley, 1980.
FINLEY, M. *Early Greece: The Bronze and Archaic Age*, New York, 1970.
FINLEY, M. *The World of Odysseus*, New York, 1965.
HOPPER, R. *Trade and Industry in Classical Greece*, London, 1979.
HUTCHINSON, R. *Prehistoric Crete*, Baltimore, 1962.

NILSSON, M. *Homer and Mycenae*, London, 1933.
PAGE, D. *History and the Homeric Iliad*, Berkeley and Los Angeles, 1959.
SAMUEL, A. *The Mycenaeans in History*, Englewood Cliffs, N.J., 1966.
STARR, C. *The Economic and Social Growth of Early Greece, 800–500 B.C.*, Oxford, 1977.
TAYLOUR, W. *The Mycenaeans*, rev. ed., London, 1983.
VERMEULE, E. *Greece in the Bronze Age*, Chicago, 1964.
WEBSTER, T. *From Mycenae to Homer*, New York, 1964.

7

SPARTA AND ATHENS:

order or freedom?

A writer of fiction could scarcely conjure up two states exhibiting greater contrast than Athens and Sparta in their heyday. Sparta chose order, stability, a controlled society; Athens chose freedom, kaleidoscopic and creative change, sometimes catastrophic individualism. Antecedents played a part in their development: The Spartans were Dorian, and the Athenians were Ionian. Still, the two peoples spoke dialects of the same language, worshiped the same gods, and lived less than one hundred miles apart, in straight-line distance. Neither was a typical Greek state—indeed, there was no typical state. They participated little in early colonization and trade, though Sparta did establish a colony in southern Italy (Taras = Taranto), and both exported excellent pottery. In both states experiments in government embodied unique features.

A. EARLY SPARTA

In the Mycenaean age and in Homeric times, Sparta was, like the other Greek states, a monarchy. The story of King Menelaus and Helen begins there. Later, when the none-too-brilliant light of history finally casts dim illumination on the scene, Sparta was still a monarchy, but there were two kings, with greatly restricted powers. Elected officials had greater domestic authority, and a council and the assembly had strong positions as well.

The Spartans traced their developed state back to a great reformer and lawgiver, Lycurgus. A cursory reading of the early paragraphs of Plutarch's life of Lycurgus, however, shows clearly enough that even in antiquity he was a shadowy figure. It is possible to doubt he ever actually existed, though the soundest scholars are not quite that skeptical. Another Spartan tradition made the governmental reform the response to an answer of the oracle of Apollo at Delphi, called the Great Rhetra. Although the oracle's cryptic sentence can hardly have served as a constitution, it might have supported some proposed scheme or a controversial, recent change. Obviously, we have both contradictory and vague information about early Sparta, and, for that matter, about Sparta in its heyday as well. The task of the historian is complicated by the deliberate efforts of the Spartans to create a public image that was to some extent false; this was notably the case in the third century B.C. and after, when Spartans as citizens of a state then important only for its history looked back nostalgically to a mythical, ideal state that had never really existed. Half a century ago a French scholar coined a much-used term for this contrived image: the Spartan *mirage*. Still, we do know the general outlines of the evolution of the Spartan system and the major reasons for them.

Archaeology has demonstrated that in the eighth, seventh, and part of the sixth centuries B.C., Sparta was neither the backward and isolated place it had earlier been nor the culturally deprived, repressive place it later became. Poets, sculptors, and vase painters of great artistic ability lived and worked there. More than any other single factor, it was Sparta's imperialism that inexorably changed the city and shaped its future course.

During the eighth century B.C. Sparta became the dominant power in the plain of the Eurotas River in the southeast Peloponnese, absorbing the smaller states there. Then followed an extension of power, if not of territory, to the north and northeast. Except for the towns closest to Sparta, the peoples were left more or less autonomous (see *perioeci*, p. 134) but subject to Spartan intervention and were not allowed full citizenship. Messenia, to the west, possessed a productive plain that Sparta coveted and took, thereby precipitating a long war. When it drew to an end in the late eighth century B.C., Sparta had already made some military and political changes. As we have noted, all the hoplite class, desperately needed in the fighting, was enfranchised. A second Messenian war in the following century, similarly long and hard, produced further political changes; for example, elected officials (*ephors*) now became the chief magistrates.

The Consequences of Imperialism

The state of Argos, northeast of Sparta, had also achieved a considerable growth in land and dominance during the mid-seventh century when it was ruled by the legendary King Pheidon. After his death Argos declined somewhat but long remained Sparta's chief rival. The time of Sparta's military dominance of all Greece lay far in the future; for a time, in fact, even some of the lesser states to the north, notably Tegea, managed to block Spartan expansion northward.

After the Second Messenian War, when Spartan hoplites had become full

Spartan Soldier. (Courtesy Wadsworth Atheneum, Hartford, Conn.)

citizens and elected ephors the state's chief executive officers, Sparta was—internally—a relatively liberal oligarchy. Along with a degree of political liberalization, however, came a set of conditions that gradually fossilized the state. The Spartiates—full citizens—were a distinct minority, forming perhaps only about 3 percent of the population of the expanded state. To retain control over the subject peoples, they had to band themselves into a military caste, exercising rigorous discipline. Their whole purpose in life became the conservation of their own privileged position, but in the name of stability. Every Spartan thus became a professional soldier and nothing more. His education was designed to make him a soldier, and his duty was to the system—or the state, as he would have put it. Trade and commerce were to be discouraged because they would produce uncontrollable change. When philosophy and free education were later embraced in Athens, these ideals became anathema in Sparta—too dangerous. The result for Sparta was indeed order; there were only a few serious revolts over several centuries. But its price was the substantial loss of individual freedom, not only for the subject peoples but for the Spartiates as well.

Government and Society

In developed form, the government of Sparta included two kings of separate families, whose duties at home were primarily religious and advisory. They led the army on campaigns and thus were also rather important in foreign affairs. The chief executives at home were the five annually elected ephors. A council of elders, called the *gerousia,* made up of twenty-eight men over sixty years of age plus the kings, debated matters as it programmed the work of the assembly and served judicial functions. The assembly of all full citizens, or Spartiates, voted without debate on matters presented to it. The ephors were elected by the assembly, along with the elders of the gerousia. The constitution was thus a mixed one, including democratic, aristocratic, and monarchical aspects.

Besides the Spartiates, other major social classes were the *perioeci* ("dwellers around"), who were free but not citizens, and the *helots,* or state serf-slaves who formed the largest group of all. The helots worked plots of publicly owned land that were assigned to the Spartiates, who lived off the produce. These helots, located mostly in eastern Messenia and vastly outnumbering their rulers, were a continual danger to the Spartans. If they should revolt, the threat they posed was not merely military; it was economic and social as well. Yet it is notable that in times of crisis, the Spartans did not hesitate to arm the perioeci, and in the Peloponnesian war, some helots even served in the heavy infantry.

Most of the full-status Spartans lived off the proceeds from the public lands. Beginning in their seventh year (or as we would say, at age six), when they left their homes permanently to live in training barracks, Spartan boys—like the adult Spartiates supported by the helots—gave full attention to their education. They learned military arts and military virtues: discipline, obedience, toughness, endurance. At age twenty they entered the army. They could now marry but must still live in their communal barracks and contribute to its support; only at age thirty could they live with their wives. This, too, was the age when they gained the right to vote in the assembly. If they were fit, they served in the army until age sixty.

Spartans did not completely ignore such cultural activities as music, but theirs were old-fashioned martial tunes and dances. Religion was taken very seriously; an important festival was not to be interrupted. Most important were the rites to Artemis Orthia.

The system inculcated a pride in self and city that is not altogether to be disparaged. Spartans, sure of their superiority, for centuries proved they were the best soldiers anywhere. On one occasion when an Athenian twitted a Spartan by saying there were a good many Spartans buried on Athenian territory, the Spartan replied, "There are *no* Athenians buried on Spartan territory." That is, no Athenian army—or for that matter, any other alien force—had reached Sparta in human memory. The Spartans actually gloried in their rough clothing and tasteless food. A visiting Sybarite, after he had eaten a Spartan meal, exclaimed, "Now I know why Spartans are not afraid to die!"

Yet this social and political image—created not merely to impress others, for the Spartans did try to live up to it—turned out to be indeed a mirage. Spartan leaders could not resist the lures of wealth and power when these presented themselves, and the tensions that developed were in time to weaken and alter the state.

Formation of the Peloponnesian League

Perhaps because the minority of Spartiates had no need for additional territory, or because they felt they could not exercise adequate control over more helots, Spartan policy changed during the sixth century B.C. A defeat or two played a part in this change as well. Spartan imperialism continued within the Peloponnese, but in a new form. Defeated states—first Tegea, then Mantinea, Orchomenus, and others—were forced into alliance, with Sparta itself dominating the system. This alliance system (the league) was formalized by the Spartan King Cleomenes I (c. 519– 487 B.C.) a few years before 500 B.C.

King Cleomenes I not only brought most of the Peloponnese into the Spartan alliance but also intervened in Athens and Aegina; moreover, he defeated Argos, Sparta's most inveterate enemy in the Peloponnese. Though he was ambitious and capable, Sparta's complicated political system at last defeated him. At one point he was frustrated by Demaratus, his colleague as king, and at another by the ephors.

As we shall see (in the section on Athens), Cleomenes, with a Spartan army, expelled the Athenian tyrant Hippias in 510 B.C. Two years later he intervened again in Athenian politics with a small force that was, however, expelled by the Athenians. A third expedition to the same city two years after that was blocked by Demaratus, and a fourth in 504 B.C., mounted with the stated purpose of restoring the tyrant Hippias to power in Athens, was stymied by the amazed Corinthians. That sort of unruliness subsided after 494 B.C. when Cleomenes won a victory over Sparta's inveterate enemy Argos, and the league began to seem an instrument of Cleomenes' imperialism. Though he was the most adventurous and imperialistic Spartan king yet, Cleomenes still would not intervene to help the Ionians in their revolt against the Persians (499–494 B.C.), nor would he go as far as Samos (earlier) on a similar mission. However, he did venture as far as the island Aegina in 491 B.C.—though he had to bribe the oracle of Delphi and get his fellow king Demaratus deposed as illegitimate to keep him from obstructing his plans. This sacrilege, when exposed, caused the ephors to imprison Cleomenes. The king persuaded a helot guard to give him a dagger, with which he mutilated himself and so committed suicide.

The historian Herodotus reported the incident; he obviously thought it was retribution from the gods for Cleomenes' irreligious acts—especially against sacred groves, temples, and priests at Argos—but he reported also that the Spartans thought it was caused by the king's habit of drinking his wine straight, like the Scythians, rather than mixed with water in the usual Greek manner.

B. EARLY ATHENS

The Athenians preserved a tradition regarding their political development which probably is in a fundamental way accurate—though not in its details—and which is also rather typical of the evolution of many other Greek states in the same period. The Athenian monarchy was diminished in power at a time of crisis, when the king's power to lead the army was turned over to another official, the *polemarch*. At some later time, this office became elective. Royal administrative powers went next, to the *archon eponymos*, another elected official, after whom the calendar year was named. Finally the kingship itself became elective, first for ten years, then annually, like the other two magistracies. The *archon basileus* (king-archon) retained primarily religious and ceremonial functions. There were also an advisory council, the Areopagus, and an assembly of the full citizens. At some point, six other archons, called *thesmothetae*, were provided for; their functions were judicial. There was thus eventually a board of nine archons.

Though Athens was ultimately the greatest sea power among the Greek states and, of course, a leader in maritime commerce, this was not the case during the pioneer eighth and seventh centuries B.C. The various communities of Attica had come together by the end of that period to form a unified state, or polis, which of course was centered on Athens itself. Henceforth the city and the state were virtually identical.

Toward the end of the seventh century, certain disturbances in Athens indicate some degree of economic and social unrest. About 632 B.C. a nobleman named Cylon attempted to make himself tyrant. He failed and fled, and his followers were executed. The leaders in the purge, members of the Alcmaeonid family, were said to have violated the sacred right of sanctuary, since the condemned had taken refuge at the altar of Athena. The family was afterward considered, by its enemies at least, to be accursed. This unsuccessful attempt at tyranny, even though led by a member of the aristocracy, implies the rise of a group who might oppose the entrenched nobles. Similar implications may be seen in a written law code drawn up under the archon Draco about 621 B.C., which was notorious for its harshness (hence the English adjective *draconian*, of something barbarously severe). The death penalty was instituted for numerous civil infractions, even for petty theft. The harshness of the code may have made it palatable to the aristocrats, but the need for it indicates that the old tribal system was breaking down.

Solon

The first great constitutional reformer of Athenian history was Solon, elected archon for the year 594 B.C., a liberal aristocrat given broad power to shake up government and society. His acts and his own words, preserved in poems he composed in defense of his measures, indicate clearly that it was a time of deep economic distress and incipient revolt. Solon wrote of those who

> grow rich through deeds of injustice . . .
> they spare neither sacred nor public property . . .
> they have no regard for the revered foundations of justice. . . .

Athens was ripe for tyranny, and Solon's task was to stave it off by compromise. Though there is considerable information regarding his year in office, it is certain that Solon did not do all that is attributed to him in the sources, and much else about his career is doubtful—even the date of his reforms, which may have occurred later than his archonship.

One change that Solon assuredly accomplished was to rearrange the social classes, for political purposes, on a timocratic basis; that is, political classification was made according to wealth, not birth. It is likely that some form of classification by wealth existed earlier; still, Solon's more complete rearrangement must inevitably have reduced the power of the aristocrats and correspondingly increased that of nonaristocratic but well-to-do landowners, as well as of the relatively tiny but growing group of tradespeople, who could now serve along with the others in the highest offices. At the bottom level, Solon increased the number of full citizens who could vote in the *ecclesia*, or assembly. A new *heliaea*, or people's court drawn from the assembly, heard appeals from decisions of the archons. Middle-level groups were given the right, along with the upper class, to serve in the *boule*, or Council of 400 (according to Aristotle), which functioned as a steering committee for the assembly.

Solon naturally had to deal with the economic situation. He redeemed men who had been sold into slavery for debt and voided mortgages (probably all of them) in which a human being's freedom was collateral. Though urged by many to do so, he did not seize and redistribute land holdings. He forbade the export of agricultural products other than olive oil; this suggests that other Greek states had been purchasing Attic grain, thus producing an artificial shortage in Athens. He encouraged foreign artisans to settle in Athens. His new system of weights and measures and his new law code—less harsh than Draco's—were perhaps beneficial to the rising group of traders and merchants. Despite these liberal measures, Athens continued to be rocked by troubles. In the ensuing decades, official archon lists twice record a state of *anarchia*, when no archons could be elected, doubtless because of civil disorders. Ultimately Athens did experience the tyranny Solon had tried to forestall.

Peisistratus

Athens' first tyrant was Peisistratus, a noble who sought the support of the poor farmers of the "Hill" (perhaps this familiar term at first referred to a geographical sector east of Athens). Eventually he also gained the support of most of the city's poor and of the "Shore" (a group which included some merchants and traders). The "Plain," however, dominated by the landed aristocracy, mostly opposed him. After an initial failure to take power about 562 B.C., Peisistratus was tyrant more or less continuously from 560 B.C. to 527 B.C., except for two periods of exile, briefly early in his tyranny and then for ten years (556–546 B.C.).

Peisistratus had a flair for opportunistic publicity. He was thought to have faked the dramatic beating that persuaded the Athenians to give him a personal bodyguard—which he then used to seize power. He married the daughter of one of the major noble families to gain badly needed support. On his return after his first expulsion, proclaiming that the goddess Athena herself was sponsoring his resumption of power, he entered the city in a chariot with a beautiful, statuesque woman clad in armor. His ten-year exile was spent on his own estates in Thrace. From his silver mines and timberland, he acquired enough wealth to hire a band of mercenaries, mostly from Argos; his second return, thus, was something of an invasion.

Peisistratus was careful not to exercise power too nakedly. If he made constitutional changes, they were comparatively minor (though some attributed to Solon may actually have been his). He courted popularity in his building program and in his support of public festivals, including the first of the great theatrical contests (in 534 B.C., won by Thespis), which were to make Athens the drama center of the world.

Much of what Peisistratus did was made possible through the expenditure of his substantial personal fortune in the public interest—that is, the income from his silver mines in Thrace. It is often overlooked that one reason for the Peisistratid decline in popularity was the loss of these mines by his successors in 513 B.C. to Darius of Persia. The important silver mines at Laurium, within Attica, were exploited to an extent by Peisistratus, but the rich finds there came only in the fifth century B.C. The tyrant did impose a new land tax, which bore most heavily on the aristocracy. It seems, too, that he seized and redistributed some private land. Probably it was Peisistratus who first introduced coinage at Athens, and in other ways he encouraged trade and commerce.

At Peisistratus' death in 527 B.C., his two sons, Hippias and Hipparchus, assumed their father's role. Hippias was the political leader, and Hipparchus the patron of the arts. An attempt to assassinate Hippias went wrong, and instead Hipparchus was killed. The would-be tyrant killers hardly murdered Hipparchus out of idealism: A love affair was said to have been involved. Nevertheless, the pair of assassins—Harmodius and Aristogeiton—became heroes, and a fifth century sculpture by Polycleitus helped to perpetuate their heroic image.

Hippias afterward grew suspicious and vengeful. Economic distress caused by loss of the family silver mines must have hurt. In the end, it was the Spartans under King Cleomenes, conservative but opposed to tyranny, who sent troops to expel Hippias, about 510 B.C. The fleeing tyrant took refuge with the Persians and later accompanied them on invasions of his native Greece.

Cleisthenes' Reforms: Structures for Freedom

The ejection of the tyrant of course signaled the return of aristocratic oligarchy. Unfortunately, the aristocrats were divided into bitterly opposing groups: One was led by Isagoras, and the other by Cleisthenes, an Alcmaeonid. The latter and his faction had done the most to expel the tyrant. After the Temple of Apollo at Delphi had burned, he contracted to build a new one. He threw in such extras as a marble front, which were not called for in the contract. The grateful oracle, it was said, began to add to every answer given to any Spartan the words "But first, Athens must be freed." Perhaps King Cleomenes did not need such a spur. At any rate, Cleisthenes was unwilling to see Isagoras and his party installed in power by the Spartans. To thwart them, he courted the lower-class supporters of the Peisistratids and thus gained power. Like Solon, he made major changes in the constitution, which perhaps gained easy acceptance because of anti-Spartan feeling in the state.

Cleisthenes did not foolishly attempt to turn back to some sort of pre-Solonian oligarchy. His greatest concern was to set up governmental machinery that would not further polarize the classes. He therefore made the *boule*, now enlarged to a Council of 500, a more important body, chosen in a balanced fashion from ten newly created, artificial tribes. The new tribes meant an end to any lingering, aristocratic influence exercised through the old tribes; a local, residential arrangement replaced the previous kinship pattern. These tribes were created with local districts, the *demes*, as the basic residential units. Each tribe contained some demes largely dominated by aristocrats, some by the middle class, and some by the lower classes. Fifty persons from each of the ten tribes, chosen by a combination of election and lot, made up the boule. Demes were represented in the boule according to population—a sort of proportional representation.

The boule or Council of 500 served as the chief deliberative body and steering committee for the assembly comprising all citizens, and it furnished numerous officials. Foreign affairs and most internal matters came under its jurisdiction. The Council of 500 was divided into ten *prytaneis* of fifty men each. One prytany was always on duty, with each serving for the tenth part of the year. The chairmanship changed on a daily rotation. Since one could sit only two years on the council—and those not in succession—a large number of persons were thus able to serve on this important body. The citizens in this way learned the workings of the government. Athens was not yet a complete democracy, but Cleisthenes' innovations took a long stride in that direction.

The nine archons, still the chief executives of the state, were elected only from the top classes as before, so that wealth was still a prerequisite for this office. Moreover, much power remained with the council known as the *Areopagus*, composed of ex-archons. And it must not be forgotten that votes can be controlled by the powerful.

It was perhaps Cleisthenes who also established a new procedure, *ostrak-*

ismos (ostracism), so called because votes were written on *ostraka*, or potsherds. The purpose was to prevent the return of tyranny by making possible a general balloting for the banishment of overpopular leaders. Some scholars have thought that this institution belonged to a later period because it was not actually used until 487 B.C., but it could at first have served its purpose simply as a deterrent. It worked this way: Each year the assembly voted on whether to have a special secret balloting for ostracism. If one was held and if a quorum of at least 6,000 citizens voted, the person receiving the most votes had to go into exile for ten years. Ostracism became a factional tool, of course, but it was not used excessively.

King Cleomenes of Sparta, obviously aghast at such reforms, again intervened in Athens, at least on a personal basis. He engineered the exile not only of Cleisthenes but also of 700 other Athenians with their families. But when he attempted to undo some of Cleisthenes' reforms, the populace reacted indignantly, and soon Cleomenes, along with those whom he supported—the Athenian aristocrat Isagoras and his party—found themselves besieged atop the Acropolis. Cleomenes (with Isagoras) was forced to withdraw, and Isagoras' followers were captured and executed. Cleisthenes and the 700 returned from exile. The Athenians, still in reaction against Sparta, even attempted to ally themselves with the Persians, for they were sure that Cleomenes would be back. They were right: In 506 B.C. the Spartan brought a major expedition to punish the responsible Athenians and, according to Herodotus, to set up Isagoras as tyrant. But this was one of the times that Corinth refused to cooperate with its ally (as we have seen), and Demaratus, the other Spartan king, also obstructed his colleague. The expedition came to nothing. A couple of years later, Cleomenes—who was nothing if not persistent— again attempted to invade Attica, with the intention, he eventually let it be known, of restoring Hippias as tyrant. The Corinthians, who had rid themselves of tyranny not many years before, along with others of the Peloponnesian League went home, and so this attempt also failed.

Later reforms at Athens, based on the constitution of Cleisthenes, may be mentioned here for the sake of convenience, though they belong mostly to the years after the Persian wars. Army organization was soon based on the ten new tribes, and officials called *strategoi* were elected as commanders of the tribal army units. The ten strategoi could be reelected year after year. In the fifth century B.C., when Athens had an imperialistic policy and was often involved in war, it was inevitable that these officials, especially any one strategos who could dominate the group, should become the chief officers of the state. This was markedly so after about 487 B.C., when the archons began to be chosen by a procedure that included drawings by lot. In 462 B.C., certain judicial powers of the Areopagus were taken away and put into the hands of the popular courts, which became more important. The third-class citizens became eligible for election to the top offices about the same time. By the time of Pericles, it seems that any citizen, even of the lowest class—in fact, though perhaps not by law—could hold any office except that of treasurer.

Except for the fact that women, foreign residents, and slaves did not have

Attic lekythos, red-on-black ("red-figured") as developed by Athenian artists. Hunter with dog. Fifth century B.C. (Boston Museum of Fine Arts)

the rights of citizenship, by the mid-fifth century B.C. Athens had become a rather thoroughgoing, direct democracy in a unique way that set it apart from other states.

BOOKS FOR FURTHER READING

BOARDMAN, J. *The Greeks Overseas*, Baltimore, 1964.

CARTLEDGE, P. *Sparta and Laconia: A Regional History, 1300–362 B.C.*, London, 1979.

EHRENBERG, V. *The Greek State*, New York, 1964.

EHRENBERG, V. *From Solon to Socrates*, 2nd ed., London, 1973.

FINLEY, M. *The Legacy of Greece: A New Appraisal*, Oxford, 1981.

FORREST, W. *The Emergence of Greek Democracy*, London, 1966.

FORREST, W. *A History of Sparta, 950–121 B.C.*, London, 1968.

HOOKER, J. *The Ancient Spartans*, London, 1980.

JONES, A. *Athenian Democracy*, London, 1957.

8

FROM THE PERSIAN WARS
TO 431 B.C.

The Persians must often have found their Greek subjects in Asia Minor exasperating. These Greeks had always found it difficult to adjust to Persian rule. Their brothers across the Aegean found it dangerous enough to live at that distance from a huge, acquisitive, imperial state. In those home city-states, Greeks were expressing their freedom in new political forms, away from oligarchy, sometimes by means of tyranny, and toward some form of democracy. The Ionian Greeks pressed for similar change. The Persians belatedly went along with tyranny; they doubtless observed that tyrants can be controlled more easily than oligarchs. Eventually the Persian overlords even accepted some local democracy. A truly democratic state must, by definition, be free, however. The Ionian revolt, which broke out in 499 B.C., was said by Greek sources to have been instigated by Aristagoras, a tyrant of Miletus under the Persians who fell into disfavor; but the inherent Greek drive toward freedom must have been a significant factor in the rebellion.

Once the revolt broke out, Aristagoras sought help from other Greeks. King Cleomenes of Sparta listened sympathetically to his request; but when he learned that the Persian capital, target of a proposed expedition, was three months' march into the interior of Asia, he told Aristagoras to get out of town. The Athenians did send twenty ships, and the men from these ships joined a raiding force that captured and sacked Sardis, a Persian administrative center. Later, when the Persians put down the revolt and in turn sacked Miletus, the Athenians reproached themselves for not having sent more help to their fellow Ionians.

Persian motives for invading Greece proper soon afterward were partly a desire for revenge, partly the wish to prevent similar revolts in the future, and partly a continuation of their usual imperialistic policy. A first invasion force, proceeding by sea along the northern Aegean coast, came to grief when storms heavily damaged the Persian fleet in 492 B.C. The Persians had to call a halt, but they had already successfully occupied additional lands along the northern Aegean littoral.

A. THE INVASION OF DARIUS

Marathon (490 B.C.)

Persian invaders came again by sea in 490 B.C., this time directly across the Aegean. They took an island or two and then made their base on Euboea, just across from Attica. Soon they debarked an army on the Plain of Marathon, in Athenian territory and only twenty-six miles from Athens itself. The Greeks knew of the threat; they were never without general information on Persian movements, even in Asia. No well-organized defensive arrangements had been made, however. Cleomenes had held Sparta to an anti-Persian policy, and the Peloponnesian alliance could mostly be counted on for aid, even though Athens was the chief target. A runner sent by the Athenians to Sparta brought a promise of help, but a religious festival then in progress was not to be interrupted. It has been suggested—and there is some slight evidence—that the real reason the Spartans delayed was that they were having trouble with some helots. Religious scruple, however, would have been important to the ultra-conservative Spartans. The Spartan troops were soon sent north but arrived too late to fight alongside the Athenians. Meanwhile the Athenians, with the help of the Plataeans, faced the enemy at Marathon, blocking the road that led to Athens. A complication developed when, according to one theory, the Persians decided to use their superior fleet to bypass the Athenian army. They began to embark a portion of their army, including all their excellent cavalry. While the remainder of their force stayed at Marathon to pin down the Athenians, the Persian ships would sail around Cape Sunium and perhaps take the ill-defended capital. The plan implies that in Athens there were Persian sympathizers—or at least sympathizers of the cause of the ex-tyrant Hippias, who had accompanied the Persians.

One of the Athenian generals, Miltiades, persuaded the rest to fight, even though the remaining Persian force still greatly outnumbered the Greeks. The disposition of troops and the manner of attack show that the Greek generals understood very well the nature of the two quite different armies. The Persians were light-armed and depended mostly on missiles; the Greek hoplites were heavy-armed and depended on spear thrusts at close quarter. The advantages of the light-armed troops were mobility and flexibility; hence the Greeks extended their battle line dangerously thin to prevent being outflanked. The wings were kept strong, however, and the weak center was held back somewhat. Then the Athenians attacked at a double-quick pace, no doubt to keep casualties from arrows and other missiles at a minimum as they closed in. The hoplites were able to pin the Persians and Medes back against the sea and won a resounding victory. Casualty figures reported by Herodotus were 6,400 Persian dead, as against 192 Greeks. (Some of the latter's graves were found a few years ago.) A late tradition of doubtful value has it that a runner named Pheidippides (or Philippides) took the news of victory back to Athens (the first "Marathon") and then died on the spot. Pheidippides does deserve to be remembered for an earlier achievement: It was he who took the request for help to Sparta, running about 150 miles in two days.

The victorious army also hurried back to Athens to meet the threat from the sea, and the Persians then called off their faltering expedition. They could still claim important gains in the Aegean islands. They would not attempt to avenge their loss for ten years; but the Greeks, who could not know this, expected an avenging Persian expedition to be sent as quickly as it could be organized.

Themistocles and the New Military Policy

During the decade that intervened between the two major Persian invasions of Greece, a man of an obscure but noble family, Themistocles, made use of democratic processes to rise to power. He ostracized some of his opponents, including the moderate aristocrat Aristeides. Perhaps influenced by the fact that hoplite forces tended to be dominated by oligarchical leaders, but also recognizing that Athenian weakness at sea had almost brought disaster in the Marathon campaign, Themistocles pressed for a completely new military strategy. Athens should, he thought, emphasize sea power at the expense of the army and take a defensive stance on land. He perhaps engineered a small war—a renewal of a prolonged conflict, actually—with the neighboring island of Aegina to gain his point. After the small Athenian fleet was defeated, his proposals to spend the profits from Athenian silver mines near Laurium on ships, port facilities, and fortifications were adopted. By 480 B.C., therefore, Athens had constructed many new ships and had a navy of about two hundred vessels, mostly triremes (ships with three banks of oars) of the latest design.

Since the rowers of the naval ships were lower class, both the navy and the imperialism based on it came to be connected particularly with the democracy. Themistocles' strategic policy was similarly identified with his party, and as long as Athens remained an important power in Greece it was generally followed. Perhaps this rise to power of a brilliant man born of a family of no importance under the oligarchy illustrates, as well as anything, the strengths of democracy.

The Hellenic League

The Persians were prevented by revolts, internal problems, and the death of Darius from mounting another invasion before 480 B.C. Preparations for this were extensive and required several years. The Greeks, who had of course learned of the Persian mobilization, made more organized preparation this time to meet the threat. The Peloponnesian alliance served as the nucleus for a defense organization; Athens and perhaps a few other states now allied themselves with it, to form the Hellenic League. The Spartans therefore provided the leadership for the combined force, even for the fleet, though it was dominated by the Athenians.

B. XERXES' INVASION: THE RAZOR'S EDGE (480 B.C.)

The polyglot army that Xerxes put together for the great invasion of 480 B.C. may well have been the largest single army ever collected until modern times. Greek scouts were overawed. Herodotus reported an estimate for the total force, including service personnel but excluding camp followers, of more than five million. There were terrifying reports of whole streams and lakes drunk dry by men and horses. Although the wide-eyed Greek scouts exaggerated, the actual figures, even if only a tenth of Herodotus' estimate, were still overwhelming.

This vast horde crossed the Hellespont on a bridge of ships; there were far too many troops to be transported any distance by a fleet. There were a naval fleet and hundreds of supply ships as well, for no army of that size could live off the land in the fashion that was usual in antiquity. Vast baggage trains trailed the marching troops. The army moved ponderously across Thrace and Macedonia, down into Hellas. Before it, most Greek cities in the areas occupied offered earth and water in submission to the Persian monarch. Other states farther south, even Argos in the Peloponnese, "Medized" meekly.

Greek Efforts to Halt the Persians:
Thermopylae and Artemisium

A decision was made by the Hellenic League to try to stop the Persians at the Vale of Tempe, a pass from Macedonia into Thessaly, in order to keep the Thessalians and their valued cavalry safely on the Greek side. But Xerxes' immense forces used other passes, and the Greeks had to abandon the area to the enemy without a fight. To the south, however, where the main road from Thessaly enters Boeotia through a narrow pass along the sea at Thermopylae, a small Greek force under King Leonidas of Sparta opposed the Persian hordes. Just offshore, the Greek fleet, with its nucleus of new Athenian triremes, took up its station off Cape Artemisium, at the northern tip of the island of Euboea.

The 300 Spartans (each doubtless accompanied by helots), with about 5,000 Thespians, Thebans, and others, held off the Persians for a time at Thermopylae, until a Greek guide showed the invaders how to outflank their position. King Leonidas was aware of the danger, but true to the Spartan ideal, elected to fight to the end. Most of the other Greeks were ordered to retreat, however. One of the monuments later set up at Thermopylae seems to symbolize Greek restraint, as well as Spartan concepts of virtue: "Go, passing stranger, and tell the Lacedaemonians that we lie here, obedient to their word." The Greek fleet also was forced back by superior numbers. The Persians, however, suffered greatly from the elements: Fierce storms destroyed a large number of their ships.

The Battle of Salamis

As the Persian army swept through Boeotia, the Athenians withdrew from their city and abandoned it to the enemy. It was a hard decision. They had asked the advice of Apollo from the Delphic oracle and had received a terrifying warning to flee. When they persisted in seeking a more heartening answer, the oracle somewhat tempered its advice: The Athenians were told to trust to wooden walls. Themistocles persuaded them that this meant their fleet. The noncombatant population was therefore evacuated to the island of Salamis, just offshore in the bay, and to other locations. The Greek fleet took up a position in the bay, while the Athenians on Salamis could only watch in dismay as the enemy sacked and burned their city.

The Spartans were now pressing for all Greek forces to withdraw within the Peloponnese, behind a wall being constructed across the Isthmus of Corinth. They urged that the fleet move south also. Themistocles, in order to induce the invaders to attack, we are told, secretly informed the Persians of the Greek intent to withdraw. Xerxes did decide to attack and had a throne set on a high point where he could watch the fateful panorama in the straits below. The numerically inferior Greek ships outmaneuvered the Persian vessels—mostly Phoenician—in the narrow waters and won a resounding victory. The Greek naval force rammed and sank many of the enemy ships. In his tragedy entitled *The Persians*, Aeschylus tells how the Greeks killed Persians thrashing about in the water by battering them with the butts of their spears. Herodotus adds that most of the enemy forces could not swim. Though his defeat was not decisive, since much of his fleet and all his land army were intact, Xerxes, furious and fearful for his own safety, concluded that no more could be done that year. With most of his army, he returned as he had come, but a considerable Persian force was left behind in Thessaly under his general Mardonius.

Plataea and Mycale (479 B.C.)

The largest single army ever raised by the Greeks in antiquity assembled during the early months of 479 B.C. The Spartans were still inclined to defend only the Peloponnese, at the fortified isthmus, but the Athenians threatened to go over to the Persians unless the Greek army moved north, so that Sparta was finally forced to agree. The Greek force that took up positions some time later at Plataea on Mount Cithaeron, northwest of Attica, numbered about 100,000 according to Herodotus (probably including supply personnel) and surely was not much smaller than Mardonius' army.

After several days of preliminary maneuvering and skirmishing, the Spartan commander Pausanias decided on a minor pullback from flatland to hilly ground to escape the attacks of the strong Persian cavalry. At dawn, seeing only the withdrawing rear guard, the Persians attacked. The main body of Spartans quickly moved forward to a strong position and split the Persian line. Then the Greeks charged, killed many, and sent the rest reeling. The Athenian hoplites, the second-strongest contingent on the Greek side, met the Theban allies of the Persians and defeated them. But the chief glory in this victory went to the Spartans. Although Herodotus presents the whole situation as fortuitous, it may have been at least partly planned by the Spartan command. The Persian remnants now withdrew into Asia, never to return. Greece had been saved.

This victory was, actually, a double triumph for the Greeks. On the very same day that the battle of Plataea was fought, as the Greeks reckoned it, a second decisive battle of Mycale in Asia Minor brought added disaster on the Persians. Much of their fleet was destroyed, along with substantial ground forces, by the Greek fleet and marines. Several of the Aegean islands passed from Persian control at this time, and it did not seem unreasonable that the Greeks might even take the offensive against mighty Persia.

As it happened, Greeks in the West, on Sicily, also won a great victory in these years. Over a period of two or three centuries, the Carthaginians had backed their fellow Phoenicians in western Sicily in competition with the Greeks, who held most of the eastern part of that island. In 480 B.C. the Carthaginian general Hamilcar brought a large army to Sicily, which was challenged and decisively defeated at Himera in north-central Sicily by Gelon, tyrant-general of Syracuse.

The combination of victories against odds, by land and by sea, in the East and in the West, proved tremendously exhilarating to the victors. Greeks, it seemed for the moment, could do almost anything they put their minds to. A new atmosphere of confidence and enthusiasm invigorated the Hellenes.

C. DELIAN LEAGUE TO ATHENIAN EMPIRE

Sparta Fails as Leader of All Greece

Just after the twin victories of Plataea and Mycale, Sparta had an opportunity to assume the leadership of all Greece in a great counteroffensive against the Persians. Pausanias was willing and led a Greek force that expelled the Persians from some towns in the north Aegean area. Sparta also requested Athens not to rebuild its walls and suggested that other cities' walls be demolished. Sparta itself did not have encircling walls. Themistocles fooled the Spartans: He was part of an embassy to discuss the matter; at the same time all able-bodied citizens were rebuilding the Athenian walls in great haste. The Spartans subsequently accepted the accomplished fact.

Spartan ephors always tended to fear extended foreign involvement. When they heard rumors that Pausanias had assumed the airs of a Persian potentate, they recalled him and appointed a nonentity in his place. Soon the replacement, too, was recalled, and Sparta virtually abdicated the leadership of the general Hellenic coalition. When some of the other allies asked Athens to assume the leadership role, it willingly did so.

Founding of the Delian League

The new confederation, formed in 478/477 B.C., was in truth the brain-child of Themistocles, who had made Athens the foremost sea power in the Aegean. But it was the moderate aristocrat Aristeides who actually brought the organization itself into being, and another aristocrat, Kimon, the son of Miltiades, was its first vigorous leader. As for Themistocles, who over the years had been often accused both of giving and taking bribes, he was ostracized and went into exile at Argos. Thereafter, ironically, both he and Pausanias were charged with "Medizing"—working in the interests of Persia. Pausanias took refuge in a temple, where the ephors starved him to death. Themistocles fled to Magnesia in Persian-controlled Asia Minor, where at length he died, reportedly a suicide.

Though theoretically an alliance among equals, the Delian League was dominated by Athens from its inception. Its headquarters was on the island of Delos (hence the name), but Athens furnished all the important officials, including the commander-in-chief, and most of the naval power. The treasurers also were Athenians. Many of the league members were to regret they had all tossed red-hot pieces of iron hissing into the sea and had sworn to abide by the alliance until the iron should float.

Under Kimon's generalship, the league was notably successful. All the Greek states in the Aegean area were freed from Persian domination, and most joined the league. About 468 B.C., a high point in the counteroffensive occurred at the battle of Eurymedon, in southern Asia Minor, where the Persian fleet and army were decisively defeated. The very success of the Delian League, however, brought problems. When the Persian threat receded, some members wanted to withdraw. Kimon established a principle of "no secession" and used military power to enforce it. He also arranged that some states, including two that had rebelled, Naxos and Thasos, would no longer furnish contingents of ships and men, but money only. This practice was more convenient for many small states, but it left them entirely at Athens' mercy. The amount of their contributions could be determined by Athens alone, and collections were made under threat of force. The league was growing into an empire, with imperialist coercions.

Sparta at first acquiesced in the formation of an Athenian-led league, probably because the Athenian leaders in charge were rather conservative aristocrats (Aristeides and Kimon), whose basic philosophy called for cooperation with Sparta and other nonallied Greek states in a common offensive against the real enemy, Persia. As the league developed into an empire, however, Sparta seems to have made preparations to intervene, perhaps intending to aid Thasos when that city rebelled and was besieged by Athenian forces after 465 B.C. But then Sparta was hit by a destructive earthquake, followed by a helot revolt; so weakened, she was forced to ask for help from her allies. When Kimon led an infantry force from Athens to help, however, the Spartan leaders spurned his assistance. This snub brought a political reaction in Athens, and Kimon was blamed; in 462 B.C. he was ostracized and went into exile for a decade.

The Leadership of Pericles

The exile of Kimon meant also a change in party dominance. Democratic leaders Ephialtes and Pericles now assumed leadership of the state and the Delian League. Democratic political reforms we have alluded to earlier were put into effect, limiting the power of the Areopagus. It is uncertain exactly what was done; perhaps its general guardianship of the laws (whatever that meant) or its power to hear charges against the magistrates was eliminated. This action seems to have stirred some group against Ephialtes, and he was soon assassinated. Presumably Athenian policy now came under the predominant influence of Pericles. We can be certain of his preeminence only for the period after about 454 B.C., when as strategos he led a campaign in the Gulf of Corinth. From 443 B.C. to his death in 429 B.C. he was strategos every year and so dominated affairs that his power was compared by some to that of a tyrant.

Continuing War Abroad; New Wars in Greece

After Kimon's ostracism in 462/461 B.C., Athens adopted an anti-Spartan policy within Greece, and even went so far as to enter into alliance with Argos, Sparta's inveterate enemy in the Peloponnese. This amounted to a declaration of war against Sparta and resulted in the so-called First Peloponnesian War (460–446 B.C.). In pursuit of this policy the Athenians created something of a land empire to go with their sea empire; it was based on alliances with mainland Greek states, and it directly challenged Sparta's basic position of power. The Athenian allies included Boeotia (except Thebes), Phocis, Thessaly, Megara, Argos, and others. At the same time the Athenians continued the offensive against Persia and engaged in risky campaigns even into Egypt in aid of a revolt against the Persian King Artaxerxes.

Athens overreached itself in this attempt to carry on war in three widely separated areas. There was a tremendous disaster in Egypt, where the Persians, at first largely expelled, managed to recover Egypt and in the process destroy 250 league ships, killing or capturing many Greeks (c. 454 B.C.). In Greece itself neither side prosecuted the war strenuously. Sparta and its allies won the single most important land battle at Tanagra in Boeotia in 457 B.C. and broke up the Athenian alliance on the mainland. The most serious consequence of this conflict for Athens was the growing enmity of Corinth. It will be remembered that Corinth, in the days of Cleomenes, had once or twice blocked Spartan aggression against Athens. Now all the Peloponnesians except the Argives were uniformly anti-Athenian.

Athenian Dominance of the Delian League

In the war, though they lost most of their mainland allies, the Athenians' control over the remaining Delian League members in fact tightened. When a Persian fleet threatened to enter the Aegean, the Delian League treasury was moved to Athens, and league members were charged a percentage for the protection of that city's tutelary goddess. Moreover, once peace was again established, Pericles felt free to use at least some Delian League funds for strictly Athenian purposes, such as building temples.

This war was costly, not only in money but also in men. An extant inscription, probably of the year 459 B.C.—not one in which there was any major battle—illustrates both the wide range of Athenian operations and their human toll. It states that just one Athenian tribe had 177 men killed in that year; the losses occurred in six actions in four countries: Cyprus, Egypt, Phoenicia, and three locations in Greece itself.

Policies of Pericles other than moving the treasury to Athens also grated on Delian League members. Athenian colonies called *klerouchoi* (cleruchies; from *kleroi*, plots of land assigned to colonizing citizens) were sent out to various allied territories, beginning with the Chersonese. The land on which these Athenians settled was purchased by the mother city, but only through a reduction in the subject region's tribute, not by direct payment of funds. The settlers retained their Athenian citizenship and served almost like garrison troops in their new homes, thereby consolidating Athenian domination. It rankled, also, that any protest against the tribute levied on the subject states (at the height of the Delian League there were about three hundred of them) could be decided only at Athens, before an Athenian court. Athenian weights and measures were made the required standard, and Athens, to its economic benefit, dominated the minting of all coins.

Rebuilding of Athenian Temples

After about 445 B.C. Athens was at peace with both Persia and Sparta. Perhaps as a means of giving work to unemployed sailors or simply to embellish the city, Pericles, serving as strategos year after year, proposed to rebuild the temples on the Acropolis destroyed by the Persians thirty-five years earlier. He had previously suggested that other Greek states assist in this restoration, but without response. Surplus tribute funds from league members and income from other sources, especially the silver mines, provided the necessary capital.

The Parthenon, the Temple of Athena on the Acropolis, begun in 447 B.C., was of course the most important structure built during the age of Pericles. Its chief architect was Ictinus, and its chief sculptor was Pheidias, who also sculptured the chryselephantine (gold and ivory) statue of Zeus for the temple at Olympia, considered one of the Seven Wonders of the ancient world. He placed a similar huge statue of Athena in the cella of the Parthenon and did most of the frieze

The Parthenon, Doric style temple of Athena on the Acropolis, Athens. The most celebrated temple of antiquity. (Built 447–443 B.C.)

sculpture, much of which is now in the British Museum. The so-called Theseum (the best-preserved temple at Athens) was erected near the Agora below the Acropolis during the same years. The magnificent Propylaea, or templelike entrance to the Acropolis, was also built by Pericles (finished about 432 B.C.), along with an odeum (music hall) near the Acropolis. During the Peloponnesian wars, after the death of Pericles, the Temple of Athena Nike and the Erechtheum (with its splendid caryatid porch), both on the Acropolis, were constructed.

The Brilliance of Periclean Athens

The physical setting, beautiful even in ruins, is still impressive, but even more astonishing is what we know of the intellectual atmosphere of Pericles' Athens. In the years around 440 B.C., Sophocles and Euripides were writing tragedy; Socrates, then in his twenties, may already have been teaching; Herodotus (originally from Halicarnassus) was writing his *History*; Protagoras and other Sophists (popular philosopher-teachers) were lecturing to eager young men; Pheidias and other celebrated artists went about their work. At no other time in the history of mankind has such a galaxy of intellectuals and artists been concentrated within so small a political entity during such a short period. Intellectuals from other cities were drawn to Athens as if by a magnet. About the time Pericles died, Xenophon and Plato were infants or soon to be born, and Thucydides was a grown man.

Even lower-class Athenians could take advantage of the opportunities of their city, become prosperous through the tribute of empire. Many citizens, holding the numerous offices, were on the public payroll. The democracy employed hundreds of jurors (*dicasts*); numerous other citizens served in the fleet. Citizens were eligible, also, for a small payment from a special fund (*theoricon*) that made it possible for them to attend the great theatrical spectacles put on at Athens. And, of course, stipends for public office made it possible for relatively poor men to serve.

It was indeed a brilliant age; but there were dark spots. To some degree, Athenians as a group lived off the labor of their subjects, and many citizens kept slaves. Women played mostly a subordinate, domestic role. Even the system of salaried public office, without which democracy is impossible, was attacked as a questionable use of state funds by Pericles to build a political machine—a kind of early patronage system. There is some justice in these various attacks, which even today appear occasionally in newspapers and magazines. But whatever Athens' weaknesses in this glorious era, they were more than compensated by its strengths. Nothing can quite tarnish the brilliant luster that history has given to Periclean Athens. The democratic ideal—the concept of government of and by the people as the best form—was not to last for many years, and once submerged by a changing world, would not be revived again until modern times.

Workaday Athens

Much is known also of the less glorious quarters of Athens, with their mundane affairs; areas were named for their activities or the crafts produced and sold there. In the agora (marketplace and public square) were the ceramicus, where potters hawked their wares, and areas for silversmiths, tanners with their leather goods, and other artisans. Some of these skilled workers lived, worked, and sold their goods from a single location. Other goods also were purchased in specified areas; there were places for the fishmonger, for the butcher, for the seller of foreign goods; grain, mostly imported from a distance—Thrace or the Black Sea region mostly—was sold at an assigned spot, as were vegetables, baked goods, tools, charcoal, vinegar, wine, salt, cheese, oil, fabrics, wreaths for religious purposes, birds, and various luxury items. The whole area of the agora, with streets leading to and from it, was full of activity.

D. ART AND ARCHITECTURE OUTSIDE ATHENS IN THE SIXTH AND FIFTH CENTURIES B.C.

Although Athens rose in the time of Pericles to become the single most important cultural center, the most active area of evolving culture earlier, in the sixth century B.C., was the Ionian region of western Asia Minor and the adjacent islands. The leading city was probably Miletus. Here, the influences of the older civilizations of Mesopotamia and Egypt—transmitted in part through Phoenicia and Syria—could most strongly bear upon Greeks, who already were receptive to change. Important progress in the arts was being made on the Greek mainland, as well. In vase painting, notably, but also in other areas in this late archaic period, the home-land Greeks were advanced. No doubt they learned from what remained of the Mycenaean monuments, but they also, through innovative ideas and techniques, created fresh, attractive forms.

Sculpture

The dual influences of the earlier Aegean (Mycenaean on the mainland) and ancient Near Eastern civilizations are obvious in both sculpture and architecture. Life-size sculpture developed earliest in the Ionian areas; the two schools of sculpture at Miletus and Chios set the pace for other Greek artists. The earliest remaining figures from the period seem to reflect a still earlier time when full-sized figures were carved out of tree trunks: The stone statues are rounded, with a trunklike configuration. Both on the mainland and in Ionia, *kouros* figures (nude young males) look so much like the Egyptian statuary of the New Kingdom or even earlier periods that almost no one doubts that Greek sculptors, traveling with traders to Egypt, had learned much from Egyptian models. The figures stand in a typically Egyptian pose: They are stiffly erect, one leg advanced, arms held straight down the sides; moreover, the shoulders, neck, lower legs, and feet show Egyptian characteristics.

By the mid-fifth century B.C., Athens was one of several centers for sculpture. The two best-known artists working in Athens in those years were Pheidias and Myron. Pheidias, as has been noted, sculptured the chryselephantine (ivory and gold overlay) figure of Zeus in the temple at Olympia—regarded by the ancients as one of the Seven Wonders of the world—and that of Athena in the Parthenon at Athens, as well as the great bronze statue of the same goddess, about thirty feet high, that stood prominently outside the temple on the Acropolis. He also did some of the frieze on the Parthenon. Myron is best known for his Discus Thrower. Other important mainland centers of sculpture included Argos, where Polycleitus sculptured a chryselephantine statue of Hera for the Argive Heraeum and a Doryphoros (spear-bearer) that became a model for proportion in nude male figures. Along with Argos, Sicyon and Aegina were famous for large bronzes.

Kouros figure, Delphi Museum. (Art Resource)

Architecture

Greek architecture naturally was varied, and the Greeks produced many different types of public buildings. Discussion usually—and justifiably—tends to focus on temples, since many of these were renowned in antiquity and, in their ruins, still impress tourists. The ground plan of the classic temple is the *megaron,* the basic design of structures erected both by the Mycenaeans and by other Aegeans elsewhere; a megaron unearthed at Troy antedates any such known building on the mainland. Greek travelers to Egypt had surely seen such works as the colonnades of the Hypostyle Hall of Ramses II at Karnak and those of the Temple of Hatshepsut at Deir el Bahri; they must have learned from these as they did from Egyptian statuary.

The Ionians developed a somewhat more ornate style for their temples than did the mainland Greeks. Called Ionic, it features slender columns and scroll capitals. In Greece itself, the more prominently favored style was the Doric, with

Ionic style porch of the Erechtheum, fifth century B.C., on the Acropolis, Athens. (Art Resource)

its thicker, deeply fluted columns and simple capitals. This is the style of the Parthenon, as of several of the best-preserved temples in Italy and Sicily.

These magnificent structures served both as shrines to the gods or goddesses (Athena, in the case of the Parthenon) and, often, in a more utilitarian function, such as housing a state treasury—as the Parthenon. Mostly, however, they were created as things of beauty, which often symbolized the unity of the polis. To the modern eye they speak eloquently of the remarkable flowering of Greek genius in the classical period.

E. EARLY SCIENCE AND PHILOSOPHY

Thales and the Early Milesians

What traits of mind, what influences of environment, could cause one lone man, perhaps for the first time in history, to attempt to see and explain the world solely on rational grounds? Such a man was Thales of Miletus, who flourished in Ionia soon after 600 B.C.

Thales' surviving fragments reveal nothing of his motivation. As in sculpture, however, it is clear that contacts with older cultures and especially travel to Egypt brought to Greeks of his time not only a broadened horizon but even cultural shock. Two Greeks of a somewhat later period illustrate this statement and may serve to indicate what sort of influences affected Thales earlier. Xenophanes of Colophon, founder of the so-called Eleatic school of natural philosophy, realized that the gods of Homer and Hesiod must be poetic invention when he learned that other people invented gods with traits like their own. The Ethiopians, he said, made their gods black; Thracians made theirs redheaded. He went on to theorize that there must be only one god, nothing like men, a being capable of seeing, feeling, thinking of all and eternally unchanging. Hecataeus, also of Miletus, the geographer and protohistorian mentioned earlier, as we have said traveled to Egypt and was shocked to learn that the priests there considered Greek ideas about the gods crude and puerile. Men of such inquiring minds, then, learned not only to mistrust what had been handed down to them by the ancients but also to doubt even the evidence of the senses.

Thales and his successors launched on a great adventure of the mind: Through logical analysis alone, and ignoring the many-layered accumulation of myth, legend, and superstition by which people formerly explained the mysterious universe, they contemplated what is (being) and how it came to be and how it changes (becoming). Thales saw unity in what is, and he concluded that the unity must be one of substance. This basic substance, he decided, was water. The notion of a basic substance was pursued by several of Thales' successors. This idea is not so naive as it might first appear, when one troubles to think about it.

Thales is supposed to have made his reputation by a spectacular prediction of the solar eclipse that took place in the spring of 585 B.C. He must have had available to him astronomical records from either Mesopotamia or Egypt. Astronomers today doubt that he could have predicted the exact time of an eclipse on the basis of information then available; perhaps he merely predicted an approximate time, or perhaps he made a lucky guess.

Pythagoras (c. 580–500 B.C.)

Pythagoras, a generation younger than Thales, was also an Ionian Greek, born on the island of Samos, off Miletus. As a mature man, he emigrated to the west Greek colony of Croton in southern Italy and there made his mark. Pythagoreans emphasized numbers and their relations—or mathematics—as the key to the understanding of what is, rather than a theory of primal substance. Everyone knows one of Pythagoras' discoveries in geometry: As transmitted by Euclid, the so-called Pythagorean theorem is in daily use in building construction. Pythagoreans stressed harmony, which in music was shown to rest on a mathematical basis. Numbers, therefore, could be a practical guide in human affairs and could provide a mystical key to understanding the universe. The world, this school thought, was spherical—because a sphere is perfect.

Some Pythagoreans led ascetic, almost monastic lives and espoused the Orphic religion, with its belief in transmigration or cycles of reincarnation of souls (or perhaps Orphism borrowed this belief from the Pythagoreans). Pythagoreans in southern Italy attempted to impose their austere code of conduct on whole city-states. This brought a violent reaction in the fifth century B.C.; such puritanism was not for the average Greek. Nonetheless, Pythagoras influenced Plato, among many others, and there was an occasional resurgence of Pythagorean thought as late as the time of the Roman Empire.

Heracleitus and Parmenides: Polarization and Compromise

Two other natural philosophers, Heracleitus, an Ionian of Ephesus, and Parmenides of Elea in southern Italy (late sixth to early fifth century B.C.), brought to a climax the arguments on the nature of being, or reality, and of becoming, or change. Heracleitus said that change, a kind of constant flux, is the only reality; no such thing as *being* exists. That is, everything in the universe is either coming into being or passing out of being. He did see some logical unity in change, and this principle of rational order he called *logos*. His most famous aphorism was that "You can't step into the same river twice." (The most famous comeback to this, we are told, probably facetiously, was that one of his debtors refused to pay him back on the grounds that Heracleitus wasn't the same person who lent the money and he was no longer the same person who borrowed it.) Heracleitus thus rejected absolutes.

Parmenides took precisely the opposite view. There is no such thing as change, he said—only being. He completely mistrusted the evidence of the senses. Logically, he argued in his celebrated analysis, *not*-being cannot be; being thus could not derive from not-being: Whatever is, is at once, completely and eternally. All apparent change is illusion. For him, the universe was a perfect body, that is, a sphere, and the earth was also a sphere set in the middle of the universe.

Compromise views were put forward. The best-known of these pluralists was Empedocles of Agrigentum, in Sicily, who lived in the mid-fifth century B.C. He argued that there are four basic elements—fire, water, earth, and air—which never change, as Parmenides had said, but which constantly appear to change through their varying combination or dissolution, as Heracleitus had argued. Empedocles was a remarkable person, at times followed by thousands of disciples, who heeded his words as if inspired. He was said to have healed the sick, and he was thought to be in the final incarnation before union with deity.

Ionian by birth but Athenian by adoption, Anaxagoras, the friend of Pericles, held that there are an infinity of elements, which can come into or pass out of existence. In this same vein were the atomists, the best-known of whom was Democritus, a generation younger than Anaxagoras and perhaps once his pupil. He postulated an infinite number of atoms rushing through space, coagulating in vortices to form an infinite number of worlds. All things are made up of atoms, even the soul. Either he or later atomists postulated also a kind of geological and biological evolution.

The Sophists

The Sophists were a diverse group of philosophers who "brought philosophy down to earth" and became professional teachers of young men in Greece. They rejected speculations about the cosmos as unprofitable or not relevant and turned to questions of how people ought to behave on earth.

In general, the Sophists were subjective in their outlook. This is best expressed by Protagoras, who was also a friend of Pericles in Athens, just before the Peloponnesian wars. "Man is the measure of all things," he said, "of things which are, that they are; and of things which are not, that they are not." This quotation is much discussed; it appears to mean that he felt that humans have no grounds for judgment but their own perceptions and their own mind. Followed to its logical end, this view would support a humanistic relativism in morals, justice, and all other issues.

Gorgias of Leontini, in Sicily, who as an old man came to Athens late in the fifth century B.C., emphasized rhetoric and other practical virtues in his school—for which he charged very high tuition. He was totally skeptical of any possibility of real knowledge. "Nothing exists," he said. "If anything does exist, we cannot know it. If we could know it, we could not communicate it." Many of the sophists were apparently cynical and argued specious cases: for example, that justice was simply the interests of the stronger. Socrates and Plato were to oppose such skeptical, relativist teaching vigorously.

F. TRAGEDY

Every educated person in the contemporary Western world encounters the work of the great tragedians of Athens in the fifth century—Aeschylus, Sophocles, and Euripides—on several different levels. Naturally, any literary survey must give prominent place to them and to their themes, which continually reappear in *belles lettres*. In addition, they have provided models (plus terminology) for psychologists and psychiatrists and philosophers, as well as inspiration for generations of artists. Great literature deals with universals; presentations in these plays of typical human dilemmas, such as an individual's attempts to deal with conflict between religious values and demands of family or of state, are timelessly meaningful. If drama is to have an enduring impact, however, it must also be presented in a form both stirring and entertaining; moreover, the poetic lines, the themes, and the mode of presentation must all be focused in time and place. The forms of the early Greek tragedy—with its chorus that speaks lines integral to the plot; with its limited number of actors, wearing strange masks; and with equally limited action—seem somewhat alien to a twentieth-century audience. But across the centuries the sense of tragedy emerges powerfully even from translated lines.

The drama grew out of festivals to Dionysus, god of wine; the early performances were poetry recitals with chorus. At Athens, after Peisistratus first offered a prize in 534 B.C. (won by Thespis that year), the dramatic performances were supported by the state. Scripts were screened by a board, and the best plays were backed financially by prominent citizens, assigned that duty, and were presented in official contests, with prizes for winning entries. Possibly as early as Pericles' day, as noted previously, a special fund (theoric fund) established with profits from the silver mines paid small amounts to poorer citizens to permit them to take time off to enjoy the dramatic presentations.

Aeschylus (c. 525–456 B.C.)

A convenient way to remember the approximate ages of the three greatest Greek tragedians is to use the date of the Battle of Salamis (480 B.C.) as a focus. Aeschylus was present at the battle and described it in his play *The Persians*; Sophocles, fifteen or sixteen years old, led the chorus of young men who celebrated the victory; and Euripides was four or five years old at the time.

Aeschylus added a second actor, which made possible a true dialogue, with the chorus playing a background role. In *Agamemnon*, for example, the chorus represents the townspeople. This play, one of the conventional trilogy, was based on the tale of Agamemnon; his wife, Clytaemnestra; and their children, Iphigenia, Electra, and Orestes. The story itself was familiar to the audience: It occurred at the end of the Trojan War, yet the atmosphere at Mycenae was foreboding. Clytaemnestra had become alienated from Agamemnon, because he had offered Iphigenia as a sacrifice to enable the Greek fleet to sail off to war, and she had taken a lover, Aegisthus. When Agamemnon returned, with Cassandra (who knew everything that was to happen, though no one believed her forecasts), he was killed by his wife and her lover. Aeschylus' sonorous, lofty language spells out this message of proud men come to grief at the hands of Zeus, of wrong following upon wrong down through the generations. His audience knew that just as this was not the beginning of sorrows, neither was it the end: "This is no mere drizzling shower. Fate now is whetting Justice's heavy sword on a new whetstone. . . ." This play, like all the rest of the greatest Greek tragedies, somehow touches every reader (or hearer) and conveys the common tragedy that is the ultimate core of every human life.

Sophocles (c. 496–406 B.C.)

No other tragedian won more first prizes in the Athenian competitions than Sophocles, who added a third actor and painted scenery. His play *Oedipus Tyrannus* (or *Oedipus Rex*), perhaps the best-known and most widely performed ancient tragedy, tells the story of a man who was predestined, according to an oracle of Apollo to kill his own father and marry his own mother. All of them took desperate measures to prevent these events from coming to pass, but in vain. Yet the play's message is not merely that man is a tool in the hands of Fate or the gods, for Oedipus says, "Apollo brought these ills to pass; But the right hand that dealt the blow was mine" (referring to the killing of the man who he later discovered was his father). The whole play has all the suspense of a murder mystery. The chief investigator, King Oedipus, not only is himself the murderer but also, unknowing, is the husband of his own mother. Tension builds as, step by step, the evidence falls into place and finally brings Oedipus face to face with the horrifying truth. *Antigone*, deservedly, is perhaps second only to *Oedipus* in popularity. It is a story of the duties of religion and family loyalty confronting loyalty to the state and society.

Euripides (c. 485–406 B.C.)

Much less lofty, but just as meaningful, are Euripides' plays. He won few first prizes, but more of his plays have survived than those of Aeschylus and Sophocles together—which says something for his later reputation. One of the most interesting of his tragedies is *The Bacchae*, which tells the story of the introduction of the wild rites of Dionysus, in which the Bacchae, or Maenads, worked themselves into a frenzy (or the wine god did it for them) and afterward ran to the woods, where they tore to pieces the first living thing they saw and consumed it raw. In the play a young king who has heard scandalous things about what transpired during the Dionysian rites attempts to stop the quickly spreading rites by going into the woods in pursuit of some Bacchantes, including his own mother. But he is found there and torn to pieces. His mother carries his head back to the city, thinking it is the head of an animal. In the most electric moment of the play she comes to her senses and recognizes what she holds. The message, as so often in Euripides, is ambiguous: Did he mean to suggest it was useless to fight against the gods? or did he criticize traditional concepts of the behavior of the gods? Certainly the latter intention is possible, for Euripides was influenced by the Sophists.

G. RELIGION

Students of ancient Greece sometimes note the rationalism of the philosophers, the ridicule of the gods implicit in Homer and explicit in the playwrights Euripides and Aristophanes, and the attitudes of intellectuals like the historian Thucydides and conclude that religion was no longer of any real importance to the Greeks. Such a conclusion is totally wrong. The greatest of the philosophers were quite religious even if skeptical of much that passed for religion. The last thing Socrates did was to ask a friend to offer a cock to Aesculapius, the god of healing, to satisfy a vow he had made. Plato was very nearly a monotheist—if a unique one. The charge of impiety was still a serious accusation in enlightened Athens and could bring exile to friends of Pericles, the death sentence to Alcibiades, indictment (by Cleon) of Euripides, death to Socrates, and the threat of death to Aristotle. The Greeks were not so arrogant as to think that because they had learned a bit about the physical world, they had proved the nonexistence of the deity.

Religion was inextricably bound up with ordinary life and with the state in ancient Greece. Thus, for example, proper reverent treatment of gods, temples, and images was involved in simple patriotism; to offend deity was to threaten the state.

On the other hand, no Greek religionist ever claimed that he alone had found the true way. The Greeks in general had no received dogma, not even about the origins of the gods. They had, then, no heresy; toleration came naturally to them, except when they saw some threat to traditional institutions or the state. Greeks had no priestly hierarchies; their temples were served by lay priests. In a few places, however, the priests were professionals, as were those of Apollo at Delphi.

The Twelve Olympians

The Olympians appear already fully developed in Homer, composite deities with long traditions. Zeus was the great sky god of the Indo-Europeans, wielder of thunder and lightning, Nordic but associated also with Crete, where he was said to have been born and to have died. Yet like the rest he lived on as an immortal. Associated with the bull, Zeus was a god of justice and a symbol of humanity. Athena, patron deity of Athens, was a war goddess, but also a goddess of wisdom and crafts. As Athena Parthenos, she was the virgin goddess. She was associated, appropriately, with the owl. Apollo—who along with Aphrodite was on the side of the Trojans in the Trojan War—was a war god, a god of law and right, and the god of purity of young men, connected especially with Delphi and Delos. Equally complex were the other Olympian deities: Hera, Hestia, Hephaestus, Poseidon, Artemis, Ares, Demeter, and Hermes, the messenger of the gods. Also important was Heracles (Hercules), a symbol of man-become-god as the result of great labors in the interests of others. Alexander the Great and certain of the Roman emperors later would consciously imitate him. Dionysus, god of wine, was sometimes included among the twelve Olympians in place of Hestia, goddess of the hearth.

Oracles held an important place in the religious activity of the ancient world. One of renown was that of Ammon at the Oasis of Siwah in Egypt; almost all others of importance were Greek. Among them were those of Zeus at Dodona and at Olympia; that of Asclepius, the god of healing, at Epidaurus; and the most famous of all, that of the Pythian Apollo at Delphi. Questions were addressed to the oracles through various mechanisms, and responses came in varying ways. At Dodona, answers were interpreted from the rustlings of a sacred oak. At Epidaurus, sick persons slept in the temple and hoped for something—perhaps even a miracle—that might bring healing. Doubtless the priests there were experts in medical science; Greek physicians were much sought after in the ancient world. At Delphi the Pythia, or priestess, heard the questions as she sat in a transport of ecstasy, possessed by the god, on a tripod said to be located over a fissure that was the navel of the earth. Her responses were interpreted by priests, and the answers were delivered to the questioner in verse form.

Enough has already been said about Delphi to emphasize this oracle's great importance in the political, social, and cultural life of Greece. The responses of the Delphic oracle, as we have seen in the case of its opposition to the Athenian tyranny, could be quite politically motivated; inevitably the oracle took sides in the great struggles within Greece. The amphictyony, or religious league formed to protect the oracle, was itself much involved with interstate politics. But the oracle also was much concerned with moral questions and upheld high standards. Carved on the front of the great Temple of Apollo were two aphorisms symbolizing at its best the Greek outlook on life: "Know thyself" and "Nothing too much."

The popularity of Delphi at its height reflects, of course, the wisdom of the responses given there. Part of its attraction surely related to the magnificent site, on the flank of Mount Parnassus, overlooking the Gulf of Corinth. The great games held there every fourth year (Pythian Games) were almost as popular as the better-known ones at Olympia. Those at Olympia, founded in 776 B.C., were initiated almost two centuries earlier than those at Delphi.

Delphi and the other Greek oracles predictably declined as Greece itself did. Plutarch and other later Greeks discussed with some nostalgia the decline of the oracle at Delphi. The operation continued, nevertheless, until the Christian emperor Theodosius closed it down in A.D. 390.

The Mystery Religions

Orphism was a mystery religion. The Orphics generally believed in cycles of reincarnation to higher or lower levels, according to behavior in any particular life. Little remains of its lore because the knowledge leading to higher levels was secret (hence the term *mystery*). Orpheus himself, the legendary sweet singer, was a kind of prophet; Dionysus was the god of this cult.

Eleusis became a center of a mystery cult in connection with the myth of Demeter and her daughter Persephone, who was carried off to the underworld by Hades. Since Demeter was goddess of grain and fertility, the earth did not bring forth its fruits while she wandered in her sorrow. At Eleusis, the Attic Greeks claimed, she first partook of some barley water and began to return to her former self. The Eleusinian rites were, of course, secret but somehow involved the barley water, a grain of wheat, a washing or purification, and the hope of a life beyond. So humanistic a man as the Roman Cicero, when initiated into the mystery rites in the first century B.C., was impressed by them.

BOOKS FOR FURTHER READING

ADCOCK, F. *The Greek and Macedonian Art of War*, Berkeley, 1957.

BOARDMAN, J. *Greek Art*, London, 1964.

BIERS, W. *The Archaeology of Greece*, Ithaca, N.Y., 1980.

BURN, A. *Persia and the Greeks: The Defense of the West*, London, 1967.

CASSON, L. *Ships and Seamanship in the Ancient World*, Princeton, 1971.

COOK, R. *Greek Art*, 2nd ed., Harmondsworth, England, 1979.

COULTON, J. *Greek Architects at Work*, London, 1977.

EHRENBERG, V. *From Solon to Socrates*, 2nd ed., London, 1973.

FINLEY, M. *The Legacy of Greece: A New Appraisal*, Oxford, 1981.

GODWIN, J. *Mystery Religions in the Ancient World*, London & San Francisco, 1981.

GUTHRIE, W. *The Greeks and Their Gods*, Boston, 1965.

GUTHRIE, W. *The History of Greek Philosophy*, 6 vols., Cambridge, 1962–1981.

GUTHRIE, W. *The Sophists*, Cambridge, 1971.

HIGNETT, C. *Xerxes' Invasion of Greece*, Oxford, 1963.

LENARDON, R. *The Sage of Themistocles*, London, 1978.

MEIGGS, R. *The Athenian Empire*, reprint, Oxford, 1975.

MURRAY, G. *The Five Stages of Greek Religion*, New York, 1955.

NAQUET, P. *Economic and Social History of Ancient Greece: An Introduction*, Berkeley, 1978.

RICHTER, G. *A Handbook of Greek Art*, 4th ed., New York, 1965.

SELTMAN, C. *The Twelve Olympians*, New York, 1960.

SNELL, B. *The Discovery of the Mind*, New York, 1960.

WEBSTER, T. *Athenian Culture and Society*, Berkeley, 1973.

9

HELLENIC FAILURES AND SUCCESSES:

recurring war and cultural heights

A. THE PELOPONNESIAN WAR (431–404 B.C.)

In retrospect and in the light of the usual trends in human history, there seems to have been something almost inevitable about the Peloponnesian War. When geography and circumstance throw together two approximately equal powers, they usually contend for supremacy. And when the two states are as unlike as Athens and Sparta, this tendency is even stronger. Athens symbolized all that was liberal, or even radical: freedom (at least for Athenians), individualism, willingness to try out new ideas. Sparta stood solidly against these things and nurtured conservative ideals: order, stability, obedience. The Spartans were suspicious of anything novel. They were slow to act, however, and it was Athens that forced the ultimate confrontation.

The moving spirit behind that Athenian policy was Pericles. Though he continued to be elected to the *strategia* every year, his position just prior to the war was not so strong as before. He had to fight unpopular little wars to keep the Delian League members in line. His political enemies combined to attack him viciously, sometimes sniping at him through his friends. The sculptor Pheidias was accused of embezzling precious materials; the outcome of the trial is not known, but he went into exile. The courtesan Aspasia, a beautiful and intellectual woman from Miletus who was a sort of unofficial second wife to Pericles, was accused of impiety. The philosopher Anaxagoras, Pericles' friend, was charged with atheism.

Still, Periclean rhetoric generally controlled the Athenian assembly, and the power politics the "Olympian" espoused became state policy.

Trouble Spots: Immediate Causes of the War

Athenian presence in western waters always disturbed the Corinthians, who were chief among the allies of Sparta in the Peloponnese. As early as the time of Themistocles, Athens had cultivated good relations with the island of Corcyra—which much earlier had been colonized by Corinth. When Corinth and Corcyra had a falling out that came to war and engaged in a major sea battle in 433 B.C., Athens chose to intervene in the interests of Corcyra. The challenge to Corinth in the Ionian Sea and the west was clear.

Potidaea, another former colony of Corinth located in the Chalcidice, at the northwestern corner of the Aegean Sea, was also a sore spot. It had become a member of the Delian League. When Potidaea later rebelled against Athens' continued domination, Corinth sent aid. Megara, a small state at the Attic end of the isthmus just opposite Corinth, at one point left the Peloponnesian League over a dispute with Corinth and joined the Athenian alliance. Later it left Athens and rejoined the Peloponnese alliance. In retaliation, Pericles decreed that Megara could not trade with any member of the Delian confederacy. This was a severe economic blow to Megara, which joined with Corinth in demanding a meeting of the Peloponnesian League, at which it persuaded the Spartans to send an ultimatum to Athens. Pericles in turn convinced the Athenians to reject any compromise, and soon the prolonged and ruinous war was on.

The First Stage (431–421 B.C.)

Pericles seems to have felt that a full-scale war with Sparta and the Peloponnesian League was inevitable, and that it might as well come while he was still around to lead it. Certainly Athens was more nearly ready for the conflict than Sparta was. Despite the enormous cost of beautifying Athens and, more recently, of the siege of Potidaea, there were still 6,000 talents in the Athenian treasury; and the fleet of Athens was invincible. The strategy was to be that which had been spelled out by Themistocles much earlier, with some modifications: Athens was not to attempt to defeat the Peloponnesian army, which was probably unbeatable on land, but was to rely mainly on its navy. When the enemy invaded Attica, all its citizens were to withdraw within the walls of Athens or the Piraeus, or inside the "Long Walls" (about five miles long), which in recent decades had been constructed to connect Athens with its port. The outlying land would not be defended. Supplies would be shipped in from overseas possessions. Income from the silver mines, from tribute, and from customs duties in various places was to sustain Athens for the long haul.

Sparta, on the other hand, did not have the economic resources even for long campaigns, much less for a long war. Yet Sparta had men and dependable allies.

Tyche—Fortune—dealt Athens an early, severe blow. The expected invasion came, led by the Spartan King Archidamus II. The Athenians took refuge within the walls as planned, and they allowed their land to be ravaged. The scene was repeated the following year. Then plague struck the crowded city. Within a few months a considerable percentage—possibly a third—of the populace had died. Though Athens fought on and made an apparent recovery, the state was never so strong again. One of those who died during this time (429 B.C.) was Pericles himself. Athens never found another Pericles. A tanner named Cleon rose to leadership in the city; his chief political rival there was the general Nicias, a conservative aristocrat.

One campaign of 425 B.C. somehow symbolizes the pointlessness and the ultimate destructive futility of this war. The Athenian admiral Demosthenes decided to seize the harbor and spit of land at Pylos in the southwestern Peloponnese, as a way station for naval squadrons and a base for raiding Spartan territory. The Spartans reacted by sending an army to the area, so near to the lands worked by helots. For some months the two forces fought over this spit of land and a neighboring island (Sphacteria), which were both so poor they had no permanent inhabitants. At length the Athenians, under Cleon now, not only won but even took a number of Spartans as prisoners. True, the Spartans were isolated on the island and almost starved to death, but the idea of Spartans surrendering under any circumstance astonished the Greek world. Although the victory really meant nothing, Cleon's reputation stood high; therefore when he recommended that the Athenians refuse to negotiate a peace that Sparta would probably have accepted at this point, he carried the day.

The Spartans found a vigorous general of their own, Brasidas. He realized that Athens was most vulnerable in the northern Aegean area, where its fleet could not bar the entry of the Peloponnesian army. The fighting thus came to focus on Amphipolis, just above the Chalcidice in the northern Aegean, where Cleon brought Athenian troops to oppose Brasidas. In the ensuing battle (422 B.C.) both these leaders were killed, and the Athenian commander, Nicias, soon negotiated the peace treaty named for him (421 B.C.). Unfortunately it did not really settle any of the problems that had caused the war, and though intended to endure fifty years, it lasted only eight.

The Second Stage (415–404 B.C.)

The resumption of war was in part the work of another Athenian leader, Alcibiades. This youthful charmer learned from his teacher Socrates everything except his main message—virtue—and had all the abilities to be another Pericles, except for integrity. He persuaded the Athenians to undertake a risky and ultimately disastrous adventure in the west, in Sicily. Just as back home, Greeks in

Sicily were divided along Dorian-Ionian lines. When Athens got an appeal for help from Ionian Segesta against Dorian Syracuse, Alcibiades persuaded the citizens not only to give aid but also to attempt to conquer Sicily for Athens. If this were done, Athens would become too powerful for the Peloponnesians.

Alcibiades, unfortunately, at the last minute was charged with profaning the Eleusinian mysteries in a drunken burlesque at a party. He was also suspected of defacing some Herms—pillars topped with busts of Hermes that served as protectors of houses—and he was deposed from leadership of the expedition (415 B.C.). Fearing the death penalty, Alcibiades fled—to Sparta. He charmed his way into the confidence of the Spartan leaders; he advised them to resume the war, to send aid to Syracuse, to appeal for help from Persia, and to establish a permanent base within Attica. His advice helped Sparta to win the war. In Sicily, the Athenian expedition laid siege to Syracuse but gradually lost the initiative to an augmented defense force led by the Spartan General Gylippus. Athens strained its resources and sent more ships and men. Through a combination of ill fortune and bad generalship, these forces were bottled up and then destroyed during an attempted retreat. Allied troops were either sold into slavery or eventually redeemed by family or friends, but the Athenians were killed outright or otherwise sentenced to death. This was a terrific blow, from which Athens never quite recovered.

The heavy losses at Syracuse brought a strong reaction against the democracy of Athens. With the help of Persia, Sparta built a fleet and began to challenge Athens even in the Aegean, so that things looked blacker still. Some Athenian allies, especially those nearest Persia, began to revolt with Persian and Spartan aid. Yet Athens somehow managed to rebuild its fleet and actually won several important victories over the Peloponnesian fleet.

During this period, Alcibiades left Sparta (it was said that he left the king's wife pregnant) and went on to Persia, where he persuaded the Persians not to help Sparta too much. They would, he said, simply exchange Athens for Sparta as their chief opponent in the Aegean. Alcibiades now entered into negotiation with some Athenian leaders, first at the base at Samos and then in Athens. He intimated that if Athens were to replace the democracy with an oligarchy he might find it possible to get the Persians to switch sides—all important, since their money was financing the Peloponnesian navy. A conspiracy was formed, a chief opponent was assassinated, and soon Athens became an oligarchy, for the first time since Solon. Still, moderates such as Theramenes retained positions of leadership, and on Samos the democrats maintained control. After a time, when it became apparent the Persians would not support Athens, and after the Athenian navy regained a degree of control over the Aegean, the democracy was restored.

Alcibiades played a role in the naval successes. As a reward, he was absolved of the sentence and the curse that had been placed on him. Once again he was elected to the strategia and given command of the main fleet. At last, however, when the Persians again were bankrolling the Spartan naval forces, Alcibiades lost a major naval battle. It was not his fault—he was absent, and his lieutenant fought against his orders; yet since Athenians had the occasional habit of executing or exiling unsuccessful commanders, Alcibiades fled to a refuge in the Hellespont. After the war the Persians procured his assassination.

For Athens, the decisive defeat came in 405 B.C., when their fleet was destroyed at Aegospotami (Goat's River), on the Hellespont. Soon after, the Spartan admiral, Lysander, put Athens itself under siege, with a naval blockade this time, and in a few months starved the Athenians into surrender.

B. SPARTAN DOMINANCE

A New Order for Athens and the Former Members of the Delian League

In the aftermath of these defeats, Lysander and the leadership of Sparta naturally dissolved the Athenian Empire. In every "liberated" state, oligarchies were put in control. *Decarchies* (ten-man boards) supported by Spartan *harmosts*, who were commanders of garrisons, ruled the "liberated" states. These oligarchical boards exiled or otherwise got rid of their most likely enemies, the democratic leaders.

The Spartan allies, especially Corinth, who had contributed much to the conduct of the war, were unhappy with the peace settlement. As they viewed it, Athens was treated too gently; moreover, it was Sparta that gained most of the booty as well as the tribute and continuing hegemony. It was another source of dissatisfaction that the Greek states in Asia Minor were virtually abandoned to the Persians—as the price Sparta paid for renewed Persian support in the later years of the war. As we shall see, however, Sparta was later to attempt to renege on that agreement.

At Athens, the ruling clique comprised thirty, rather than ten, oligarchs. These thirty were supposed to set up a rather broad oligarchy, but they believed no such government could endure while the democratic leaders lived. They began a reign of terror and executed hundreds of their possible opponents. Their nickname, the "Thirty Tyrants," was well earned.

A reaction inevitably occurred. An exiled moderate politician, Thrasybulus, took refuge in a frontier fortress and began to build up a military force. He soon moved on to Piraeus and fortified this important position. The oligarchs attempted to stop him but failed; they then called on the Spartans for aid. It was sent, but the leader was King Pausanias, who disapproved of Lysander's policies. He noted, quite correctly, that those policies were alienating most Greeks from any feeling of loyalty to Sparta or sympathy for its aims. Thebes and Corinth, in fact, had refused to support the expedition. The king superseded Lysander and allowed a compromise. The democracy was restored in Athens (403 B.C.), and amnesty was granted to all oligarchs, who were also given permanent asylum at Eleusis.

Compared with prewar Athens, the restored democracy, however, was a weak state. The population had probably been halved, or even worse. The Athenian empire was gone, and so was the navy. The Long Walls had been torn down. Economically, the city was stricken. Only the beauty of the Acropolis and several public buildings in the agora nearby, some shreds of the intellectual structure—and memories—remained of the glory that had been.

Sparta Attempts to Lead a Panhellenic Crusade

The end of the Thirty Tyrants at Athens was followed by the elimination also of many of the decarchies throughout the Aegean, in what was now the Spartan—no longer the Athenian—Empire. Sparta maintained in theory the principle of sovereignty for its allies, but in practice, often domineered over them. If Spartans were to become truly leaders of a unified Greece, they felt that they must organize a crusade against a common enemy. This could be none other than Persia, which had begun to impose its will on the Asian Greek states. King Artaxerxes II, on his part, had reason to move against the Greeks in general, and especially the Spartans, because of a recent expedition against him—the famous "March of the Ten Thousand"—which had the support of Sparta.

The Greek mercenaries who comprised the Ten Thousand were in the service of the Persian king's brother, Cyrus, who in 401 B.C. attempted to seize the throne from Artaxerxes with the aid of the Greek soldiers. The latter were in ample supply because of the recent end of the Peloponnesian War. Cyrus' expedition was well documented by the historian Xenophon, who participated in it. The army marched deep into the interior of the vast empire and met Artaxerxes' army in battle at Cunaxa, far down into Mesopotamia. The Greeks won the battle with almost no losses, but unfortunately for them Cyrus was so anxious to kill his brother that he recklessly exposed himself and was slain. With their royal paymaster dead, the Greeks had little reason to stay in hostile territory. Under guise of a parley, the Persians treacherously killed the Greek generals. The Greek soldiers then elected new ones and escaped in a desperate march northward that took them to the Black Sea. Many of the survivors joined the Spartan expedition in Asia Minor, to which we now return.

A Spartan expeditionary force under Thibron had arrived in Asia Minor in 400 B.C.. His successor, Dercyllidas, accomplished little. The Spartan king who next led this expedition was Agesilaus; surprisingly, for a Spartan king, he was wizened and crippled; yet he was quite competent. It was Lysander who had gotten him the throne, by charging that the dead King Agis's son was really the child of Alcibiades, the renegade Athenian. Lysander hoped to control Agesilaus (Agis' brother), but he soon learned that the new king was his own man. Agesilaus' campaigns in 396 and 395 B.C. were models of deception and achieved more than might have been expected, given the rather small size of the Greek—and Spartan—contributions to the army. But the Persians were not to be counted out easily.

The Corinthian War (394–387 B.C.)

Persian diplomacy and Persian money, combined with the unpopularity of Sparta's hegemony, stirred up a war against the Spartans in Greece itself, and in 394 B.C. King Agesilaus was recalled from Asia Minor. A coalition of Athens, Thebes, Corinth, Argos, and other states fought indecisively with Sparta for several years. Athens used Persian help to regain some naval power and rebuilt the Long Walls. Sparta won the chief land engagements, but the Athenian general Iphicrates, in a portentous battle, used light-armed troops to destroy an entire Spartan regiment in 390 B.C. Lysander was killed in an early engagement.

When peace came at last (387/386 B.C.; called the King's Peace), it was virtually imposed by Artaxerxes, with the connivance of Sparta. Persia gained most from the war: an end to Spartan aggression in Asia Minor and control of the Greek states there. Sparta gained a few more years as the dominant power in Greece. But Sparta had been weakened. During the war there had been an attempted rebellion of the non-Spartiate elements of the population, supported by the "Inferiors"—former Spartiates who somehow because of poverty had lost their full citizenship. Though unsuccessful, the attempt reflects internal disaffection. The Spartan ideal—never perfectly adhered to—also was eroded by the twin tempters, power and money, which corrupted numbers of Spartiates, including some leaders. Yet there was no upheaval, and Sparta still seemed strong.

Renewed War (378–371 B.C.)

Sparta reaped great unpopularity throughout Greece because of its agreement to leave Ionia to the Persians. Sparta's Greek allies were put off also by Spartan interference in their internal affairs and by the tendency of Spartan leaders to treat them more and more as subjects. One of Sparta's generals seized an opportunity to put a garrison in Thebes in support of the oligarchic faction, which drove out the democrats. A similar attempt to put a garrison in Athens' port, Piraeus, alienated the Athenians. After Theban democrats regained control of Thebes in a coup and expelled the Spartan garrison, a new coalition was put together to end the Spartan dominance; Athens and Thebes were the chief allies.

Athens was able to form a second Athenian confederacy (378/377 B.C.), much like the old Delian League, but with safeguards for the allied states against possible Athenian domination. Thebes also strengthened its position in Boeotia and dominated a reconstituted Boeotian League. In the only important land battle, in 375 B.C., a Theban force defeated a Spartan army of 1,000 hoplites. The loss was not seen as portentous: After all, only one Spartan unit was involved. Soon after, the peace of 387 was reestablished. But it did not last, and war resumed the following year.

When Thebes began to expand outside Boeotia, Athens grew cool to the alliance and sought a peace conference. This conference included representatives from many Greek states, and a real effort was made to end the constant war and repression. Unfortunately, when Epaminondas, the representative for Thebes, attempted to sign for all members of the Boeotian League, Agesilaus would not permit it, and the Theban delegation walked out of the conference. The others signed anyway and left Thebes to the tender mercies of Sparta.

C. THEBAN DOMINANCE (371–362 B.C.)

Victory over Sparta at Leuctra

As everyone at the peace conference had anticipated, the Spartans quickly mobilized an army and marched north to deal with Thebes. The results, however, were wholly unanticipated. For the first time in memory, a main army of Sparta was defeated and driven from the field at the Battle of Leuctra, in 371 B.C. By keeping Thebes at war for years, Sparta itself had helped to forge the army that defeated it. Two Theban leaders deserve mention as architects of victory. Epaminondas, serving as *boeotarch* in the generally democratic Theban state, supplied the tactical genius. Pelopidas, a dashing and sometimes rash warrior, had helped to train the army, especially the elite Sacred Band of 300 picked men who played a key role in the battle.

The tactics of Epaminondas were unusual enough to be worth a note. Normally, Greek armies depended on a strong right wing to crush the opposing left. This seemed necessary because of the tendency of the troops to close to the right as they advanced, with each man seeking the protection not only of his own shield but also that of the nearest man on his right. The generals chose to use rather than try to counter this tendency—hence the strong right. Before Leuctra, however, Epaminondas vastly strengthened his left wing and actually withheld his right from battle, since it was made up of allies who might not be dependable. The Sacred Band and the other men on the left were fifty shields deep, compared with the twelve shields of the Spartans. As the startled Spartan commander attempted, just before the battle, to strengthen his right, a cavalry charge threw his ranks into disorder, and the Thebans were suddenly on them in overwhelming force.

The Humiliation of Sparta

Disastrous defeat is demoralizing for any state; but for Sparta, with its whole society organized on a military basis, the blow was especially severe. King Agesilaus, who was not at Leuctra, put down with difficulty a rebellion of young men at home. He and the ephors then reviewed the stringent laws that disgraced anyone who retreated from a battlefield. It was then announced that the laws should "sleep" for one day; otherwise all the survivors would have been cashiered. Plutarch says—on what information we do not know—that those at home whose relatives fell at Leuctra rejoiced and that those whose relatives survived felt disgraced, regardless of the official decision to let the laws "sleep."

Epaminondas now invaded Laconia itself—the first such invasion since the Dorians had occupied the Peloponnese—but was prevented from taking the unwalled city of Sparta proper by energetic defense measures and a fortuitous flood of the Eurotas River near the city. Epaminondas helped organize a new Arcadian League as rival to Sparta in the peninsula, with headquarters at Megalopolis. Moreover, he freed Messenia, with its hordes of helots. Sparta's power went into a decline that was permanent, except for a brief period of resurgence near the end of the following century. The inability of the city to recover from these losses is proof of the seriousness of Sparta's long-term problems, chiefly the shortage of manpower in the Spartiate, or full-citizen class.

Theban Ascendancy and Decline

The only possible contender with Thebes for the premier position among the Greek states at this point was Jason of Pherae. He began as tyrant of that city, located in Thessaly, and by a combination of genius, force, and threats of force, he had in recent years made himself ruler of all Thessaly in a typical sort of alliance. He appeared with an army just after the battle of Leuctra and mediated a temporary truce that permitted the Spartans to retreat to the Peloponnese. Certainly his ambitions would soon have brought him to a confrontation with the Thebans, even though the two leagues were on friendly terms. In 370 B.C. he planned some important military venture; some thought he even intended to seize the treasure of the Delphic priests to use it to finance a large-scale conquest. But he was assassinated, and no significant figure was found to take his place. Much of his territory was soon under the control of the Thebans.

The power of Thebes rested chiefly in its leaders: Epaminondas, the cool and competent general, and Pelopidas, the impulsive but equally competent tactician. Epaminondas was austere, reportedly something of a philosopher. His views were liberal. He could hold the top office of boeotarch no more frequently than every second year, however, and thus his recommendations were not always followed. Thebes generally used the army instead of persuasive leadership to force its rule on others. It therefore became just another aggressive city-state, muscling its coercive way to the top.

Thebes' control outside Boeotia extended to Thessaly and even Macedonia. At one point a young Macedonian of royal family was brought to Thebes as a hostage; later he would be King Philip, father of Alexander the Great. Pelopidas had much to do with success in this area, but unfortunately he was killed in a rash charge against superior numbers in Thessaly. The very success of Thebes ensured a coalition against that city. Athens joined Sparta and others in an anti-Theban alliance. Though landlocked, Thebes even built a navy in an attempt to counter Athens' power at sea. Sparta gradually strengthened its position in the Peloponnese, and Thebes found it necessary to intervene there twice more.

Epaminondas led the final thrust into the Peloponnese, where he hoped to regain control without a fight; but this was not to be. At Mantinea, in Arcadia, he was brought to battle in 362 B.C. Astonishingly, through a series of maneuvers before the battle, he succeeded in again surprising the allies with precisely the same tactics he had used at Leuctra. The Thebans swept the field, in what would have been a great victory had Epaminondas himself not been killed. Before he died, he learned that others he considered capable of assuming command had been killed, too; he therefore counseled that the Thebans make peace and return home.

The Thebans could no longer aspire to the leadership of all Greece. The Athenians perhaps did, and once again edged toward domination of the members of their reconstituted confederacy. But a rebellion in 357 B.C., abetted by the enemies of Athens, left the state much weakened. Another would-be leader, the small state of Phocis on the borders of Delphi, plunged into meteoric political adventure for a few short years. After a dispute with the priests of Delphi, the Phocians virtually took over the oracle. An ancient league, originally set up on a tribal basis and called the Delphic Amphictyony (it included the Phocians), could be depended on to come to the rescue of the oracle, in spite of its loose organization. A "sacred war" therefore followed, between the Phocians and some members of the Amphictyony; the Phocians used the Delphic treasure to hire mercenaries and for a

Socrates. (Art Resource)

time were astonishingly successful. Ultimately, Phocis was defeated by Philip II of Macedonia, who used the alleged religious war as an opportunity for massive intervention in Greek affairs (next chapter).

D. THE GREAT AGE OF PHILOSOPHY

In classical Greece (the period before Alexander), Athens was the intellectual center, not only in the days of Pericles, as we have seen, but also for a century and longer after his death. Here the finest plays continued to be presented; here the best history was written; here the great philosophers lived, taught, and founded their schools—which emphasized not just philosophy proper but other liberal arts such as mathematics, science, and music. The important schools were not just those of Plato and Aristotle, the best known; there were several others; for example, that of the influential orator, publicist, and political scientist Isocrates.

Socrates (469–399 B.C.)

Socrates surely ranks as one of the most influential persons in the history of Western civilization, yet we do not know him well. He left no writings, and we learn of him chiefly through the works of Plato and Xenophon. But Xenophon had only a shallow perception of his teacher, and Plato nearly always used Socrates as the chief character in his dialogues, so it is difficult to separate Socrates the protagonist from Plato in these creations.

Socrates was a stonemason who made an indifferent living for his family. No wonder his wife, Xanthippe, had a reputation as a nag. He taught an important array of pupils; besides Plato and Xenophon, Alcibiades and Critias were among them. But unlike the Sophists, he taught without pay. Moreover, his teaching was infused with a high moral purpose: Education, he insisted, had the improvement of the individual as its sole purpose. His didactic method was unusual. He felt that knowledge was already somehow immanent within each person and needed only to be elicited. He therefore used a question-and-answer method to lead his students to see for themselves. He also used the same sort of system in debating with others, with ironical effect, and the great teacher made enemies when he demonstrated publicly that many self-declared experts did not know what they were talking about.

Socrates' great emphasis was on virtue, which he felt could be elicited from every person. Wrong behavior was simply ignorance. For example, persons who commit murder may understand that it is "wrong" to do so, but at the moment of their crime they believe that at this place and time, it is right for them. Socrates taught, and strictly adhered to, the principle that it is never right to do wrong. Curiously, he declared that he was sometimes guided by an inner voice, a *daimon*, which told him only what *not* to do.

Socrates' trial and subsequent execution took place in the disillusionment following the Athenian loss of the Peloponnesian War. In this vengeful atmosphere, he was accused of introducing strange gods and of corrupting the youth of Athens. If we can believe Plato, he ignored these charges and instead chose to defend his whole life and purpose. Perhaps the real reason for such crude accusations was that Alcibiades and Critias turned out so badly after having been instructed by Socrates. The jury that convicted him did not expect he would die as a result. He had the right of suggesting an alternate sentence, which was usually exile; instead, he said they really ought to reward him, not penalize him, but if they insisted, he would pay a small fine. The jury was so irritated it confirmed the death sentence. Socrates could still have escaped (his friends arranged to bribe the jailor), and probably even his accusers would have preferred that he go into exile. However, he insisted that all his life he had taught that one should obey the laws and that it is never right to do wrong. How could he now turn his back on his own teachings? He drank the hemlock and died a martyr to his own cause.

Plato (c. 429–347 B.C.)

By common consent, Plato is the greatest philosopher in the Western tradition. Some of his work in systematic thought seems so much like musings from an ivory tower that one forgets how much he was influenced by events of his own day and by his efforts to confront contemporary problems. The failure and defeat of Athenian democracy, the dismal performance of oligarchy at the time of the Thirty Tyrants (some of whom were friends and relatives, for Plato was of the Athenian aristocracy), the execution of his beloved teacher Socrates, and the continued bloodletting in Greek politics all affected his thinking.

Socrates had taught his pupils to go to the root of any problem, to look for its essence. Plato did not attempt, piecemeal, to consider the world's ills; he sought ultimate reality and the manner in which humans might learn of that and attempt to perfect themselves and their institutions. His theory of Ideas is at the center of his philosophical thought. In this usage, the word *idea* is a transliteration from the Greek and does not mean "idea" in our modern sense at all, but rather signifies "form." Plato taught that the world of sensation is part illusion; reality lies in a separate world perceived only through the trained mind. Thus beauty, for him, was a thing in itself; things that are called beautiful are so only as they partake of the true or ideal form, Beauty. Other such forms include the four cardinal virtues: Wisdom, Restraint, Bravery, Justice. The highest of forms, almost like a monotheistic deity, was the Form of the Good. Plato was influenced by Orphism and believed (perhaps from Socrates) in the immortality of the soul.

The historian, of course, is interested in the great philosopher's ideas on government, a topic Plato treated in several of his dialogues, including the greatest of all, *The Republic*. In this essay, Plato's search for the best form of government was essentially the search for Justice. He argued the necessity that kings should become philosophers—or philosophers, kings. He outlined educational curricula, in which he eliminated Homer and all such "nonsense." The Greek polis was the ideal size for his perfect state, which was a single community. His society comprised two main classes, the workers and the guardians. Some of the latter would also be the rulers of the state. This upper class would be an elite of superior persons properly educated. They would possess all things in common; marriage would be eliminated; their children would be reared under the tutelage of the state. This sort of Utopia has been much imitated in literatue but seldom in practice.

In his later dialogues, Plato argued for a mixed constitution. He attempted to put his views into actual practice in Syracuse, which he appears to have visited three times, during the reigns of Dionysius I, his son-in-law Dion, and his son Dionysius II. Unfortunately the philosopher's counsel seems to have had little impact on the government there.

At Athens Plato established the Academy, where he lectured for most of his mature life. The Academy, along with the Lyceum later established by Aristotle, endured until the Christian emperor Justinian shut down both schools some nine hundred years later.

Aristotle (384–322 B.C.)

Best remembered as the pupil of Plato and the teacher of Alexander the Great, Aristotle ranks close behind Plato as an important philosopher in his own right. He is notable for common sense, a respect for the common views of men, a keen ability to analyze and classify, and exhaustive thoroughness. Aristotle was much more interested than his master was in physical research, and his works are much more diverse. A mere list of the subjects of his works (which, unlike Plato's, are far from complete) is impressive: he wrote on physics, botany, biology, geology, astronomy, politics, logic, poetics, metaphysics, ethics, and other topics.

Rather typically, when Aristotle began to investigate government, he researched the constitutions of 158 states, including Carthage. His analysis, also typical, seems impeccable; there are good forms and bad forms, distinguished by whether those ruling do so in their own interests or in the interests of the people as a whole. Basically, there are governments that consist of one person, of a few, or of many—three each of good and bad forms:

Good forms	Bad forms
Monarchy	Tyranny
Aristocracy	Oligarchy (or plutocracy)
Constitutional government	Democracy (or mobocracy)

Though this is an oversimplification (and Aristotle also oversimplified), it is an impressive and deceptively simple analysis. Aristotle himself rather favored the constitutional government, with checks and balances and a large, stable middle class.

Aristotle rejected Plato's theory of Ideas and held that his ideal pure forms were just universals. In many ways Aristotle was a reconciler of opposing views and, in fact, strongly emphasized that extremes were likely to be the worse alternative, whereas the mean was generally the better position.

E. HISTORY

It is often said that true history begins with the Greeks. This may seem a puzzling assertion, since many earlier documents, from Sumerian clay tablets to the Hebrew Bible, are basically historical in nature. History as a category of literature and as a discipline, however, does have its beginning with the Greeks. In this sense, history is the systematic investigation of a specific topic, with the selection of material to be included made according to the purpose of the study.

Herodotus (c. 485–c. 425 B.C.)

The "Father of History," Herodotus, has already been quoted several times in this book. His chronicle of the Persian Wars is not only the first real work of *historia* (the word itself, used by Herodotus in his opening sentence, in Greek means "research") but also the oldest extant Greek prose. Poetry was the earlier vehicle for conveying information in written form, even by such a figure as Solon when defending his acts as archon.

Herodotus came from Halicarnassus in Asia Minor; he may have been a travel lecturer, and some of his work seems to incorporate lecture material. The work is nevertheless unified and structured toward goals that are literary as well as strictly historical. Herodotus wrote interestingly, even delightfully, and his writings include much that moderns tend to dismiss as legendary, mythical, or fantastic. Yet he was by no means gullible, for he often remarks something to the effect that this is what they say but he doesn't believe it. His interests ranged widely: he included information that was geographic, social, economic, religious, and psychological as well as political. Much of what we know of Persia and Egypt in the decades before Herodotus comes from the acccounts of this historian. He managed to be remarkably objective, even toward the Persians, the chief enemy of the Greeks in the period of his research. Some later critics consider him biased toward Athens, where he lived and wrote during his middle years.

One might wish that Herodotus had included more "solid" information in place of some of his more dubious tales or that he had done a little more research in connection with the actual campaigns of the Persian War. However, keeping in mind that he was something of a pioneer, we realize that this achievement was indeed tremendous.

Thucydides (c. 460–c. 403 B.C.)

Thucydides was the greatest historian in antiquity and one of the greatest historians of all time—certainly one of the most influential. An Athenian, he lived and was educated in the Periclean age, served as a general in the early years of the

Peloponnesian War, and wrote his history of the war while in exile as a result of an unsuccessful military campaign. His work (which extends to 411 B.C.) shows the influence of the skeptical Sophists and, in structure, the influence of the forms adopted by the great dramatists. What he had to chronicle, after all, was a great fratricidal tragedy.

In contrast to Herodotus, Thucydides had almost nothing to say about the influence of religion or oracles or of the intervention of the gods; his approach was strictly rational. He discussed remote and immediate causes of the war and looked for underlying influences, just as a modern historian would. When reading Thucydides, one feels that here was a great mind at work—objective, rational, methodical, and above all believable.

Thucydides' greatest fault was that he gave conclusions, often with little indication of supporting evidence. We have to trust him. In Herodotus it is often possible to decide, on the basis of information he himself included, that he was mistaken and that the truth must lie in another direction. This sort of independent analysis usually is not possible with Thucydides' work. In fact, the large gaps concerning religious, social, and economic matters make one fearful at times—even while admiring his obvious great competence as a historian—that he allowed his mental set to keep from his readers data they might judge important to the truth.

It is even possible to suspect that since Thucydides was tremendously clever, he may very subtly have conveyed impressions, under cover of apparent objectivity, that are not objective at all. This could have been done in the speeches, for example, which are so well done they are often accepted as the exact words of the speaker. So many times even modern historians quote Pericles—when, in fact, they are quoting Thucydides. Though the latter himself tells us in the introduction what his general policy was in regard to the speeches, we have absolutely no way of knowing whether, in any instance, Thucydides was trying to give the actual content of a speech as he heard it or as someone else heard it whom the historian had interviewed—or whether he is simply presenting sentiments he thinks "appropriate to the occasion." Unfortunately, Thucydides' imitators, especially in antiquity, followed him in this practice. The speeches are very important in conveying a sense of immediacy; the reader almost feels he is there. Still, they may tell us more about Thucydides' own great ability than about history.

Xenophon (c. 434–c. 355 B.C.)

Though a student of Socrates, the Athenian historian Xenophon had no great depth of mind, as his works well show. He was quite influential, nevertheless, because he wrote well and because he was widely read. Doubtless the most significant of Xenophon's works was his *Anabasis,* the story of the march of the 10,000 Greek soldiers hired by Cyrus into the interior of Persia. Xenophon himself was elected one of the commanders before the arduous retreat toward the Black Sea. The *Anabasis* underlined the vulnerability of the great empire. Alexander the Great was to read and be impressed by this story.

Xenophon also wrote the *Hellenica,* a continuation of Thucydides' narrative to the Battle of Mantinea in 362 B.C. Though only a shadowy imitation of his great predecessor's work, it helps greatly to fill in an otherwise obscure period. Xenophon also wrote eulogistic works on Agesilaus, king of Sparta, and on Cyrus the Great of Persia. The latter book, called the *Cyropaedia*, was considered useful reading by Cicero centuries later. Xenophon wrote about the constitution of Sparta, the teaching of Socrates, and other practical topics such as cavalry tactics. Readable, useful to a degree, and third-rate is the general modern judgment of Xenophon's body of work.

F. THE THEATRE AT ATHENS AFTER PERICLES

Tragedy

The great tragedians Sophocles and Euripides were still active up to the year they both died, 406 B.C. For example, both produced works entitled *Electra* around 415 B.C., in the middle of the Peloponnesian War. Athens must have been a less happy place to be in this time, when the war was going badly; repression uncharacteristic of the freer atmosphere of mid-century was introduced. Euripides is said to have been prosecuted for impiety by the democratic leader Cleon, and as we have seen, spent his last years in Macedonia. Since Cleon was killed several years before Euripides left Athens, this specific attack cannot have caused his departure. Others must have continued the criticism. The repressive atmosphere in the later years of the war had its greatest effect, however, on comedy.

Comedy

Though we know the names of several writers of the *old comedy* of the fifth century B.C., the only extant plays are those of Aristophanes; we have eleven of the forty or more plays he wrote. Full of allusions to contemporary conditions, they are immensely valuable to the historian, but their exaggeration and distortion make their comment difficult to assess. The comedy is bawdy, sometimes obscene, but also at times serious and even lofty.

Aristophanes opposed the Peloponnesian War. His early plays expressing that opposition were allowed to be presented even as the war went on. *The Acharnians* presented the viewpoint of Attic farmers whose lands were ravaged by the Peloponnesians. *The Knights* made an open attack on Cleon; in the play he is defeated in an election by a sausage seller, who wins by making even more outrageous promises to the common people than Cleon himself. The piqued politician is said to have prosecuted Aristophanes, unsuccessfully. In the later years of the war, however, Aristophanes' plays are escapist and lack the earlier pointed, scathing attacks on public figures and public policy.

Aristophanes' best-known play is probably *The Clouds*; it may be his best play as well. In it he lampoons Socrates specifically and the Sophists in general.

Socrates runs a "thought factory" with doubtful intent. Two of his pupils want to learn how to swindle people better. The play perhaps did damage the great philosopher's reputation; Socrates himself thought so, if his pupil Plato reported him accurately.

Lysistrata is a celebrated tale in which the women of Greece decide to end the war by withholding sex from their husbands until they make peace. In *Ecclesiazusae*, women take over the government and set up a communistic system. This and *Plutus*, the last play of Aristophanes now extant, are quite different from the earlier plays, with little reference to the real world and no insult to any living person. Sometimes referred to as *middle comedy*, they belong to the period of disillusionment following the Peloponnesian War.

BOOKS FOR FURTHER READING

ALLAN, D. *The Philosophy of Aristotle*, 2nd ed., Oxford, 1970.

ANDERSON, J. *Xenophon*, New York, 1974.

BROWN, T. *The Greek Historians*, New York, 1973.

BURN, A. and M. *The Living Past of Greece*, London, 1980.

DOVER, K. *Aristophanic Comedy*, London, 1972.

DOVER, K. *Thucydides*, Oxford, 1973.

EHRENBERG, V. *The People of Aristophanes: A Sociology of Old Attic Comedy*, rev. ed., New York, 1974.

FINDLAY, J. *Plato and Platonism*, New York, 1978.

FROST, F. *Greek Society*, 2nd ed., Lexington, Mass., 1980.

GUTHRIE, W. *A History of Greek Philosophy*, 6 vols., Cambridge, 1962–1981.

KAGAN, D. *The Archidamian War*, Ithaca, N.Y., 1974.

KAGAN, D. *Outbreak of the Peloponnesian War*, Ithaca, N.Y., 1969.

KAGAN, D. *The Peace of Nicias and the Sicilian Expedition*, Ithaca, N.Y., 1981.

SUTTON, D. *Self and Society in Aristophanes*, Washington, D.C., 1980.

TAYLOR, A. *Plato*, New York, 1927.

TAYLOR, A. *Socrates*, New York, 1933.

WOODHEAD, A. *Thucydides on the Nature of Power*, Cambridge, Mass., 1970.

Chart 4 Rise of Macedonia; Alexander the Great and the Hellenistic Age

PERIOD	MACEDONIA	OTHER
359 B.C.	Rise of Macedonia under Philip II. Intervention in Sacred War. Victory over Greek cities at Chaeronea. League of Corinth established.	Demosthenes' speeches against Philip. Athens, Thebes, other states subjugated by Macedonia. Macedonian garrisons in Corinth and Thebes.
336 B.C.	Philip assassinated. Alexander takes over, becomes head of Corinthian League, defeats Thebans, destroys Thebes.	
334 B.C.	Alexander begins campaign against Persia. Granicus, Issus, sieges of Tyre, Gaza, occupation of Egypt. Visit to oracle of Ammon.	
331 B.C.	Gaugamela; end of Persian Empire. Campaigns in the east; defeat of Porus; return to Babylon. Plans for further campaigns.	Sparta leads rebellion against Macedonia; suppressed by Antipater, Macedonian general.
323 B.C.	Death of Alexander; Perdiccas and Antipater regents. Antipater defeats Athenians et al. in Lamian War. Death of Antipater; struggle for control, Polyperchon, Cassander. Death of Philip III, Olympias, Roxana, Alexander IV.	Demosthenes leads another rebellion, Lamian War; defeat; suicide. Ptolemy satrap in Egypt, Antigonus in Asia Minor; his son Demetrius at Athens and the islands; Seleucus satrap of Babylon; Perdiccas not able to control. Ipsus; Antigonus killed. All major successors now call themselves kings.
300 B.C.	Continued struggle for throne; death of Cassander; later rulers include Demetrius, Pyrrhus, Lysimmachus, Seleucus, Ceraunus.	In theatre, new comedy: Menander and others. Zeno founds Stoic school of philosophy; Epicurus founds Epicurean school of philosophy.
281 B.C.		Battle of Corupedion.

	MACEDONIA	GREECE	SYRIA	EGYPT
280 B.C.	Antigonus Gonatas establishes Antigonid dynasty. Philip V makes alliance with Hannibal against Rome.	Formation of Achaean, Aetolian Leagues. In Sparta, Agis and Cleomenes try to restore the old order. Aetolians ally with Rome against Philip V, then against Rome with Antiochus. League dissolved.	Seleucus I assassinated. Antiochus I.	Ptolemy II king. Height of power under Ptolemies II and III. Alexandria a great city. Aristarchus, Eratosthenes at Museum. Six Syrian wars during this entire period.
200 B.C.	In a second war, Philip V defeated by Rome. Perseus; war with Rome, defeat. Macedonia, 4 republics. Fourth war with Rome; becomes a Roman province.	Polybius, other Greeks taken hostage to Rome. Achaeans rebel against Rome. Corinth destroyed all Greece subordinated.	Antiochus III; conquests. War with Rome, defeat. Antiochus IV; forced out of Egypt by Rome. Religious imperialism, trouble with the Jews under the Maccabees.	Loss of Palestine to Antiochus III. Low prices for wheat bring economic crisis.
100 B.C.		Athens joins Mithradates; sacked by Sulla, Romans. Achaea a separate province.	Pompey annexes Syria as a Roman province. Judea becomes a client state of Rome.	Caesar in Egypt. Antony, Cleopatra defeated. Egypt a Roman province.

10

THE RISE OF MACEDONIA: ALEXANDER THE GREAT

Macedonia had become an important kingdom in the days of King Archelaus (c. 413–399 B.C.). He built up the army, constructed fortified cities, established the capital at Pella, and developed trade and a new system of coinage. Although Archelaus expanded in the region in part because of Athenian losses in the late stages of the Peloponnesian War, he maintained good relations with Athens. In his time also, Macedonia to a degree entered into the mainstream of Greek culture. The playwright Euripides spent the last years of his life there, still writing plays; the *Bacchae* was composed in this period. Archelaus was murdered, however, and the next several decades saw repeated foreign invasions and internal struggle as well.

A. PHILIP II (359–336 B.C.) DOMINATES GREECE

The king who made Macedonia the chief power of the Greek peninsula was Philip II. He became head of state when he was about twenty-three, first as regent for his nephew Amyntas and then, quite soon, as king himself. The two years Philip spent as a hostage in Thebes during its years of ascendancy were decisive in shaping his career. He learned more of military matters than of the philosophy he studied in Epaminondas' house. An eminently pragmatic person, he saw that what Macedonia really needed was a better army.

Macedonia had many enemies, and there were formidable obstacles to any rise to significance. The country was more rural than Greece to the south, and tribal influences were still strong. Macedonia had been effectively unified only in the late fifth century B.C.—but as a monarchy, not as a city-state. Illyrians to the west, Thracians to the north and east, Thessalians to the south, and Athenians, who had strong interests in the entire northern Aegean area—all these would oppose any powerful development of Macedonia.

Philip's Reorganization of the Army

All the Greek states by this time relied heavily on mercenary troops, especially archers, slingers, and other light-armed specialists. Philip used them, too. But in a period when the Greeks used fewer and fewer citizens in their armies, Philip was able to make Macedonians the core of his phalanx and to keep them in service on a year-round basis. Recently acquired silver and gold mines made possible this heavy military expenditure. To instill group loyalty, the units were organized by tribe. A longer thrusting spear than was normal in the south made his phalanx quite formidable. More close-order drill was needed, but this was no problem. In addition, Philip—having learned this, among other things, from Epaminondas—developed a very strong cavalry contingent, which he used to break the opposing line of battle and throw it into disorder—much the way Epaminondas did at Leuctra and Mantinea, but with even more decisive impact.

With this army Philip soon defeated the Illyrians and Thracians, despite Athenian support for some of the latter. He gained access to the sea on both sides of the Chalcidice, first to the east and later at Pydna on the west. He captured Amphipolis, which the Athenians had once ruled and still claimed. A town a few miles east, Crenides was captured by Philip and renamed Philippi; it was to become one of the most important Macedonian cities. Near Philippi were more of the rich gold and silver mines that gave Philip at least 1,000 talents a year—the financial sinew he needed for his aggressive policies. His power soon was felt toward the south, also, as he expanded into Thessaly.

Philip Intervenes in the Sacred War;
Demosthenes' Opposition

As we have seen, the Phocians, fighting against certain members of the Delphic amphictyony, won several quick victories and soon pressed north into Thessaly. The Thessalians called on Philip and Macedonia to aid them (353 B.C.). After an initial defeat, the next year Philip was able to drive the Phocians out of Thessaly. He hoped to use the Sacred War, by playing the role of defender of Apollo and the Delphic oracle, to gain a powerful position in central Greece. Temporarily, however, he was unable to proceed into Phocis proper. A group of allies, including Athens, sent troops to the pass at Thermopylae and blocked him. Philip returned home to Macedonia and to further campaigning against Thrace and other neighboring areas on the north and west. Macedonia's territory, wealth, and power were increasing rapidly, and soon Philip felt capable of moving against the Chalcidian League (around Chalcidice), the most important city of which was Olynthus. Athens had long had a vital interest in the area.

The most indefatigable opponent of Macedonia in the days of both Philip II and Alexander after him was that greatest of all Athenian orators, Demosthenes. In a series of famous orations delivered over a period of about a decade—his famous *Philippics*—the Athenian thundered against the Macedonian. The first was given in 351 B.C. or 350 B.C. Demosthenes tried almost in vain to arouse the Athenians to their old glory. In one way the orator seems, in retrospect, to have been prescient, patriotic, and courageous, but in another way, he seems more a man who lived in the past, who was attempting to call the Athenians to a war they could not sustain and had no chance of winning—perhaps a bit out of touch with reality.

When Philip turned on Olynthus in 349 B.C., in his three Olynthiac orations Demosthenes urged the Athenians to intervene, even though Olynthus had been allied with Philip against Athens only a short time before. Athens did send help to Olynthus (more mercenaries than citizens), but the aid was too little and too late. Philip diverted the Athenians by promoting a revolt in Euboea against its pro-Athenian leader. In 348 B.C. Philip was able to destroy Olynthus. The whole campaign illustrates Philip's consummate if somewhat unscrupulous methods: He took advantage of weather—moving his army at a time when the Athenians could not counter with their fleet—as well as of money, diplomacy, trickery, bribery, and of course military power to achieve his goals.

By now most Athenian leaders—including Demosthenes; his inveterate orator-enemy Aeschines; and Eubulus, the cautious and moderate financial expert—recognized the necessity for peace. An embassy under Philocrates (Demosthenes and Aeschines were also members) traveled to Macedonia and negotiated a peace in 346 B.C. Athens and Macedonia became allies; the effect of the peace was to abandon Phocis to Philip. The Macedonians soon reduced Phocis, thereby ending the Sacred War. Philip was given the vacant place on the amphictyonic council and, in fact, a few months later was allowed to preside over the Pythian festival at Delphi.

Demosthenes and other Athenians, perhaps feeling guilty over the fate of Phocis and with good reason mistrusting Philip, began to have second thoughts. Demosthenes now delivered a second *Philippic* (343 B.C.), in which he charged that Philip intended nothing less than the destruction of Athens, and he called into question the justice of some of Philip's recently acquired holdings in the northern Aegean. Philocrates, the chief negotiator of the peace, was charged with treason and went into exile. Demosthenes next initiated one of the most famous trials in all the classical world, a proceeding in which he impeached his rival Aeschines. The latter was acquitted, however. The published orations of the two, with their bitter charges and countercharges, in a biased way provide much of the information we have for this period. The works of Isocrates, another great orator—or rather, publicist, for his speaking voice was poor and others presented his orations—who saw Philip as a possible savior of Greece from itself, present additional information, quite different in tone.

In succeeding years Demosthenes continued his campaign to create an anti-Macedonian alliance. His third *Philippic* was given in 341 B.C. Philip's continuing expansionist tactics caused friction, but specific incidents in the deteriorating relationship were as much the fault of Athens as of Philip, who seemed genuinely to respect the great cultural traditions of that city. Philip's moves against the straits of the Bosporus and the Hellespont, so important to the Athenian grain supply, did much to bring Athenians around to the views of their great orator. Other Greek states also began to side with Athens.

Battle of Chaeronea (338 B.C.); The Corinthian League

The crucial point came when Philip prepared to intervene in another Sacred War, against Amphissa, which like Phocis earlier had a dispute with the Delphic priests. Demosthenes was able to get even Thebes to join with Athens to stop the southward thrust of the Macedonians. At Chaeronea, before Thebes, in 338 B.C. the Macedonian army crushed the allies, and Macedonia soon dominated virtually all Greece. The Theban sacred band fought valiantly to the last man. The Athenians, including Demosthenes, fled the battlefield.

Except for Thebes, the Greek states—Athens especially—were lucky to receive treatment no more severe than a forced alliance with Macedonia. Philip's leniency was perhaps in part due to the advice given him by the aged Isocrates, who had long hoped for a great leader, not a tyrant over Greece but a statesman and unifier.

Philip, at any rate, took little vengeance except on the Thebans. Demosthenes escaped punishment. The Macedonian king did force the Greeks into an alliance called, conventionally, the Corinthian League, whose member states were to remain autonomous. There were a league council and a league army, but no central taxation. Philip was to be the *hegemon* (guide, leader) of both the political structure and the army of this alliance. Macedonian garrisons were to be stationed at key points in Greece: Corinth, Thebes, Chalcis, and Thermopylae. To many of the smaller Greek states, long tyrannized by the Spartans or the Thebans or the Athenians, the Macedonian dominance meant greater freedom, for Philip really demanded little of the Greeks except an end to rivalry and some minimal cooperation in a unified crusade against the Persians. Perhaps the advice of Isocrates may be seen here, too. The liberation of the Greeks in Asia Minor from the Persian yoke had long been a popular cause.

King Philip, however, was not destined to lead the crusade. As he made preparations for the campaign, he was struck down by an assassin (336 B.C.). It was his young son and heir, Alexander, who would eventually lead the combined army of Macedonians and Greeks against the sprawling Persian Empire.

Philip's Achievement

Any judicious assessment of the work of Philip II must admit that his accomplishments are impressive and that it was he who really made possible Alexander's meteoric career. It is not so easy to judge fairly of character. In general, modern scholars have tended to accept Demosthenes' views, according to which Philip was unscrupulous, untrustworthy, treacherous, and a destroyer of liberty and anything else that stood in his way. Even a sympathetic biographer must agree that Philip could be ruthless and also Machiavellian, for he was capable of fooling his enemies by deception and misdirection.

Let us look at three quotations from Demosthenes: The first is from the *Fourth Philippic* (62), which may be spurious but certainly expresses Demosthenes'

Demosthenes, greatest of all Athenian orators. Best known for his famous Philippics. (Art Resource)

point of view; the second is from his speech *On the Chersonese* (59); the last is from the *Third Philippic* (23, 25, 30–1).[1]

> It is not your subjection that Philip aims at; no, but your complete annihilation. For he is well assured that you will not consent to be slaves; or if you consent, will never learn how to be slaves, for you are accustomed to rule others. . . .
>
> We like to pretend that he is not at war with us. . . . But when our turn comes . . . of course he will deny that he is attacking us, just as he denied that he was attacking the men of Oreus, when his troops were already in their territory, or the Pheraeans before that, when he was actually assaulting their walls, or the Olynthians at the start, until he was inside their frontiers with his army.
>
> Your hegemony [that is, Athens'] in Greece lasted seventy-three years, that of Sparta twenty-nine, and in these later times Thebes too gained some sort of authority after the battle of Leuctra. . . . Yet all the faults committed by the Lacedaemonians in those thirty years, and by our ancestors in their seventy years of supremacy, are fewer, men of Athens, than the wrongs which Philip has done to the Greeks in thirteen years. . . . The wrongs which the Greeks suffered from the Lacedaemonians or from us, they suffered at all events at the hands of true-born sons of Greece. . . . Philip . . . is not only no Greek, nor related to the Greeks, but not even a barbarian from any place that can be named with honor, but a pestilent knave from Macedonia, whence it was never yet possible to buy a decent slave.

Hardly the presentations of an unbiased observer!

Perhaps we may balance the scales a bit with some of the purported words of Alexander, speaking of his father to his mutinous troops in 321 B.C. The passage, from the ancient historian Arrian, at least reflects a different and valid point of view.[2]

> When Philip took you over you were nomadic and poor, the majority of you clad in skins and grazing sparse herds on the mountains. . . . He gave you cloaks to wear . . . making you a match in battle for neighboring barbarians. . . . He made you dwellers in cities and graced your lives with good laws and customs. . . . He added most of Thrace to Macedon. Seizing the best-situated places on the seaboard he opened up the land to trade. . . . He made you rulers of the Thessalians . . . humbling the Phocian people he made the way into Greece for you broad and easy. . . . The Athenians and the Thebans . . . he humbled. . . . He brought as great glory on the Macedonian state as on himself.

For Alexander (if this is a genuine expression of his sentiment), obviously, allegations of bad character were unimportant in the face of such success.

---

[1]The translations of J. H. Vince in the Loeb Classical Library edition (Cambridge, Mass., 1930).
[2]As translated (with slight modifications) in G. Cawkwell, *Philip of Macedon* (London, 1978), pp. 17–18.

B. ALEXANDER USHERS IN A NEW AGE

Individuals, it often seems today, have little impact on history. Presidents and premiers struggle with problems not of their making, often with small success. To the modern observer, events appear to control men. The world careers on blindly in a kind of inexorable, staggering course toward nobody knows what goal. It is instructive, however, to note the weighty influence of some leaders of the past—leaders whose achievements are not to be explained solely in terms of environment or upbringing. Alexander the Great is one such figure.

So great were the changes Alexander initiated that historians give a different name to the period after him: The age in the Greek world before Alexander is called Hellenic; that after him is called Hellenistic. Though the term *Hellenistic* is usually applied specifically to the period after Alexander's death, it seems most logical to use it for the age beginning in 334 B.C., when Alexander, the Macedonian king, crossed the Hellespont and began his fateful invasion of the Asian mainland.

Young Alexander Takes Control

Philip II of Macedon had groomed Alexander to command by taking him along on military campaigns, leaving him as regent in his absence, and even making him second-in-command, in charge of the cavalry, at the crucial battle of Chaeronea (338 B.C.), when his son was only eighteen years old. In the following two years, however, increasing tension had built up in the family. Philip's relations with Alexander's fiery mother, Olympias, had never been ideal. He always had other women. She was intense, passionate, and attracted to the exotic and unusual, as in religion. Philip had five wives—legal in Macedonia, perhaps because there was likely to be a shortage of heirs to the royal family in a kingdom almost constantly at war. It seems that Olympias long held the first rank. However, at age forty-five, in 337 B.C., Philip chose to make yet another marriage, this one to the niece of Attalus, one of his higher officers. There were implications both for Olympias and for Alexander, and both, some sources say, reacted bitterly. Olympias now was completely estranged from her husband. As for Alexander, the story was told that he attended the wedding feast, and when Attalus proposed a toast that the new union might result in a legitimate heir to the throne, Alexander stood up and threw his goblet at the man. "What do you think I am," he demanded, "a bastard?"

Even if this story is distorted or untrue, it is not surprising that when Philip was assassinated the following year, 336 B.C., some thought that Olympias and Alexander were implicated. But there is no evidence of that: The best account we have places the blame on Pausanias, one of Philip's closest guardsmen, who was said to have had some rivalry with the bride's father. Pausanias was quickly killed by other guards. Alexander vigorously tracked down and executed others adjudged to be fellow conspirators. In a pattern not unusual, he also killed Attalus, his niece (Philip's latest wife), and her infant son (a possible rival). If the tomb recently unearthed at Vergina is (as it appears to be) that of Philip, then Alexander buried his father with all appropriate splendor.

Tetradrachm of Alexander the Great. Presumably an engraving of the young king, horns on his head in the style of Zeus-Ammon. (Hirmer Foto Archiv, Munich)

Alexander was accepted as king by the army in the Macedonian tradition, and he quickly took over the reins of government. He soon moved south with units of the army and succeeded his father as president of the Thessalian League, as a member of the Delphic amphictyony, and most important, as *hegemon* of the League of Corinth. In that capacity he announced his intention to proceed with the invasion of Asia that his father had planned. But the news of Philip's death had brought troubles in various areas. Alexander, not yet twenty years old and still untried, soon proved equal to the challenges in campaigns against the Thracians to the northeast and then against Danubian barbarians to the north. A campaign against Illyria to the west was necessary; there his forces fell into a topographical trap, but he extricated them by adroit maneuvering.

Now a rumor reached the Greek cities to the south that Alexander was dead. Demosthenes, of course, was quick to try to organize a drive for freedom from Macedonian dominance, but Alexander moved very swiftly—it had already become one of his trademarks—and was at Thebes before a coalition army could be put together. He defeated the Thebans and took the city. As an object lesson, it was destroyed, except for the temples and the house that had belonged to the poet Pindar. Again Athens escaped Macedonian wrath, and once again Demosthenes was lucky to keep his life and freedom.

Invasion of Asia: Battle of Granicus (334 B.C.)

Alexander's attack on the massive and still strong Persian Empire was something of a confident gamble. Macedonia's finances could not support a long campaign; quick victories were necessary. The Hellenic fleet of about 160 ships was numerically inferior to that of the Persians, which was chiefly Phoenician in its makeup. The Greek army was large by Hellenic standards but diminutive compared with the hordes that Persia could field, given time. Alexander had fewer than 40,000 men, including cavalry and specialized units. About half of these were Macedonian, and the rest were allies. The Greek infantry was the best in the world, but the Persians too would have thousands of Greeks in phalanx in any army they raised. Perhaps the Macedonians were superior enough to give Alexander the edge here, but since they were fighting against superior numbers and far from home, one must say that the odds were not on Alexander's side.

The crossing of the Hellespont was itself surprisingly easy. Philip had sent Parmenion, one of his senior generals, across with an army two or three years before. Though hard-pressed, Parmenion still held a bridgehead in Asia Minor. The Persian commanders, who must have known of Alexander's movements, did not mobilize their navy to oppose the crossing. Alexander himself, playing the new Achilles, went to Troy to make a landing. There, symbolically, he threw a spear into the sand and sacrificed to the specter of King Priam, who had been slain by the son of Achilles. Even at this early date, Alexander saw himself as no mere man; at the very least, he cast himself in a heroic mold.

The Persian commanders elected to oppose Alexander at the Granicus River. To attack, Alexander would have to cross the stream and storm the banks on the opposite side. Rejecting any suggestion of caution, Alexander launched his attack as soon as his forces were set. He led the heavy cavalry of his right wing in a headlong, oblique (diagonal) assault that disarrayed the opposing forces enough to permit his infantry to make its crossing. Then, with the opposing center held fast, he used his cavalry to roll up the line from the now-exposed flank. Rashly and impetuously, Alexander charged into the melee himself and would have lost his life except for the quick action of one of his lieutenants, "Black" Cleitus. Among those slain on the Persian side were thousands of Greek soldiers, who were looked on as traitors to their homeland. Surviving Greeks were put to work as slaves in Macedonia. One of Alexander's characteristics was a willingness to learn and to change. And he soon changed his attitude toward Greek mercenaries who had fought for the Persians; in fact, he enlisted some in his own army, though he did not use them in key units such as the phalanx.

By the end of that year, the whole western half of Asia Minor was in Alexander's hands; once liberated from Persian rule, the Greek cities there perhaps joined the Corinthian League. Macedonians replaced Persians as satraps in most western regions. The supplies and money captured made it possible for Alexander to go on with his campaign as planned. He wintered at Gordium, where he is reputed to have cut—rather than untied—the famous Gordian knot (of which it was said that he who learned its secret would someday rule Asia).

From Issus to Egypt (333–332 B.C.)

The world waited for the great battle that was sure to come in 333 B.C., when the fully mobilized army of Darius III of Persia would meet the somewhat augmented forces of Alexander. The clash came in late fall at Issus, on the Mediterranean shore just south of the mountain passes leading from Asia Minor into Syria. Darius had superior forces but allowed himself to be brought to battle on a field too narrow to make maximum use of his numbers. Again Alexander, leading the heavy cavalry on the right wing, smashed the forces opposite and then rolled up the line. It did not help Persian morale much when Darius, conspicuous in his chariot, fled before the contest was fairly decided. In the confrontation of personalities, Alexander won hands down. Darius even abandoned his wife and daughters; captured by Alexander, they were treated with studied courtesy.

That winter and most of the next year were spent in besieging the port cities that gave Persia its troublesome naval superiority. Tyre required a siege of seven months; Gaza, three. The main sector of Tyre was situated on an island; Alexander at length decided to build a mole out to the island and did so, under great difficulties. Not until he achieved naval supremacy in the locality, however, did the city fall. The captured populace of these cities was either killed or sold into slavery.

Jerusalem and Judea seem to have gone over to Alexander's camp peacefully. Egypt, too, surrendered to Alexander without a struggle. Alexander sacrificed to Apis, the bull god of Memphis, and was made king with the traditional coronation. In fact, he always sacrificed to local deities and was quite scrupulous in his treatment of priests. He seems to have believed strongly in oracles and soothsayers, one of whom had accurately predicted the date he would take Gaza and had warned him it would be a dangerous day for him personally—and he was wounded in the fray.

Some biographers, both ancient and modern, have made much of the psychological effects of a trip Alexander made to the oracle of Ammon (the old Amon god of Thebes) at the oasis of Siwah, in the western desert of Egypt. Quite probably the priests there hailed Alexander as "son of Ammon," which would translate into Greek as "son of Zeus," since the Greeks identified Ammon with Zeus. Except for the Persian dynasty, all the kings of Egypt for two thousand years had been "sons of Ammon." Certainly the priests of the oracle told the young king whatever else he wanted to hear.

The first of the cities named Alexandria was established in a strategic location on the Nile delta to serve as the Greek administrative capital; this ultimately became the most important city of Egypt. Alexander eventually established eighteen cities bearing his name—which indicates a healthy ego.

Gaugamela—The Decisive Battle (331 B.C.)

Near the end of 332 B.C., when Tyre and Gaza had fallen, Alexander received a communication from Darius offering a negotiated peace. Darius would pay 10,000 talents as ransom for his family and would cede to Alexander all the land west of the Euphrates. At a council meeting, Parmenion suggested that if he were Alexander, he would accept the terms. Alexander's much-repeated reply was that were he Parmenion, he probably would. Only death would put an end to Alexander's imperialist quest.

Mosaic of Alexander fighting Darius in battle, found at Pompeii. Now in the National Museum, Naples. (Art Resource)

Late the following year Alexander's army crossed the Euphrates, next the Tigris, and then turned south. At Gaugamela his troops encountered the main Persian force, the largest army yet. This time it was the Persian generals who chose the battleground: They took up their position on a broad, flat plain. They hoped to make maximum use of their numerically superior cavalry and immense forces. They had cleared the ground for their scythed chariots, with which they hoped to cut up the array of the Hellenes. This battle, above all, tested Alexander's generalship and the mettle of his men.

Alexander accepted the fact that his army would be outflanked and arranged for defense not only on the flanks but also at the rear. He approached the enemy while moving obliquely to the right, which forced the Persians to move also—but less skillfully. A gap opened near their center. Alexander charged the gap with his heavy cavalry, followed by the phalanx, and with this bold tactic won the battle. However, his oblique advance had made things difficult for Parmenion on the left wing, which was surrounded, and the camp was taken. Thus Alexander could not pursue Darius when he fled, but the news of the crushing defeat of the Persian center spread, and the rout became general. Eventually Alexander captured the Persian camp and, a little later, its base of operations farther south. His victory was complete, although Darius still lived.

Alexander spent a little time at Babylon; he ordered the rebuilding of the dilapidated temples of the ancient city, which the Persian kings had deliberately neglected because of revolts. Alexander planned to make it a regional capital. But soon he moved on to Susa, where he saw the spoils that Xerxes had taken from Athens 150 years before. He wintered further on still, after some difficult skirmishing at Persepolis, where for some curious reason the palace of Darius and Xerxes was burned. Perhaps this was meant as a symbol of the fall of the Persian Empire, but more likely it was simply an accident—after all, it belonged to Alexander now.

At Susa and at Persepolis also, Alexander came into possession of the main Persian treasury, with vast quantities of gold and silver. He was rather prodigal with it, both in gifts and in general expenditures. So much of the raw metal was coined and put into circulation that over the next quarter-century prices in the entire eastern Mediterranean area were inflated by about 100 percent.

Alexander, the Great King

Early the following year, Alexander and his army were once more on the move. Unable to organize effective opposition, Darius again fled, only to be killed by one of his own lieutenants, the satrap Bessus. Alexander could now take over the titles, as well as the office and accouterments, of the dead monarch.

But the campaigning went on. The army, now somewhat smaller and including native contingents, moved east and northeast in the next four years and penetrated as far as the area of modern Pakistan. Across the Indus and some of its tributaries they marched, sometimes against bitter opposition but finally always victorious.

A battle at the Hydaspes River, a branch of the Indus farther to the east, was the most desperate Alexander ever fought. The east bank of the river was held by Porus, the region's king, with a force larger than the Macedonian, including 200 elephants and 300 chariots. After passing days and nights of deliberate false alarms, Alexander quietly led a major portion of his army by night to an uncontested crossing several miles upstream, while one of his generals remained to hold the bank opposite Porus as usual. Alexander, superior only in cavalry, managed to lure the enemy cavalry into a preliminary battle and threw it back on the center, with Porus' elephants and infantry, just as the phalanx arrived on the attack. Meanwhile the rest of his army made the river crossing and attacked from the rear. Alexander captured Porus but later confirmed him as king and even enlarged his kingdom. He remained a faithful ally.

By then (326 B.C.), Alexander's army was tired of the eternal campaigning that took it ever farther from home. Though many of the soldiers doubtless were replacements, there was a veteran core that had marched all the way from Macedonia and fought in all the major battles. The straight-line distance was 3,000 miles; in all, these men had walked at least 10,000 miles during eight years of campaigning. It is not surprising that one day when Alexander ordered his troops to continue the march eastward, they mutinied. The king at last gave in but decreed the army return by another route; so they marched down the Indus Valley, to return westward part by land and part by sea.

One incident that occurred on the march down the Indus seems very revealing of Alexander's character and of the army's feelings also. When a small walled town of the Mallians refused to surrender, Alexander ordered it taken. Two ladders were constructed to scale the walls. When the command to attack came, his men were reluctant to climb the ladders. Alexander himself went up first, accompanied by two aides, and fought his way atop the walls. Looking back, he saw that his men still were not following, so he leaped down inside. Suddenly the Macedonian soldiers realized how serious the situation was and stormed up the ladders in such numbers that both broke. By the time they had mended them and rescued Alexander, he was seriously wounded, with an arrow piercing a lung.

The march home across southern Iran, mostly desert, was a terrible nightmare for most of the army and even worse for the camp followers, and cannot have improved the king's health. Yet, once back at Susa and Babylon, Alexander began to plan future conquests, while at the same time reorganizing his imperial administration. After a year's rest (324 B.C.) for the army, he would undertake a great campaign into Arabia; later he would gain more complete control of the Black Sea area. In the more distant future would come, possibly, ambitious campaigns against Carthage and other powers of the western Mediterranean. But weakened by his wounds and fever as well as by dissipation, Alexander died in June of 323 B.C. at Babylon—not yet thirty-three years old.

Alexander's View of Himself

It is amazing what different pictures are presented of Alexander by his numerous modern biographers, all of whom of course rely on the same basic body of evidence. The diversity of their views is greatest when they attempt to evaluate Alexander's motives and aims.

It has already been mentioned that Achilles was Alexander's hero and that he sought consciously to imitate him. From the beginning Alexander claimed descent from Heracles, the great example of the man-become-god. After his visit to the oracle of Ammon in Egypt, he began to claim a position as the son of Zeus; in fact, Olympias is said to have encouraged him in this, telling him that Philip was not his father. Alexander went so far as to send messages to the Greek states asking them to acknowledge his deity. In most states the populace shrugged its shoulders collectively in response and said, "Why not?"

Along the way farther east from Ecbatana, Alexander began to require his subjects to practice *proskynesis*, bowing or prostrating themselves when approaching his presence. He called himself by the Persian title "Great King" and even began to wear Persian dress. He made considerable use of Persians in high position, and when he reorganized the army in 330 B.C., started training natives as fighting men and eventually used some even in the heavy-infantry phalanx.

All this conduct displeased his own men. In fact, one of Alexander's continuing problems was the strong feelings against absolutism among Macedonians of all levels. Alexander's pretensions provoked more than one conspiracy against him. One involved Philotas, the son of Parmenion, and the senior general himself was executed on mere suspicion of involvement. Another apparently involved Callisthenes, the nephew of Aristotle, one of a corps of scientists, engineers, and historians who accompanied the army on the great Asian campaign. The rank-and-file Macedonians objected most to the equal treatment accorded some of the "barbarians," and only slightly less objectionable to them were Alexander's pretensions to deity and the proskynesis. Alexander exempted the Macedonians from all such requirements. Still, down to the last days of his life, he had difficulty in conciliating his troops on these matters.

What of this evidence for Alexander's view of himself? How does it all add up? Alexander had a tremendous job to do. He could not do it merely as king of Macedonia; he must make something more of himself. Nor could he function to his fullest potential as *hegemon* of the Corinthian League. It might have been all right to settle for that after his first campaign, but a league official could neither administer the world's greatest empire nor unify it. And surely Alexander's chief goal was just that—to organize this empire and to function as its monarch. He had to be king of all his far-flung subjects, not only of Greeks or Macedonians. These aims surely explain his new titles and seeming pretensions.

Alexander's Ideals

It is impossible to discover any of Aristotle's influence in Alexander's ordering and administration of the new empire. Alexander wished to be acceptable to all his subjects, and this may explain much: his attempts to deify himself, his adoption of exotic native dress, and his use of natives in high position and in the army.

Did Alexander believe in a true brotherhood of men, as some historians think? Alexander did encourage his men to marry native women in the conquered lands; it was said that at Susa in 324 B.C. he had 10,000 marriages celebrated at one time between his men and native women. Although this most likely meant a regularization of existing irregular alliances, Alexander may have felt that children of mixed parentage would be loyal to him and to his new regime. He himself married both the Bactrian princess Roxana and a daughter of Darius. In many ways Alexander tried to demonstrate that the peoples of Asia he ruled were more to him than mere barbarians, but whether any lofty humane ideal inspired him or he was only trying to unify his dominions in order to control them we cannot know.

Alexander's Impact on the World

The bringing down of the Achaemenid dynasty of Persian kings and its replacement with Greco-Macedonian rule, of course, changed conditions drastically for almost everyone in the eastern Mediterranean regions. Greeks and Macedonians had triumphed over the barbarians and had proved their right to dominate. The opportunities for these Hellenes now exceeded anything they might once have imagined. Soldiers and politicians, merchants and traders, all could now advance and prosper. Even Greek intellectuals, patronized by Alexander and his successors, had new vistas opened to them.

The subjugated Asian peoples were not oppressed by Alexander. As we have seen, he used many of them even in high office and in the army. Merchants and traders among the native Asians must have prospered along with the Greeks. The precious bullion the Persian monarchs had hoarded was coined and put into circulation, with a quickening economic effect over the entire area. No official policy of restraint or discrimination prevented Asians from sharing in this economic growth, though Greeks perhaps often managed to gain favored status.

Alexander shook up the Greek world along with that of the Asians. In his wake, Greeks were forced to rethink their politics, their society, their religion, and their culture; but they were likely to remain unchanged at home and to accept new views only in overseas posts. The parochial city-state mentality persisted in Greece proper. Perhaps Greece could never have been truly unified, even by Alexander and even if he had lived three or four decades more. Abroad, however, where Greeks ruled as a superior class, the typical political unit became the one Alexander had established: an absolute, divine monarchy.

The great migration of Greeks, who took along with them the Greek language and Greek literature, art, and architecture, changed the world and produced the Hellenistic age. Throughout the Near East, Greek became the lingua franca. Everywhere there developed a class of natives who were thoroughly Hellenized, and thus were looked on with favor by their rulers, though perhaps sneered at contemptuously by their more conservative compatriots. The capitals of the Hellenistic kingdoms grew into cosmopolitan centers of great size. These tremendous urban centers, especially Alexandria in Egypt and Antioch in Syria, became not only political capitals but also centers of diffusion for Greek culture.

Greeks were, in turn, tremendously influenced by Oriental ways. That is, as Moses Hadas has emphasized,[3] the age after Alexander was one of fusion as well as diffusion. In many ways, but most notably in religion and philosophy, the Greeks themselves learned from their subjects and were gradually changed.

It has been suggested that Alexander overextended the resources of the Greco-Macedonian world. There were simply not enough Hellenes to furnish the manpower necessary to consolidate the tremendous empire he had conquered. Even a fusion of races could not soon have made it possible for this great state to endure, or even for the fragmented successor states to endure for long. In consequence, it is argued, Alexander weakened the Hellenic world itself and opened it to eventual Roman aggression and conquest.

Alexander's greatest legacy was his vision of a united world. To a degree, at least by the time of the early empire, the Romans were actuated by the one-world view Alexander had created. The idea, in Roman dress, survived the fall of

[3]*Hellenistic Culture: Fusion and Diffusion* (New York: Columbia University Press, 1959).

Rome, and in some ways this vision has endured into modern times. The youthful Napoleon's Near Eastern adventures were to a degree inspired by Alexander's ambitious vision. The various one-world hopes and dreams of the present century, though no longer based on a single great unified empire, nevertheless are in part heir to the one-world view inspired by Alexander. In short, it would be hard to point to any other individual in world history (in a political role) who has been more influential than Alexander the Great, the charismatic conqueror who died before completing his thirty-third year.

BOOKS FOR FURTHER READING

BADIAN, E. *Studies in Greek and Roman History*, Oxford, 1964.

BURN, A. *Alexander the Great and the Hellenistic World*, New York, 1962.

CAWKWELL, G. *Philip of Macedon*, London, 1978.

EHRENBERG, V. *Alexander and the Greeks*, Oxford, 1938.

FOX, R. *Alexander the Great*, London, 1973.

GRANT, M. *From Alexander to Cleopatra: The Hellenistic World*, New York, 1982.

GREEN, P. *Alexander the Great*, rev. ed., Harmondsworth, Eng., 1974.

GRIFFITH, G., ed. *Alexander the Great: The Main Problems*, New York, 1966.

HAMMOND, N. *Alexander the Great: King, Commander, and Statesman*, Park Ridge, N.J., 1980.

HAMMOND, N., and GRIFFITH, G. *A History of Macedonia, vol. ii: 550–336 B.C.*, Oxford, 1979.

TARN, W. *Alexander the Great*, Cambridge, 1948.

WILCKEN, U. *Alexander the Great*, New York, 1932.

11

THE HELLENISTIC STATES

The far flung empire of Alexander fell apart at his death. There was no logical successor, and he had made no arrangements for the succession. Perhaps he refused to believe that he too could die. His half-brother, Philip III Arrhidaeus, unfortunately was of moronic intelligence. Roxana had been left pregnant, and a short time after Alexander's death she produced a son, Alexander Aegus.

The officers and cavalry of the army, representing the nobility of Macedonia, favored making the young Alexander king, though a long and doubtful regency would be necessary. The common soldiers, however, who in Macedonian fashion constituted an assembly, favored making Philip Arrhidaeus king. (Probably it was not generally known just how low the prince's intellect was.) By way of compromise, therefore, the two were made joint rulers, and a council of generals was named to act as regents. Chief among these were Perdiccas, one of the senior generals with the main army, and Antipater, who had been in command in Macedonia since 334 B.C., when the army left for Asia.

In a relatively short time a power struggle began. For decades a number of generals, some of them very competent, fought for the right to be the new Alexander. Olympias, the mother of the dead Alexander, played a role, by championing the cause of young Alexander IV, Roxana's child. But he, Philip Arrhidaeus, Olympias herself, Roxana, and even another child claimed to be a bastard of Alexander, became pawns in a lethal game that saw them all dead within a few years.

The struggles of Alexander's successors, inconclusive and prolonged, raged over personal goals—survival or self-aggrandizement. Whatever idealism may have motivated Alexander was lost to his successors, who had no time to consider impractical and unattainable dreams. One result was a widening of the gulf between the Greeks as a master race and their subjects. But as we shall see in the next chapter, on an intellectual level the ideal of brotherhood was emphasized and widely propagated.

The political history of the Hellenistic age is so scrambled and complex that it seems not only fruitless but also impossible to give even a general sketch of it. This chapter will therefore attempt to indicate only typical patterns and record a few important events. Actually, the most significant political movement in the period was the gradual encroachment by Rome, which continued until all the great Hellenistic powers were absorbed into the Roman Empire. This topic will be discussed more thoroughly in the subsequent chapters on Rome.

A. GREECE AND MACEDONIA

The Period Immediately After Alexander's Death

Even while Alexander was alive and winning his greatest victories, Sparta had led a rebellion against Macedonian dominance in Greece (331 B.C.). Antipater, Alexander's lieutenant in Macedonia, put down the rebellion. The Athenians had been tempted to join the Spartans, and under the leadership of Demosthenes and others, remained ready to join any anti-Macedonian alliance that had a chance of success. News of the death of Alexander, therefore, ignited another attempt to throw off the Macedonian yoke.

This war was a serious threat to Antipater. It is called the Lamian War because much of the activity took place around Lamia, a fortified city in southern Thessaly controlling the major route from central Greece. Athens had built up its sea power and had some of the latest types of vessels, quadriremes and quinqueremes. A mobilization of the resources of several imperial satraps, however, made it possible to defeat Athens at sea and eventually to invest the Attic capital itself and force its surrender. The other allies had mostly given up earlier. This time Demosthenes and several other leaders who were notoriously anti-Macedonian were marked for death. Demosthenes fled, and when about to be captured, took poison. During this time Aristotle also left Athens; his connections with Macedonia made him most unpopular, and he was charged with impiety. He is reported to have said as he departed that he could not allow Athens to sin twice against philosophy.

So long as he lived, Antipater, though much disliked, managed not only to keep the Greeks in proper subjection but also to hold the throne for the corulers, Philip III and young Alexander IV, the son of Roxana. On Antipater's death, however, everything changed. His successor, at his own recommendation, was Polyperchon. But Antipater's son Cassander chose to dispute power with Polyperchon, intending, it would seem, to rule himself. He gained the support of many Greek states by proclaiming the principle that all these states should be free; and he got the support also of Antigonus, a powerful satrap in Asia Minor.

At this point Olympias intervened from her homeland in Epirus. She took over Macedonia briefly, in the interest of her grandson Alexander, and had Philip III assassinated. But then Cassander appeared with an army and drove out Olympias and her forces. Eventually he captured her and had the army condemn her to death in 316 B.C. Cassander was now the unrivaled ruler of Macedonia. Not until 310 B.C., however, did he kill the young Alexander and his mother Roxana.

Greece and Macedonia in the 3rd Century B.C.

Cassander controlled Macedonia until his death in 297 B.C. In the usual fashion he attempted to dominate all Greece, partly through the League of Corinth. He was opposed in this effort by a son of Antigonus, Demetrius Poliorcetes (the Besieger), who was trying to make himself king over all the empire of Alexander. This new contender, who conducted operations in the islands and in Greece proper, made his headquarters at Athens and was for a time accorded divine honors and in effect made tyrant. Demetrius succeeded brilliantly in gaining influence and alliances among the Greek states, while his father had a major part in the struggle for Asia. However, in 301 B.C. the battle of Ipsus in Asia Minor changed the situation. Antigonus and Demetrius faced a formidable coalition: Cassander; Seleucus, satrap of Babylon; Lysimachus of Thrace; and Ptolemy, satrap of Egypt. All these local rulers were calling themselves kings by now. Antigonus was killed at Ipsus, and Demetrius' power was much reduced as a result of their defeat by Lysimachus and the others. The Athenians refused to receive him; perhaps they were repelled by the way he had lived so dissolutely in the Parthenon on the Acropolis.

Demetrius' fortunes revived, however, when he made an alliance with Seleucus, who now saw Ptolemy of Egypt as his chief enemy. Demetrius seized Macedonia from Cassander's younger brothers, who were fighting over the kingdom, and resumed his efforts to control all Greece. About 287 B.C., he was driven from the kingdom by King Pyrrhus of Epirus, who is better remembered for his invasion of Italy a few years later, and by Lysimachus, one of the Alexandrian successors, who ruled Thrace. Lysimachus then became king of Macedonia.

A second major battle (there were many lesser ones) among the successors, at Corupedion in Asia Minor in 281 B.C., ended Lysimachus' reign and his life at the hands of Seleucus, who proclaimed himself king of Macedonia. Shortly after, however, Seleucus was assassinated by a renegade son of Ptolemy, called Ptolemy Ceraunus, who also ruled Macedonia briefly. Finally, Antigonus, called Gonatas (the "Knock-Kneed"), a son of Demetrius I and grandson of Antigonus I of Syria, the general of Alexander, gained the throne of Macedonia to establish the Antigonid dynasty there. He had to fight against a Gallic invasion that devastated much of Greece and Asia Minor. He was also temporarily displaced by Pyrrhus when the latter returned from his ill-fated Italian venture; but by 272 B.C. Antigonus Gonatas was firmly established in Macedonia. This Antigonus early was a pupil of a philosopher and former student of Plato, Menedemes of Chalcis, and he was later influenced by Zeno, the founder of Stoicism, and by a later Stoic leader and poet, Aratus. The experience perhaps showed in his sense of personal responsibility, but it hardly influenced his foreign policy, which was typical of the age. The Antigonid dynasty endured for about a century.

Two federal-style leagues were constituted in Greece during the mid-third century B.C. and played important political roles for several decades. The Aetolian League exercised its power to the north of the Gulf of Corinth and ultimately reached to the Aegean. The Achaean League flourished in the Peloponnese. Both these federations had league officials, league assemblies, and league armies. Neither was dominated by a single state, as earlier leagues had been. Both played a part in reducing Macedonian power over Greece.

The city-states that had been so powerful in the classical period were now comparatively weak. Thebes, rebuilt after its destruction by Alexander, was again reduced by the Aetolian League. Athens led still another rebellion against Macedonian dominance in the middle of the century and found the attempt ruinous. Thereafter Athens played no further important role in world politics but remained a cultural university center.

Social and Economic Problems

The weakness of the older Greek city-states was not merely political. There was some depopulation of the area, no doubt in part because of emigration, as fortune beckoned the most energetic and adventurous young men to service in the armies or the upper bureaucracies of the great monarchies. Perhaps, too, infanticide was practiced more frequently; in any case, the major reason for the decline was economic. Greece was not a land of opportunity in this age.

Especially in the third and early second centuries B.C. a kind of class struggle arose (to which the Marxist historians naturally have devoted much attention), pitting the poor and the debtors against the rich. All over Greece, agitation welled up again and again, the lower classes demanding a cancellation of debts and a redistribution of property—presumably the larger, private estates. When political leaders arose who espoused these popular demands, the results could be totally unsettling.

Interestingly, the most successful efforts to effect such reforms were seen in Sparta, although the kings who carried them through were really conservatives who wanted to restore what they thought was the ancient constitution put in place by Lycurgus.

Sparta had declined since classical days, and its legendary ideals had been eroded. The love of money, ancient writers declare, infected many of the Spartiate class, which was much diminished in numbers through profligacy and extravagance. Some Spartiates sold or somehow lost their allotted public lands and, impoverished, were then unable to contribute their share to the public barracks. Such Spartans lost their first-class citizenship and were classed as "inferiors." Much of the Spartan wealth was now in the hands of women. Two kings, Agis IV and Cleomenes III, who ruled Sparta between 244 B.C. and 221 B.C., despite strong opposition cancelled some debts, seized land and redistributed it to an enlarged body of Spartiates, and reinstituted the old training.

As the old Sparta had been dominant in the Peloponnese, so, they thought, must the new. This meant conflict with the Achaean League. King Cleomenes at first defeated the league and seemed on the point of raising Sparta to its old eminence. But then the chief leader of the Achaean League, Aratus, reluctantly called on Macedonia to aid against Sparta. Giving up Corinth to occupation by Macedonia was the price paid for this support. The situation was ironic, for some decades earlier Aratus had made his reputation by expelling a Macedonian garrison from Corinth. Cleomenes was defeated by the combined forces in 222 B.C. at Sellasia, a few miles north of Sparta.

This did not quite end Sparta's ambitions. Under the tyrant Nabis at the beginning of the second century B.C., Sparta was still a power to be reckoned with. Nabis attempted to continue the conservative restoration of Cleomenes III and also to restore Spartan dominance over the Peloponnese. He succeeded in gaining control of Argos and other territories. But later in his reign (207–192 B.C.) Rome effectively restricted Nabis' power, and finally the Aetolians procured his assassination. Eventually Rome swallowed up Sparta along with the rest of Greece and curtailed much more than the expansionist dreams of the Spartans. The Roman policy of supporting existing aristocracy (if not oligarchy) effectively and deliberately smothered any possibility of true social and economic reform in Greece or anywhere else in the Hellenistic east. But peace brought its blessings.

Macedonia and Greece Fall to Rome

Philip V of Macedonia (221–179 B.C.) was at once one of the most competent and the most unfortunate of the Antigonid kings. As usual for Macedonian rulers, he felt he must dominate all Greece and exercise a major influence in a larger sphere encompassing all the Balkan Peninsula. About the time he came to power, the Roman Republic intervened on the eastern shore of the Adriatic to eliminate some pirate nests there. Philip considered this an intolerable incursion into his sphere of influence and therefore allied himself with Hannibal during the Second Punic War. The Romans retaliated first by making alliances with the Aetolians and other of his adversaries and then by declaring war on Macedonia itself once Hannibal had been defeated. The Macedonian phalanx fell before the Roman legions at Cynoscephalae in Thessaly in 197 B.C. Philip was not treated severely by the Romans, however, and all the Greek states were declared by Rome to be free. The Romans felt the Greeks should all be duly grateful for this generosity, and thereafter they resented any action by a Greek state that might be construed as being against Rome's best interests. The Aetolians, who had fought

Hellenistic World
200 B.C.

with the Romans at Cynoscephalae, were bitterly resentful because they were not allowed to occupy large chunks of Macedonian border territories as a reward.

The Romans forced a third Macedonian war on the son of Philip, Perseus (r. 179–167 B.C.), who, they felt, was preparing for war against them. By this time both the Greek leagues were in disfavor at Rome. After a Roman victory over Perseus at Pydna in 168 B.C., Macedonia was made over into four separate republics. An unsuccessful rebellion in 149/148 B.C. was followed by the conversion of Macedonia into a Roman province. The Aetolian League had already been dissolved by Rome following the Syrian War, discussed later in this chapter. The Achaean League also rebelled against Roman influence in 148 B.C., and in the war that followed, Corinth was destroyed as an object lesson. Greece outside Macedonia (later called Achaea) became in effect a Roman province also, though it was not officially organized as such until the time of the Emperor Augustus.

B. SYRIA, PERGAMUM, AND EGYPT

Syria Under the Seleucids (301–63 B.C.)

The founder of the Seleucid dynasty of Syria was Seleucus I Nicator, one of Alexander's generals. From a position as satrap of Babylon, he gradually extended his power until all the empire eastward to the Indus came under his control. In India, however, a remarkable native king, Chandragupta of the Mauryan dynasty, withstood Seleucus. They came to an understanding by which Chandragupta was confirmed sovereign over all the provinces in the vicinity of the Indus and Seleucus got war elephants (by tradition, five hundred of them). He used these battle animals in struggles in the west against Antigonus and Lysimachus. He profited from both the major battles mentioned earlier, Ipsus (301 B.C.) and Corupedion (281 B.C.). By the latter date he was actually in control of, or in a position to control, all Alexander's dominions except Egypt and India. But then he was assassinated by Ptolemy Ceraunus and was succeeded by his son Antiochus I. Most subsequent rulers of the dynasty were named either Seleucus or Antiochus.

The sixth in the Seleucid line was Antiochus III (r. 223–187 B.C.), eventually surnamed "the Great." His predecessors had not been able to keep all the territories ruled by Seleucus I, and Antiochus III made a serious effort to recover them. His greatest successes came in the east. In the west the chief enemy of Syria was Egypt, for the Ptolemies held the Palestine-Lower Syria region, along with other territories in Syria and Cilicia. Antiochus gained control of all these, though not easily. His first major effort against Egypt in 217 B.C. came to grief; only in 200 B.C. did he succeed in defeating the forces of young Ptolemy V and in annexing the disputed lands.

A second Seleucid opponent of note was the Attalid kingdom in western Asia Minor, the kingdom of Pergamum. (See page 214 for a discussion of the city of Pergamum.) Though it was established on an independent basis somewhat earlier, the true founder of this monarchy was Attalus I (r. 241–197 B.C.). Only a period of weakness in Syria made the creation of this kingdom possible, and its every expansion was at the expense of at least the pretentions of the Seleucids and was a challenge to them. Antiochus the Great never got around to destroying Pergamum, but its kings were acutely aware that he might undertake such reprisal at any time. Eumenes II (c. 195–159 B.C.) of Pergamum helped to persuade the Romans to intervene in Asia against Antiochus, whose power he much exaggerated.

The reasons for the clash of Rome with Syria were several. For one, Antiochus had given asylum to Hannibal when that enemy of Rome fled to the east soon after the end of the Second Punic War (201 B.C.). For another, in attempting to regain all the territory held by Seleucus I, Antiochus moved into Thrace, and Rome professed to be perturbed by any such invasion of Europe. Third, Antiochus was allied with the Aetolians, who had become anti-Roman after Macedonia was let off easily following Philip V's defeat in 197 B.C.. And then, as we have said, Eumenes II played a role of intriguer.

Antiochus III actually took an army of several thousand men to Greece. But neither he nor the Aetolians mobilized anywhere near the number of men each had promised. Rome declared war and crushed the allied force at Thermopylae in 191 B.C. Then the Roman army crossed into Asia Minor, where with the aid of Eumenes' cavalry it defeated Antiochus' main army. The Seleucid king had to give up all territories in Asia Minor, pay a large indemnity of 15,000 talents, reduce his fleet, and get rid of his war elephants. He died a short time later, still trying to raise money to pay the heavy installments of the indemnity.

From this time on, Syria declined. A son of Antiochus III, Antiochus IV Epiphanes (r. 175–164 B.C.), made a great effort to stem this decline. He fought successfully against Egypt, only to be forced out of that country by a warning from Rome. He tried to unify his diverse dominions with a syncretic religious policy. This perhaps was successful in some places; but at Jerusalem, where the Syrian monarch sacrificed pigs and set up his own statue in the temple precincts, it produced rebellion, led by anti-Hellenist Jewish conservatives. The Jewish feast of Channukah in December celebrates the date in 164 B.C. when, under the leadership of the Maccabees, the Jews purified the temple. Meanwhile Antiochus campaigned against another revolt to the east but died, reputedly mad, before he could recover the situation.

The Seleucid dynasty endured, though continually beset by dynastic strife, rebellious subject peoples, and economic troubles, until 63 B.C. In that year Syria was made a province of Rome by Pompey the Great, almost as an afterthought. While conducting a war against Mithradates of Pontus to the north, Pompey noted the power vacuum to the south and simply moved into the area without serious opposition. So ended the second of the great Hellenistic monarchies. Palestine became a client state of Rome; as for Pergamum, when the last of the Attalids died in 133 B.C., his will made Rome heir to the kingdom. Rome first had to fight a small war to convince the Pergamenes that the will was valid, and thereafter Pergamum became a Roman province called Asia.

In Pergamum—eventually in all Asia Minor—and Syria, as in Greece, the Romans bolstered the faltering Greco-Macedonian upper class against the natives and suppressed all attempts to achieve social and economic reform. In Pergamum the suppression was with arms at the time of the Roman takeover, 133 B.C. to 129 B.C. Again, however, it should be added that the Roman peace allowed greater prosperity, and as we shall see, the Roman system allowed social mobility for some.

Egypt Under the Ptolemies (305–30 B.C.)

The first Ptolemy, another of the Macedonian generals of Alexander, was named satrap of Egypt after the death of Alexander. As Ptolemy I Soter, he soon began to act independently, like a monarch ruling his own kingdom, and in 305 B.C. he openly proclaimed himself king. His conduct in the early years brought efforts by Perdiccas to discipline him, but Ptolemy was able to hold the naturally protected Egypt against that general, and later against Antigonus as well. He seized

Ptolemy I, Lagos (Soter); tetradrachm of Ptolemy II.

Cyrene and, during the maneuvering before the battle of Ipsus (301 B.C.), occupied Palestine and Lower Syria as well. He had given Seleucus I refuge from Antigonus at a critical moment and had also lent Seleucus forces to reconquer his satrapy, Babylon. Thus Seleucus did not attempt to dislodge Ptolemy after Ipsus, when he gained full control of North Syria and most of the rest of Alexander's empire.

Egypt reached a height of power in the first half of the third century B.C., under Ptolemy II (r. 282–246 B.C.) and Ptolemy III (246–222 B.C.). It seems that it was really the second wife of Ptolemy II, Arsinoë II, who organized the strong and aggressive policy of the king. She was also his sister. This was only one of a whole series of brother-sister marriages that characterized the Ptolemaic dynasty, and Arsinoë was only one of a series of strong-minded women who helped make Hellenistic history. Egypt's power now extended north along the Phoenician coast and into the Aegean.

Ptolemy III continued this aggressive drive. However, Antigonus Gonatas of Macedonia defeated the Egyptian fleet in the Aegean, and a few years later Antiochus III of Syria, as we have seen, began to push the Ptolemaic forces out of their positions along the eastern Mediterranean coastline. Even when the Ptolemaic kingdom was reduced to Egypt proper, Cyrene, and a few islands (after 200 B.C.), however, Egypt remained strong.

Internal problems followed one of Egypt's great victories, that over Antiochus III of Syria in 217 B.C., at Raphia, along the coast of what is now the Gaza Strip. The young Ptolemy IV was at this time under the influence of native ministers, who armed the indigenous populace in putting together the army that defeated the Seleucid force. As a consequence of this participation, native Egyptians aspired to higher posts and even tried to expel the alien Macedonian dynasty. One of the rather meager sources of information for this period is the famed Rosetta stone. It tells of the building of a temple on which construction was halted numerous times because of internal disorders. Much is sometimes made of the fact, too, that the first known worker-organized work stoppages that can properly be called strikes occurred in Egypt during the Hellenistic age.

Friendship with Rome saved Egypt from Antiochus IV in 167 B.C., as we have seen. But a little later, a profound economic depression—drastically low prices for Egypt's major export, wheat, followed by several successive bad crop years—made it impossible for Egypt ever to recover its strong position of the third century B.C. The quality of its rulers seems also to have declined from this time on.

In one significant respect, Egypt under the Ptolemies differed from the other two major Hellenistic monarchies. Its economy was controlled down to the last detail by the government, in a system somewhat comparable to state socialism. It was nothing new in Egypt, of course, for the pharaoh to claim title to most of the land; this was true even in remote antiquity. The Ptolemies, however, also placed tight controls on imports and exports and so strictly controlled the monetary system that no foreign currency at all was allowed to circulate within Egypt. Numerous monopolies were either directly operated by the state or were granted as special privileges or for monetary consideration to individuals. The chief imports so controlled included olive oil, wine, and lumber. The chief exports, wheat and paper, were closely controlled as well. So completely was every economic activity monitored that natives even had to buy permits each day they fished in the Nile.

On the plus side, some of the Ptolemies spent considerable sums to improve the irrigation systems, as for example, in the Fayum area. As we shall see in the next chapter, Ptolemaic rulers sometimes also spent large sums for the benefit of scholars, schools, and libraries. On the minus side, the enormous revenues furnished opportunity for grandiose foreign ventures to some of the dynasts, who used Egypt simply as a base of operations. For the native populace, Macedonian rule was an episode; they did as they have always done—endured.

Everyone knows the last ruler of the Ptolemaic line, Cleopatra VII, who will be dealt with further in the later chapters on Rome. Ambitious and competent, she had great plans that might well have come to fruition had she not backed the loser in a major civil war in Rome. Octavian (later to be Emperor Augustus) could not forgive Cleopatra her support of Antony, whom she had married. He therefore invaded Egypt, and the ill-fated lovers committed suicide. The last of the great Hellenistic monarchies thus fell to Rome, in 30 B.C., and became another of the provinces.

BOOKS FOR FURTHER READING

BURN, A. *Alexander the Great and the Hellenistic World*, New York, 1962.

CARY, M. *A History of the Greek World from 323 to 146 B.C.*, London, 1932.

GRANT, M. *From Alexander to Cleopatra: The Hellenistic World*, New York, 1982.

GRIMAL, P. *Hellenism and the Rise of Rome*, Eng. ed., New York, 1968.

LARSEN, J.   *Greek Federal States,* Oxford, 1968.

LARSEN, J.   *Representative Government in Greek and Roman History,* Berkeley and Los Angeles, 1955.

MACURDY, G.   *Hellenistic Queens,* Baltimore, 1932.

PETERS, F.   *The Harvest of Hellenism,* New York, 1970.

ROSTOVTZEFF, M.   *The Social and Economic History of the Hellenistic World,* 2nd ed., Oxford, 1959.

TARN, W.   *Hellenistic Civilization,* New York, 1952.

TARN, W.   *Hellenistic Military and Naval Developments,* Cambridge, 1930.

WALBANK, F.   *The Hellenistic World,* Atlantic Highlands, N.J., 1981.

12

HELLENISTIC CULTURE:

currents and crosscurrents

One might imagine that balance-of-power politics and the frequent wars among the Hellenistic powers caused such constant turmoil that the creative mind could not function. They did not. These wars were dynastic struggles fought with professional armies. The entire populace was not involved in the way the people of Athens and Sparta were caught up in the Peloponnesian War. The actual theaters of conflict experienced much depredation and destruction, but battles seldom touched the great centers that served as the capitals for Hellenistic monarchies. Intellectual activity was almost uninhibited, and even commerce was seldom seriously affected.

A. THE GREAT CITIES OF THE HELLENISTIC WORLD

Just as the cities produced the first civilizations in an earlier era, so the Hellenistic cities were cultural centers of fusion and diffusion, synthesis and syncretism. These cities, the largest the world had yet seen, were the natural creations of absolutist monarchies. Great centralization of power required great concentration of administrative offices, soldiers, arms and armament, businesses, and warehousing facilities. Necessarily, there followed a similar concentration of population. This pattern of urbanization is seen everywhere in the Hellenistic world, even in hitherto almost totally rural Macedonia.

The Macedonian and Greek ruling class, the people who manned the mercenary armies and all the major political offices, lived in these—often new—cities. The cities therefore were organized on Greek models, with local officials and city councils and sometimes even with citizen assemblies. However, the local governments were always subject to the edicts of the monarch or even to his actual intervention. Most paid tribute to the king. As in Greece, the cities frequently relied on the benefactions of the richer citizens for construction of public buildings or presentation of festivals or even for the ordinary expenses of government.

Many of the urban upper class were absentee landowners (or lessors, as in Egypt); their lands were directly overseen by a native who could communicate with the peasants. Although the cities used the voluminous and standard coinage issued by each state on the Alexandrian model, the rural areas everywhere still depended chiefly on barter for local exchange.

Alexandria

Egypt, with its centralized government and highly centralized economic system, developed the largest capital city, Alexandria. Located in the Nile Delta on a site with an excellent harbor, it was also connected to one of the branches of the river by a canal. Egypt's low and undifferentiated coastline made it difficult at times for ships at sea to locate the harbor. The Ptolemaic solution was a lighthouse nearly 400 feet high on the harbor island of Pharos—one of the Seven Wonders of the ancient world. The lighthouse was only one of the wonders of Alexandria. It was the most cosmopolitan of cities as well as the largest; perhaps a million inhabitants crowded into its quarters by the end of the Hellenistic period. It was the city with the largest Greek and the largest Jewish populations in the world, and its broad streets were planned on a rectangular pattern. A letter preserved on papyrus in Egypt's dry sands, written by a woman who had just moved to the city, complains to a country relative that the city's broad streets made shopping too difficult: One's feet were tired all the time!

The patronage of the early Ptolemies made Alexandria a leading cultural capital. The library, the largest in ancient times with at least 700,000 volumes, drew scholars like a magnet. The museum (home of the Muses) supported research and teaching of enormous importance. To be head of the museum at Alexandria was to hold the most important academic position in the world—with the possible exception of leadership of the Academy and the Lyceum in Athens. The foremost scholars in both cities were likely to be more than purely philosophers; they were scientists as well—men of broad interests and attainments.

It was at Alexandria that Jewish scholars produced the Greek translation of the Hebrew Bible, the Septuagint. This collection, which contained extra books now called the Apocrypha, was much used by Hellenized Jews and even by Palestinian Jews, though the latter subsequently rejected the Apocrypha. Many of the quotations in the Christian New Testament are from the Septuagint. When Saint Jerome translated the Bible into Latin—the Vulgate, which is still the official Bible of the Roman Catholic church—he used the arrangement of the Septuagint.

Antioch, Pergamum

The sprawling Syrian Empire spawned a number of important cities, among them Seleucia on the Tigris. The chief administrative center, however, was Antioch on the Orontes River in Syria. Situated on an easily defended site, Antioch was one of a complex of four cities founded in Syria by the Seleucids, each, like Alexandria, planned on a grid pattern. It too was cosmopolitan, with native, Jewish, and Greek quarters. Like Alexandria it was something of an intellectual center, with library, museum, and gymnasia. Two of the new cities were ports, the busiest being Laodicea. The other inland city, Apamea, was chiefly a military base.

The greatest city in Asia Minor was Pergamum. At the beginning of the reign of Attalus I (mid-third century B.C.) it was only a hill fortress from which Attalus made a reputation by defying invading Gauls—the Galatians. Much of the Attalid income, derived from a relentless tax system and the export of parchment, fine textiles, and pitch, was put to the enrichment of this capital. Its most famous edifice was the altar of Zeus, excavated in the present century and taken to Berlin. It also contained several gymnasia and celebrated temples. The library at Pergamum grew until it was second in size only to that at Alexandria. There were, of course, other notable cities in Asia Minor, in particular Ephesus with its huge temple to Artemis, another of the Seven Wonders. Still another of the wonders, the mausoleum built for King Mausolus in the middle of the fourth century B.C., was located in Halicarnassus.

In Macedonia, the most important urban centers were Thessalonica and Cassandreia. Both cities had populations that included many foreigners, especially Greeks, and both had typically Greek, democratic institutions—for local matters only, to be sure.

B. SCIENCE

The significant—sometimes astonishing—advances in basic and applied sciences, medicine, mathematics, and mechanics during the Hellenistic period can only be indicated here. The work of a few of the most eminent figures must be permitted to symbolize the whole.

Aristarchus of Samos (c. 310–230 B.C.)

Many otherwise well-informed persons today believe that all men before Columbus thought that the world was flat. Greek thinkers after Pythagoras, however, conceived of the earth as a sphere, perhaps primarily because they considered the sphere a perfect figure. A pupil of Plato, Eudoxus, attempted to reconstruct the entire universe mathematically. He gave special attention to the *planets*—a word derived from a Greek word meaning "wanderers," because, as compared with stars, planets do not remain in relatively fixed positions. Eudoxus and some contemporaries postulated an earth revolving on its axis every twenty-four hours.

Aristarchus of Samos, working at the museum in Alexandria, went further in his theories than Eudoxus. He conceived the system that bears the name of Copernicus, who lived 1,800 years later. That is, he thought that the sun was much larger than the earth and that the earth, along with the planets, revolved about the sun. The chief objection to this view was that the stars did not seem to change positions, as they would (and do, imperceptibly) if the earth moved in an orbit. Aristarchus replied, it seems, by arguing for a much larger universe than anyone suspected. His figures for the size of the sun and its distance from the earth fall short of reality (311 times the earth's mass and 18 to 20 times the distance from the earth to the moon), but his errors were due solely to the lack of instruments for precise measurement. Unfortunately, his views were not generally accepted, partly because it did not occur to him that the whole universe is moving and that therefore the planets' orbits are elliptical.

Eratosthenes of Cyrene (c. 275–195 B.C.)

Eratosthenes, head of the library at Alexandria, was almost as versatile as Aristotle. He was nicknamed "Beta," which indeed implied that he was second best, but then he was second in so many areas that it became a backhanded compliment. Eratosthenes worked out a historical chronology widely accepted in antiquity. Most striking of his other achievements was his measurement, with considerable accuracy, of the circumference of the earth: He missed by only a few hundred miles. Again, as in Aristarchus' work, the system was perfect and only the measurements were faulty. Eratosthenes computed the difference in the declination of the sun's shadow at two cities in Egypt on the day of the summer solstice. The two cities, he thought, were in exactly the same latitude. The resulting angle, converted into a fraction of a circle, needed only to be inverted and multiplied by the distance between the two cities to give him the correct figure.

Archimedes of Syracuse (c. 287–212 B.C.)

The achievements of Archimedes surpass even those of Eratosthenes, who was his friend. It is ironical that Archimedes is best remembered for certain practical engineering devices—inventions he considered trifling. His greatest accomplishments were in mathematics; indeed he was quite possibly the greatest mathematician of antiquity. Some of the problems he solved would now be demonstrated by analytical geometry or integral calculus. He did much work in relation to cylinders, spheres, spirals, and conic sections. His predecessor, Euclid, whose work on the *Elements of Geometry* was much less original, is better remembered as a mathematician.

Whatever Archimedes thought of it, his practical work deserves to be remembered, nevertheless. He discovered the principle, named after him, that an object immersed in water is lighter by the weight of the water displaced. His discovery evolved after King Hiero of Syracuse asked him to determine whether a certain metalsmith had cheated him. The king feared that the smith had used different proportions of gold and silver than were given to him to make an elaborate crown. Archimedes was able to demonstrate that the smith was honest. Hiero was also much impressed when Archimedes, using either levers or pulleys (he worked out the principles of both), launched a huge ship the king had built; one of the largest constructed in antiquity, it must have displaced at least 4,000 tons. Archimedes also designed a revolutionary screw pump to make irrigation from the Nile River easier. And at the siege of Syracuse by the Romans in 212 B.C. he made bigger and better war machines—grappling cranes, missile throwers—than had yet been used. He was killed by a Roman soldier when Syracuse fell, reportedly when he shouted at the man not to disturb the figures he had drawn in the sand for study.

Hellenistic engineers, in fact, after a pattern that seems valid for all human history, unlike Archimedes, gave most of their attention to the development of weapons of war, and they developed an astonishing variety of missile throwers, catapults, heavy siege equipment, and the like.

Industrial Revolution in 200 B.C.?

The practical inventions of Archimedes and others in the Hellenistic age are impressive. Water power, harnessed in various ways, operated machinery. Even a slot machine, which operated by the insertion of a coin, was developed. Hero, an Alexandrian scholar, discovered more than one way to make mechanical use of steam. There is little doubt, in fact, that the technological knowledge then existed to initiate an industrial revolution 2,000 years before it actually occurred. Much work would have been required in metallurgy and in the manufacture of instruments, for example, but it could have been done. What primarily prevented it from occurring was the cheapness of human labor, especially slaves. Only profitable operations endure and prompt the further improvement of machinery. As so often in history, though, one is led to speculate how different the world might have been if men like Archimedes and Hero had sparked a continuing revolution in labor-saving devices.

The crucial role of slavery as an impediment to mechanical and economic progress in antiquity has been denied by some modern scholars, but without sufficient reason. It is true that learned men like Archimedes scorned the practical side of their work, and it is equally true that the Ptolemies and other patrons subsidized science as a matter of intellectual curiosity. Nonetheless, the availability of cheap labor was the main reason the Industrial Revolution did not begin about 200 B.C.

C. PHILOSOPHY

Cynicism and Skepticism

Several schools of philosophy were established in the Hellenistic era, including those of the Cynics and the Skeptics. The founder of the Cynic school was Antisthenes, a pupil of both Socrates and Gorgias the Sophist. It was said that Antisthenes and Plato disliked each other cordially, and for approximately the same reasons. Antisthenes thought Plato a rich snob; Plato thought the other a flaunter of poverty, for Antisthenes taught the absolute unimportance of everything except virtue. Birth, rearing, money, property, even convention and good manners were nothing.

A cynic far better known than Antisthenes was Diogenes of Sinope, who spent most of his life in Corinth. Diogenes dramatized the Cynic beliefs through his style of life. He reduced his needs to the minimum, lived in a barrel, and ate with a single dish and spoon whatever anyone gave to him, uncooked. Legend has it that he carried a lighted lantern in the daytime, "looking for an honest man," and that he gave Alexander his comeuppance when the young king arrived in Corinth. He asked Diogenes what the philosopher would have from him. Diogenes demanded that Alexander get out of his sunlight. Alexander is reported to have said then that if he were not Alexander he would be Diogenes; more likely, it was perhaps fortunate for Diogenes that he was an old man at the time. Diogenes' frequently shocking behavior probably made him something of a tourist attraction. But he was well enough liked by the Corinthians; when some rowdy boys once broke up his barrel, local persons took up a collection for a new one.

Skepticism was advocated by the leaders of the Academy, a century or two after Plato. Those heads of the "Middle" Academy, like Carneades in the second century B.C., who propounded their views on the impossibility of perception of truth, surely would have pained the founder of the school. Plato had fought against similar ideas in the Sophism of his own day.

Stoicism and Epicureanism

Two great schools of philosophy developed in the Hellenistic age: Stoicism—named from the porch (*stoa*) in Athens where its Cyprian founder, Zeno, taught—and Epicureanism—named for its founder, Epicurus, an Athenian from Samos. Both Zeno and Epicurus were teaching in Athens by 300 B.C. Both philosophical systems had a great impact over a long period. Stoicism influenced many Roman leaders and helped to mold Roman institutions, especially legal ones. Christian views, of a later time, of course, bear a marked similarity to Stoic ones.

Both Stoicism and Epicureanism were concerned primarily with helping individuals decide how they should behave in a world they never made; that is, their emphasis was on ethics. Zeno and Epicurus were, quite understandably, re-acting to the world Alexander left as a legacy. Both developed a materialistic view of the universe, with an accompanying cosmogony. But in ultimate ways the two systems were vastly different.

Stoic Beliefs

Zeno, and more especially his successors Cleanthes and Aratus, pro-pounded beliefs that were as much religious as philosophical. The one-world view fostered by Alexander's conquests meant for them the basic equality of all races of people under the universal and benevolent dominion of a father-god. The ma-terialistic universe they envisioned, though cyclical in nature, was nevertheless guided by God—or Zeus or Mind or Providence—in rational ways often hidden to men. These Stoics were not really monotheists, though they frequently talked as if they were. One unfortunate consequence of their religious emphasis was an often quite superstitious belief in divination and in astrology, the pseudoscience of the influence of the stars on human destiny.

Humanity's position in the Stoic's universe was distinctly subordinate. The individuals must accept their lot without complaint; one must not cry out against destiny (hence the modern meaning of *stoic*). One should play one's assigned role with dignity and courage. Things that seem evil, even disease and death, are not really so; people must always keep in mind the rational nature of the universe. Mind, not the emotions, must rule the individual. The suppression of emotions such as anger and bitterness seems to us laudable, but Stoicism also taught the suppression of the finer emotions such as mercy and love. To be a Stoic was not easy. Self-control, the greatest virtue, was to be supplemented with temperance, modesty, and honesty. Stoics did argue, however, that people might work to im-prove their lot and that of their neighbors. Public service, they taught, was noble and enriching. The true Stoic was a good citizen, and when opportunity afforded, a good magistrate or judge. The Good Man who accepted his destiny, who saw God in all that is and in all that he experienced—that was the Stoic, and in the Stoic conception, a happy man.

Epicurean Views

Epicurus lived and taught in a pleasant garden withdrawn from the world—a fact that seems to symbolize all of Epicureanism. The universe, he said, is ma-terial and mechanistic; it came to its present state by chance evolution. The gods, if they exist (Epicureans were not atheists exactly, but often sounded as if they were), live apart from people and have nothing to do with them or their lives, Epicurus believed. People's chief goal in life must be to seek their own happiness. This they could best do by recognizing the basic evils of the world and of the mass of humanity and by withdrawing from public affairs to whatever retreats they might find with others of similar views.

Like the Stoics, Epicureans who followed Epicurus believed in a high personal code of ethics, for Epicurus taught that no person could be happy unless he or she was also virtuous. The philosophy itself, however, which is basically selfish in nature, attracted many who interpreted the conclusions of Epicurus to mean that they should "eat, drink, and be merry." It is difficult to know just how influential Epicureanism was. Not a great many specific followers of the philosophy are known, but its influence seems to have been quite pervasive.

Both philosophies spread to the Roman west. Possibly Caesar and certainly Lucretius stand out as Epicureans of the first century B.C. The younger Cato, Seneca, and Marcus Aurelius are among the longer list of noted Roman Stoics.

D. RELIGION

The tendency toward a species of monotheism was not confined to the Stoics. Any period in which there is considerable trade and intercommunication among people of distant areas manifests this trend—through the identification of the different principal deities—toward syncretism. The conquests of Alexander and the thinking that accompanied it, of one world and of one people of the world, gave impetus to monotheistic thought. Perhaps the growing familiarity with the Jewish religion, with its well-developed monotheism, may also have contributed something to the trend. Large, absolutist states, however, have their own built-in impulses toward a universal, if not monotheistic, deity, especially if the rulers manage to associate themselves with the dominant god, as Egyptian pharaohs had done from far antiquity.

Syncretism: Sarapis

As the chief deity of their kingdom, the Ptolemies chose a god neither wholly Greek nor wholly Egyptian—Sarapis. The name apparently came from a combination of two ancient Egyptian gods: Osiris, god of the underworld and judge of the dead, and Apis, the bull god of Memphis. The attributes of Sarapis were universal: He too was judge of the dead, but he blessed humanity in all ways and was considered a creator. His greatest temple was, naturally, in Alexandria. Just as naturally, the temple was in the Greek style. The worship of Sarapis and the construction of shrines to him spread over the Mediterranean, following the trade routes. One important temple was built at Delos, for example, and by the first century B.C. his devotees were to be found at Rome. Thereafter, the popularity of Sarapis began to fade; he was partially replaced by another old Egyptian deity, the goddess Isis.

In the great days of Egypt two millennia earlier, Isis had been the wife of Osiris and mother of Horus, one of the riverine deities who was also associated with fertility and motherhood. In the Hellenistic age Isis, along with Sarapis and several other eastern deities, developed into a universal god who was worshipped throughout the Mediterranean in Roman days. Identified by the Greeks with Aphrodite (earlier with Demeter), Isis was also the goddess with whom Cleopatra chose to be identified, probably in a pattern set previously by consorts of the Ptolemies. She was especially important to women in pregnancy and childbirth and also to travelers. An extant prayer addressed to her reads like one that might have been composed by a Jew or a Christian. In it, Isis seems omnipotent, benevolent, merciful; exclusivism, however, necessarily one element of real monotheism, is absent.

The King as God: Antiochus IV of Syria

The priests of any well-organized religion are always men of some power and influence, not only religious but economic and social. Kings and other heads of state have thus often believed that for their own protection religion must be closely supervised or controlled. In the Kingdoms of Egypt and Syria in the Hellenistic era, the association or even identification of the king with the chief deity was considered vital to sound statecraft.

The Syrian king Antiochus IV (175–164 B.C.) tried to make his diverse empire more unified by artificially syncretizing religion. (See also p. 219.) All the major deities were to be considered as one; thus, the Jews' god, Yahweh, was to be identified with the Syrians' Baal Shamin and the Greeks' Zeus, and so on. Antiochus took the surname of Epiphanes, which with "Theos" understood means "the god made manifest," and completed the godhead by including himself in its identification. Apparently, statues of himself were to be erected at every major religious site in the kingdom, and worship accorded the king in this way.

Most peoples of the empire no doubt accepted the identification with a shrug as nothing new. The Jews, however, rebelled under the Maccabees against both their own Hellenizers and the king. Antiochus never did regain control of the area before he died, so the Jews for the most part retained their independence until the Romans asserted control over Palestine.

Judaism itself became widespread, chiefly through the emigration of Jews to Alexandria, Antioch, and other cities of the Hellenistic east and, eventually, to Rome as well. The religion remained everywhere the strict monotheism it was in Palestine, but it was influenced in its outward forms by the cultures of various areas. The very term *synagogue*, which describes the local organization typically used by the Jews of the dispersion, is Greek.

Other Oriental Religions

The Asia Minor–Syria region exported its own forms of religion to Greece and the western Mediterranean during the Hellenistic age and the Roman period that followed. The goddess Cybele is typical of this influence. Called also the Great Mother, the Mother of the Gods, or the Great Mother of Pessinus (from the town in Asia Minor where the mythical stories about her centered), Cybele ranked almost with the Twelve Olympians from a rather early period. Yet she gained even more adherents in Hellenistic times.

The reasons why Cybele and other oriental deities grew in importance were perhaps related to the religious needs of the common people. These needs were not satisfied by the cold, formal rites to the state deities or the parochial local gods. The worship of Cybele began in Rome in 204 B.C. under the tutelage of two of its leading noble families. There Cybele became a sort of upper-class goddess, and her spring festival was one of the most celebrated in that city.

Cybele's priests, *galli*, were self-emasculated. Her rites were sometimes emotional and orgiastic. At Rome they were somewhat more dignified but still noisy, as we learn from the poets. The most important characteristic of the Cybele and similar cults was that of "mystery." Participants in the mysteries were given promises of blessings in this life and privileges in the next.

E. LITERATURE

Much of the more significant literary work of the Hellenistic age was philological in nature, especially that at Alexandria. There scholars collected the great works of the past and established definitive texts, expunging and emending with skill. They wrote critiques and commentaries, compiled dictionaries and bibliographies. Unfortunately, most of their labor was lost in antiquity. Even so, had not an Alexandrian scholar discovered a moldering part of Aristotle's library, we would be even poorer today in the treasures of the past.

History

Two great writers compiled oriental histories: Manetho and Berossus, both Hellenized natives of Egypt and Mesopotamia, respectively. Their works survive only in fragments, but it is obvious that they helped to keep alive much that would otherwise have been irretrievably lost.

The greatest Greek historian of the age was Polybius. Large sections of what survives of his *Histories* deal with Rome, but the account as written embraced the Graeco-Roman world. Substantial fragments illuminate such crucial periods as that in which the Ptolemies and Seleucids fought for control of Egypt, 220–200 B.C. Polybius was especially well qualified to write of all the Mediterranean. He was a Greek who lived in Rome for a number of years and was friendly with Romans who held high positions. He himself had previously held office in the Achaean League. In addition to traveling throughout his Greek homeland, Polybius visited Spain and North Africa. His theory of cycles in political evolution, which modified Plato's and Aristotle's conclusions, is interesting. He thought the most stable and enduring constitution, like the Roman and the earlier Spartan, should contain a balanced mixture of the elements of monarchy, oligarchy, and democracy. However, the soundness of such a constitution, he thought, would at last be undermined when one element—most likely the democratic—overshadowed the others.

Poetry

Some of the best poetry of the age was written by the great Stoic teachers, Cleanthes and Aratus. Their hymns of praise and prayers to Zeus as God rank with the great psalms of the Hebrews. And it was probably this age, incidentally, in which some poet of the Hebrews was producing the Song of Songs.

At Alexandria, the pastoral idylls of Callimachus and Theocritus (who was born in Sicily), composed in the third century B.C., exercised great influence on the later Latin poets of the Augustan period. Callimachus was also a scholar, and perhaps the first to organize the collection of rolls in the library at Alexandria. Apollonius, who lived some years in Alexandria before retiring to Rhodes after quarreling bitterly with Callimachus, wrote the epic *Argonautica*, which relates in Homeric rhythms the familiar story of Jason's search for the Golden Fleece and his love affair with Medea.

Drama

Many forms of drama continued to be produced in the Hellenistic age, with Athens, through sheer tradition, still the theatrical center. Of tragedy little remains, probably testimony enough to the general quality. The third century saw the development of the so-called New Comedy, which is much more like the modern forms of comedy than are the plays of Aristophanes. The appeal of such drama, as in most movies and television programs today, was to the lower strata of society. The common people of earlier Athens could become absorbed with ultimate concerns, but after the Peloponnesian War, most citizens watched comedy as an escape from the real world. Only the philosophers gave much thought to the great problems, and no one paid much attention to important social issues.

The best-known writer of these comedies was Menander. Not until about thirty-five years ago did we have a full play of Menander's—when the sands of Egypt yielded up one almost entire. But it is a disappointment. Clearly, some of his other works, of which we have sizeable fragments, were much better. Again, much of the importance of the author lies in his influence on later writers in Latin, especially Plautus and Terence. The New Comedy was rather frivolous, filled with sex intrigues and impudent slaves and turning on plots that often involved fortuitous solutions to not-very-serious problems. Will the aristocratic young man be able to marry the slave girl he loves? After many adventures the answer is that he will, because she turns out to be the long-lost daughter of a friend of the family. The humor depended on pun-filled dialogue, exquisite timing, and crowd-pleasing actors.

F. HELLENISTIC ART

Restraint had been the guiding principle of the culture of the Hellenic period. "Nothing too much" was carved, along with "Know thyself," on the temple of Apollo at Delphi, and restraint was one of the four cardinal virtues of Plato. That same canon had guided the artists and architects of the age. The great temples displayed the clean lines and uncluttered appearance of the Doric and Ionic style, and the sculpture presented neutral features and idealized figures in formal pose. The art primarily glorified the states with their gods and heroes.

The Hellenistic artists emphasized humans, human emotion, and human needs. In sculpture, painting, and engraving there was a new emphasis on portraits of real persons. Some of the finest portraits remaining are cut into gemstones or engraved in high relief on the fine coinage of the age. Full-size sculpture frequently reveals sensuous lines—even if of the gods, as the famed Victory of Samothrace—or realistic emotion or pathos. The contorted anguish of the figures in the Laocöon group, the Trojan and his two sons struggling with two fearsome

The Laocoon, restored. (Vatican Museums)

serpents, and the statues of the Gaul and his wife—he has just killed her with his sword and is in the act of killing himself—illustrate the typical art of the time. Some modern critics find the work of this period, and these two groups in particular, overpowering, overdone: The Laocöon is almost painful to look upon, and the blood wells from the wound of the Gaul.

Hellenistic architects preferred more elaboration than the earlier Hellenic designers. The Corinthian style predominated in temple architecture. Structures such as the Great Altar of Zeus at Pergamum (in Ionic style) were almost completely covered with relief sculpture, often projecting emotion. Several of the greatest structures of the age had practical, purely human purpose, such as those at Alexandria mentioned earlier: the library, the museum, and the lighthouse. Gymnasia—the museum was an elaborate gymnasium—for lectures, exercise, and instruction were built everywhere in this time, as were *stoae,* or covered colonnades, that flanked the major squares in the cities. The Painted Stoa at Athens, it will be recalled, gave Zeno's philosophical system its name.

The Hellenistic age has often been compared with the nineteenth and twentieth centuries. Parallels, indeed, are easy to see: balance-of-power politics; large urban centers that were beehives of scholarly activity, emphasizing science and literature; fast-paced comedy in the theatre; simplicity and functionalism in architecture (though more elaborate in that age). But as always in history, it is well to notice also the differences, for they are vast.

BOOKS FOR FURTHER READING

AVI-YONAH, M. *Hellenism and the East,* Ann Arbor, 1978.

BEVAN, E. *Later Greek Religion,* New York, 1927.

BIEBER, M. *The Sculpture of the Hellenistic Age,* rev. ed., New York, 1969.

BOARDMAN, J. *Greek Art,* New York, 1964.

BROCK, A. *Greek Medicine,* New York, 1929.

CLAGETT, M. *Greek Science in Antiquity,* London, 1957.

COOK, R. *Greek Art,* 2nd ed., Harmondsworth, Eng., 1979.

DAVIS, N., and C. KRAAY *The Hellenistic Kingdoms: Portrait Coins and History,* London, 1973.

DIJKSTERHUIS, E. *Archimedes,* Copenhagen, 1956.

DRACHMANN, A. *The Mechanical Technology of Greek and Roman Antiquity,* Copenhagen, 1961.

GRANT, M. *From Alexander to Cleopatra: The Hellenistic World,* New York, 1982.

HADAS, M. *Hellenistic Culture: Fusion and Diffusion,* New York, 1959.

LLOYD, G. *Greek Science after Aristotle,* London, 1973.

LONG, A. *Hellenistic Philosophy: Stoics, Epicureans, Sceptics,* London, 1974.

RIST, J. *Epicurus,* Cambridge, 1972.

RIST, J. *The Stoics,* Berkeley, 1978.

SAYRE, F. *The Greek Cynics,* Baltimore, 1948.

THOMPSON, J. *Ancient Libraries,* Berkeley and Los Angeles, 1940.

WALBANK, F. W. *The Hellenistic World,* Atlantic Highlands, N.J., 1981.

WEBSTER, T. B. L. *Studies in Menander,* Manchester, Eng., 1950.

PART III   Rome

13

EARLIEST ROME

History is not always—perhaps not often—specifically useful. (Of course, it is in a general sense valuable.) Still, hordes of amateur and professional scholars, politicians, and common individuals have used the history of Rome, especially the decline and fall of the empire, as an analog of the present. For several reasons, the history of Rome suits such comparison better than most other histories. We have been left a fairly detailed account of the rise of a small village on the Tiber to world power and dominion, followed by its agonizing deterioration, accelerating decline, and reverberating collapse. Roman history presents what seems a complete unit, the tale of the entire life cycle of a political organism. The historians Spengler and Toynbee found in it a model when they looked for cycles in history.

But political units, though fashioned by men, are not biological organisms. Seldom exact, analogies are often more misleading than illuminating. This sort of speculative misuse of Roman history does not, however, detract from its enduring importance.

A. GEOGRAPHICAL SETTING

Rome now seems an unlikely spot for the center of a world empire. Italy does not have the resources for a first-rank power in the twentieth century; but by ancient standards, and especially in comparison with Greece, the Italian Peninsula was both richly endowed and strategically located. Greek travelers who visited Italy in

Chart 5 The Roman Republic

PERIOD	ROME	ELSEWHERE
800 B.C.	Rome a tiny village on the Palatine Hill.	Carthage founded by Phoenicians; Greek colonies in south Italy, east Sicily, elsewhere. Etruscans powerful north of Rome.
700 B.C.	Petty kings; Etruscans gain control, make Rome into an important political and economic center.	Assyrian Empire reaching its height.
600 B.C.		Fall of Assyria to Medes, Babylonians; Nebuchadnezzar. Babylonia falls to Cyrus and Persians.
500 B.C.	Rome freed of Etruscan kings; becomes a republican oligarchy; period of economic depression, decline follows. Struggle of the orders begins.	Persian wars with Greeks; Athenian Empire. Etruscans decline under attack from Gauls, Greeks, and Romans. Peloponnesian War; Spartan dominance in Greece.
400 B.C.	Romans take Veii, then lose to Gauls; city burned and sacked. Rome achieves dominance over Latin peoples; suppresses revolt; sets up alliance system.	Theban dominance; rise of Macedonia. Alexander becomes king; conquest of Persian Empire.
300 B.C.	Samnite wars; Roman expansion of power in Italy. End of struggle of the orders (Hortensian Law). Wars with Pyrrhus and others lead to Roman dominance of all Italy south of the Po Valley. First Punic War; Sicily becomes a province, then Sardinia and Corsica. Earliest Latinized productions of Greek theatre. Occupation of the Po Valley.	The successor states: Ptolemaic dynasty in Egypt Seleucid dynasty in Syria and much of Near East Antigonid dynasty in Macedonia Attalid dynasty in Pergamum Achaean and Aetolian Leagues in Greece.
200 B.C.	Second Punic War; two provinces in Spain; First Macedonian War concurrent; Second Macedonian War follows.	Antiochus III recovers much land previously lost; acquires Palestine from Egypt; loses war to Rome, in alliance with Aetolians.

226

Syrian War; playwrights Plautus and Terence.
Polybius at Rome, becomes member of "Scipionic circle."
Third Macedonian War.
Culmination of career of Cato; Greek cultural penetration.
Fourth Macedonian War, Achaean War, Third Punic War; North Africa and Macedonia become provinces.

The Gracchi; land and grain laws.

100 B.C. Marius; Jugurthan and Celtic Wars; Saturninus.
The Italian War; Italian and Latin allies enfranchised.
Mithridatic War; civil strife in Rome.
Sulla's return; civil war; conservative reforms.
Reforms mostly scuttled; Third Mithradatic War, height of Pompey's career; Cicero consul; Catiline.
First Triumvirate: Caesar, Crassus, Pompey; period of Lucretius, Sallust, Catullus.
Civil war between Pompey and Caesar; Pharsalus; Pompey dies.
Assassination of dictator Caesar; renewed civil war; Second Triumvirate against Brutus and Cassius.
Octavian victorious over Antony and Cleopatra.

27 B.C. Octavian becomes Augustus; controls Roman world.

Philip V of Macedonia chooses Perseus as successor.
Perseus killed; Macedonia broken down into four republics.
Antiochus IV of Syria; Jewish revolt.
Macedonia a Roman province; Greece subordinate.
Attalus III dies, wills Kingdom of Pergamum to Rome; this becomes province of Asia.

Cilicia taken over by Rome as a province.
Mithradates of Pontus "liberates" peoples subject to Rome in Asia Minor; defeated by Rome.
Bithynia also willed to Rome in Asia Minor; Mithradates reacts with war.
Cyrene becomes Roman territory. Cyprus taken over by Rome.
Parthians defeat Crassus in war and kill him.

Cleopatra cooperates with Caesar, then with Brutus and Cassius; forgiven by Antony, marries him; defeated by Octavian, the couple are suicides; Egypt becomes Roman province.

Italy
in the 6th Century B.C.

Areas dominated by

- Greeks
- Etruscans

ALPS

Adige R.

Po R.

LIGURIA

ILLYRIA

Arno R.

ETRURIA

PICENUM

UMBRIA

Adriatic Sea

ELBA   Bolsena
(Volsinii)

Tiber R.

APENNINES

CORSICA

Rome

LATIUM

CAMPANIA

SAMNIUM

APULIA

CALABRIA

Volturnus R.
Naples

LUCANIA

Tarentum

SARDINIA

Tyrrhenian Sea

BRUTIUM

LIPARI
ISLANDS

Messina

MT. ETNA

SICILY

Syracuse

Mediterranean Sea

antiquity marveled that the land seemed one vast garden. Though the Apennine Mountains form a spine for the 600-mile-long peninsula, they do not compartmentalize the country as do the mountain ranges of Greece; moreover, the rich agricultural areas of Italy are larger than the productive valleys of Greece. Italy yielded iron ore, copper, and precious metals, but its true wealth was more a matter of cropland, pasture, forests, and above all, men to fill the ranks of army after army.

The location of Rome influenced its development throughout ancient history. In the earliest period the city's position on the Tiber about eighteen miles inland gave it both security from piracy and a valuable outlet to the sea. The roads west of the Apennines tended to converge on Rome also, for the lowest point to ford the Tiber was there. The Tiber Island also made it easy, later, to bridge the stream. From remote antiquity, roads had come down along both sides of the Tiber as well. In the next phase, the age of expansion within Italy, Rome's central location and good communications were important. Beyond Italy, the Romans first expanded westward, because in its natural geography Rome faced west. This meant that Rome waxed strong in the West before it turned to confront the sophisticated and powerful Hellenistic states in the East. Still later, when Rome's empire embraced the whole Mediterranean basin, Italy's central position eased the task of governing. It should not be thought, however, that geography alone, in any mechanical way, determined the history of Rome. Physical setting was just one important factor.

From the Alps to the heel of its bootlike peninsula, Italy stretches about 750 miles. It is relatively narrow, however, averaging only about 120 miles in width. On the east is the Adriatic Sea, with Illyria and Epirus lying beyond in ancient times; Greece lies farther to the southeast. On the west the Tyrhennian Sea is marked off by large islands: Sicily at the toe of the boot, and Sardinia and Corsica. The Alps, higher than any mountains in the United States outside Alaska, provide some natural protection for Italy, but there are numerous passes. The Apennines, less lofty, connect with the Alps on the west. Between the Alps and the Apennines nestles the Po Valley, the richest agricultural region of ancient and modern Italy; in the earliest history of Rome, however, it played almost no part.

Important areas along the west coast of ancient Italy included Etruria, located north of Rome and named after the Etruscans; Latium, where Rome was situated; Campania, a quite rich agricultural area farther south; Lucania, just south of Campania; and at the toe of the boot, Bruttium (modern-day Calabria). On the opposite side, the heel of the boot was occupied by ancient Calabria (that is, Calabria and Bruttium are reversed in modern Italy). North of Calabria, along the eastern, Adriatic coast lay Apulia; in the rough hill country inland southeast from Latium between Apulia and Campania rose Samnium; and farther north along the Adriatic lay Picenum and Umbria.

The climate of much of peninsular Italy is typically Mediterranean: Summers are dry and hot; winters are wet and cold. There is somewhat more rainfall than in Greece. In the southernmost regions, desert winds off the Sahara (the sirocco) sometimes desiccate the land. In the north, on the other hand, winds off the Alps can be freezing cold.

B. CIVILIZATION MOVES WEST: ETRUSCANS, GREEKS, PHOENICIANS

The high civilization that first developed in the ancient Near East was diffused gradually—perhaps *percolated* would be a better word—into the western Mediterranean. The Bronze Age arrived in Italy about 1800 B.C.; the Iron Age, about 900

B.C. The Bronze Age in Italy did not rest on a brilliant urban culture as it did in Mesopotamia. There were urban settlements, and excavation of some of them, as in the Neolithic Terremare culture of northern Italy, has furnished evidence of planning and orderly development. (Archaeologists of a century ago were too glowing in their reports, however.) Not until the Iron Age did the western Mediterranean achieve a high culture, largely brought in by traders and settlers. Rome was to be much influenced by these settlers: Etruscans, Greeks, and Phoenicians.

Etruscans

The mystery of Etruscan origins titillates the curiosity of everyone who studies them. Both in antiquity and in modern times scholars have argued the question. Two opposing views get the support of most scholars: Some think the Etruscans were an indigenous people, and others hold they came as immigrants to Italy in the early Iron Age, probably from the east, most likely Asia Minor. Herodotus and most other ancient historians thought the latter. Archaeology can now tell us a great deal about the physical world of the Etruscans and the development of their culture, but it has yet to verify their origins. Nor have we learned much about their government and modes of behavior from the quite extensive remains. Whatever their views, most scholars now think the question of origins is not very important, for it is likely—probably one should say certain—that the most significant aspects of Etruscan government, society, art, and craftsmanship developed within Italy in the seventh and sixth centuries B.C.

Etruscan culture first appeared in Italy in Etruria, a region named after them by the Romans. (Etruscans called themselves the Rasenna.) In the archaeological strata of Etruria this culture is superimposed immediately over an early Iron Age culture called Villanovan. Scholars who think the Etruscans were indigenous see Etruscan culture simply as a late and distinctive phase of the Villanovan; yet in other areas, Villanovan culture did not develop such distinctive features. It is hard, then, to see how the two groups could have a similar history.

Some facets of Etruscan life seem oriental. Their distinctive sculpture shows an oriental cast, and Etruscans are known to have imported art objects from Egypt and elsewhere in the East. Many of their religious practices, especially the reading of omens in the study of animal livers and entrails and their manner of burial, derived from the East. The most frustrating element of the Etruscan enigma is their language, which might help to solve the mystery if it could be read and compared with other similar languages. Since they used, basically, the Phoenician characters already adopted by the Greeks, the words themselves can easily be spelled out, and even their grammar can be partly discerned. The language may be similar to one used in the Aegean area and in Phrygia, but evidence for this is slight and indecisive.

Etruscan government rested on a loose league of twelve cities, held together more by religious than by political ties. A chief festival was the annual gathering to honor the goddess Voltumna at a site called Volsinii, probably near

Bolsena on the modern map. The priest-rulers of each of the twelve cities, who were called *lucumones,* conferred in council under the chairmanship of an official called *rex* and made common plans. Action apparently required unanimous approval. The Etruscans thus were not tightly organized politically, and different cities of the league not only pursued isolated goals but sometimes actually fought against each other.

Etruscan power reached its height in the sixth century B.C. Though never very numerous as a people, the Etruscans ruled over an extended area. They expanded north toward present-day Bologna and then across the Apennines into the rich Po Valley. They competed with the Greeks in southern Italy and won control of Campania, the richest agricultural region of the south. Rome, too, and probably all Latium came under their influence.

The Etruscans were a great trading people. For export they made objects of bronze and iron; the best deposits of copper and iron ore in all Italy lay in Etruria and on the island of Elba, just offshore. Great slag piles remain to testify to the huge amounts of iron produced in the area in antiquity. Important silver-bearing lead deposits were also exploited. Etruria produced an abundance of farm crops, and her great forests were so dense that the Romans feared them for centuries. The Etruscans maintained a merchant fleet and shared with Greeks and Carthaginians the sea trade of the West.

Trade rivalry led to conflict at sea, in which the Etruscans and the Carthaginians fought in alliance against the Greeks. In 535 B.C. the allied fleet attacked some Phocaeans who had established themselves on Corsica and forced them out of the area. Later, however, after the Greeks on Sicily had defeated the Carthaginians in a great land battle (see p. 148), an Etruscan fleet fought alone against Greeks off Cumae, about a hundred miles south of Rome (474 B.C.) and was routed. For Carthage, the defeat was only a temporary setback, but the Etruscans began a gradual but permanent decline. The revolt of Rome and other Latin states from Etruscan dominance (see pp. 235–237) was helped by Greek land and naval victories over the Etruscans in Campania and offshore during this period, and obviously, the Etruscan decline is due in considerable part to these defeats.

Planned layouts for towns were an Etruscan specialty, as the visible remains show. Settlement sites were shrewdly chosen, and fortifications were carefully designed to fit the terrain. Etruscan architecture is impressive and, again, distinctive. Through archaeological remains, tomb paintings, and reproductions on later Roman coins, we know with some certainty how an Etruscan temple looked. It was more nearly square than the Greek temple and had fewer columns and more decoration, especially on gables and friezes. Terra-cotta antefixes, more elaborate than those on Greek temples, are often found. A full-scale reconstruction of a small Etruscan temple may be seen at the Villa Giulia Museum in Rome. To the modern eye these temples, as vestiges of antiquity, seem somewhat baroque yet attractive.

The enormous hemispherical vaulted tombs, sometimes completely underground, in which the Etruscan upper classes interred their dead, have yielded most of the Etruscan art that remains to us. The best site for the tourist to inspect these fascinating tombs is at modern Cerveteri (ancient Caere), where the local museum preserves some fine objects salvaged in the vicinity. The Villa Giulia is the most comprehensive Etruscan museum. Preserved there are excellent examples of terra-cotta sculpture, especially on sarcophagi; beautiful examples of Etruscan pottery, somewhat imitative of the best Greek ware but with a distinctive oriental cast; detached wall paintings, which decorated the tombs in profusion; and the fine bronze ware the Etruscans loved.

The Romans were to learn much and borrow much from the Etruscans. They made use of Etruscan *haruspices,* or takers of omens; borrowed their temple architecture and even certain deities; and learned from them to make statues of their gods. Elements of Roman government derived from the Etruscans also: names for officials, the Senate, accouterments of office. In the field of entertainment Romans were influenced by Etruscan music, dancing, theater, and contests of various sorts, including—unfortunately—gladiatorial combats. Such influence was greatest and most direct about the sixth century B.C., when Rome was ruled by Etruscan kings, but it continued over a span of centuries. Gaius Maecenas, the friend and counselor of the Emperor Augustus, was Etruscan, and he still maintained the reputation Etruscans had as connoisseurs of sensual pleasure. The Emperor Claudius in his early life studied and wrote on both Etruscan history and language. By that time, however, there was something antiquarian about Etruscan studies, since as a people they had dissolved in Rome's melting pot.

The Greeks in the West

Arnold Toynbee, in his A *Study of History,* argues that the proper unit of historical study is the society or civilization, not individual states. Thus, he listed Rome under "Hellenic society." Whether or not this division is proper, it does underline the undoubted fact that Rome owed more to the Greeks than to any other people, that Roman culture was in many important respects a continuation of Greek culture.

The Roman debt to Greece, however, was often not a debt to the Greeks in their mainland home, but to Greeks in the West. Many first-rank Greek philosophers, poets, architects, painters, mathematicians, scientists, and politicians resided in Sicily or southern Italy. Familiar names leap to mind: Pythagoras, Parmenides, Zeno, Empedocles, Gorgias, Archimedes, Timaeus, and Diodorus, among others. Western Greeks were traders and explorers; they informed the Romans about geography. Western Greek potters, painters, town planners, and other artists and artisans often worked for the Romans. Ultimately the greatest influences did come from Greece itself, for it was there that the greatest thinkers and most of the greatest artists lived.

An increasing number of archaeological sites show that Greeks had penetrated the West already in the Mycenaean age. Homer's *Odyssey* perhaps indicates some continued familiarity with Sicily and southern Italy during the dark age that followed. Beginning in the eighth century B.C., Greeks moved westward

Detail of a sixth-century B.C. Etruscan relief; wood overlaid with bronze. (The Metropolitan Museum of Art, Rogers Fund, 1903)

in large numbers, as we have seen. Sites on the island of Ischia and at Cumae in Campania were colonized in the mid-eighth century B.C. and a large number of important sites elsewhere in southern Italy and Sicily within the following century. Greeks also settled in what is today eastern Spain and southern France. In these new lands they organized city-states like those developed in Greece; fought each other with the same abandon that Spartans, Athenians, and Thebans did; and warred against the Etruscans and Carthaginians as well.

Greek influence reached Rome first through the Etruscans, later through

Roman alliance with the Samnites in Campania (still under strong Greek influence), and still later through Roman conquest of southern Italy and Sicily. When, in the second century B.C., Rome's power enveloped Greece and Macedonia, another surge of cultural penetration resulted, and this persisted into the period of the Roman Empire.

Phoenicians

By Greek reckoning, the Phoenician colonization of the western Mediterranean occurred earlier than their own. In moving westward, Phoenicians appear to have been interested mostly in trade, whereas many Greeks simply wanted land for agriculture. Yet the Phoenicians, too, needed an agricultural base and so came to control much land around Carthage, elsewhere along the North African coast, and in western Sicily and southern Spain. Neither Greek nor Phoenician colonies were controlled from the mother city, though religious and commercial ties were strong.

When Tyre and Sidon and other Phoenician home cities were weakened and then conquered by the Assyrians and later the Babylonians, Carthage emerged as leader of the Phoenicians in the West. In western Sicily, for example, Phoenician colonists looked to nearby Carthage for assistance whenever they found themselves in conflict with the Greeks at the other end of the island. As noted previously, Carthage, in alliance with some Etruscan cities, helped to defeat Greeks based at Alalia on Corsica; Corsica went to the Etruscans, but the Carthaginians got Sardinia. However, Carthage suffered a sharp setback in Sicily in 480 B.C. when Greeks beat its army soundly in a land battle at Himera; still, the Carthaginians clung to the western third of the island, and the contest for control of Sicily went on intermittently for two more centuries, when the Romans took it over.

With both a rich trade and a productive agriculture, Carthage was well equipped to lead. Most of the land owned by Carthaginian aristocrats was worked by the native populace; Carthaginian citizenship was restricted, so that the total number of Carthaginian citizens was relatively small. A core of citizens staffed the navy and the officer corps of the army, but most soldiers were hired mercenaries from Libya, Iberia, Greece, and elsewhere. The long heritage of Phoenician seafaring and extensive trade made the navy important in Carthaginian eyes; hence, more care was given to ships and harbor facilities than to the development of a land army.

The government of Carthage was a close-knit oligarchy. The popular assembly had little power; the aristocratic senate had more, but most power resided in an inner council of the senate called "the Hundred" and in a still smaller group, known as "the Thirty." The assembly elected the chief magistrates, called *suffetes*, and also the generals. This mixed constitution was stable, at least as compared with the Greek states in the West, which alternated—sometimes *gyrated* would better describe the process—from oligarchy to democracy to tyranny.

The Carthaginians influenced the Romans most through warfare. They forced the Romans to build a navy and thus to turn to the sea. Carthage gave Rome its most severe tests. Spoils and territory won from Carthage made Rome rich and gave it the base for eventual world dominion. In some specific areas, however, the Romans learned from the Carthaginians in peace. Long before the Romans, for instance, Carthaginians developed plantation-type agriculture. The Romans found quite instructive an important book on the subject written by a man named Mago and translated into Latin in the second century B.C. In addition, some of the procedures of the Roman system of provincial government were adapted from Carthaginian ones.

C. THE MONARCHY: LEGEND AND FACT (c. 753–509 B.C.)

As everyone "knows," Rome was founded by Romulus, twin brother of Remus, in 753 B.C. This date was decided on by Marcus Terentius Varro, a Roman intellectual of the first century B.C., on the basis of available data, including that of researchers during the preceding century or two who had concerned themselves with the same problem. Some of this evidence was tenuous indeed. As for Romulus—he may have been invented a few centuries earlier to account for the name of the city. Modern archaeology provides us with some solid information unavailable to Varro; but he, in turn, had access to other important materials that are no longer available. We are forced to rely on the accounts, in particular, of the historians Livy and Dionysius of Halicarnassus, and to winnow as best we can the scanty wheat from their abundant chaff.

The Romans listed seven kings, from Romulus to Tarquinius Superbus, who ruled from 753 B.C. to 509 B.C. Each of these rulers seems rather stereotyped in the accounts. Romulus, one of twin sons of Mars by a vestal virgin, was a vigorous conqueror and assimilator. His successor Numa Pompilius, a Sabine, was a religious and political organizer. Tarquinius Superbus, the last king, was the prototype of the tyrant, who ran roughshod over the rights of other Romans—meaning, of course, the aristocracy. Although we cannot give strong credence to these stories, the king list itself may be approximately correct.

It is clear from archaeology that Rome was no more than a tiny village on a hill above a ford in the Tiber in the mid-eighth century B.C. The celebrated Forum was at this time a burial ground. As the legends said, the earliest settlement was on the Palatine. But these ancient accounts make of Rome much more than it was at a given time. The first pebble-paved streets probably were laid only in the last century of the monarchy. Contrary to the traditional Roman view, it is very doubtful that in this early era Rome dominated the other Latin states in the area. In the days of the later kings, who were probably Etruscans, Rome did develop into an important town; in comparative terms, it would be proper to call it a city. One significant piece of solid evidence is the temple of Jupiter Optimus Maximus, Juno, and Minerva, built in Etruscan style and by tradition dedicated in the year the monarchy ended and the republic was established. At the time of its construction, and consistently through several later reconstructions, it was the largest temple in all Italy.

The three Etruscan kings made Rome a prosperous city. Etruscan trade and manufacturing were centered in Etruria, of course; but as we have seen, Etruscans also controlled the rich area of Campania south of Rome. The natural land routes passed through Rome, and its strategic site made the city one of the more important regional centers in the Etruscan system. On the other hand, when Rome eventually asserted its independence, Etruscan trade bypassed the city. The result for Rome was a gradual economic decline, which has been attested to by archaeology. Romans of the early republic, for example, could no longer afford expensive imported Greek pottery. For several decades, Rome remained within the general Etruscan economic and cultural sphere of influence. Etruscan defeats by the Greeks at sea, ending the earlier, more prosperous age, had effects also in Rome, bringing a more severe economic decline by the 460s and 450s B.C.

D. THE EARLY REPUBLIC (c. 509 + B.C.)

Expulsion of the Etruscan Kingship

A primary cause for the expulsion of the Etruscans, it seems, was a change in military tactics all over Italy, similar to changes that had occurred in Greece even earlier. Armies grew larger and began to depend less on aristocratic cavalry than on heavy-armed infantry. Extremely important to the new tactics was the size of the phalanx; this meant the use of ever-larger numbers of men—mostly commoners, naturally. Etruscan kings who developed such armies necessarily depended less on the nobility. The nobles felt their power and status slipping away and reacted. The expulsion of Tarquin, then, was not so much a patriotic uprising against a foreign tyrant as it was a reactionary effort by Rome's nobles to retain their dominant position in the state. The story of Tarquin's son Sextus raping the fair Lucretia, whose suicide then actuated the heroic Lucius Junius Brutus to free the country, is most likely a romantic invention. As for the traditional date of 509 B.C., though most scholars today accept it as approximately correct, others note that Etruscan cultural influence continued into the middle of the following century and so date the beginning of the republic at about 475 B.C. to 450 B.C.

Struggle of the Orders

The Roman aristocrats who engineered the expulsion of the Tarquins and the establishment of the republic were called *patricians*; probably the leaders of patrician families had served on the Senate or advisory council to the king under the monarchy. Patricians made up the major *gentes*, or clans; those who belonged to the minor gentes were called *plebeians*. (We know of some instances in which different branches of a single *gens* were both patrician and plebeian.) The patrician class soon became a closed group which could be entered only by birth.

The struggle of the orders developed between patricians and plebeians in the early republic because of the patrician monopoly of power: Only they could serve in the top offices, the Senate, and the important priesthoods. The economic depression of the middle fifth century B.C. (and after) brought heavy loads of debt to some plebeians, and this too contributed to the conflict. Harsh laws that permitted debtors to be sold into slavery or perhaps even executed exacerbated the problem.

The patrician officials could not defend the state without a large body of infantry any more than could the kings. Using this need as leverage, the Roman plebeians over a period of time extracted concessions from the aristocrats and gradually got a greater share in government. As Rome expanded in central Italy and gave citizenship to the conquered, the struggle of the orders was refueled by new plebeians. Some of the newly assimilated citizens had been aristocrats at home, but they became plebeians in Rome. Such men often furnished the leadership for the Roman "plebs" as a whole. Plebeians eventually gained the right to hold all offices and participate in all the institutions of the state.

The struggle of the orders continued intermittently from the beginning of the republic to about 287 B.C., when the Hortensian Law (see p. 238) marked its successful end. At the same time, it should be emphasized, the plebeian class came to include many important and wealthy men. Along with the patricians, those who reached the highest offices formed an expanded aristocracy, the *nobilitas*. In time these *nobiles* guarded their acquired privileges almost as jealously as the patricians had done.

Let us look at some of the major plebeian gains in the struggle of the orders. In the fifth century B.C. plebeians gained the right to elect ten tribunes of the plebs annually. The chief function of these officials was to protect plebeian rights. Their concern, of course, was most often for upper-level plebeians; only a few tribunes interested themselves in helping lower-class plebeians. Other rights gained in this century were the codification of law (the XII Tables of 451–450 B.C., by traditional dating), the right of intermarriage with patricians, and the right to be elected military tribunes with consular power—officials who replaced consuls in most years between 444 and 367 B.C. The fourth century brought further advance: In 367 B.C. one of the Licinian-Sextian Laws provided that one consul *could* be a plebeian, and later legislation stipulated that one (at least) of the consuls *must* be a plebeian. By the end of the century, plebeians could legally serve in any elective office. The Publilian Law of 338 B.C. and the Hortensian Law of 287 B.C. gave the two popular assemblies the right to pass laws without prior approval of the Senate, as was previously required.

Government after the Struggle of the Orders

Aside from the moribund curiate assembly, which had been more important under the kings, there were two citizen assemblies in the Roman state: the Assembly of the Centuries (*comitia centuriata*) and the Assembly of the Tribes (*comitia tributa*). The centuriate assembly elected the chief magistrates, declared war, served as a court in capital cases, and passed laws. A consul usually presided over its sessions. The tribal assembly, which comprised all citizens also, was more democratic than the centuriate assembly. In the latter, the centuries were organized on the army model into cavalry and five classes of infantry. Voting began at the top and stopped when a majority was reached, so that rich patricians and plebeians usually determined the outcome. In the Assembly of the Tribes, however, placement in the tribes was on the basis of residence, not wealth, and the voting order was determined by lot. Under the presidency of a tribune, the tribal assembly without the patricians—a body usually referred to as the *concilium plebis*—elected the tribunes of the plebs. The tribal assembly, however, was usually under the presidency of a consul, and it also chose other officials, passed laws, and served as a court.

A most important body, with about three hundred members during most of the republic, was the Senate. It was composed of ex-magistrates, who served for life. Its members were appointed by the censors, who could also remove members for cause, such as immoral behavior. The Senate always gave its opinion in the form of advice to the convening magistrate, usually one of the consuls. Its decrees, called *senatus consulta,* were seldom disregarded by the magistrates and therefore usually had the force of law. As Rome expanded into empire, the Senate gradually arrogated to itself the right of assigning duties to the chief magistrates, the power of controlling state money, and (eventually) of controlling the provinces. It gained this extensive power partly because of the great experience and influence (*auctoritas*) its members possessed and partly because it could, when necessary, be in almost continuous session, whereas the citizen assemblies were unwieldy and slow to act.

The chief magistrates, elected annually, were consuls and praetors. The two consuls were the chief executives and frequently served as generals in the army. The praetors within the city were judges; outside the city they, too, might lead armies. Later, praetors and consuls often governed provinces. Consuls and praetors had *imperium,* the right to command troops. Dictators, chosen in emergencies to replace both consuls for a maximum period of six months, had *imperium* also, and more arbitrary authority. Censors, elected about every five years, took the census; assessed property for taxes; let out government contracts; and assigned men to the Senate, the cavalry, and their place in the assemblies. Like consuls and praetors, *censors* were elected in the Assembly of the Centuries. The *aediles* and *quaestors* were elected in the Assembly of the Tribes. Aediles organized major festivals and supervised trading in the Forum. Quaestors were financial officials. One quaestor was assigned to each general; two city quaestors supervised the treasury, and later, the port of Ostia, with particular attention to the important matter of grain imports. Consuls, praetors, and quaestors might on occasion have their offices extended, or prorogued, by the Senate. They were then called *proconsuls, propraetors, proquaestors.* Such an extension of command was usually for one year.

Along with the adoption of the Hortensian Law of 287 B.C., the potential power of the tribunes of the plebs increased greatly, for they could now convene the plebeian assembly and pass laws even over the objection of the Senate. At some point their veto powers were extended so that they could obstruct the action of the other assemblies or even of the Senate; they could themselves convene the Senate and put questions to it. These powers were rarely used, however, for many years.

Social Organization of the Early Republic

Early Rome was basically rural; in society, government, and religion there were tribal vestiges of sorts. One such institution, which not only survived but evolved with changing society, was the patron-client system. Most patricians, and later many plebeians, were patrons to numbers of clients. Patrons looked out for their clients' welfare, especially in connection with the courts. Clients supported their patrons; in early times, they probably did so with weapons, but in the historic period, they responded chiefly through their votes. The patron-client relationship had a religious aspect and was hereditary. This helped the aristocracy to control votes in the assemblies; the timocratic arrangement in the centuriate assembly, of course, made it easier to control the important elections in that body. The nobility thus controlled the offices, the Senate, the assemblies, and also the army, which they led. The social organization simply reflected the realities of power.

The great power and pervading influence of the family was another tribal leftover from remote antiquity. The *pater familias* retained his control over grown and married sons. It is always stressed that his power even allowed him to take the life of any member of the family, but known examples of this can be counted on the fingers of one hand. The great emphasis on family extended into the sphere of religion, leading to ancestor worship at the family hearth, and into politics, where alliances of families were able to control elections.

Early Romans worshipped a multitude of deities. Most were *numina*, powers or spirits; there were numina of fountains, streams, woods, pools, crossroads, and so on. The family gods are best known: Vesta, goddess of the hearth; the *lares* and *penates,* gods of the property boundaries and storerooms; and Janus, god of the threshold. Jupiter Capitolinus was the chief deity of the state, and there were state cults of Vesta and Janus also.

Etruscan and Greek influence led the early Romans to identify many of their deities with those of these two more civilized peoples. They taught the Romans to conceive of their gods in anthropomorphic style and provided sculptors to create their images. Jupiter was equated with Zeus, Juno became one with Hera, and Mars found analogy in Ares. Yet in many instances the Romans retained views of their gods or gave them attributes that had no counterpart in Greek conceptions. As we have seen, they began to build temples also, first in the Etruscan and later in a modified Greek manner.

Romans had a conviction that they were more religious than those peoples they conquered, especially the Greeks—and they were probably right. The chief priest at Rome, the *pontifex maximus,* was always an important official with duties going beyond pure religion. This and other priestly offices (usually in colleges), as well as the college of augurs, were always filled with laymen, not professionals. Members of an important college of women, the vestal virgins, served thirty years each and thus were actually professionals, since they had no other major pursuits.

Struggle to Survive in the Early Republic

The expulsion of the Tarquins brought not only economic depression, as we have seen, but also attempts of Etruscan leaders to regain control of the city. The Romans later told much-embellished stories of their heroic efforts to safe-guard the new freedom. Horatius, who held off an Etruscan army at the Tiber bridge, and Cincinnatus, who left his plowing to rescue a besieged Roman army, were held up to generations of Roman boys as examples of their ancestors' in-domitable courage, which they were expected to imitate.

The early books of Livy emphasize that the new republic was in constant danger from the Etruscans and other nearby peoples: the Sabines, the Volsci, and the Aequi, among others. Some sort of martial campaign was a yearly affair. Even though tradition may exaggerate, it is not unlikely that for most ancient Italian peoples, a summer's campaign was a routine part of the yearly military training for youths. Rome at length made headway against neighboring Etruscan powers. The first important victory across the Tiber in Etruscan territory was the taking of Veii, on a strongly fortified eminence north of Rome. According to tradition, a siege of ten years was required to reduce this Etruscan stronghold, which fell to the forces of another hero type, Camillus, in 396 B.C. (by the traditional dating).

The Romans did not have long to celebrate, for the most serious threat in their early history soon descended on them. Gauls from central Europe had poured into the Po Valley in recent years, thereby weakening the Etruscans as they drove them out of that area. In 390 B.C. the Gauls (Senones) moved down

The reverse of this first century B.C. denarius shows the temple of Jupiter Optimus Maximus as it was before the fire and reconstruction after Sulla.

into central Italy; their chief aim was perhaps to despoil the Etruscan cities north of Rome, and they sought alliance with Rome. But the Romans chose to oppose rather than cooperate with them. The result was a disastrous battle just north of Rome at the Allia, a tributary of the Tiber. Rome itself was then taken and burned, except for the citadel on the Capitoline Hill.

After a time, the Romans scraped together a rich ransom to negotiate the withdrawal of the Gauls. Camillus, who was made dictator, reorganized the army and defeated the Gauls the following year. Then the city was rebuilt. Rome now grew stronger than ever. The later Romans thought their city had dominated the Latins even during the reign of the kings, and that this dominance was maintained through alliances formed in the early years of the republic. The facts, however, seem to indicate that Roman conquest of the Latins came about only in the middle decades of the fourth century B.C.

BOOKS FOR FURTHER READING

BANTI, L. *Etruscan Cities and Their Culture*, Berkeley, 1973.

BLOCH, R. *The Etruscans*, London, 1958.

BLOCH, R. *The Origins of Rome*, New York, 1960.

GRIMAL, P. *In Search of Ancient Italy*, London, 1964.

HARRIS, W. *Rome in Etruria and Umbria*, Oxford, 1971.

HUS, A. *The Etruscans*, New York, 1961.

MACKENDRICK, P. *The Mute Stones Speak; The Story of Archaeology in Italy*, New York, 1960.

OGILVIE, R. *Early Rome and the Etruscans*, Atlantic Highlands, N.J., 1976.

PALLOTTINO, M. *The Etruscans*, rev. ed., Bloomington, Ind., 1975.

PALMER, R. *The Archaic Community of the Romans*, Cambridge, 1970.

RICHARDSON, E. *The Etruscans: Their Art and Civilization*, Chicago, 1964.

SCULLARD, H. *The Etruscan Cities and Rome*, Ithaca, N.Y., 1967.

WOODHEAD, A. *The Greeks in the West*, New York, 1962.

14

IMPERIAL EXPANSION:

rome creates a republican empire

The reasons why Rome expanded into a world empire are of course manifold. For almost any people in antiquity, expansion required no justification. If opportunity presented itself for successful penetration of a region worth the taking, moral scruples rarely hindered action. Much of Rome's expansion was of just that sort—opportunistic. Certainly there was no overall blueprint for conquest, no master plan; no one foresaw the end from the beginning. Quite often, it was a matter of one thing leading to another. Alliance against a common foe often brought with it responsibility to aid the ally against a new foe. Possession of new territory brought with it the responsibility to protect it. In any age, when semicivilized areas abut lands controlled by a highly organized power, the latter is drawn into the less-developed areas as if by a kind of magnet.

Most of the time Roman statesmen pursued a step-by-step course, solving immediate problems in the forthright, sometimes crude and cruel, Roman way. Principles did guide the Romans: They would never surrender nor negotiate from weakness, but always fight to a successful end; they were as firm (or cruel) as necessary to accomplish the goal; they punished any disorder like rebellion severely.

It must be admitted that in some wars, especially during the late republic, Roman leaders were motivated by conscious imperialism. "To the victor belong the spoils" was a concept generally accepted in antiquity. Sometimes Romans fought chiefly because victory would bring profit to individuals as well as to the state. Whatever the reasons, Romans fought often and usually won. Gradually they raised the city on the Tiber to world dominion.

**Growth of Roman Dominions
under the Republic
509-44 B.C.**

Rome, 500 B.C.

264 B.C. (start of First Punic War)

146 B.C. (close of Third Punic War)

44 B.C. (at death of Caesar)

■ Battle sites

A. TOWARD DOMINANCE IN ITALY

The Latin Revolt (341–338 B.C.)

Rome's relationship with its nearest neighbors, as we have seen, had been forged through struggle and alliance over a rather long period. The "revolt" of 341 B.C. grew out of Latin resentment because Rome's increased strength was changing the real conditions of their alliances. The treaties were no longer between equals; they only ensured Roman domination. Most important was the outcome of the struggle. Once the Romans had won, they cemented ties with these nearby Latin and some Italian states and so set the pattern—comparatively enlightened and therefore enduring—for the later organization of all Italy.

The sensible, restrained settlement of 338 B.C. permitted almost all the states involved to retain autonomy at home, to continue to elect their own officials, and to collect their own taxes. None of them could make treaties with anyone else, however, and all had to supply troops to serve with Roman armies in the field. The nearest Latin states were actually incorporated into Rome, and their citizens received full Roman citizenship. The *fasti*—lists of officeholders in Rome—soon began to include the names of some of these new citizens. This demonstrates to us that they had equal opportunity to reach high office; in this way some new citizens even entered the nobility, though they could not become patricians, of course.

Latin states not incorporated into Rome became close and respected, though dependent, allies with rights of trade and intermarriage as well as self-government. Inhabitants of Italian states which had participated on the side of the rebellious Latins were made citizens without the right to vote or hold office in Rome. Though they controlled their own affairs, they were directly subject to Roman magistrates, whereas the Latin allies were not. Within a period of a century and a half, however, citizens of these states also gained the vote in Rome.

This wise policy ensured the loyalty of Rome's neighbors in the heart of Italy. The bonds created were to withstand even the terrific stresses created by Hannibal's invasion in the next century. As Rome conquered the Italian Peninsula, the subjugated peoples were given similar treaties and brought into the alliance system on the same strong basis: autonomy in internal affairs at home, treaties with Rome only, and a commitment to serve with Rome's armies.

The Samnites

The most stubborn opponents blocking Rome's rise to dominance in Italy were the Samnites. Kinspeople of the Romans and other Italians, the Samnites mainly inhabited the hill country east and south of Rome; some Samnites lived in Campania, which they had seized when Etruscan control faltered. The Samnite League, in area and population, was perhaps double the size of Rome with its Latin allies. Romans and Samnites made an alliance in 354 B.C., perhaps against the Gauls, who occasionally ravaged Italian cities from Umbria, where they had settled.

The First Samnite War (343–341 B.C.) seems to have been caused by Roman willingness to offend the Samnite hillfolk in order to gain a foothold in Campania through alliance with the plains Samnites (Oscans), who dominated Campania from their capital at Capua. Some of the hill Samnites attacked the Oscans (they were competing for iron-rich border country), and Rome came to the rescue. The war was decided in a single battle, obviously a Roman victory, though the ensuing peace was a negotiated one. Rome now held Campania in firm alliance, and her extended power equalled that of the weakened Samnite League.

Both Romans and Samnites fought to keep their own allies in line in the period immediately following the First Samnite War. Rome's struggle with its Latin and nearby Italian allies was just discussed. At the same time, both Romans and Samnites prepared for a second conflict. Rome irritated the Samnites by planting colonies on the fringes of Samnite territory to strengthen its communications corridor to Campania, and the Samnites encroached on central and southern Campania to strengthen their position against Rome.

The Second Samnite War (c. 327–304 B.C.) severely tested Rome. At the Caudine Forks, a few miles east of Capua, a full-size Roman army of perhaps 10,000 men—Roman historians said 20,000—with both consuls was forced to surrender (321 B.C.). Late in the war the Etruscans joined the Samnites, thus forcing Rome to fight on two fronts. But Rome gained allies in Apulia and elsewhere in south Italy, doggedly persevered, and won a favorable peace. Some territory on the western fringes of Samnium became Roman, and Rome established Latin colonies in Apulia east of Samnium, hemming it in. The Roman strategic position was therefore distinctly improved.

Rome's burgeoning power alarmed all her neighbors and quickly brought on the Third Samnite War (298–290 B.C.). Only the Romans' superior manpower reserves enabled them to win this conflict, since they had to maintain three separate armies, dangerously dispersed, in Apulia, Campania, and Latium, for the Samnites had persuaded both Etruscans and Gauls to ally with them. The Romans won a crucial battle in 295 B.C. at Sentinum in Umbria, which prevented the linkup of all three allies. It was a desperate fight, won only after the Roman consul Publius Decius Mus inspired his flagging men by "devoting" himself—and the enemy!—to the inferior gods; he then plunged to a sacrificial death amid the ranks of the enemy. The Roman troops, reinvigorated by this sure omen, fought on to victory. In the peace settlement, Rome took some of the best Samnite and Gallic lands. The remaining Samnite states, along with some Etruscan ones, were forced into the Roman alliance system. Roman dominance over Italy was now assured, though the fighting was far from over.

The Pyrrhic War (281–275 B.C.)

The alliances made during the Samnite wars and the conquest of Samnium itself involved Rome with south Italy. The Greek states there had always contended with each other and with their neighbors, the Lucanians. The most powerful of the Greek states was Tarentum, which three times within the previous century had hired whole mercenary armies to come to Italy from Greece and fight its land battles. In fourth-century Greece, even King Agesilaus of Sparta had led an army in the pay of a king of Egypt; and after Alexander the Great, Greek mercenary armies fought all over the Mediterranean. The Tarentines, then, fearing the growing power of the state on the Tiber and certain that Greeks could be found to fight for their cause, decided to challenge Rome. When a small Roman naval fleet sailed into southern waters, ostensibly to aid the Greek city Thurii against the Lucanians, Tarentum invoked an old treaty limiting the range of Roman ships, then attacked and sank the Roman fleet. A Roman embassy, according to Roman sources, lodged a protest, only to be insulted by the Tarentines. And the war was soon on.

The army brought in by the Tarentines was that of King Pyrrhus of Epirus, across the Adriatic. Pyrrhus, related by marriage to Alexander the Great, was a great but capricious general who was always seeking new adventures before present business was settled. Twice he had the throne of Macedonia within his grasp, but each time he withdrew prematurely. Now he saw a great opportunity; apparently he hoped to control all of southern Italy and Sicily.

Pyrrhus's superior cavalry and his elephants gave him the edge in a first battle against the Romans at Heraclea in 280 B.C. The following year he won a second battle, at Asculum in Apulia. Both battles were hard-fought and indecisive. The Romans may have invented the story of the Greek general's remark that if he won another such battle he was lost, but the term *Pyrrhic victory* still describes a battle won at too great a cost to the victor.

Pyrrhus now took his army off to fight for Greeks in Sicily against the Carthaginians. There also he was successful but found it tiresome to reduce the Carthaginian forts along the western coast. Nor did the Sicilian Greeks, in wild gratitude, declare him monarch of all he surveyed. Meanwhile, Rome was again making headway in southern Italy. Pyrrhus returned in response to the call for help and fought the Romans once more. This battle, at Beneventum in 275 B.C., Pyrrhus lost, though his army was by no means destroyed. He went back to what seemed better opportunities in Macedonia and the Peloponnese. A short time later, just as his troops were successfully storming the Greek city of Argos, Pyrrhus was killed—ironically, by an old woman. She threw a roof tile that hit him on the head and someone with a sword finished him off.

Rome now forced the defeated Greek cities of southern Italy into alliance in the familiar pattern. The only difference was that whereas most allies furnished troops to fight with the Roman army, the Greeks contributed ships and men to the Roman navy. During this same period the Romans also subdued the remaining Etruscan states, in a struggle that continued until 265 B.C.—a date that marks the end of their Italic phase of expansion. Rome now controlled all of the Italian Peninsula south of the Po Valley through its alliance system.

B. ROME'S GREATEST CHALLENGE: THE PUNIC WARS

Carthage was a great sea power, concerned primarily with trade. Rome was still a nation of small farmers with only a minuscule navy, reflecting slight interest in seaborne commerce. The two nations had made treaties of alliance on at least three occasions, most recently against Pyrrhus, when he had invaded Sicily. It is one of history's anomalies that within a decade these recent allies were locked in protracted, bitter struggle.

With Rome's growing alliances, however, interests and responsibilities had increased. No longer was this a small state on the Tiber primarily concerned with Latium. The same factors that caused the Greeks to struggle with Carthage over a period of two centuries—mostly in Sicily—could now induce a serious confrontation between Rome and Carthage. A minor crisis at a strategically sensitive spot that both states might wish to control would make this clear.

First Punic War (264–241 B.C.)

The focus of the trouble we refer to was Messina, the Sicilian city on the vital straits between Sicily and the Italian mainland. These straits control the Tyrrhenian Sea, off the western Italian and northern Sicilian shores. At that point, Messina was in the hands of the Mamertines, Campanian (Samnite) mercenaries formerly in the service of Syracuse, who sometime before had massacred the men of Messina and taken the women for themselves. Young King Hiero of Syracuse attempted to take the city and punish the renegades. The Mamertines called on Carthage for support; then, for good measure, they also called on Rome. Always interested in curbing Greek power in Sicily, Carthage responded. After some delay, the Romans did so also and, by trickery, gained control of the city. Carthage called home its general in command and executed him, presumably for stupidity, and then declared war.

King Hiero first sought alliance with Carthage. Later, under threat of siege, he allied himself with the Romans, an alliance he was to keep for fifty years. Rome soon discovered how hard it was to win a land war in Sicily without control of the seas. With this incentive, the Romans built their first real fleet, equipping the ships with a special boarding bridge, nicknamed the *corvus* ("crow") from its beaklike appearance. This made possible unorthodox tactics involving the use of more infantrymen aboard ship. The Roman fleet defeated the Carthaginian, but its vessels were soon lost to the elements. Throughout the war, a major problem for Rome was to build ships and to find admirals: Roman generals were versed only in land warfare. Carthage's main difficulty was altogether different: to hire enough mercenaries and to find capable generals to lead them.

The Romans opened a new phase of this costly war with an invasion of North Africa under the consul Marcus Atilius Regulus in 256 B.C., following the example of an earlier Greek tyrant of Syracuse, Agathocles. Carthage's unpopularity with the African natives who were her subjects made such invasions feasible. Regulus gained local support and defeated a Carthaginian army. Carthage now wished to negotiate peace, but Regulus demanded nothing less than unconditional surrender. The Carthaginians therefore sent out recruiters to collect mercenaries and hired a Spartan general, Xanthippus, to lead them. The next year Regulus was soundly defeated and captured along with most of his army. This event points up a common misconception—that citizen troops were better than mercenaries. The mercenaries were in fact better, but Rome and its allies could muster more men than the Carthaginians could hire.

Members of Regulus's family may later have invented the story of how the general was sent back to Rome with peace terms, which he then recommended that the Senate reject—this in spite of the fact that he had given his word that he would return to Carthage, and also in spite of the fact that he could expect severe treatment from his captors. The tale has it that he was tortured to death on his return. The story entered the canon of patriotic tales reiterated to every generation of Roman youngsters to teach them hardihood and dedication to the state above all.

Rome had mobilized a fleet of fighting ships and transports and succeeded in saving a part of the army of Regulus. Ironically, the rescue fleet was then almost entirely destroyed in a storm. In this disastrous campaign alone, Rome lost nearly 100,000 men. By 250 B.C. Rome had lost two more fleets with most of the men aboard, partly because of enemy action and partly because of storms. After a lull, Rome managed one last desperate effort, building another fleet of ships of improved design with money scraped up partly by private contributions. A Carthaginian fleet was defeated near Sicily, off Drepana; the fortified cities of western Sicily began to fall one by one. Suddenly the exhausting struggle was over (242 B.C.). Rome got Sicily and an indemnity of 3,200 talents, to be paid by Carthage in installments over a ten-year period.

The Carthaginians soon were embroiled in a bitter war with their own mercenaries; they had promised them large bonuses but now refused to pay because the war was lost. This mercenary war extended even to Sardinia. When the Romans saw Carthage sending troops to that island, so near the Italian coast, they declared the action a breach of the peace and sent an ultimatum. Carthage could only back down and accept terms. Rome now seized Sardinia and Corsica also and added another 1,200 talents to the indemnity Carthage was to pay. This action of Rome in 238 B.C. naturally infuriated the Carthaginians, and none more than Hamilcar Barca, an effective general who had kept the Romans off-balance in Sicily in the last phase of the recent war for as long as Carthage's fleet brought supplies. Hamilcar took his young son before an altar of Tanit, Carthage's chief deity, and made the nine-year-old swear he would always be an enemy of Rome. The son's name? Hannibal.

Second Punic War (219–201 B.C.)

Once the mercenary war was settled at Carthage, Hamilcar Barca led the Carthaginians in a vigorous attempt to restore their prosperity and power. He took an army into Spain, reasserted Carthage's former control there, and expanded north along the eastern coast. He extracted silver from mines in the area and found new ones. When he died in 231 B.C., he was succeeded by his son-in-law, Hasdrubal. Ten years later he too was killed, and Hannibal became commander. Perhaps the Barcids ruled Spain as a sort of personal empire, but their success brought them support in Carthage.

The Romans, though preoccupied with other matters in this period, nevertheless were concerned over the Carthaginian conquest of Spain. To a Roman query about this expansion, Hasdrubal answered that they were only trying to get enough money to pay the Roman indemnity—a reasonable enough reply. About

225 B.C., however, the Romans were prodded by their Greek allies of Massilia (modern Marseilles) to curb the Carthaginian expansion. A treaty was drawn up by which the Carthaginians agreed to stay south of the Ebro River. A complication, however, was left unsettled; Rome had another commitment in the area: an alliance with the city of Saguntum, south of the Ebro. From the Carthaginian point of view, if this commitment was made before the Ebro accord, it was cancelled by the treaty; if the alliance was made after the treaty, it was a clear violation of it. (Some later Roman historians felt sensitive enough about this to falsify the location of Saguntum, placing it *north* of the Ebro.)

However it was, Hannibal understood well enough when he attacked Saguntum in 219 B.C. that his action would mean a second war with Rome. Perhaps the time seemed propitious. The Romans had just repelled a Gallic invasion from the Po Valley and were attempting to colonize that region. Thus, all the Gauls in the valley were now enemies of Rome. Moreover, Rome was embroiled in Illyria. Piracy in the Adriatic had brought complaints from allies, and when diplomacy failed to suppress the freebooters, Rome sent military units to do the job. In addition, Hannibal had a large army, trained to a fine edge, and was ready for revenge on the Romans. To get full support from Carthage itself, however, he wanted the Romans to force the issue. Saguntum was just the instrument he needed. During several months of the siege of Saguntum, the Romans mopped up as best they could in Illyria and the Po Valley; then the Roman Senate sent an embassy to Carthage. The two sides could agree only to go to war.

The Romans planned to invade North Africa again, but Hannibal's famous march changed their plans. In the summer of 218 B.C., with 30,000 or 40,000 men, including some fine cavalry and elephants, Hannibal moved across the Pyrenees and through southern France; in early fall he crossed the Alps and proceeded down into the Po Valley. His army had suffered from the rigors of early snows in the Alps and even more by the opposition of Alpine tribesmen. The latter were not pro-Roman, but they automatically fought any army passing through their territory. A Roman army sent out from Italy had missed Hannibal's army because the Romans thought the Carthaginian objective was Massilia, an ally in southern France. Most of this Roman army then went on into Spain. This decision, to create a second theater of operations there, was decisive for the ultimate victory, but there were long intervening years when it must have seemed a mistake.

In November Hannibal crushed a full-sized Roman army at the battle of the Trebia River (a tributary of the upper Po), where he set an ambush and overwhelmed the unwary Romans. Then he spent the winter recruiting Gauls. In 217 B.C. Hannibal moved south into central Italy by an unexpected path. In the marshes he contracted a fungus infection and lost an eye. Near Lake Trasimene he won a second major battle. Again, the Romans were ambushed and driven into the lake, where many drowned. After this disaster the Romans chose a dictator, Quintus Fabius Maximus, whose delaying, harassing tactics against Hannibal gained him the surname Cunctator ("Delayer") and the reputation of having saved Rome.

What Hannibal chiefly desired was to break up the Roman alliance system.

Fabius tried to prevent this. It was most significant that all of Rome's older allies save one—Capua—stuck firmly with Rome. These allies furnished about half the manpower that made possible the eventual victory.

In the fateful year 216 B.C., two consuls at the head of a reinforced army decided to engage Hannibal in battle once more. At Cannae in Apulia, on ground chosen by Hannibal, a Roman army superior in size to the Carthaginian pushed its way into a tactical trap; most of the Romans, squeezed tightly into a milling mass by Hannibal's superior cavalry, never got into the fight, and most were slaughtered. Rome reported its losses that day at 80,000; actual losses were considerably less, but this was the most severe defeat the Romans ever suffered in their rise to power.

The situation worsened; now Rome's most recent allies in southern Italy went over to Hannibal. The City of Syracuse in Sicily (its ruler Hiero had just died) joined the Carthaginian side. Worst of all, potentially, Philip V of Macedonia, irritated by Roman penetration of Illyria, east of the Adriatic, in what he considered his sphere of influence, made formal alliance with Hannibal. Rome's fortunes reached their lowest ebb; but Rome, as always, fought on doggedly. The Senate even refused to ransom the prisoners captured at Cannae.

After Cannae, Rome gradually recovered ground against Hannibal's best efforts. In Sicily, Marcus Claudius Marcellus besieged and took Syracuse (212 B.C.); it was in the capture that Archimedes was killed. On the Italian mainland, Rome was able to besiege and recover Capua, even though Hannibal made a feint to the walls of Rome to draw the Roman army away from the city. A little later, Tarentum fell into Roman hands. Marcellus won two or three unimportant battles against Hannibal himself in southern Italy. The Carthaginian general Hanno even lost his camp at Beneventum. Yet, amazingly, though without adequate reserves and money, Hannibal's mixed army never faltered. There is no mention of mutiny in any of the accounts.

Philip of Macedonia never sent aid to Hannibal. Rome sent a few troops to Greece, made an alliance with the Aetolian League, and won minor successes against Philip's allies. Roman control of the Adriatic prevented more vigorous action by Macedonia; then, too, Philip had other fish to fry (see p. 250).

It was in Spain that the most portentous events took place in these years. Two Scipio brothers, one the father of the great Scipio, fell in battle in 212 B.C. Thereupon, in 210 B.C. Publius Cornelius Scipio (later known as Scipio Africanus Major) was by a vote of the Roman people given the Spanish command, though he was young and had not held the usual offices. Scipio swiftly conquered New Carthage, the main base of the Carthaginians. He was sure that he had the help of the gods: An unusually low water level left the city's sea walls vulnerable. Scipio attributed his good fortune to a close relationship with Jupiter Optimus Maximus, with whom he had communed in the temple on the Capitol before leaving Rome. By 206 B.C. Scipio had driven all Carthaginians from Spain.

Scipio made only one major error: He permitted Hasdrubal, the brother of Hannibal, to escape from the Iberian Peninsula with an army in 208 B.C. The following year, having followed Hannibal's earlier path, Hasdrubal was in Italy. Roman counterintelligence, by intercepting a message, prevented Hannibal from learning accurately of Hasdrubal's movements. In a daring maneuver, the Roman army facing Hannibal left its camp, marched 240 miles in six days, and joined another force opposing Hasdrubal near the Metaurus River in Umbria. The combined armies annihilated the Carthaginian troops (207 B.C.). Hannibal was informed of the catastrophe when Hasdrubal's head was tossed over the wall of his camp. Another effort to reinforce Hannibal by sea led by his other brother, Mago, failed (205–203 B.C.).

Scipio returned to Rome in 206 B.C., in time to be chosen consul for the year 205 B.C. and to receive command of an invasion force. Late the following year (now as proconsul) he crossed from Sicily into North Africa. In 203 B.C., Hannibal was recalled by the Carthaginians to undertake the defense of Carthage itself. For more than fifteen years he had suffered no major defeat during his stay in Italy, but in 202 B.C., at Zama Regia, Hannibal was defeated by Scipio in a decisive battle. Scipio had the aid of Numidian cavalry; moreover, Hannibal's elephants misbehaved and did more damage to the Carthaginian troops than to the Romans. Yet it was Scipio's flexible tactics that earned the victory. Scipio soon took the rather grandiose surname "Africanus." Carthage had no options left and capitulated.

By the peace treaty drawn up in 201 B.C., Carthage gave up Spain, which Rome soon converted into two provinces, Hither and Farther Spain. Carthage had to reduce the size of its fleet and army and had to pay, over a period of fifty years, an indemnity of 10,000 talents. Carthage also was forbidden to wage war without Rome's permission.

The Second Punic War against the forces of Hannibal was the most important that Rome ever fought, and Zama was one of the most important battles. Though the battle on the Metaurus River had meant the turn of fortune in Italy, right up to the end of the war it was questionable whether Rome would emerge merely as a survivor of the most serious threat it had ever faced or as the dominant power in the western Mediterranean. The victory at Zama ensured that Rome would be dominant. As events would soon show, Rome could now dominate not only the western but also the whole Mediterranean basin. A loss at Zama would still have left Rome one of the great Mediterranean powers; victory made possible the eventual vast empire.

C. ROMAN PENETRATION OF THE EASTERN MEDITERRANEAN

Second Macedonian War (200–196 B.C.)

Rome had concluded a separate peace with Philip of Macedonia in 205 B.C., ending the First Macedonian War; yet some Roman leaders felt that Philip's alliance with Hannibal after Cannae was a low blow that merited sterner retri-

The standard early type of the silver denarius, Rome's major coin during the middle centuries. First struck during the Second Punic War. On the obverse, left, the goddess Roma, on the reverse, right, the gods Castor and Pollux as horsemen.

bution. Moreover, Rome's Greek allies clamored for action. A Senate recommendation to the assembly for war against Macedonia came in 200 B.C., only a year after the peace with Carthage. The war-weary Romans voted down the motion. A few months later, however, with impassioned oratory a Roman consul assured the assembly that it was not a question of whether there would be war but, rather, whether it would be fought in Greece or, if Rome delayed, in Italy itself. With Hannibal's successes still fresh in their minds, the Romans now voted for war.

Decisive action did not come until 198 B.C. The young consul Titus Quinctius Flamininus persuaded the Achaean League to join the alliance Rome already had with the Aetolian League. The following year, at Cynoscephalae in Thessaly, the Roman legions first met the Macedonian phalanx. With considerable help from the Aetolians, the more flexible legions took advantage of a break in the phalanx and won a resounding victory, which virtually ended the war. Afterward Flamininus persuaded the Senate to adopt a liberal policy for all Greece. The Romans did not wish to disturb the existing balance of power, and so Philip was let off with only the loss of recently acquired territory and a small indemnity of 1,000 talents.

Many Greeks feared they had exchanged one master—Macedonia—for another, but at the Isthmian games of 196 B.C., Flamininus announced dramatically that Rome would withdraw entirely, leaving all the Greek states free. This announcement brought such wild rejoicing that the games were cancelled. Surviving inscriptions show that some Greeks made Flamininus a god. The Greeks were to learn, however, that Rome expected such beneficence to bring its reward. The Greek states were expected to behave much as client behaved toward patron within the Roman social structure. Overt ingratitude to the Romans would be considered disloyalty, deserving punishment. But the jubilant Greeks could hardly know this—yet.

The Syrian War (192–189 B.C.)

Members of the Aetolian League were disgruntled by the peace terms. They had expected to profit handsomely from the defeat of Macedonia, since they had been allied with Rome for many years and had fought at Cynoscephalae. Instead, Rome's liberal policy meant little booty and almost no territorial gain for them. Despite Flamininus' fancy phrases, it became evident that Roman influence in the eastern Mediterranean would remain great. The Aetolians therefore sought a way to redress the balance and found it, they thought, in King Antiochus III (r. 223–c. 187 B.C.), the Seleucid ruler of Syria.

Antiochus' prime political and military objective was to rule the largest possible territory—at least all that was dominated by his most successful Seleucid ancestors, and possibly all that was ruled by Alexander the Great. He had recently taken lower Syria and Palestine from the Ptolemies of Egypt; now he needed a foothold in Europe. He wanted control of Thrace, and perhaps he wanted much more. Certainly Antiochus wished an end to Roman intervention in the eastern Mediterranean. To this end he concluded an alliance with the Aetolians.

This alliance would assuredly mean war with Rome if Antiochus brought troops to Greece. Rome had already given the Syrian king an ultimatum. Probably the chief reason for Rome's concern was Hannibal, for about him some Romans were almost psychotic. Hannibal had stayed in Carthage for a few years after the peace of 201 B.C., but then he heard—whether correctly, we cannot say—that the Romans intended to demand that he be surrendered to them. Therefore he fled and found refuge at the court of Antiochus, where of course he schemed against Rome.

Another element in Rome's opposition to Antiochus was the role of Pergamum. This kingdom in Asia Minor had joined the alliance against Philip in the First Macedonian War (concurrent with the Second Punic War) and had fought with a Greek coalition against Philip and Antiochus, who had begun gobbling up territory in Asia Minor and the Aegean islands toward the end of the third century B.C. Now the Attalid King Eumenes II (r. 197–159 B.C.) feared that Antiochus' ambitions included the acquisition of Pergamum; hence he played on Roman fears and fought along with them in the war.

First Rome and its allies defeated the inadequate army assembled by Antiochus and the Aetolians in Greece, at Thermopylae (191 B.C.). Then Rome sent an army into Asia Minor. There, at Magnesia, with great help from Eumenes' cavalry, the Romans crushed Antiochus in a major battle at the end of 190 B.C. The Roman commander was Lucius Scipio, brother of Africanus—who, of course, became "Asiaticus." In the peace that followed, Rome again took over no territory, though Antiochus was deprived of all his lands in Asia Minor. Most of these were given to Eumenes and the Rhodians, whose fleet had helped defeat Antiochus' navy, which was under the command of Hannibal. The Carthaginian exile fled again and took refuge with Prusias, king of Bithynia, whom he urged to war against Eumenes of Pergamum, Rome's friend and ally. When Rome demanded that Prusias deliver Hannibal up, the great Carthaginian leader ended his life with poison about 182 B.C.

If the Romans took no lands they did take a tremendous indemnity (15,000 talents), to be paid on the installment plan, and required that Antiochus' fleet be reduced and his elephant corps eliminated. A year later, as he was taking treasure from a temple in an effort to pay off the Romans, Antiochus was killed by a priest.

The Roman army took a tour about Asia Minor, accepting or forcing the surrender of various territories—and accepting "gifts" from the cities as well. Such pacification was needed, however; some Gallic tribes there were unstable and warlike. Not only Roman commanders but also individual soldiers profited tremendously from this war, especially in the subsequent military tour. Some later Roman historians date the moral decline of Rome from these campaigns, with their debilitating spoils.

Third Macedonian War (171–167 B.C.)

Though King Philip cooperated without actually participating in the war against Antiochus, relations between Macedonia and Rome were always strained. Inhabitants of border territories were continually appealing to Rome against Philip's ambitions, and Rome usually ruled against the Macedonian king. During these decades every Greek who had a grievance tended to present his case at Rome. The Romans were contemptuous of what they thought of as sniveling Greeks, but they were flattered too; and it was noticed that the decisions tended to favor those who first appealed to Rome. Thus Rome was constantly involved in Greek affairs.

Philip greatly strengthened his army and his treasury, and the Romans thought he was building up to another challenge. They were offended, also, at Philip's decision on a successor. His elder son, Perseus, was born of a secondary wife, whereas the younger, Demetrius, was wellborn. Demetrius, who had spent some years in Rome as a hostage and had made friends with influential Romans, attempted to persuade his father to follow a pro-Roman course. Perseus, with forged documents, convinced his father that Demetrius was traitorous; Philip thereupon had his younger son executed. Thus, when Perseus succeeded Philip at his death in 179 B.C., he was already in bad odor with Rome. The Romans interpreted his continuation of Philip's policies as proof that he also intended to fight Rome when ready. The Greeks brought numerous charges against Perseus at Rome, and the Romans believed some of them. King Eumenes of Pergamum even made a special journey to Rome to accuse Perseus before the Senate. When Eumenes was waylaid afterward and nearly killed as he journeyed toward Delphi in Greece, the Romans were ready to believe that Perseus had ordered the murder attempt and that the incident confirmed the charges Eumenes had made.

There seems little doubt that Perseus did not want to fight, and that he was forced into an unjustified war. As Rome prepared to declare war (171 B.C.), he offered to capitulate on the same terms given his father after Cynoscephalae, but the Romans would have none of it. From the vantage point of history it often seems that there was a kind of inevitability about Roman victory. But if Perseus had been a little freer with his money and a little more adept at diplomacy, Rome might well have lost—and thereafter might have stayed out of the eastern Mediterranean. However, under command of the consul Lucius Aemilius Paullus, son of the consul of the same name killed at Cannae, a Roman army in a close-fought battle again crushed the Macedonian phalanx, at Pydna in 168 B.C. Perseus was eventually captured and led in a triumph into Rome, where he died or was killed.

Rome still did not annex Macedonia, which was instead divided up into four separate republics. Of course, Perseus' property became spoils for Rome; his treasury, more or less intact, was seized, and his library was sent to Rome, to become the first important one in that city. Paullus also inflicted punishment on the Epirotes, who had supported Perseus. Scores of their towns were destroyed, and 150,000 of their men were sold into slavery. Part of the reason for this unwarranted brutality was that the Roman soldiers did not feel they had been given enough loot after the combat in Macedonia.

Even without annexation of land, imperialism was quite profitable—so much so that from this time on (167 B.C.), no Romans living in Italy paid any direct taxes into the state treasury.

Wars Against Macedonia, the Achaean League, and Carthage (149–146 B.C.)

No long explanation is needed for the Fourth, and last, Macedonian War. Division of the country had meant artificial restraints on trade; the silver mines had been closed down. Economically, the country was in ruins. A man who claimed to be a son of Perseus raised a rebellion, which the Romans put down (149–148 B.C.). The commanding general was one Metellus, who naturally then called himself "Macedonicus." Now at last Macedonia became a province of Rome.

The Greek war, waged mostly against members of the Achaean League, came about because the Greeks were goaded beyond endurance by restrictive Roman policies. Rome's troubles with Macedonia and Carthage also made the timing seem propitious. Hence, Roman ambassadors were insulted, and war ensued. As an object lesson, the Roman General Lucius Mummius destroyed Corinth, a center of the revolt (146 B.C.). Greece was not formally organized as a province but was in the same situation, under the tutelage of the governor of Macedonia. A little more than a century later, Augustus organized it into a separate imperial province called Achaea.

The origins of the Third Punic War are more complicated than can be fully discussed here. Scipio Africanus had made an ally in North Africa of King Masinissa of Numidia. At the end of the Second Punic War, Numidian territory had been increased at the expense of Carthage. In the following decades Masinissa often encroached on Carthaginian territory, and since the Carthaginians could not go to war without Roman approval, they could only appeal to Rome—and Roman commissions usually decided in Masinissa's favor. In 149 B.C. an anti-Roman party gained ascendancy in Carthage in the wake of Masinissa's latest land grab, raised an army, and went to war with Numidia, contrary to the treaty with Rome. Masinissa, of course, called on his ally, and Rome responded. It is well known that some Romans, notably old Cato (see p. 264), already favored war.

When Rome declared war, there was a reaction in Carthage. The men in the city responsible for the policy that had brought down on them Rome's declaration of war were executed. Ambassadors were sent to Rome to offer a negotiated surrender, only to be told that the consul would see them back in Africa. Once arrived there with an army, the consul called on the Carthaginians to surrender their arms. They surrendered 100,000 sets—which does seem a large quantity, since Carthage had already outfitted a well-equipped army then in the field against Numidia. Once they had given up their arms, the Carthaginians were told to evacuate their city: It was to be destroyed. In revulsion, another overturn brought new leaders to power in the city. The appeasers were executed, Carthage's gates were closed, and her walls were manned. Men and women worked desperately to make arms and equipment; amazingly, the Carthaginians held out for three years against the much superior Roman forces. The Roman general who finally took and destroyed the city in 146 B.C. was Publius Cornelius Scipio, called Aemilianus because he was a Scipio only by adoption; he was actually the son of the Aemilius Paullus who had defeated Perseus. Like his adoptive grandfather, he took the surname Africanus.

Carthaginians who survived the ruin were transplanted elsewhere in North Africa. The city was leveled, its site cursed and strewn with salt. Some traces of Carthaginian culture lingered on. The territory itself, however, became a Roman province called Africa. Rome's superiority, both in the West and the East, could no longer be questioned.

Yet it should not be implied that all was now peaceful. The Romans continued to have trouble with the Illyrians on the eastern shores of the Adriatic and for decades maintained armies there much of the time. Spain put the Romans to the test even more, for the Celt-Iberians reacted fiercely against continual Roman encroachment. Guerrilla-type warfare, like running sores, persisted there during much of the second century B.C. Governors of both Spanish provinces had to maintain standing armies and were often in the field on campaign. Several Roman generals lost their reputations in this restless arena. Much of Spain was pacified by 132 B.C., when Numantia was destroyed, but the peninsula as a whole was finally conquered only in 19 B.C., more than a century later.

BOOKS FOR FURTHER READING

ADCOCK, F. *The Roman Art of War Under the Republic*, rev. ed., Cambridge, Mass., 1963.

ASTIN, A. *Cato the Censor*, Oxford, 1978.
ASTIN, A. *Scipio Aemilianus*, Oxford, 1967.

BADIAN, E.   *Foreign Clientelae*, Oxford, 1958.

DE BEER, G.   *Hannibal: Challenging Rome's Supremacy*, New York, 1969.

HARRIS, W.   *War and Imperialism in Republican Rome 327–70 B.C.*, Oxford, 1979.

HEURGON, J.   *The Rise of Rome to 264 B.C.*, trans. J. Willis, Berkeley, 1973.

LAZENBY, J.   *Hannibal's War: A Military History of the Second Punic War*, Warminster, Eng., 1978.

SALMON, E.   *The Making of Roman Italy*, Ithaca, N.Y., 1982.

SALMON, E.   *Roman Colonization Under the Republic*, Ithaca, N.Y., 1970.

SALMON, E.   *Samnium and the Samnites*, Cambridge, 1967.

SCULLARD, H.   *Scipio Africanus: Soldier and Politician*, Ithaca, N.Y., 1970.

WARMINGTON, B.   *Carthage*, rev. ed., London, 1969.

15

STATE AND SOCIETY:

the impact of empire

The Rome of 146 B.C. was vastly different from the Rome of a century or so earlier, when Rome had only dominated Italy south of the Po Valley. The Romans ruled the Italian states indirectly, through an alliance structure, but got no income from them. In the intervening period, Rome fought wars on three continents and came to dominate the whole Mediterranean littoral. Eight provinces now sprawled from Spain to Macedonia, from all of which regular tribute flowed to Rome. Earlier in the second century B.C. this income had been greatly augmented by spoils and indemnities; as we have seen, Carthage was made to pay 10,000 talents after the Second Punic War, and Syria 15,000 talents after 189 B.C. Rome had become a world capital, and bustled with general prosperity. It was an exciting city, too, for in the Roman Forum were made decisions that affected the entire civilized world. The Roman calendar was crowded with festivals, games, theater, gladiatorial combats, and races. The city on the Tiber was decidedly the place to be in this era.

A. SOCIAL AND ECONOMIC TRANSFORMATIONS

The Upper Classes

The Roman aristocrats who belonged to the "establishment," who held the highest offices, commanded the armies, served on embassies, and sat in the Senate, found their positions enormously enhanced by the republic's gradual expansion into empire. Roman officials were the most important people in the world, with unequaled opportunities for profit and prestige. Consuls and praetors, once local magistrates whose power was limited by law and tradition, now ruled provinces with almost absolute authority. Inevitably, such men developed new conceptions of themselves as representatives of the dominant power in the Mediterranean and acquired new standards and tastes in their personal lives. As a matter of course, they acquired finer homes and clothing, personal slaves—in short, luxury and status quite beyond anything known to their grandparents.

The greater benefits now conferred by high office brought increased competition at the polls. A few "new men" reached the top offices as new plebeian families shouldered their way into the select circle of aristocracy, which by now included both patricians and plebeians, for it was an officeholding aristocracy. Family-political alliances of an informal sort were formed around nuclei of older families. Although these coalitions shifted constantly and involved complex personal relationships, their goals were clear: to see that the right persons gained the right offices and were given the best assignments. Sometimes these family-political groups can be identified with continuing policies, but for the most part their sole objectives were the control of elections and offices, and thus the Senate. Among the leaders of such informal factions in the second century B.C. were the Claudii and the Scipionii.

A Rising Equestrian Group

In most of history the term *middle class* refers to a group who have money but who are not aristocrats. In Rome such people came of plebeian families who were nonpolitical and whose members did not often attain high office. (Senators by law were barred from certain important commercial activity.) By the first century B.C., men of upper middle class were usually called *equestrians*; that is, they owned sufficient property to be ranked with the cavalry contingents of the Roman army. But to use the term *middle class* here would be misleading, for many—perhaps most—equestrians were not middle-class businessmen at all; they were landowners who had close relationships with the senatorial aristocracy.

Rome's expansion, the great wars, the vast building projects, commercial opportunities created by Rome's new position—these were the factors that fostered the rise of a moneyed middle group. The contractors who built the ships for Rome's great fleets; supplied its armies; constructed roads, bridges, and public buildings; or bought up slaves and spoils for later sale at a profit almost all prospered, and a few became economically powerful. By the first century B.C. among them were bankers, tax collectors, and moneylenders.

A lower middle class, made up of enterpreneurs on a small scale, flourished also. These people might own a few fishing boats, operate small shops, or build olive and grape presses or other machinery. One of the misfortunes of Rome was the failure of these middle groups in society to continue to grow and flourish. Too many equestrians confined their activities to banking, tax collecting, and money-lending. Many of the rest were ruined by civil war and, ultimately, by competition from the developing western provinces as well.

Growth of the Latifundia

An important economic change on the rural scene after the Second Punic, or Hannibalic, War involved the development of capitalistic agriculture. Since upper-class Romans by custom, station, and law were restricted in their business activity, they turned to landholding; this was always respectable, for land was the basic form of wealth throughout ancient (and medieval) times. To those with money, land was available. State-owned land (*ager publicus*) could be leased. Some, in fact, had been used to pay off war debts contracted when the state borrowed from private individuals during war emergencies. Land also could be purchased, sometimes at low rates, from small owners who left or were forced off their farms. Besides capital and land, a third requirement for the new-style farm was manpower—slaves or tenants. Slaves were available in large quantity during the second century B.C. from the sale of war prisoners. Those used as farm labor came mostly from less-civilized areas such as Spain, Cisalpine Gaul, or Illyria. Supervisors, bookkeepers, cooks, physicians, and tutors of children would probably be Greek or Asian.

The object of capital investment is profit. In human terms, this meant that the slaves had to be adequately cared for, but also that the maximum amount of labor was extracted. Some slaves worked in irons and slept in prisons. In economic terms, this system of agriculture meant an emphasis on cash crops, that is, livestock, grapes for wine, and olives. Grain was unprofitable, partly because large quantities were brought in as tribute from the provinces, especially Sicily, and sold by the state, and partly because it could not be transported far by land conveyance economically. In social terms, the new *latifundia* (that is, large landed estates) meant a decline in numbers of small independent farmers, who were replaced by tenants and slaves. In political terms, this latter change tended to destroy the old patron-client system, in which lay much of the power of the aristocrats. The family-political alliances helped to offset the decline of the old system; but these political effects were nonetheless portentous.

The Lower Classes

The reduction in numbers of the small citizen-farmers has sometimes been overemphasized, for this group remained the basic ingredient in Rome's political, economic, and military systems. Yet all these systems were changed and weakened. Consider the army. Rome did not draft the poorest citizens for military service but kept the army in the hands of those who had some stake in the existing system. Terrific losses in battle, especially during the Hannibalic War, and the displacement of small property owners by slaves meant a shortage of draftable military manpower. During the second century B.C. the property qualification for military service was drastically reduced; still there were scarcely enough men, for Rome now required soldiers not merely in war emergencies but also for standing armies in the provinces. In consequence, military conscription bore excessively hard on the draft-eligible citizens.

Many propertyless men drifted or migrated to the cities, particularly Rome, and the capital soon was bursting at the seams. The population pressure made it necessary, in 144 B.C. to 140 B.C., to build a new aqueduct for the city and refurbish the two old ones. Since for most of the century Rome was prosperous, a man could find work or go into business in a small way. Ambitious public and private construction and the service needs of the expanding population meant opportunity even for simple day laborers.

A new class thus arose in Rome: *Proles*, the Romans called them, day laborers without property. There had always been propertyless laborers, of course, but previously they were scattered in rural areas. As long as times were good, these lower-class city workers did well; but they had no reserves. Their lodgings were likely to be miserable, and they were subject to the whims of economic fortune. It is significant, too, that they lost former ties of clientage while retaining the right to vote. This new class of proletarians constituted an unstable mass in the capital. One day its members would starve, riot, and follow demagogues and military leaders in civil commotion. For the time, however, they did not suffer inordinately; their precarious situation was brought home to them only with the economic depression that was to come in the 130s B.C.

Women in Rome: A Growing Freedom

Given the overwhelming legal power assigned to the *pater familias* in Rome, it might be expected that women would have been repressed there as thoroughly as in any male-dominated society. Yet this was not so. The position of the Roman matron was highly respected, and the list of Roman women who were influential not only in the family but also in society at large is longer than that of any other people in antiquity.

Under stress of the Hannibalic War, when most men were away in the army and women necessarily assumed control over family and property, an effort was made to restrict upper-class women. The Oppian Law of 215 B.C. forbade women to wear varicolored clothing, to drive chariots in or around the city, or to own more than one-half ounce of gold. Women forced the repeal of the law in 195 B.C., despite the opposition of several important Romans including the elder Cato. They demonstrated in the Forum in raucous crowds that grew day by day. Cato's speech to the Senate, as reported by the historian Livy (it is doubtful that we have the exact wording), protests that women should stay at home and calls their protests a sedition. Cato seemed to think it especially bad that women should yell at men other than their husbands. Obviously, the law was symbolic for women in more general ways, and they persuaded the senate to vote their way.

As early as the mid-fifth century B.C. the Twelve Tables of law had granted women the right to inherit property equally with men. Under one form of marriage, increasingly utilized (no law controlled the marriage contract), women did not come under the legal guardianship of their husbands and retained control of their property, though such women remained, technically, under the authority of their fathers. This view is perhaps reflected in the virtual end in the middle republic of the practice of women taking the names of their husbands. Divorce, once rare, became more common; women as well as men could initiate the simple process, which, like marriage, was not controlled by law or courts.

Most notable of the noblewomen reported to have been influential in public ways in this period was Cornelia, daughter of Scipio Africanus Major and mother of the Gracchi (see later in this chapter). Her husband was gone much of the time, and she seems to have attended to the education of her children, choosing the tutors. She herself was well educated in both Latin and Greek. The period of her greatest eminence came after the death of her husband, when she maintained in her home in Rome a kind of intellectual salon which Greeks and other foreigners frequented. She certainly had strong influence on her famous sons.

Women were to be even freer and more influential in the future (see pp. 340-341)—and, along with the rest of society, less inhibited morally than their ancestors.

B. INTELLECTUAL AND MORAL CHANGE

An emergent world capital eventually is likely to become something of an intellectual center as well. In the second century B.C., however, this development was only beginning in Rome, which in many ways had long absorbed intellectual impulses from other peoples. The Etruscans, Greeks, and Carthaginians had all contributed something to Roman culture. But now, when so many Romans traveled in Greece and the Hellenistic East and when so many Greek pedagogues, scholars, and physicians were imported into Rome proper, a new wave of influence was felt.

Literature

Soon after the First Punic War, Latin translations of Greek dramas were presented in Rome. After a few years dramatists began to modify these plays and put them in Roman dress, so to speak. Ennius (239-169 B.C.), a Greek poet from Tarentum, was brought to Rome and made a citizen. He presented numerous tragedies based on the older Greek masters. Plautus (254-184 B.C.) and Terence (195-159 B.C.) used Greek plots from the New Comedy of Menander and others, but they were original in their brilliant mastery of the Latin language. Social historians are acutely interested in what they changed from the Greek plays that were their models. No Latin counterparts existed for the Greek *hetaira,* or courtesan; and no Roman pater familias would ever put up with the impudent slaves and disobedient sons that appear in the plays. Greek settings were the rule; to put such plays into a Roman setting would have outraged Roman sensibilities. Roman tragedy, some considered quite good by ancient writers, was also produced later in the century, but none of it has survived.

The oldest extant Latin prose is *De Agricultura,* a work of Cato the Elder dealing with all aspects of the new agriculture. This work (also often called *De Re Rustica*) is unpolished and owes very little to Greek stylistic models. It does owe a great deal to the Carthaginian Mago, however, whose work had circulated in Rome in translation for some years.

The history of Polybius (discussed in Chapter 12, on Hellenistic culture) hardly belongs to Roman literature; yet Polybius well illustrates in his own person the Greek influence on intellectually inclined Romans. The exiled Greek historian lived at the house of the Roman General Aemilius Paullus and helped to tutor his son, who was later adopted into the Scipio family and known as Scipio Aemilianus. Scipio continued to cultivate the company of Polybius and other Greek and Roman intellectuals, creating an informal group now often termed the *Scipionic circle.* Besides Polybius, this circle included Panaetius, a Greek Stoic philosopher; Lucilius, the first great Roman satirist; and several others. Lucilius' work is known to us only in fragments, preserved through occasional quotation in later writers.

Philosophy

Romans were exposed to Greek philosophical teaching of all sorts during this period. The skepticism of certain Greek philosophers repelled many Romans, however. Carneades, while on an embassy to Rome about the middle of the second century B.C., horrified conservative Romans by arguing both for and against justice as a knowable and workable concept in lectures given in the capital. Stoicism was much more to their liking; Roman views of public service, personal and civic virtue, and stern self-control gave them a predilection for a philosophy emphasizing these qualities. Panaetius of Rhodes (c. 180–111 B.C.), mentioned previously as a member of the Scipionic circle, was a house guest of Scipio for some years. He, more than any other person, introduced Stoicism to the Romans and, to some degree, popularized its doctrine. The greatest influence of this philosophical school, however, was to be during the next three centuries.

Religion

The stresses of the Hannibalic War produced unorthodox religious behavior in Rome, some of which the officials tried to suppress. On the highest levels, however, one religious innovation was welcomed in Rome. The goddess Cybele, said the keepers of the Sibylline Books (of oracles), if brought to Rome would help it to victory. The priests of the goddess in Asia Minor agreed to send to Rome her effigy—perhaps a meteorite. After a few years the goddess was housed in a new temple on the Palatine Hill.

During the decade 190 B.C. to 180 B.C., devotees of the wine god Bacchus attempted to draw in Roman young people to his orgiastic worship. Conservative

Romans brought charges of immorality and even conspiracy, so that the Bacchic rites were sternly curtailed by decree of the senate. Large numbers of persons, mostly in the Greek areas of southern Italy, were summarily tried and executed on conspiratorial charges.

By the middle of the second century B.C. there was a changed, more relaxed attitude toward religion among some upper-class intellectuals. Polybius makes it clear that Romans he knew had come to feel that the state religion was useful primarily to keep the masses in disciplined control. This attitude gradually spread, and by the middle of the next century two consequences were apparent: The governing class was neglecting temples, rites, and the priesthood; the unexpected corollary was a weakening of the constitution itself, of which the state religion was so integral a part.

Morals

It is almost a truism of history that each generation thinks that the world is "going to the dogs." One must necessarily believe that unless morals have declined in each generation since the beginning of time, such gloomy and pessimistic views are usually wrong. In any contemporary setting it is very difficult to gauge such trends. However, the historian, using hindsight, can sometimes make a more accurate assessment. It does indeed appear now that the greater affluence and widened horizons of Romans in the second century B.C. did cause some erosion of old values and a greater emphasis on material status and possessions.

The Romans whose opinions have been preserved had differing explanations for this worsened moral climate. Some attributed it to the influx of rich spoils from the Syrian War; others saw Greek contacts and Greek influence as the prime cause; and still others thought the defeat of Carthage removed the last strong enemy of Rome, with the unfortunate result that the Roman young no longer cultivated the military virtues.

Two Men, Differing Views: Cato and Scipio Aemilianus

Two great Romans, a generation apart in age, will symbolize for us the inertia and strength of Roman conservatism and the dynamics of change.

Marcus Porcius Cato (234–149 B.C.), as a "new man," rose from an undistinguished family to the top offices of Rome—and thereby to a place for his family in the aristocracy. He advanced through sheer ability, displayed most effectively in speeches before the people and in the law courts. He was sponsored by a patrician closely associated with the great Fabius Maximus. As praetor and consul, Cato performed well, but he is best remembered for his use of the office of censor in 184 B.C. and for his long-continued, mostly conservative influence.

Most Roman censors in these decades took stern positions on mores and morals. Cato, convinced it was Greek influence that was eroding the fiber of the

Roman young, was the sternest of the lot. As censor he assessed at ten times their real value all luxuries, such items as pretty young slaves, often bought to permit the masters to indulge their sexual appetites. He carefully winnowed the lists of members of the senate and the *equites,* or cavalry. For a moral lapse, he even excluded a brother of the Flamininus who had defeated Philip in the Second Macedonian War. Two years earlier Cato had played a part in the Bacchanalian investigations and the resulting harsh decree. Three years after his censorship he instigated a book burning of Pythagorean writings accidently discovered and judged subversive.

Cato had only scorn for the "Greeklings" who aped Hellenic ways and worshiped Hellenic philosophy and literature. He felt it impossible to imbibe the culture of the Greeks without picking up their vices as well. When the academic skeptic Carneades visited Rome on the previously mentioned embassy and charmed the young with his lectures, Cato saw that his business was expedited so he would not stay long in Rome. He seems to have been behind passage of a decree requiring all Greek philosophers to leave Rome. Yet Cato himself knew the Greek language and sent his own son—with much warning—to study in Athens.

In one way, moreover, Cato actually encouraged change. His book *De Agricultura* gave sound advice to those who would buy slaves and organize latifundia to grow olives or grapes. He seemed unaware that these slave-operated plantations had deleterious effects on the old Roman constitution.

Scipio Aemilianus (185–129 B.C.), as we have seen, was the grandson of the first Scipio by adoption and the natural son of the Aemilius Paullus who defeated Perseus of Macedonia in 168 B.C. He grew up with privileges of family and prestige that Cato lacked. His career took him to the top offices, but not merely because of family connections. Though Cato and the Fabian family group with which he was associated generally opposed the Scipios, the old orator felt that Scipio the Younger was one of the few capable military men and politicians left in Rome. It was Scipio who destroyed Carthage, as Cato had desired and the Senate ordered, at the end of the Third Punic War (146 B.C.). His views on the importance of maintaining the old morality were the same as Cato's. Though he occasionally supported a liberal measure—for example, one of three bills that extended the secret ballot in voting—he supported the *mos maiorum* (ancestral custom) almost as strongly as Cato did.

Scipio and Cato, however, had quite different views about the Greeks. Scipio was to a degree philhellene; that is, he admired and embraced Greek philosophy and literature and hoped to see them emulated in Rome. The "Scipionic circle, as has been noted, included Panaetius, the philosopher who popularized Stoicism in Rome, as well as the Greek historian Polybius and the Roman playwright Terence and the satirist Lucilius.

Of Cato, Scipio, and other Romans of the second century B.C., it may be said that, as in so many other times and places, these men embraced certain elements of change without desiring or perceiving what other transformations would inevitably follow.

C. THE GRACCHI: CHALLENGE TO THE OLD ORDER

Economic Downturn: An Accumulation of Problems

The number and seriousness of the long-neglected internal problems in Rome were masked by prosperity for some years. The decline of the small farmer and the growth of the city proletariat produced the obvious difficulty that the number of draft-eligible men was steadily dropping; but the parallel deterioration of the constitution because the city proles no longer had any real attachment to the ancestral state was not so obvious. The unequal benefits of empire and the growing gap between the status of rich and poor did not seem so acute as long as the poor were not in fact starving. The coming of economic depression, however, did reveal at least partially the depth of the trouble.

The economic depression was caused by several factors. The end of profitable wars and spoils, much of which had been spent in Rome, was one cause. Another was a worldwide grain shortage, which caused prices of this staple to go up. Most important for the city of Rome itself was a slave rebellion in Sicily. Perhaps as much as half the grain supply for Rome came from Sicily, either through tribute or through additional purchases. The slave revolt came at a time when grain prices were already high from scarcity and, moreover, during a period when pirates were quite active. In consequence, the city suffered from an acute grain shortage and soaring prices at a time when these could not easily be rectified.

Tiberius Gracchus, Tribune of the Plebs (133 B.C.)

It would not have been without precedent if an official had proposed that the state make an extraordinary effort to import grain and sell it at a loss to relieve the economic crisis. Nor is it impossible that this was done, at least on a small scale. Young Tiberius Sempronius Gracchus, who took office as tribune of the plebs on December 10, 134 B.C., felt that any enduring solution must also deal with long-range problems and underlying causes. As he saw it, the most serious problems all related to the decline of the small farmer and the large-scale migration to the city. The shortage of men for the draft and the lack of grain grown in Italy itself were both connected with the decline of the small farmer, for owners of the new latifundia, profit-motivated, seldom raised grain. Partly in consequence, there was an overdependence on Sicily for wheat. Gracchus wanted to reestablish the peasant class, protect Rome's reservoir of manpower for the army, and reduce the dependency on Sicilian grain. To these ends he proposed an agrarian law he thought would achieve it all.

Tiberius Gracchus' land law was not revolutionary. It dealt with public land, not at all with privately owned land. Like earlier laws, it limited the amount of public land any one Roman could hold; it also provided for distribution of the rest of the public land (or the best of it) to the Roman poor, on a lease basis. Whatever injustice there was in the law was a consequence of the sloppy way in which the public land had been leased or neglected in the past. Persons who expected to be able to hold their leases indefinitely had poured capital into the land. In other cases, land that had been proclaimed as confiscated by Rome had never actually been taken over. By the Gracchan law, persons would be dispossessed whose ancestors had lived on their land for perhaps centuries. This situation applied especially to Rome's Italian allies, who were bitter about it. Much land in southern Italy had been confiscated on paper after the war with Hannibal, as punishment for states that had deserted the cause of Rome, but it was never actually taken from the Italian owners. Now, two-thirds of a century later, this land was to be taken over by Rome.

The initial outcry against Gracchus' proposal came primarily from Romans. Quick passage of the measure was prevented by the veto of another tribune of the plebs. Tiberius, sure of his cause and encouraged, it seems, by Blossius of Cumae, a Stoic and democratic theorist who was his adviser, carried through an unprecedented recall election, got rid of the offending tribune, and put another in his place. This, as much as anything Tiberius did, aroused his political enemies. Roman aristocrats always feared as a potential tyrant anyone who offered great benefits to the general public. This recall election seemed to confirm their fears. Most of the aristocracy opposed Tiberius (who was also an aristocrat and had the support of other senators); his bill became law, but only a tiny sum of money was voted to help his agrarian commission carry out its terms. The majority of the Senate remained firmly opposed to the tribune's efforts.

Tiberius pressed on, nevertheless, and used private funds. Then he got an unusual opportunity: Attalus III of Pergamum died in 133 B.C., the year of Gracchus' tribunate, and willed his kingdom to Rome. Tiberius, ignoring the Senate (which usually controlled both finance and the provinces), got a law passed which would have the new province settled by action of the Assembly, not the Senate, and also would use Attalus' treasure in carrying out the agrarian law. On top of this, Tiberius announced he was running for reelection. His enemies considered this illegal. At the time of the elections disorders broke out. The senators heard rumors that Tiberius was demanding a crown. Tiberius was defended before the Senate by the consul, who refused to take action. The chief priest (*pontifex maximus*), however, got together a crowd of persons and assassinated Tiberius and his friends. For centuries Rome had witnessed no political assassination, but officials did nothing about it, since too many important Romans were involved. The chief priest found it expedient to leave the city soon afterward, perhaps because of threats to his life.

The agrarian commission was reconstituted and continued to operate for a time, but owing to persistent complaints of the Italians, Scipio Aemilianus got its power reduced. Some land was indeed distributed to the poor, but not enough to reverse the trends already mentioned—if that was possible at all.

Gaius Gracchus, Tribune of the Plebs (123–122 B.C.)

Gaius, the younger brother of Tiberius Gracchus, eventually took up his brother's cause. The immediate crisis involving the grain supply in Rome had been somewhat alleviated by the end of the slave revolt in Sicily. The condition of the Roman poor was still very bad, however, for grain prices did not come down much and many were doubtless still unemployed. To them, a mass of voters of some consequence, Gaius Gracchus offered hope.

Elected tribune for 123 B.C., Gaius quickly initiated a rather extensive program. This included a restoration of power to the agrarian commission, but there is no evidence that it did much to distribute public land to individuals after this time. Gaius depended primarily on a price-fixing measure for grain to relieve the hungry. The state would sell the grain received as tribute at a price much lower than the current market—about the market price before the shortage began. He hoped this would force all prices down. Unfortunately, it did not, and the state had to buy grain at high prices and sell it at low prices, with resulting strain on the treasury.

Gaius also constructed granaries, roads, and bridges, with a double intent: to obviate future shortages of food and to give immediate employment to the jobless. Other measures he initiated included colonization on a considerable scale; a change in the tax structure of Pergamum, the new province the Romans called Asia, to produce more income for the treasury; and weakening the power of the Senate by staffing the jury panels of the permanent courts with equestrians of nonpolitical families, excluding senators and their close relatives.

After serving two consecutive years as tribune, Gaius failed to be reelected for a third year, in a bitter campaign. No sooner was he out of office than his political enemies began to try to annul some of his laws. During his efforts to prevent this, a messenger of the consul was killed by one of Gaius' followers. Gaius and his friends, about to be "railroaded" (they felt) for complicity in the murder, refused to give up and barricaded themselves in a temple on the Aventine Hill. Acting under the authority of the Senate's final decree, which declared something like martial law, the consul, Lucius Opimius, an old enemy of the Gracchi, collected troops and stormed the temple. Gracchus fled but was killed (121 B.C.).

The Gracchan Heritage

In their brief careers the Gracchus brothers had effected some changes destined to be permanent. Leaders continued to arise who emulated them. Typically they used the office of plebeian tribune, bypassed the senate, and proposed popular measures. They were thus called *populares*. Actually, the populares did not at any time constitute a true party in the modern sense. Popular leaders mostly used this approach as an alternate route to power. Some of them, however, did benefit lower-class Romans, and no doubt some of them sincerely wished to do so. One should not doubt, either, that their opponents, who eventually called themselves *optimates*, sincerely believed that only their own conservative approach could preserve the republic and that most of the popular leaders were would-be tyrant-demagogues of the Greek stamp.

What the Gracchi most definitely did was to point up the dual nature of the Roman constitution. Magistrates and Senate, tribunes and Assembly—both groups had power either by custom or by law to do many of the same things. Before the Gracchi came to power, the chief officials were the consuls and praetors, and the chief deliberative body was the Senate. The primary assemblies elected the officials but did little else. After the Gracchi, a tribune (or a popular consul) might well be the most important official, able to use the primary assemblies as legislative bodies to bypass the Senate. Before the Gracchi, despite occasional clashes, political leaders cooperated to make the constitution—defective as it was—work. After the Gracchi, the kind of tolerance that is always needed to make any republican constitution work was often lacking. Violence in the Forum became common. Ultimately it led to civil war and the end of the republic.

Who was to blame for the century of unrest and civil war that followed the Gracchi? The blame lies at so many doors it is futile to attempt to focus on one person or two or on a single group. The oligarchy seems, in retrospect, to have been extraordinarily shortsighted and greedy at times. But the popular leaders also seem, sometimes, to have sought personal power, to have aimed at nothing short of overturning the traditional state. One thing is certain: We do not have in the Roman Republic a simple contest between democracy and oligarchy, as sometimes portrayed. Nor is it quite true, as is also often said, that the senatorial oligarchy resisted and did not change to meet the needs of empire. It did—but admittedly not enough—and thus it may be true that such an oligarchy could not long govern a far-flung empire.

After the Gracchi, at any rate, things were never the same again.

BOOKS FOR FUTHER READING

ASTIN, A. *Scipio Aemilianus*, Oxford, 1967.

BADIAN, E. *Foreign Clientelae*, Oxford, 1958.

BALSDON, J. *Roman Women*, rev. ed., London, 1974.

BERNSTEIN, A. *Tiberius Sempronius Gracchus: Tradition and Apostasy*, Ithaca, N.Y., 1978.

BOREN, H. *The Gracchi*, New York, 1969.

BRUNT, P. *Social Conflicts in the Roman Republic*, London, 1971.

D'ARMS, J. *Commerce and Social Standing in Ancient Rome*, Cambridge, Mass., 1981.

DILKE, O. *The Ancient Romans: How They Lived and Worked*, London, 1975.

FRANK, T. *Aspects of Social Behavior in Ancient Rome*, Cambridge, Mass., 1932.

FRANK, T. *Life and Literature in the Roman Republic*, Berkeley, 1930.

GRIMAL, P., ed. *Hellenism and the Rise of Rome*, New York, 1969.

GRUEN, E. *Roman Politics and the Criminal Courts, 149–78 B.C.*, Cambridge, Mass., 1968.

LEFKOWITZ, M., and M. FANT *Women's Life in Greece and Rome* (readings from ancient sources), Baltimore, 1982.

ORMEROD, H. *Piracy in the Ancient World*, London, 1924.

POMEROY, S. *Goddesses, Whores, Wives, and Slaves: Women in Classical Antiquity*, New York, 1976.

SCULLARD, H. *Festivals and Ceremonies of the Roman Republic*, Ithaca, N.Y., 1981.

SMITH, R. *The Failure of the Roman Republic*, Cambridge, 1955.

STOCKTON, D. *The Gracchi*, Oxford, 1979.

TAYLOR, L. *Roman Voting Assemblies*, Ann Arbor, 1966.

16

DEATH THROES OF A REPUBLIC

The violence employed by the opponents of the Gracchi was a two-edged sword. In succeeding decades popular leaders made good use of it against the traditional oligarchy. Small-scale violence became an almost acceptable part of the Roman political scene. One reason for this continuing violence was the lack of an effective police force for the capital. The Romans felt no need for such control. Important persons moved about only with a sizable group of retainers and hangers-on. Lower-class citizens were rather primitively expected to protect themselves or seek the aid of bystanders when trouble arose.

Violence has byproducts. In such an unruly age, less "reprehensible" methods of influencing elections and legislation—such as bribery—came to seem harmless, almost proper, conduct. Escalating violence and disregard for law brought armed clashes, and finally civil war, on such a scale that the inevitable consequence, no matter which side won, was the end of the republic. The cynical historian may say that, after all, the fall of the republic meant only the replacement of one set of oligarchs with another set. But there was a difference: The republic did at least incorporate safeguards—which, to be sure, did not always work—against the control of the government by paranoid individuals, unlike the authoritarian form of government that followed.

A. THE JUGURTHAN WAR AND GAIUS MARIUS

Outbreak of the War (112–111 B.C.)

It must have been a surprise to many Romans when they found them-selves at war with Jugurtha, king of Numidia. This north African kingdom, under the patronage of the Scipios, had been a friend and ally of Rome ever since the Second Punic (Hannibalic) War. Rome had often supported Numidia in border disputes with Carthage. Jugurtha, the illegitimate grandson of King Masinissa, had fought with the Romans as a cavalry officer under the younger Scipio Africanus (Aemilianus), and the latter's high commendation caused Micipsa, then ruler of Numidia, to adopt Jugurtha and give him an equal inheritance with his own two sons. Soon after Micipsa's death, however, the ambitious Jugurtha had one of these heirs, his cousin Hiempsal, slain. Rome's entry into the North African war was a consequence of the struggle between Jugurtha and Adherbal, his surviving foster brother, over their shares of the kingdom.

Whatever the problems in Numidia, it was still an independent state, and thus Rome had no legal right to intervene. Its reasons for doing so were at least three. First, Rome was now the next-door neighbor of Numidia, since the former Carthaginian homeland had become the Roman province of Africa. Second, cer-tain Italians, longstanding allies of Rome who engaged in trade in Numidia, had for some reason chosen to support Adherbal's cause. Jugurtha apprehended several hundred of these supporters at Cirta in 112 B.C. and massacred all of them. Finally, the whole question was taken up by popular politicians suspicious of the motives of the central oligarchy, and so it entered the arena of partisan politics in Rome. Highly placed Romans were accused of taking bribes from Jugurtha on a lavish scale to influence the outcome. At this distance, we cannot reliably determine the truth of these charges.

Marius and the War

When the fratricidal conflict in Numidia began, Roman officials at first only remonstrated. But when Italian allies were killed, a Roman army sailed for Numidia. Jugurtha "surrendered" to the Roman commander, who left him in con-trol of the kingdom—and not much weaker than before. Bribery charges brought an investigation, during which Jugurtha was summoned to Rome; while there he inadvisedly arranged the assassination of a cousin who might have made a legiti-mate claim to the Numidian throne, and the war resumed. In command of the Roman forces was Quintus Caecilius Metellus (later surnamed "Numidicus"), who took Gaius Marius along as his legate.

Marius came of a family which had held Roman citizenship for only a couple of generations. Since none of his ancestors had reached high office in Rome, he was not of the nobility but of equestrian rank. He had served with distinction in Spain with Scipio Aemilianus and must have known Jugurtha. His official career in Rome had proceeded slowly. He served as tribune in 119 B.C. but was probably the oldest man in the college. After failing to be elected to higher office once, he finally made it—sources say through bribery—to the praetorship.

Marius quarreled with Metellus in Africa, and against the latter's wishes, returned to Rome to campaign for the consulship. "New men" rarely reached the office of consul without powerful sponsorship, but Marius criticized the way in which the guerrilla-type war in Numidia was being bungled and gained office on a "win the war" theme. The Assembly voted (doubtless against the wishes of the Senate) to put Marius himself in charge of the war, superseding in command his former patron, Metellus.

Between 107 B.C., the year of his consulship, and 104 B.C., Marius managed to bring the Jugurthan War to an end. Jugurtha himself was captured, ironically, by the man destined to be Marius' greatest enemy—Lucius Cornelius Sulla. Numidia was reduced in size, and an unambitious king was found for its throne. Marius had again demonstrated his military competence.

Threat from the North: Gallic Migrations

By this time Marius was needed in Italy once more, to face an enemy much stronger and more terrifying than the king of Numidia. As early as 118 B.C. masses of Celtic tribes whom the Romans called Gauls had moved into what is now southern France. The main tribes were the Cimbri and the Teutones. Roman armies trying to support Roman allies against these invaders suffered a series of defeats. A major effort to turn back the migrating tribes was made in 105 B.C. under the consul Mallius and the proconsul Caepio. But in a battle at Arausio (modern Orange, in southern France), the Gauls were able to fight the two Roman armies separately and won a tremendous victory. It was said that 80,000 Romans were killed in this debacle. The way was then open for invasion of Italy, but fortunately for Rome the Gauls first went west into Spain. In desperation the Romans turned to Marius, who was elected consul *in absentia* and put in charge of the war when he returned from Africa. While serving as consul five years in a row (104–100 B.C.), he put together a new army, and in two great battles in 102 B.C. and 101 B.C., annihilated the barbarians.

Marius reorganized the army in a way that had political consequences that were probably inadvertent. In order to recruit enough Romans in good health and of military age, he enlisted men who had no property. He also reorganized the training and structure of the legions. Significantly, he now tended to become the patron of these thousands of Romans, who had no loyalty to any other patron or even to the traditional state. He is reported to have treated them well, and so one must presume they had something to do with his reelection year after year. They supported his cause in confrontations in the Forum. Though Marius did not make the most of his newly developed support, he showed Romans what tremendous political possibilities now existed for successful generals assigned to important commands.

Saturninus

An army of propertyless men must be taken care of, both in and out of service. Soldiers who had nothing expected to gain booty, and they wanted a bonus on discharge. Small plots of land had often been given to veterans in the past. Marius prudently saw to it that his men received land as a discharge benefit; however, in order to get the necessary legislation passed, he needed political friends. One man willing to help in exchange for political support was Lucius Appuleius Saturninus, who had begun his career in the usual fashion and reached the quaestorship in 105 B.C. or 104 B.C. He was put in charge of the grain supply at Rome's port, Ostia. A shortage pushed prices up, and the Senate relieved him of this assignment. Doubtless, this would have meant the end of his elective career if he had not resorted to extraordinary measures.

Saturninus now became a popular demagogue, supporting popular measures—and the aims of Marius—as tribune of the plebs in 103 B.C. and 100 B.C. Saturninus passed a law giving Marius' veterans 100 *iugera* (about 63 acres) each in Africa. Another law provided for sale of grain to the poor at a nominal price, much lower than that established by Gaius Gracchus. Saturninus also supported a man who falsely claimed to be a son of Tiberius Gracchus. In the elections of 100 B.C., his followers killed one of the candidates for the consulship, an opponent of Saturninus' own candidate.

This blatant violence was more than the senators could tolerate. They passed the Final Decree, demanding that the consul take action against Saturninus and the culprits. The consul in Rome at the time was Marius. He took Saturninus and several others into custody, and they were shut up in the Senate house. What Marius intended to do with them no one knows; probably he wanted to give them a fair trial. However, a mob, probably abetted by important senators, climbed onto the Senate roof and killed the imprisoned men by hurling the heavy roofing tiles down through the rafters.

Marius now found himself unpopular, though he had acted neither as a popular ally of Saturninus nor as a member of the inner oligarchy—and did not really fit into either category. It has often been said that he was a great general but a poor politician. He retired from office and played a small part in public affairs for several years. The land law for his veterans was not carried through.

B. THE ITALIAN WAR (90–88 B.C.)

Rome's Allies—Their Changed Position

At the time when Rome conquered the Italian peninsula and formed an alliance system with the Italian states, that system seemed quite liberal. If these Italians were not true equals with Rome, they almost were. Free from internal interference on the whole, they were required only to furnish troops to fight alongside the Romans. By the beginning of the first century B.C., however, this relationship had changed vastly. Rome had not deliberately put down her allies; but Rome's new position of dominance in the world and the new opportunities open to Roman citizens meant that, relatively, the position of its allies had worsened. Not only had Italians fought alongside the Romans to repel homeland invaders such as Hannibal; they also had gone off to fight in Spain, Greece, the Near East, and North Africa. Their reward was to see Rome prosper and grow even stronger—and at the same time, subtly and gradually, almost inevitably exercise a tighter control over all Italy.

The Italian allies were particularly irked by the Gracchan agrarian laws, which underlined their inferior situation. When the Roman armies were disbanded and only Roman citizens were given bonuses and land, the Italians seethed; they had helped Rome to conquer and hold the Mediterranean world but did not share in the benefits. After Latins and Italians settled in Rome and were registered as citizens (some had this right), they were rudely disfranchised in 95 B.C., perhaps because their votes had been influencing elections.

The disgruntled Italians talked of rebellion but instead found a champion among Roman politicians. He was Marcus Livius Drusus, tribune of the plebs in 91 B.C. and son of a man who had shown sympathy for the Italians when as tribune he opposed Gaius Gracchus in 122 B.C. Drusus, though oligarchic in sentiment and acting with the support of many senators, passed measures of a popular sort, including a grain law and a colonization scheme. He also promoted measures to benefit the Senate itself and the equestrian class. His motive, it seems, was to build widespread support for the main objective, which was to give citizenship to the whole of the Italian peninsula. When this measure was at last put forward, however, he lost his support and, soon after, was assassinated.

The Italian War Brings Enfranchisement

The killing of Drusus sparked the revolt of the Italian allies. A government was formed—a federation called Italia, with officials comparable to those of Rome. In the early months of the war Roman civilians were killed in large numbers; and as often as not, Roman armies lost to their similarly trained and armed former allies.

Another blow struck Rome at this same time. Mithradates, king of Pontus in Asia Minor, led a rebellion against Roman power in that area, with great initial success. This forced the Romans to engage in a degree of sensible diplomacy in Italy which had been lacking before. In a series of laws the Romans enfranchised, first, all the Latins and Italians who did not join the rebellion; later, all who laid down their arms; and finally, all the Italians. Still, the fighting continued into 87 B.C. If the Romans had been as reasonable earlier, a great deal of bitter fighting and lingering animosity could have been avoided.

Even after the end of the Italian War, the Roman oligarchy, fearing the electoral power of the new voters, attempted to restrict these privileges to a few of the tribes or to put them into new tribes which would vote last. Popular politicians prevented this and so gained the general support of the new citizens.

C. THE WAR AGAINST MITHRADATES: CIVIL WAR IN ROME

Sulla Takes Command

As one of the consuls for 88 B.C., Lucius Cornelius Sulla commanded six legions of troops in the final stages of the Italian War. Since he had demonstrated his military prowess and had experience in Asia Minor as governor of Cilicia, he was named by the Senate to take command of the war against Mithradates. A tribune of the plebs named Sulpicius Rufus, however, felt that Gaius Marius should be given the command. Naturally, politics entered into the matter, for the man who got such an important post would command large numbers of soldiers and might profit both politically and economically.

The dual nature of the Roman constitution was clearly demonstrated here. The Senate traditionally made the command appointments and controlled the provinces. In theory, however, the Assembly could supersede the decrees of the Senate, and had indeed done so before, for example, when Marius in 107 B.C. was given command of the Jugurthan War. Sulpicius convened an assembly—probably a mere fraction of all the people—to pass a law that gave command of the campaign against Mithradates to Marius. Those who tried to prevent the action were manhandled, and at least a few, including Sulla's son-in-law, were killed.

Sulla considered the whole action illegal and criminal. He fled to his army and led them in a march on Rome itself—the first time a consul had invaded the city with troops. Sulpicius and several others were killed, and Marius fled for his life. Sulla made certain arrangements, including the election for the following year of consuls, whom he made take a sort of loyalty oath. Then he went off to Asia Minor to fight Mithradates.

The Cinnan Regime in Rome

Early the next year, one of the consuls Sulla had thought safe, Lucius Cornelius Cinna, attempted to pass legislation securing equal voting rights for the new citizens and so precipitated a new civil conflict. Driven out of the capital, he managed to get control of an army and then recalled Marius from his refuge in North Africa. When Marius joined him, they marched on Rome, expelled Sulla's supporters, and killed a considerable number of presumed enemies.

Cinna and Marius were elected consuls for the next year, 86 B.C. Marius no doubt intended to take over Sulla's command but died on January 13. His successor, Flaccus, raised an army and went east, presumably to replace Sulla. Flaccus was killed in a mutiny by his legate, Fimbria, who then took over the army. Sulla naturally did not accept Fimbria's claims, and Fimbria either could not or did not wish to attack Sulla. The two armies, though wary of each other, for a time co-operated loosely in the war against Mithradates.

Sulla's Victories in the East

Since Mithradates was in control of the sea, Sulla from the beginning felt he could not invade Asia Minor without a fleet. Besides, Mithradates was widely supported by the Greeks, who detested Roman rule. Athens had even made an alliance with him, and her port, Piraeus, was his major naval base in the Aegean. Sulla therefore besieged Athens in 87 B.C. and 86 B.C. When he took the city, he treated the Athenians harshly. Piraeus soon was in his hands also, and Mithradates' ships departed. Two armies that the king sent by the land route to stop Sulla, in 85 B.C., were crushed at Orchomenus and Chaeronea, though in each instance Sulla was outnumbered.

By this time Lucius Licinius Lucullus, Sulla's legate, had gathered to-gether a fleet. The army of Flaccus (soon to be Fimbria's) actually crossed the Aegean first and nearly captured Mithradates himself. Soon defeated at sea and confronted by two Roman armies, Mithradates was ready to negotiate peace. Sulla limited the vanquished ruler's navy and took some indemnity, but otherwise he reestablished the prewar boundaries. Sulla's army might then have fought that of Fimbria, but the latter's troops went over to Sulla, and their abandoned leader committed suicide.

Sulla now prepared to return to Rome. He took time to reorganize the province of Asia and punished not only collaborators with Mithradates but the whole populace, which was required to pay five years' back taxes at once (paid to Mithradates) and an additional indemnity. The provincial cities had to borrow the necessary money—mostly from Romans—and were still trying to pay off this debt two decades later.

Sulla's Return: Civil War and a New Order

Cinna served as consul each year while Sulla was gone. With other mod-erate leaders he tried to prepare for the civil war that now seemed inevitable. In 84 B.C., when he attempted to lead troops out of Italy, however, he was killed. Other leaders arose in his place, but when Sulla landed in Italy in 83 B.C., they were unable to cope with him. Sulla neutralized the Italians, who tended to support the popular leaders, by announcing that he accepted the voting arrangement for new citizens that had been enacted during his absence. Through intrigue, siege, and combat, Sulla's forces won over some of the various armies feverishly raised by his opponents and defeated others. The largest battle was at Rome itself, in 82 B.C. at the Colline Gate, where Sulla captured and slaughtered thousands of Sam-nites. He cowed the Senate, which meekly named him "Dictator for Reconstitut-ing the Republic." As dictator, Sulla ruthlessly proscribed those who had opposed him. Several thousand persons on his proscription lists were killed without trial,

Reverse, denarius of Sulla, showing a triumphal chariot, with the goddess Victory flying above, crowning the victorious general.

in a climax to the escalation of terror alternately mounted by both popular leaders and Sulla.

Sulla also revised the constitution; he tried to eliminate its dual nature by taking away most of the power of the tribunes of the plebs and the popular assemblies. He intended that the Senate should control almost all governmental functions except the elections. He enlarged the Senate, however, bringing into the government men who had not previously participated in the power structure. He attempted to restrain overly powerful politicians by a *lex annalis*, which specified age requirements for major offices, set three-year intervals between offices, and set a ten-year interval between the year of office and reelection to the same office. That would make it impossible for anyone to hold several consulships in a row, as Marius had done. Sulla voluntarily relinquished his dictatorship in 79 B.C. and retired; he died the following year.

Continued War: Sertorius and Spartacus

A decade of war for Romans—with former Italian allies, with Mithradates, and among themselves—threw the economy into complete disarray. Even the large sums brought back by Sulla from the East or gained from sale of the confiscated property of those he proscribed were not enough to restore a balance. It would be years before the province of Asia again produced the volume of tribute it once accounted for. Moreover, the civil war continued in Spain. There one of Marius' officers, Quintus Sertorius, collected troops, made allies of the Iberian natives, and defeated several Roman armies sent against him. In 74 B.C. Mithradates decided that Rome was weak enough for him to make another trial at arms. Part of Rome's problem was the lack of vigorous leadership in the restored oligarchy.

In 73 B.C. trouble broke out in Italy itself, almost serious enough to make Romans forget the challenges to their authority in Spain and Asia Minor. A Thracian gladiator named Spartacus and seventy of his fellows broke out of their barracks at Capua, south of Rome. They defeated the hastily raised local troops sent against them and captured their arms. Spartacus persuaded thousands of the slaves in the countryside to join him and equipped them with arms from the legionaries they killed. Ultimately he crushed even consular armies with his motley force, which reportedly approached 100,000 at its height. The rebels ravaged large areas from Lucania on the south to the Po Valley in the north.

Inevitably the Roman government collected stronger forces. Marcus Licinius Crassus, placed in command, trapped and destroyed the slave army in 71 B.C. He killed large numbers, perhaps including Spartacus himself; thousands of others he crucified along the roads stretching north toward Rome. A fragment of Spartacus' army escaping to the north had the misfortune to encounter a Roman army under Pompey, returning from Spain. They, too, were annihilated. Fearful slave owners, though somewhat poorer from the loss of their "property," could nonetheless breathe again.

D. NEW LEADERS FOR A FALTERING REPUBLIC

Marcus Licinius Crassus (115–53 B.C.)
and Gnaeus Pompeius Magnus (106–48 B.C.)

Crassus had spent his time in hiding in the days when Cinna and the partisans of Marius controlled Rome and Italy, and as the crisis approached, Pompey also disappeared from public view. Both came out of hiding, raised troops, and fought for Sulla in the civil wars. Pompey collected three whole legions. After he successfully carried out the various commands Sulla had given him, the dictator dubbed him Magnus ("The Great"), the surname he proudly used the rest of his life. Crassus also did well in this conflict; he commanded the victorious wing at the decisive battle of the Colline Gate.

During the years after Sulla's retirement, both these military leaders served in important commands, as we have seen; Pompey against Sertorius in Spain, and Crassus against Spartacus. In 71 B.C. both still commanded armies, and both decided to stand for the consulship. Both were ineligible, probably, by Sulla's laws: Pompey was too young and had never held any elective office at all, yet he had been given imperium and even celebrated a triumph; Crassus had held the praetorship too recently, perhaps. At this point the two decided to follow Sulla's example rather than his laws. They got together, though they disliked each other, and threatened to use their armies if they were not permitted the illegality of running for the consulship. To gain votes, they let it be known that if elected they would restore the powers of the tribunes of the plebs. In this way they were elected, and as consuls in 70 B.C., these former lieutenants of Sulla scuttled the key features of his constitution. The two-track route for political advancement was restored; the potential for constitutional conflict between tribunes and consuls, the Assembly and the Senate, was renewed.

Marcus Tullius Cicero (106–43 B.C.)
and Gaius Julius Caesar (100–44 B.C.)

Two other young men, Cicero and Caesar, also entered on their careers during or soon after Sulla's dictatorship. Both courageously opposed Sulla, though not with arms. In 81 B.C. or 80 B.C. Cicero defended Roscius, who stood accused of murdering his own father by one of Sulla's freedmen, Chrysogonus. The latter had made a good thing of handling the numerous properties of proscribed nobles, which by law were sold at auction. Skillfully treading dangerous ground, Cicero won his case and made his reputation.

Caesar from the beginning was a Marian; in fact, by marriage Marius was his uncle. Caesar had married the daughter of Cinna, and he refused Sulla's request to divorce her. To escape the latter's displeasure, both Caesar and Cicero decided to take extended tours in the Hellenistic east until Sulla retired.

Cicero was a popular politician, but not of the usual variety, for his popularity rested on his exceptional oratorical ability, used to gain friends, and on public service, rather than on advocacy of popular measures of the Gracchan sort. He was, in fact, conservative in his outlook. In 70 B.C., he successfully prosecuted an unscrupulous former governor of Sicily, Verres, and thereafter his rise was rapid. He reached the consulship in 63 B.C., at the earliest age permitted under a Sullan law still in effect. As consul he prevented passage of radical agrarian legislation that had political clientage as its real purpose, and late in the year, suppressed a conspiracy against the state. A bankrupt patrician named Catiline, who had failed three times to reach the consulship, in desperation formed the conspiracy, which eventually developed into armed revolution. Catiline proclaimed cancellation of all debts and even appealed to slaves to join his revolt.

The suppression of this conspiracy was Cicero's finest hour, as he saw it. After hearing rumors, the consul diligently sought and found evidence that made it possible for him to expose the plot before it had gone too far. Acting on a Final Decree of the Senate, Cicero took some of the conspirators into custody and put them to death. Actual military action was then required, the following year, to destroy the nondescript army Catiline had managed to put together. Cicero hoped that this threat to legitimate rule would serve as a salutary lesson to the oligarchs and businesspeople whose fortunes were endangered by Catiline, so that they would afterward unite in a more harmonious state. The renowned orator wearied even his friends with his boasts of how he had averted general disaster.

Caesar made his way upward in the usual popular manner, winning votes through a much-stressed relationship with the late Marius, his uncle, and through the fine games he put on as aedile in 65 B.C. Unlike Cicero, he wanted military command and went to Spain after his praetorship of 62 B.C. He had spent huge sums the previous year to obtain the office of pontifex maximus and, before he could proceed to Spain, had to borrow money from Crassus, who was called *Dives* ("the Rich"), to pay off creditors who had attached his baggage.

Pompey Eliminates Piracy
and Crushes Mithradates

Meanwhile Pompey emerged as the dominant figure in Rome. His position, like that of Cicero, fell between the popular one and that of the optimates; that is, he was somewhat equivocal. He attempted to stay on good terms with the Senate; yet both of the two great commands given to him during the decade 70 B.C. to 60 B.C. resulted from a vote of the Assembly, over opposition of most of the Senate.

The first of these assignments was an extraordinary command against the pirates in 67 B.C. The Romans had long neglected their responsibility of keeping the seas and seacoasts secure. However, when the pirates threatened Rome's lifeline—the grain supply—and even raided the mainland coastal cities north of Rome, something clearly had to be done. The task was made worthy of the great Pompey by the size of the forces allotted to him: hundreds of ships and many thousands of men. Pompey acted energetically and efficiently, and within ninety days the seas were cleared of the marauders. Mopping up operations continued for a time in pirate base areas such as Cilicia and the island of Crete.

The second law, in 66 B.C., put Pompey also in command of the war against Mithradates. This war had begun in 74 B.C., when by King Nicomedes' will Rome "inherited" Bithynia, on the border of Mithradates' kingdom of Pontus. Mithradates did not want Rome for a near neighbor; moreover, as we have seen, the troubled state of Rome's affairs encouraged him to think he might now succeed where he had failed before. The consul Lucullus, a lieutenant of Sulla in the First Mithradatic War, was put in charge of Rome's armies. He brilliantly defeated Mithradates and drove him out of his kingdom and into Armenia, whose king was his son-in-law and ally.

Yet the war dragged on. Some of Lucullus' troops were kept in service beyond the legal period, and their leader's strict discipline irritated the men. In consequence, part of his army mutinied. Lucullus had to withdraw, and Mithradates was able to reenter Pontus. Meanwhile Lucullus had made enemies at home by his fiscal policy in Asia; he reduced interest payments on loans that dated back to Sulla's confiscatory measures. Most of these loans had been made, of course, by important Roman moneylenders and tax collectors. This damaging combination of mutiny in his army, loss of ground to Mithradates, and influential enemies at home caused Lucullus to lose his command to Pompey.

Mithradates was actually a beaten man. Pompey, with fresh troops, made short work of the war, and Mithradates soon fled to his dominions on the north shore of the Black Sea. A short time later he was dead. Pompey now reorganized all of Asia Minor; he put part of the Pontic lands into the Roman province of Bithynia and secured the allegiance of various client kings in the area.

To the south, the old Hellenistic kingdom of Syria had almost disintegrated, with various factions vying for control. Without legal authorization Pompey moved into this power vacuum and took over; Syria became a Roman province. No one in Rome complained of this illegality, for the new province would bring in much tribute. Pompey also settled a dispute over the high priesthood at Jerusalem, but he had to besiege and take the city in order to put down the objections of some of the Jews. Thus Judea became a client state, supervised by the governor of Syria. Pompey added greatly to Rome's prestige and wealth. He, too, became enormously wealthy—a fact not totally unrelated to his conquests—and had great influence as well, though not so great as he imagined.

Cicero: Vain Hopes for a Harmonious State

The consul for 63 B.C., Marcus Tullius Cicero, was one of the few politicians in Rome who wanted to preserve the republic and who also understood what sort of policy was necessary to stay its decline. As a "new man," the first of his family to attain the consulship, he considered himself the representative of the equestrian order from which he came—made up of the second-rank country gentry plus rich and influential tax collectors (*publicani*), moneylenders, and businesspersons.

Cicero worked for a "concord of the orders," a harmonious working relationship between the aristocratic ruling class and the equestrian order. He felt that the ruling oligarchy should be broadened by the admission of more "new men" like himself. As he saw it, the concord would be an enlightened coalition that would, in a paternalistic way, look out for the interests of the lower classes, whose support they would both deserve and get. The concord would need the cooperation of a figure as powerful as Pompey. Cicero did not think this would be difficult to manage, since he had supported Pompey for the eastern command. It should only be necessary for the Senate to defer to the "great" one.

The leaders in the Senate, however, were of a different mind. The extraordinary commands Pompey held were a threat to the republic, because they resulted in a tremendous clientage. Accordingly, upon Pompey's return, they determined to bring him to heel. One of these senatorial leaders was a younger man, Marcus Porcius Cato (c. 95–46 B.C.), great-grandson of his namesake, Cato the Elder. He attempted to emulate his ancestor's blunt style and was an unbending Stoic. He did not understand that a politician must know how and when to compromise; in consequence, he was a poor politician. (Or perhaps it would be kinder to say he was an unsuccessful but highly principled statesman.)

Not suspecting that he would have difficulties with the inner oligarchy, Pompey disbanded his army as soon as he reached Italy late in 62 B.C. He celebrated a grand triumph in Rome in the following year. But when he attempted to get the Senate to ratify his eastern settlement and to find some land for his veterans, he was rebuffed and found himself unable to do anything about it. The Senate also rebuffed the publican company that contracted the taxes for the province of Asia when it asked for a review of an unprofitable bid. Cicero saw the reasons for the behavior of the senatorial oligarchs, but he understood also that the state could not function without the support of the most powerful equestrians and powerful leaders like Pompey. He feared that the concord of the orders he had labored over would collapse, and it soon did.

E. THE TRIUMVIRATE: CAESAR, POMPEY, AND CRASSUS

Caesar Puts Together a Coalition

When Caesar returned in 60 B.C. from his governorship in Spain, he wanted three things: a triumph, election as consul, and a juicy new command. Cato and his fellow optimates in the Senate chose to try to block his way, too. They refused to allow him to stand for the consulship while remaining outside the city. He could not enter the city without laying down his imperium, thus losing his chance for a triumph. Caesar decided to forego the triumph and stand for consul. He won Pompey and Crassus to his side by proposing what historians now call the First Triumvirate. A contemporary called it a "three-headed monster." With Caesar's organizational genius and popularity, Crassus' money, and Pompey's prestige, the coalition was too formidable for the oligarchy. The triumvirate was strengthened by the marriage of Pompey and Caesar's daughter Julia.

As consul for 59 B.C., Caesar turned away from a hostile Senate and through the popular assemblies got for the triumvirs what they wanted: for Pompey, ratification of his eastern settlement and land for his veterans; for Crassus, who was involved with some of the publican companies that collected taxes, a revision of the tax contracts (and no doubt repayment of some of the loan made to Caesar); and for himself, an extraordinary command—in Gaul—for five years.

In Gaul, Caesar embarked on an imperialistic adventure. Even if one discounts the reports he himself made in the finely written *Gallic Wars*, it is apparent that he did spectacularly well. In fact, his partners in the coalition soon saw that he had got the best of the bargain, and they began to angle for important commands for themselves. Caesar wisely supported them, and the two got themselves elected consuls for the year 55 B.C. Then they gave Caesar a five-year extension of his Gallic command; Crassus got a command in Syria, and Pompey, one in Spain.

Dissolution of the Triumvirate

Crassus wanted to stir up a war with Parthia, a country east of Syria that was troublesome to the Romans, and he succeeded. In 53 B.C. he led a grand campaign across the Euphrates River. The Parthians, however, used their superior cavalry, surrounded the Romans, wore them down, and won a resounding victory at Carrhae. Crassus himself was killed. A young subordinate named Gaius Cassius prevented the Parthian victory from bringing disaster to Syria. One member of the triumvirate was now gone. A little earlier, Julia had died in childbirth, along with her child. Two of the links that held Pompey and Caesar together had snapped.

Pompey had always been jealous of Caesar. The senatorial leaders therefore attempted to win over Pompey and thus break up the remains of the powerful coalition. They had earlier given Pompey another command, the charge of the grain supply, which permitted him to stay in Rome instead of going off to his

Spanish province. Now they supported an extension of his commands—but not of Caesar's.

In 52 B.C. when disorders reached an intolerable level in Rome, Pompey was made sole consul. One cause of public violence was the murder of Clodius at the hands of his arch rival, Milo. As tribune in 58 B.C. and later as leader of an organized gang, Clodius had served his own and Caesar's purposes through violence or threat of violence. During his tribunate he exiled Cicero for having put citizens to death without trial in his consulship (the conspiracy of Catiline) and sent Cato off to organize a new province, Cyprus. This prestigious pair had seemed to pose the greatest threat to the triumvirate. In their absence, Clodius' gang of ruffians became such a menace to the orderly functioning of the state that many senators supported Milo when he organized another, opposing gang. When Milo murdered Clodius after a brawl near Rome early in 52 B.C., however, his friends either abandoned him or decided they no longer needed him. Clodius' death produced a grand riot, in which his followers burned down the Senate house as a funeral pyre worthy of their dead leader. It was at this point that Pompey was made sole consul. Milo was brought to trial and exiled, despite Cicero's efforts in his defense.

Pompey, now supported by most of the Senate, apparently decided that Caesar must not be permitted to gain more power. Caesar's command in Gaul was approaching an end after ten years. What he wanted now was the right to stand again for the consulship, this time *in absentia*. He did not wish to lay down his command, since this would expose him to a politically inspired prosecution that could bring his career to an abrupt halt. The majority of senators wanted both Caesar and Pompey to lay down their commands and give up their armies, but with Pompey's influence exerted in one direction and Caesar's (through lieutenants such as Mark Antony) in another, the senators were not actually free to act. The only option open to them was the choice of mastery by one of these two powerful men—whichever one might leave the republic least damaged. Since Pompey seemed safest, they opted to support him. Accordingly, the Senate formally voted to terminate Caesar's command by replacing him. The senators did not permit Antony, one of the tribunes of the plebs, to veto the decree and, in fact, drove him from the city. They passed the "final decree" that made Caesar a public enemy and waited to see what he would do. The consul who would replace him began to raise an army, ostensibly to use in his provincial command.

F. THE CIVIL WAR OF 49–45 B.C.

From the Rubicon to Pharsalus

Caesar's positions in the negotiations before the civil war seem to have been more moderate than those of Pompey and his party. Once he crossed the boundary of his province at the Rubicon, however, on January 10, 49 B.C., he acted with great speed and vigor. Pompey, handicapped because he did not have complete authority, had to flee Italy. Caesar soon gained the allegiance of some troops Pompey had counted on if war came, and even captured the state treasury in Rome.

The greatest threat to Caesar lay in Spain, where Pompey had six legions of troops. In a quick campaign Caesar outmaneuvered and defeated the commanders loyal to Pompey. Acting with leniency toward the troops, he allowed them either to join his army or to leave. Some of them presumably went to rejoin Pompey, who was marshaling men and supplies east of the Adriatic, across from the heel of the Italian peninsula.

Caesar returned to Rome, arranged to be elected consul to legalize his position, and prepared to pursue Pompey. Since Pompey's fleet controlled the sea, the task was not easy. Caesar and his lieutenant Mark Antony got their legions across the Adriatic with difficulty and at great peril. Immediately, supply lines became a problem for Caesar; assaults on Pompey's strong position at Dyrrhachium were beaten off. During the winter his beleaguered men ate roots and anything else they could scrounge.

In late spring or early summer of 48 B.C., seeking food, Caesar moved his legions to the Thessalian grainfields of northern Greece. Pompey followed and there, at Pharsalus, the most decisive battle of the war was staged. Pompey's force was somewhat superior in numbers—especially his cavalry—but not in quality of fighting men. Caesar's men held steady under a cavalry attack on their flank, and their clever commander used reserves at a critical point to overpower the opponent's left wing. Pompey himself fled to Egypt, only to be killed by a Roman adviser to the young Ptolemy who thought it would please Caesar. When the latter arrived, he had the man responsible executed. Caesar was the victor, but the war was not over.

Caesar spent that winter in Egypt. He intervened in a dynastic struggle in Alexandria to support the claims of young Queen Cleopatra; this provoked hard fighting for the small body of troops he had with him. It seems that the child the queen bore a few months later was his. At any rate, she named her son Caesarion.

In the spring of 47 B.C., Caesar made a quick foray into Asia Minor, where Pharnaces, the son of Mithradates, had opposed his lieutenants. It was following this victory that he sent back his famous message, *"veni, vidi, vici."* Then he returned to Rome, where his presence was much needed. Antony and another lieutenant, Dolabella, were quarreling over policy, and there were problems galore. Caesar had been named dictator in 47 B.C., to maintain an appearance of legality when his consulship expired, and he arranged to keep both titles for the following year.

Final Battles: Thapsus and Munda

Under the leadership of the younger Cato and others, Caesar's enemies had collected new forces in North Africa. Caesar moved his army across the sea in late 47 B.C., and in the following year maneuvered to force his opponents to fight on ground of his own choosing, near Thapsus. The result was the customary victory for Caesar. Cato committed suicide at Utica after hearing of the disaster. Still the war flared up again. In Spain the sons of Pompey mobilized men and received refugees from Thapsus, so that Caesar had to make yet another Spanish campaign. The battle of Munda (near modern Osuna) in 45 B.C. was a severe test to his forces, but the outcome was the same. Caesar was losing his patience, however, and so were his troops; the slaughter of the losers went on for some hours.

In 46 B.C. and 45 B.C., Caesar celebrated five public triumphs—though none over Roman opponents; that would have been in bad taste. One was over Vercingetorix, the leader of the Gauls in their final rebellion against the Roman conqueror; others were over the Alexandrians, Pharnaces, King Juba of Numidia (who had aided Pompey's faction in North Africa), and finally, against the Spanish allies of the Roman army defeated at Munda. These occasions were crowd-pleasing, for Caesar had long ago learned how to put on a spectacle. He gave 100 denarii to every citizen—as much as the average laborer might make for four months' work. Moreover, he generously extended clemency to many who had opposed him, including Cicero, who had hesitantly joined Pompey on principle. After Pharsalus, the great orator had returned to Italy from Greece.

G. DICTATOR CAESAR

Caesar's New Order

Plutarch, a century and a half after Caesar's death, wrote what many of the Roman ruler's contemporaries must have believed: that the great leader was from the beginning of his career aiming at absolute power. This view is surely wrong. Caesar doubtless did want to become one of the power elite, but he was almost driven to war. Naturally he did his best to win.

Once Caesar grasped power, he embraced it wholeheartedly. There could be no turning back. The old order was moribund, and a new order had to be fashioned. Those who dislike Caesar say he was really at a loss in this constructive aspect, that he planned huge new wars because he didn't know what else to do, that most of his so-called reforms were ill-planned or presented by someone else after his death. Those who admire Caesar present a long list of significant accomplishments they attribute to him. The truth probably lies somewhere between these extremes.

Caesar doubled the number of quaestors, increased the number of praetors, and made other changes in the lists of officials. He greatly increased the size of the Senate—occasionally, of course, putting into it men to whom he owed favors—and also included some recently enfranchised Gauls. He somehow reorganized the government of the various towns within Italy (any arrangement would probably have been more logical than the hodgepodge that had grown up) and made some changes in provincial government, especially in the collection of taxes, which were needed. He planned and partially carried through grandiose projects

Caesar, the first living Roman to be honored by having his image appear on coins. (Art Resource)

in Italy. For Rome, there were to be a new basilica in the Forum and, indeed, a new forum with a temple to Venus, adjacent to the old and named, after him, the Julian Forum. An artificial harbor was to be constructed at Ostia to give Rome a more satisfactory seaport. Lake Fucinus in central Italy was to be drained, giving many acres of new and valuable farmland. These last two projects he did not even begin.

Caesar instituted a new calendar based on the solar year, for which he used Egyptian astronomers as advisers. The old calendar had gotten far out of alignment with the seasons, since the extra (or intercalary) months had not been interpolated in recent years. The result was that 46 B.C. stretched out to 445 days. With the corrections made by Pope Gregory XIII in 1582, Caesar's calendar is still in use all over the world.

When Caesar took over in Rome, 320,000 persons were getting free grain from the state. He was able to cut this figure in half, partly by sending out colonies all around the Mediterranean. Veterans were also sent to such colonies. This policy (not really initiated by Caesar), continued by Augustus and his successors, did much to Romanize the provinces. The dictator still retained a quite large army. When he was assassinated, plans were well advanced for extensive and expensive military campaigns in Dacia (in modern Romania) and against the Parthians.

The Assassination and Its Aftermath

Caesar was in general personable and amiable. His clemency during the civil wars was notable. Yet, once in power, he did not carefully enough avoid offending the sensibilities of his fellow aristocrats. He remained consul in successive years; he held the dictatorship first for single years, then for a term of ten years, and finally for life. By 44 B.C. his image was appearing on coins—the first living Roman to arrange this honor for himself—with an inscription proclaiming him perlpetual dictator. The story that he was urged to accept the title *Rex* (king) by Antony but rejected it may have been an effort to reassure the people that he would not claim that title, forever blackened in Roman history by the Tarquins. Caesar controlled the elections, and even had them conducted for three years at one time, in order to provide the magistrates and governors who would be needed while he was away on his projected military campaigns.

Caesar, then, was king in all but name. He wore regalia that belonged only to kings and triumphators. He claimed descent from Romulus and from Iulus (Ascanius, son of Aeneas)—and thus also from Venus and Mars. A priesthood was set up, with Antony at its head, to offer sacrifice to Caesar's *genius*. In view of all this panoply, it is not surprising that a large conspiracy against him was formed, including even a few men who had fought with Caesar in the civil wars (Decimus Brutus and Gaius Trebonius) as well as men who had fought against him and been forgiven (Marcus Junius Brutus and Gaius Cassius). As everyone knows, on the Ides of March in 44 B.C. Caesar was struck down by conspirators in Rome at the foot of a statue of Pompey. This took place at the Senate house built by Pompey, near the theater also built by Pompey in the Campus Martius, not far from the modern Largo Argentina.

The conspirators—or "liberators," as they chose to be called—convinced themselves and hoped to convince others that they had acted from high ethical principles. Therefore they killed Caesar only; Antony, consul with Caesar, was spared, as was Marcus Lepidus, who as *magister equitum* (commander of the cavalry) was second in command to Caesar as dictator. The assassins expected public approval and general support, both in the Senate and in the Forum. What they got instead was an ugly reaction that caused most of them to flee Rome. Some went to provinces that has been assigned to them by Caesar, such as Decimus Brutus to Cisalpine Gaul; others seized provinces and asked the Senate to confirm their hold, such as Marcus Brutus in Macedonia and Gaius Cassius in Syria. Antony and Lepidus kept order in Rome. Antony, acting realistically, made compromises with the oligarchy. The assassins, on the one hand, were given amnesty; on the other, Caesar's acts were confirmed. But beneath the surface, forces were at work that would bring on another civil war.

H. RESUMPTION OF CIVIL WAR TO THE END OF THE REPUBLIC

Second Triumvirate (43 B.C.)

A power struggle inevitably developed after Caesar was dead. The oligarchy, of course, attempted to regain control of the state; its leader was Cicero, who came out of semiretirement for the struggle. He saw the imperfections of the republic but favored it over any possible alternative.

The grandnephew of Caesar, Gaius Octavius—rather unexpectedly, for he was only nineteen years old—added a new dimension to the struggle. He was adopted by Caesar's will and became known as Gaius Julius Caesar Octavianus. Modern historians call him Octavius before his adoption, and Octavian from that point to 27 B.C., when the Senate conferred on him the name Augustus. Octavian disliked Antony's compromise with the assassins, who he felt should be punished. Moreover, he and Antony had a dispute over money; Octavian was Caesar's heir, but it was rather difficult to distinguish Caesar's funds from those of the state. Antony had just taken over all of it. Cicero and the Senate made an effort to use Octavian against Antony, for the young man was popular with Caesar's troops and veterans.

A struggle developed over Cisalpine Gaul. Decimus Brutus had taken it over, as we have noted. Antony, remembering its political importance, decided he wanted it and got a law passed giving it to him. Brutus, encouraged by the Senate, decided to fight. Cicero thundered against Antony in a series of abusive orations.

Octavian was made propraetor, and his army of Caesarian veterans was legitimized. Together with the consuls for 43 B.C., Hirtius and Pansa, he defeated Antony, but the consuls were killed in the battle. Acutely aware that the Senate meant only to use him and then get rid of him, Octavian now seized the opportunity for independent action. He marched on Rome with the army and forced the Senate to name him consul. Then he moved north, theoretically against Antony, who had taken refuge with Lepidus, serving then as governor of Transalpine Gaul.

Instead of fighting against them, Octavian joined with Antony and Lepidus to form another triumvirate, this one eventually legitimated by law. One feature of their agreement was a proscription list, and among those proscribed was Cicero, who was assassinated at the end of that year. The orator's head was taken to Rome and hung in the Forum, where Antony's wife, Fulvia, stuck pins in Cicero's tongue as vengeance for his eloquent attacks on her husband.

The following year (42 B.C.) the last opposition to the triumvirs was put down in two battles in Macedonia, the battles of Philippi. There Octavian and

Antony defeated Marcus Brutus and Cassius, who committed suicide. The war was not ended, however, for Sextus Pompey, a son of Pompey the Great, held Sicily and Sardinia with a strong naval force. From there he was able to menace the grain supply for Rome, and so could not be ignored. It was not until 36 B.C. that Octavian defeated Sextus and drove him from Sicily. At the same time Octavian also got rid of Lepidus, the third member of the triumvirate, who had been relegated to an inferior position almost from the beginning. During the campaign against Sextus Pompey, Lepidus attempted to strengthen his position by using some of Pompey's troops who had surrendered to him. However, wearing a disguise, Octavian won over the troops in a dramatic night adventure. Lepidus gave up and was forced into retirement. Probably he escaped death only because he was also pontifex maximus.

Octavian, Octavia, Antony, and Cleopatra

Immediately after Philippi, Octavian and Antony in effect divided the Roman world between them. Octavian took charge of Italy and the West, where he had to worry about Lepidus, Sextus Pompey, demobilization of veterans, and numerous other problems. His efforts to find solutions led him to confiscate private property and to carry through other unpopular measures, but he was generally successful. In the East, Antony had to concern himself with the Parthians; numerous former supporters of Brutus and Cassius; uncertain client kings such as Herod the Great; and an ally of Rome, Egypt, which under Cleopatra had supported the wrong side. Antony enjoyed his greatest success with Cleopatra and took his worst defeat at the hands of the Parthians. In general, however, he too was able to control his half of the Mediterranean world.

Octavian and Antony tended to clash with each other from the beginning. At one point, Fulvia and Antony's brother Lucius actually fought a war against Octavian in Italy over a question of the relative authority of the triumvir and the consul (Antony's brother). As it happened, Antony was in Egypt renewing his acquaintance with Cleopatra at the time, unaware of events in Italy. When he found out, he was naturally incensed—but not only at Octavian. Fulvia soon died and the leaders patched up their relationship.

To seal the renewed agreement, Antony married Octavia, the sister of Octavian. She must have seemed a bit tame after the Egyptian queen, and after a couple of years he went back to Cleopatra. At length he sent Octavia a letter of divorce and formally married Cleopatra, who by then was the mother of twins, named Helios and Selene—the Sun and the Moon. Since Octavia was a most admirable woman, like many others in Roman history, Antony's behavior cost him much of his popularity in Italy. Octavian was quick to press his advantage and circulated stories of Antony's giving away Roman territory to Cleopatra (he did give her some territory in lower Syria) and of Antony's will. He wanted to be buried in Alexandria. Imagine, a Roman!

Antony and Cleopatra prepared well for the inevitable struggle. They were strong in seapower and about equal to Octavian in the number of legions. Perhaps Octavian's greatest advantage lay in his choice of his closest lieutenant, his childhood friend, Marcus Agrippa. It was Agrippa who had really defeated Sextus Pompey, and he now organized the campaign against Antony. The latter had mobilized his sea and land forces at Actium, just across the Ionian Sea and southeast of the heel of the Italian mainland. But then, curiously, Antony became almost inactive, as if he expected an uprising in Italy that would make a battle with Octavian unnecessary.

Finally, in 31 B.C., surrounded on land and blockaded by sea, Antony and Cleopatra decided to risk all on a sea battle. Again their behavior seems curious. The battle was not yet decided when Cleopatra's squadron veered off and left for Egypt. Perhaps she panicked; perhaps she saw defeat coming. Antony quickly joined her; they abandoned their navy and twenty or so legions of troops. Back in Egypt they made little effective preparation for the inevitable arrival of Octavian's army. In 30 B.C., with no great difficulty, Octavian defeated Antony's skimpy forces and occupied Egypt. Antony soon committed suicide; Cleopatra, determined not to be led in a triumph at Rome and finding Octavian inflexible, took her own life also. (The story about the asp may be true.)

Octavian now ruled the whole empire. He would not be seriously disputed again. The old leaders, for the most part, were dead; those who remained, along with all the Roman people, were sick of war. The famous Pax Romana thus was born of despair, exhaustion, and repeated disaster that had affected almost every person in the Mediterranean world.

I. LITERARY DEVELOPMENT IN THE LATE REPUBLIC

Tragedy

Lucius Accius, who lived until about 90 B.C. to 85 B.C., long enough for Cicero to have known him, was accounted the best tragedian of Rome; only fragments of his works remain, however. Accius—and Pacuvius, another Roman tragedian about a half-century older than Accius and somewhat less well esteemed in antiquity—like the earlier comic playwrights, mostly presented free translations of the classic Greek plays. Cicero much admired the lofty, sonorous language of Accius, and it influenced his oratorical style. Accius was also a scholar of sorts, for he wrote a history of drama and was a critic of the existing texts of the great dramatists of the past.

Satire

Though earlier literature, especially that of Greece, contains satire, the literary form itself, the Romans insisted, was a creation of their own. Ennius was said to have originated the pattern, in the third century B.C., but the real creation of the genre was attributed to Lucilius, who died an old man a year or two before 100 B.C. We have only fragments of his work, about 1,300 lines, but it is enough to allow us to savor the highly personalized style and note the political as well as social content. The degree of the impact of Lucilius is best measured by his influence on later great satirists, Horace in the golden age of Latin literature and Martial and Juvenal in the silver age.

History: Sallust

The main outlines of Roman republican history to the late second century B.C. depend on the *Annales Maximi*, records kept by the pontifex maximus and containing information on officeholders, priests, and major events. Sketchy or even nonexistent for the earlier republic, they were fuller by the middle republic; in the later second century, the pontifex maximus P. Mucius Scaevola (130–115 B.C.) published the *Annales* in usable form, probably supplementing them with other archival materials. Historians began not only to use them but also to allow the form of their works to be controlled by them; that is, they wrote in an annalistic, year-to-year type of format. The annals so produced by the scholars of the next several decades are not extant, but the golden age historian Livy made much use of them. Another source of information from this period for Livy and for biographers like Plutarch, still later, was a number of autobiographical memoirs written by several of the leading politicians of the time—Sulla, for example.

The most notable historian of the late republic whose works are largely extant is Sallust (Gaius Sallustius Crispus, c. 86–35 B.C.). A not-very-successful politician who became a partisan of Caesar, he somehow grew rather rich (some say by extortion while a provincial governor in North Africa) and in semiretirement turned to writing history. He produced an account of the Jugurthan War, another of the conspiracy of Catiline, and a *History* (only fragments remain) dealing with the second quarter of the first century B.C. Sallust disliked the oligarchs, his political opponents who dominated the nobility. Perhaps he overemphasized the venality of upper-class Romans and their unbridled ambition, but his moralizing was thoroughly Roman—it set something of a vogue—and his prejudices were fairly well hidden. In style he archaized, perhaps imitating the elder Cato; in structure he followed the great Greek historian Thucydides. Sallust is a most important source for a period made difficult for modern historians because of the loss of other works produced at that time, noteworthy among these the memoirs of Sulla.

Rhetoric: Cicero

Marcus Tullius Cicero (106–43 B.C.) obviously was the greatest writer of the period named for him. In the two millennia since his death, his reputation has varied widely. Long praised extravagantly for political acumen that does not now seem so penetrating, and admired for a philosophical depth that was merely a restatement of Greek predecessors, Cicero later was condemned bitterly as a political opportunist and a borrower of ideas. In recent years, however, an interpretation both more sympathetic and realistic has presented him as a humane person who was out of place among the "direct action" politicians and generals of his day. His enduring literary greatness rests chiefly on his work of molding the Latin language and on his influence on Western intellectuals through the centuries.

Cicero's writings fall into three categories: orations, philosophical treatises, and letters. Carefully composed with measured periods and deliberate cadences, the orations are still studied as examples of speechmaking but are now valued chiefly as historical source material. The texts were edited, and sometimes published well after the speeches themselves were actually delivered; in view of this, they sometimes represent what the orator wished he had said or intended to say, rather than what he did say.

His philosophical writings, such as the *Tusculan Disputations* (a stoical dialogue on virtue and happiness), the *Academica* (a treatise on theories of knowledge), and several others, were not represented as works of original scholarship. What Cicero did was to create a Latin vocabulary that could express Greek ideas, and he presented those ideas in ways understandable to the practical Roman. Several of Cicero's essays, however, made original contributions; among these are *De Legibus* ("On the Laws"); *De Re Publica* ("On the State"), a dialogue on ideal forms of government and statesmanly qualities recalling Plato's *Republic*; and several works on oratory. These are, of course, also of great value to the historian.

It is Cicero's numerous letters, however, which are most important to history. They are like brilliant windows through which one sees the real Cicero and also an intimate view of Rome and of many important Romans, including the great Caesar. Their scenes are sometimes indistinct, and tantalizing allusions are left unexplained, but without this collection of more than seven hundred letters our knowledge of Rome during the eventful period from about 65 B.C. to Cicero's death in 43 B.C. would be much more obscure.

Caesar

Another work notable for its historical as well as literary value is Caesar's chief contribution to Latin letters, *Commentaries on the Gallic War*, written in a concise, straightforward, effective prose. The work, which recounts Caesar's conquests north to the Rhine between 58 B.C. and 50 B.C., was admired by Cicero, who also praised the dictator's speeches, only fragments of which are extant. Like the *Commentaries on the Civil War* that followed (only part of which was written by Caesar), this personal memoir was at once a history, a literary work, and an astute piece of propaganda, as a defense of the Roman leader's own actions.

Poets: Lucretius and Catullus

The Ciceronian age produced two poets of consequence whose works have survived. Titus Lucretius Carus (c. 94–55 B.C.), a convinced Epicurean, wrote his lengthy poem *De Rerum Natura* (*On the Nature of Things*) to teach that philosophy. Readers are often amazed at the apparently modern ideas set forth in this outstanding didactic poem. For example, it describes an atomic theory of the world and its creation and a sort of evolutionary theory of nature that includes the notion of the survival of the fittest. As pure science, the work of Lucretius, like that of his master of two centuries earlier, was not abreast of the most advanced work of Hellenistic scientists. The chief value of the poem today lies in its wealth of information about Epicureanism. This philosophy is otherwise not well known to us, for most of Epicurus' own writings have been lost.

Lucretius wanted to release the human mind from superstitious fear—fear of the wrath of the gods and of the dismal shades where the souls of the dead were said to dwell. With determination and almost evangelical enthusiasm, he attacked the established religious forms of his day and insisted that the soul does not live after death. A man, he taught, ought to die without fear and regret, like a banqueter who, filled with sustenance, lies down to sleep.

The other great poet of Cicero's time, Catullus (Gaius Valerius Catullus, c. 84–54 B.C.), came from the Po Valley region and wrote on lighter subjects. Catullus belonged to a group of young aristocrats in Rome who, lightheartedly rejecting stern older values, led a gay and sometimes giddy existence. Catullus fell in love with Clodia, a sister of Publius Clodius, Cicero's archenemy, and who, in the interest of late republican politics, often terrorized the capital with gangsterish methods. To Clodia, whom he called Lesbia, Catullus wrote his finest lyrics, in which he ran the gamut from passionate love to equally passionate hate (after Clodia cast him off). Intense feeling is revealed with a simplicity and directness that gave Catullus his reputation as one of the world's foremost lyric poets. Yet somehow, in comparison with other and greater poets who overshadow him, Catullus' themes seem petty and his passions shallow.

BOOKS FOR FURTHER READING

ADCOCK, F. *Marcus Crassus*, Cambridge, 1966.

BADIAN, E. *Publicans and Sinners*, Ithaca, N.Y., 1972.

BAKER, G. *Sulla the Fortunate: The Great Dictator*, reprint, New York, 1967.

CLARKE, M. *The Noblest Roman: Marcus Brutus and His Reputation*, Ithaca, N.Y., 1981.

COWELL, F. *Cicero and the Roman Republic*, London, 1948.

EARL, D. C., *The Moral and Political Tradition of Rome*, Ithaca, N.Y., 1967.

GELZER, E. *Caesar; Politician and Statesman*, London, 1968.

GRUEN, E. *The Last Generation of the Roman Republic*, Berkeley, 1974.

HUZAR, E. *Mark Antony: A Biography*, Minneapolis, 1978.

KILDAHL, P. *Caius Marius*, New York, 1967.

LEACH, J. *Pompey The Great*, Totowa, N.J., 1978.

RAWSON, E. *Cicero*, London, 1975.

SEAGER, R. *Pompey; a Political Biography*, Berkeley, 1980.

SHATZMAN, I. *Senatorial Wealth and Roman Politics*, Brussels, 1975.

STOCKTON, D. *Cicero; a Political Biography*, London, 1971.

TAYLOR, L. R. *Party Politics in the Age of Caesar*, Berkeley, 1949.

VOLKMAN, H. *Cleopatra*, New York, 1958.

WARD, A. *Marcus Crassus and the Late Roman Republic*, Columbia, Mo., 1977.

YAVETZ, Z. *Julius Caesar and His Public Image*, Ithaca, N.Y., 1983.

Chart 6 The Roman Empire

PERIOD	ROME	OTHER
27 B.C.–A.D. 14	Octavian named Augustus; announces restoration of republic; Augustan settlement; Pax Romana. Golden age of Latin Literature: Vergil, Livy, Horace, Ovid.	Parthians return standards captured from Crassus. Germany: Arminius destroys three Roman legions.
Julio-Claudians	Tiberius succeeds Augustus; Gaius Caligula. Nero. Silver age authors Lucan, Seneca. Fire at Rome.	Beginnings of Christianity. Parthian War. Jewish revolt.
68 A.D.	Civil wars; succession of emperors: Galba, Otho, Vitellius.	
69 A.D.	Vespasian; economic retrenchment and recovery.	Destruction of Jerusalem.
Flavians	Titus; eruption of Vesuvius buries Pompeii and Herculaneum.	
	Domitian.	Dacian wars.
96 A.D.	Nerva.	
	Trajan; Dacian and Parthian Wars; authors Tacitus, Martial, Plutarch.	Dacia—2 provinces; Jewish revolts in Cyrene and Egypt, later in Judea.
Five "good" emperors	Hadrian; authors Suetonius, Juvenal. Antoninus Pius. Marcus Aurelius (with L. Verus); wars with Partha, along Danube.	
180 A.D.	Commodus.	

Date		
193 A.D.	Septimius Severus; Julia Domna.	
The Severi	Caracalla; citizenship to most free persons throughout Empire.	Sassanid Persia replaces Parthia as primary foe of Rome.
	Elagabalus; Julia Maesa.	
	Alexander Severus; Julia Mamaea.	
235 A.D.	A half century of civil wars, foreign invasions, and economic breakdown; military emperors.	Persians, Goths, Franks, Alamanni invade Empire.
	Aurelian builds wall around Rome.	
284 A.D.	Diocletian restores order.	
312–337 A.D.	Constantine; first Christian emperor; building of Constantinople foreshadows division of the empire.	
337–363 A.D.	Other emperors of Constantine's family: Constantius II, Constantine II, Constans, Julian "The Apostate."	Persian War.
363–395 A.D.	Valentinian, Valens, Gratian, Theodosius; Christianity official religion of the empire.	Huns push Visigoths across Danube. Adrianople.
395–423 A.D.	Honorius, Arcadius, Galla Placidia.	
410 A.D.	Alaric and the Visigoths sack Rome.	Attila forms a Hunnish Empire.
	Barbarians flood across the Rhine.	
451 A.D.	Attila invades Gaul; repulsed.	
455 A.D.	Gaiseric and the Vandals invade by sea, take and sack Rome.	
476 A.D.	Romulus Augustulus, last "Roman" emperor; replaced by Odoacer.	Successor states being formed.

17

PAX ROMANA

The personal ascendancy of Octavian—soon to be revered as Augustus—over the Mediterranean world marks the beginning of a new era. This is true no matter what one thinks of Augustus: Some consider him an adventurer who by accident inherited a great name and by systematic elimination of his opponents managed to survive and initiate the empire; others see in him a wise, tolerant, and generally beneficent overseer who rescued Rome from chaos. Those who derogate Augustus emphasize the less commendable actions of his earlier years and refuse to believe he could really mature and change as he grew more experienced. Those who praise him excessively refuse to give reasonable weight to the more unsavory things he did, mostly before 27 B.C.

That date, 27 B.C., the year when Octavian received from the Senate the title Augustus, was also the year when he announced that he was restoring the republic. Ironically, this is the date most often taken as the beginning of the empire. Yet Augustus' announcement of a restoration of the republic was not all sham. He had learned much, and one thing he knew well was this: The ruling class must be not merely tolerated but also accepted and even enlarged. This meant retaining republican forms. He therefore made the decision to permit the Senate and the government to function in many ways as they had in the past. One must note, moreover, that what he promised to restore, the *res publica*, although usually translated "republic," really means "the state"—with an added connotation, for a Roman would have taken it to mean "like the traditional state." The point here is that Augustus should not be judged a hypocrite because of the announcement. He never promised to restore everything exactly as it was before.

The willingness of Augustus to learn, and to act on the basis of what he learned, was his greatest strength. From Caesar he learned not to exercise too much power too nakedly; from Pompey he learned that prestige alone was not enough, that a solid basis of authority was also required. Perhaps he learned most of all from Cicero. In the last two decades of his life the great orator had come to believe that coalitions dominated by powerful men—or by one man—now formed a permanent feature of the Roman political scene. It was important only that these men or one man, whom he called a *rector*, be committed to the ideals of the republic; such politicians should dominate but not destroy the ancestral state.

Augustus chose for himself an additional title, *princeps* ("chief citizen"). Historians therefore call the early empire the *principate*, to emphasize the role of the emperor as a sort of constitutional monarch, or partner with the Senate, as ruler of the state. Nevertheless, one must admit that Augustus' position became

Growth of Roman Dominions under the Empire
44 B.C.-A.D. 180

so strong that no truly free institutions could exist alongside it; the old republic could not actually be restored. Ambitious men now could advance only with the approval of the princeps. To be known as a friend (*amicus*) of Augustus—as of later rulers—was to hold prestige, influence, and power. In retrospect, it is easy to discern the growing root of absolutism in the Augustan state—and the seeds of decline and ultimate decay as well.

It should be said, too, that however Augustus restricted himself by the revival and maintenance of some republican institutions, the restrictions were applicable only to the Roman aristocracy, which had exercised effective control of the republic. As far as the provincials were concerned, Augustus was the emperor, to be appealed to for relief from imperial taxes or for help in rebuilding cities ruined by earthquake or for numerous other things; it was to him, not to the Senate, that they looked for security, for safety from robbers, pirates, or foreign invaders. From the beginning the provincials saw, not a limited monarch, but simply a ruler without rival.

A. STRUCTURE OF THE STATE UNDER AUGUSTUS

Augustus' own Power

Augustus, with clear vision, saw that although he must avoid the appearance of absolute power, he must nevertheless effectively control most of the offices, the army, and the money of the state. The legal basis for his control in the early years was provided by the consulate, which he held each year. The office of proconsul would hardly do, for the consul's power was technically superior. In 23 B.C., however, he was voted the *maius imperium,* which, with the additional powers he was given later, made his rank superior even to that of the consuls. Thus it was no longer necessary for him to retain the post of consul itself, and he held it only twice more during his long reign. As a patrician by adoption into the Julius family,

Augustus. Denarius of about 2 B.C. The inscription reads: "Caesar Augustus Divi F" (=Son of the Divine One-Caesar); "Pater Patriae" (=Father of his Country).

he could not hold the office of tribune of the plebs. However, he received the *tribunicia potestas,* the power of a tribune, by which he could summon the Assembly, propose laws, and even veto them (though we know of no instance when he did so). He exercised the power of a censor to purge the Senate of Antony's men and of some of Caesar's as well. After the death of Lepidus in 12 B.C. Augustus also became pontifex maximus.

The elections continued somewhat as in the past. Augustus himself appeared in the Forum as candidates had of old; and he paid the gratuities that were by then expected of all candidates and were not considered bribes in any pejorative sense. He did not always indicate his preferences among the other candidates; but the favor of the princeps meant more than any widespread canvass of voters. Before the end of his reign the prerogative centuries (those which voted first) were made up of senators—men whose common sense Augustus could depend on. In consequence, interest in the elections declined, and the number of Romans who exercised the suffrage declined also. When Augustus' successor Tiberius completed the transfer of the elections from the popular assembly to the Senate, it was only a formality.

The form, however, was mostly still there: Elected consuls (now usually four per year—two selected at the usual time and two more in midyear) served first in Rome, then later as provincial governors. Praetors and quaestors also were elected as before and served in routine ways. The Senate continued to make its disbursements from the traditional treasury. There were changes, too, however. The decrees of the Senate had the force of law even more than before, since the princeps saw to it that most of the decrees, screened in advance by him and his council, conformed to his own policies. Fewer and fewer laws were passed by assemblies of all the people. This latter process had, however, become almost farcical even in the late republic, when small numbers of citizens living in Rome sometimes styled themselves "assemblies of all citizens." The Senate also acquired an increasingly important role as a judicial body, policing its members.

There were other important differences. Augustus governed about half the provinces himself, sending out personal legates who did the actual governing. As it was arranged, the territories so governed included the newest provinces— the ones where Roman troops were needed. Most of the army was thus under his direct control. Egypt, richest of all the provinces, was tacitly considered Augustus' special preserve. Senators were not even permitted to travel there without special permission.

Control of Finance

Augustus did not tamper with the traditional public treasury, the Aerarium Saturni; yet the most important sources of revenue gradually came under his control. The taxes collected from each province were always, in part at least, used to meet the expenses of provincial government. Since Augustus controlled most provinces, he had access to these funds. The *fiscus* (treasury) in each province was in theory expected to send back to the state treasury in Rome all surpluses; in fact, Augustus probably assumed complete control over their operations. By the second century A.D. these were connected with a single fiscus at Rome, which by then was the main treasury. It should be noted that those provinces that required sizable army units seldom produced a surplus of income over expenditures.

Augustus also established a special military treasury (*Aerarium Militare*), with new sources of revenue, to distribute pensions to soldiers. As commander-in-chief, he naturally controlled its expenditures. The emperor also had an important source of income from Egypt, with its special status and abundant crops. Finally, the princeps had great private resources, for he had inherited rich properties from Julius Caesar and from his own family; and over the years his personal property (*patrimonium*) was vastly increased through inheritance. All important men at Rome listed the emperor in their wills, partly because it was the conventional thing to do—including important men in one's will was an old custom, going back at least a century or two—and partly because it was wise to do so. There would be no problem in validating such a will. This custom must have had a result similar to the inheritance taxes of our own day. The total disbursements personally controlled by Augustus at the end of his reign must have dwarfed the Senate's public expenditures from the Aerarium Saturni.

Control of the Army

During the republic, the most important armies were those drafted to meet emergencies. The Senate authorized a set number of men and the money to pay them; then each commander did his own recruiting, and the troops took an oath to him. In the late republic, however, a parallel practice grew up in the provinces that required standing armies. Troops there, over a period of time, might serve under two or more commanders. Augustus came to depend entirely on an adaptation of the latter system; he eliminated the traditional emergency army in favor of a larger standing army. In some senatorial provinces—Macedonia, for instance—proconsuls appointed by the Senate still had small armies under their command. Most troops, however, were under Augustus' legates, and recruiting was all managed under the authority of the princeps. Through the Aerarium Militare the troops, on discharge, were pensioned by him in the form of discharge bonuses or land. Small wonder that the army always opposed any effort at a genuine return to the republic.

Augustus also established the Praetorian Guard, nine cohorts of elite troops. Stationed in Italy (by later rulers, in Rome itself), these troops served both as imperial guards and as a strategic military reserve. During the early empire, the praetorians were recruited among Roman citizens in Italy and served for sixteen years. The legionaries, citizens recruited from all over the empire, served for twenty years. Auxiliary troops, recruited among the noncitizen population, served for twenty-four years and for the least pay but were rewarded with citizenship upon retirement. Colonies of veterans were established all over the empire and became valuable sources of call-up reserves and new recruits. Such colonies helped to Romanize the provinces—a development that was ultimately of great significance.

Augustus brought order to the city of Rome, just as he did to the entire Mediterranean world. He formed the *vigiles*, police and fire-fighting units organized by district, 7,000 in number and all freedmen. Subject to strict discipline, they could also perform in paramilitary roles. The urban prefect, who controlled these forces along with three urban cohorts of troops, held a powerful and influential position. So also did other prefects, who unlike the urban prefect were drawn from the equestrian class; most important of these were the praetorian prefect, who commanded the praetorian guard, and the prefect of Egypt, who served as the provincial governor of that important province, the only one not governed by senators.

B. SOCIETY IN THE AGE OF AUGUSTUS

Class Structures

A ruling class was an absolute necessity for the Roman Empire, and Augustus recognized this from the beginning. Moreover, he had to use as a nucleus for such a class what was left of the senatorial families important during the late republic. It might be thought that they would constitute an intransigent group. However, the carnage of the civil wars, the purges of the Senate by the princeps, and a few years of careful control of the elections that provided entry into the Senate produced an upper class that if not enthusiastically loyal, was at least mostly compliant and cooperative. No serious challenge to the new order arose among the senators, though a few dissidents propagandized against the regime and even mounted a couple of conspiracies that were handled firmly but not brutally.

In a superficial sense the upper class seemed unchanged. The patricians still provided the prestigious core; Caesar, in fact, had added to the number of patrician families. Under Augustus, members of this group could stand for office at an earlier age than the lower nobility. The senatorial class as a whole constituted the broader nobility and provided the officials needed in the government. Caesar and Antony had enlarged the senatorial group, even bringing in some newer citizens from Cisalpine and perhaps Transalpine Gaul. Augustus did not add Gauls in the same way, but following Caesar's lead, he did make extensive use of the members of Italian families that had received citizenship around 90 B.C. Later emperors added to the Senate leading citizens from all over the empire.

The equestrian order—made up of all nonnoble citizens who had sufficient property to qualify—was much enlarged under Augustus, primarily because of the extension of citizenship and the general prosperity of the age. Equestrians lived all over the empire, in contrast to the senatorial class, which was concentrated in Rome. Promising equestrians were used in the second-rank offices, political and military. A general sort of career structure was gradually elaborated for them; one might progress upward to become imperial procurator (who supervised financial matters for the princeps), or at the apex, hold one of the prefectures previously mentioned. An especially favored equestrian might even, as a "new man," move into the Senate, rise to the consulship, and govern a province—as did the later Emperor Vespasian.

A considerable degree of social mobility (it should not be overstated) for the lower social classes characterized the age. Especially through the army, an ordinary citizen who gave outstanding service could progress in rank, perhaps to become a centurion, then to serve in the Praetorian guard, then to rise to a chief centurionate with equestrian status, and on occasion to achieve even higher political rank. Provincials who served in the auxiliaries, though more limited in outlook, could attain citizenship through military service (fixed policy after Emperor Claudius) and then might, in exceptional circumstances, rise even to equestrian rank.

It will be seen immediately that from the top to the bottom of the social structure, the possibility of rise in status usually depended on the good favor of the princeps or one of his close associates and that such opportunity existed mostly within organizations closely controlled from the top. The control was direct in the case of the army but more indirect in political matters, where power to some degree was shared with the Senate.

It is often emphasized rightly that the city-states were the building blocks of the imperial structure. Imperial functions relating to finance (tax collecting) and army (recruiting) were assigned to these units. The officials in all important cities, particularly in the eastern areas, began to be rewarded with Roman citizenship. This gave greater prestige to the posts and made for healthy local government. Provincial councils were formed, made up of leading citizens; membership brought little more than prestige, but the councils naturally were supportive of the empire and in particular nourished the imperial cult.

The Imperial Cult and Imperial Unity

Whenever, as in antiquity, religious structures constitute an integral component of the state, imperialism seems always to display a religious facet. Individual loyalties are likely to be linked closely with faithfulness to the state god or gods. Imperial Rome fostered, not the worship of Jupiter Optimus Maximus, as might have been expected, but instead, emperor worship—the imperial cult. The cult did not displace other religions but functioned as a significant, universal, unifying feature of the Augustan system.

Augustus did not demand worship of himself as deity in his lifetime (the later Emperor Gaius was the first to do that), but he made much of Caesar's claimed deity, maintained a priesthood at Rome and established new ones elsewhere, and built as a cult center a temple to Caesar in the Forum. On his coinage he tagged himself "the son of the Divine one," meaning Caesar. Before his death temples to Augustus and Roma (Augustus insisted on the Roma) had been constructed by provincials in a couple of cities in Asia Minor, and in the West, at least one major shrine to him (at Lyons) had been erected. The stage was set for the acclamation of Augustus as a god upon his death, in a pattern that was to endure.

The imperial cult was naturally important in the army, which normally paraded in celebration of the birthdates of emperors; indeed these dates tended to be celebrated in festivals all over the empire. It is easy to see why the cult was thought important by the emperors, and equally easy to understand why it later became a problem for monotheists, both Jews and Christians.

Manners and Morals

Like many another strong man in the world's history, Augustus was basically a conservative. This remains true even though he introduced great changes at Rome, for he was careful to cloak his actions with an appearance of legality. The Senate approved all major changes. A considerable number of senators acting within an advisory council (the *consilium principis*) helped to set state policy.

This essential conservatism is seen also in Augustus' attachment to the ancestral state (*mos maiorum*). The princeps reconstituted priesthoods which had all but dissolved; he conscientiously observed the traditional festivals, sacrifices, and auguries; and he rebuilt scores of temples and completed several new ones. One of the latter was a temple which had been vowed to Mars by Caesar. Augustus added the name *Ultor* ("the Avenger"), to commemorate his vengeance of Caesar's

The theatre of Marcellus (Art Resource)

murder. It was placed in the new Forum of Augustus, close by the old Forum and the later one of Caesar. He put up other public structures, including a magnificent theatre dedicated to his nephew Marcellus, porticoes, and bridges. At the end of his life, he declared that he found Rome brick and left it marble.

A conservative must give attention to mores and morals; and in Rome of the early empire it was easy to view the situation with alarm. Especially among the upper classes lax morals prevailed, along with frequent divorce. Over the previous two centuries women had emancipated themselves from the most binding restrictions, and at least some made the most of their new freedom. The birthrate of senatorial families declined, as senators desired to conserve their wealth and make possible a continuation of the extravagant lifestyle all too many Romans affected.

Augustus attempted to stem the tide. He lived a rather simple life and built no great palace for himself. Laws against extravagance and loose morals were passed. Adultery was severely punished when proven; even the princeps' own daughter Julia was exiled when he learned of her illicit behavior—and later, so was his granddaughter, also called Julia. After a pattern going back to Cato the Censor, laws limiting the amounts that could be lavished on a single dinner were freshly enacted. Tax laws penalized bachelors, widowers, and married persons with fewer than three children. In his exercise of the powers of censor (three times during his reign), Augustus purged the Senate and the equestrian order of morally objectionable persons.

As in most other times and places, moralistic laws seem to have been ineffective. Yet, since the tone of society is usually set from above, Augustus' attitudes were somewhat influential. In the *Aeneid*, the poet Vergil's emphasis on the *pietas* of Aeneas toward his family and the gods reflects the pervasive attitudes of the princeps. On the other hand, the emphasis on sophisticated seduction seen in the *Ars Amatoria* of Ovid reflects the permissive mores of the younger set in Rome. This poem may have helped to draw the wrath of Augustus down on the unfortunate Ovid, who was banished to the Black Sea region.

Augustus would probably have preferred to end the free distribution of grain to the urban plebs, but he found it impossible. The distribution came to be guaranteed to hundreds of thousands of persons not as a privilege but as a right. The great festivals, which were both religious spectacles and public entertainment, he did not wish to eliminate. "Bread and circuses" remained a part of the scene in Rome as long as the city was an imperial capital. Some emperors reveled in the cheers and applause of the city's poor; a satisfied proletariat, moreover, afforded a degree of public protection to a popular ruler.

Slavery in Rome and Italy

As we have seen, the numbers of slaves in Roman society from the days of the republic tended to increase as Rome extended its empire. War captives provided the majority of slaves used in rough labor, as on the plantation-type farms that became numerous as early as the second century B.C. The arrival of the Augustan peace meant that fewer slaves now derived from this source; more were bred or purchased from dealers—who acquired them in various, sometimes disreputable ways, such as kidnaping. By the later republic the household of every Roman of importance included many domestic slaves. In the early empire even more household slaves became the rule for all who could afford them. It is possible, on the other hand (the evidence is slight), that the numbers of slaves used in farm labor decreased in favor of larger numbers of tenant farmers.

In spite of the affectation of Augustus that he lived the simple life, the household of Livia, his wife, included a very large number of slaves, as we learn from inscriptional evidence. Their responsibilities were carefully defined: She had one slave just for her sandals, for example; presumably he manufactured as well as cared for them. The larger households operated much like self-sufficient medieval manors; skilled slaves did much of the work that one might expect would have been done by hired, free laborers. This, no doubt, helps to explain why so many free persons did so badly in Rome that Augustus found it necessary to continue the debilitating practice of providing free grain for 200,000 or so of the city's poor.

Some slaves were highly educated and respected; they were given responsible jobs as managers of businesses such as brickyards or warehouses or of large farms—slaves who supervised and disciplined other, less fortunate slaves. Imperial slaves who formed the core of Augustus' household ran what there was of governmental bureaucracy in that age and had great prestige, so that a Roman noble might actually wish to be seen publicly in the company of one of them. Later, under the Emperor Claudius, government bureaus were enlarged and rationalized and put under freedmen, who became tremendously rich and powerful.

Throughout Roman history a good many slaves—those well-educated or valued for their domestic service—were customarily freed, usually at about thirty years of age. Such freedmen and freedwomen retained by law certain ties with their former owners, but they became Roman citizens, something unprecedented in earlier history. The citizenship was second class, for freedmen were under some constraints—they could not run for office, for example—but in the next generation there was no such restriction. Thus the makeup of the body of Roman citizens, especially in the city of Rome, changed so that the urban plebs included fewer and fewer citizens of old Roman stock. This change may, indeed, help to explain why the Roman populace acquiesced in the end of the republic and the establishment of a new order under Augustus.

C. FRONTIERS AND PROVINCES UNDER AUGUSTUS

For most of the 50 to 100 million residents of the Roman Empire under Augustus, the new order represented solid gain. First, of course, there was the blessing of peace. The Pax Romana, established after 30 B.C., lasted, with only brief interruptions, for nearly three centuries. What fighting did occur was on distant frontiers, and the general populace could ignore such wars. The admirable road system, though developed chiefly for military reasons, brought benefits to all. Trade restrictions within the empire were minimal; the coinage, though not completely unified, was well integrated.

Roman governors, now under better control from Rome and given excellent salaries, were on the average more competent and less avaricious than during the late republic. Many imperial administrators, especially those of second rank, were career professionals whose future depended on efficient performance. The empire was built on cities—city-states, really—everywhere except in Egypt and in the West, where tribes were the organized local units. A considerable degree of local self-government was usual. Of course, official abuses were still to be found. Every reader of the New Testament knows, for example, that Jews equated publicans (these were tax collectors) with sinners. But as long as the central government in Rome was reasonably competent, the lot of the average provincial was better than ever before—in some areas, immeasurably better.

A modern state the size of the empire under Augustus can support an immense military establishment; but an ancient state with little industry, resting on a rural economy, could not. The army with which Augustus manned Rome's sprawling frontiers was surprisingly small, averaging between twenty-two and twenty-five legions, with auxiliaries—or in all, about 250,000 to 300,000 men. In most areas, therefore, Augustus adopted a somewhat conservative diplomacy. It was rather typical of him to attempt to get back through negotiation rather than military action the three legionary standards lost by Crassus to the Parthians in 53 B.C.—and to succeed. It was also typical to publicize his success: He put *Signis receptis* on one issue of coins. The coinage became a constant vehicle of official propaganda, though mostly in good taste.

For a time Augustus pressed vigorously along the Rhine-Danube frontier to expand Rome's dominion. From the area of modern Switzerland to Thrace, Rome's armies "pacified" all the lands south of the Danube. Roman expeditions moved eastward across the Rhine and even beyond the Elbe. A disaster in the Teutoburger Forest in A.D. 9, however, brought the destruction of three entire legions. There the Roman commander, Varus, lost to the German tribal leader, Arminius, who had previously served in the Roman army, had been made a Roman citizen, and had even attained equestrian status. After this serious defeat Augustus adopted a conservative policy in the north and set the Rhine as the Roman frontier.

The whole of the Iberian peninsula came under Roman control by 19 B.C. In one way or another, most of coastal North Africa was also Roman, held for the empire with only a single legion, backed up by two more in Egypt. Toward the end of Augustus' reign Germanicus, the princeps' grandson by adoption, again ventured east of the Rhine—perhaps to the old emperor's disapproval. A year after Augustus died, Germanicus nearly met disaster on the same battlefield where Varus had fallen. In general, however, at the death of Augustus peace reigned along all the imperial frontiers.

D. LITERATURE IN THE AUGUSTAN AGE

Latin literature and its vehicle, the Latin language, have exercised a lasting influence. The language endured without lapse as the language of the Church and of medieval scholarship in western Europe. The ancient literature, however, was often lost or survived only in fragmentary form. It was recovered as far as possible in the early modern period when searches of monasteries and other repositories yielded up the little known or forgotten texts. The Latin literary works, more readily available and more easily read in the West than the Greek works that were often of higher quality, had a great impact on Western writers. Seneca, for example (see the silver age, next chapter), was a greater influence on Shakespeare than the earlier—and greater—Greek tragedians such as Sophocles. Cicero influenced oratory more than Demosthenes, and Vergil's influence on poetry was at least as great as that of Homer. Moreover, the influence continues: It is not only in the high schools and colleges that the important Latin authors are read for intellectual profit—and pleasure.

The great age of Latin literature, often called the golden age, arrived with the prolonged peace of the Augustan era (after 27 B.C.). One of Augustus' ministers and close friends, Gaius Maecenas, by his generous patronage helped to make possible the sustained effort necessary for the creation of several important literary works, such as those of Horace and Vergil. Won over to the belief that the new order had brought substantial blessings, the Augustan poets not only produced great works of literature but also sang the praises of their emperor and the Roman dominion. That means that to a degree they were propagandists for the empire, but they did not really (as sometimes is charged) prostitute themselves to the regime. Calculated propaganda seldom adds up to great art. Vergil (Publius Vergilius Maro, 70–19 B.C.), born near Mantua in northern Italy, was educated there, at Cremona and Mediolanum (Milan), and in Rome. The family suffered a blow when its farm was confiscated by Octavian about 41 B.C., along with many other estates belonging to men of republican sympathies, to provide colonies for veterans of the victorious armies. Through the interest of Maecenas, it seems, Vergil was later given another farm in rich Campania and was received almost as court poet by the Emperor Augustus.

Vergil's first major works, the *Eclogues,* are pastoral poems written in imitation of the Greek idylls of Theocritus. These are generally inferior to his later works, though the Fourth Eclogue was popular even until early modern times because of its similarity to Messianic passages in Isaiah. In it Vergil predicted a golden age of peace and prosperity under the beneficent rule of an infant yet to be born. Rather than Christ (as interpreted by early Christian writers), however, it appears that Vergil referred to the unborn child of Octavian, who unfortunately turned out to be the notorious Julia.

The *Georgics*, didactic poems on farming, appeared next. Modeled after the Greek poet Hesiod's *Works and Days*, Vergil's poetic cycle has little of the gloom and stern practicality of the earlier work. Instead, he presents farming as a glorious activity in a happy, well-ordered world of nature. The technique is flawless, and many have considered these poems the most perfect works in all Latin literature.

Vergil's fame rests chiefly on the *Aeneid*, the great Roman epic that gained for the poet the preeminent position in Latin letters he has ever held. Like Homer's *Iliad* and *Odyssey*, the *Aeneid* may be read for its gripping story, for its poetic excellence, or for the light it throws on the civilization that produced it. The poem links Roman civilization—quite properly, if somewhat fancifully—with the Greek, through the person of Aeneas, who fled burning Troy and ultimately settled in Latium. Vergil made it clear that the Roman branch was from this very early time (soon after the fall of Troy, traditionally set about 1184 B.C.) fated to be far greater than its Greek predecessor. Praising the glories and eminence of the Romans, the poet managed to exalt Augustus also—going so far as to have him named in an underworld prophecy by the dead Anchises, father of Aeneas, as one who would bring a golden age and finally live in heaven as a god. Yet, despite these propagandistic overtones, we need not doubt Vergil's sincerity or his deep loyalty to Rome and his faith in its destiny to rule men well. The *Aeneid* seems to reflect accurately the thoughtful Roman's view of imperial Rome's mission in the world.

Horace

Another of Maecenas' circle, the poet Horace (Quintus Horatius Flaccus, 65–8 B.C.) similarly became a strong supporter of the new order, although he had served with the republican forces of Brutus at Philippi in 42 B.C. He too found his family farm in southern Italy confiscated, but through Maecenas, was given another in the Sabine Hills, which he much loved. His poetry, much of it satire, lacks the biting sarcasm of Gaius Lucilius or of Juvenal. His *Epodes*, based on the early Greek poet Archilochus, contain political and personal mockery and invective, but it is mostly sham. His urbane *Satires* deal mostly with harmless topics and are filled with laughter, more than contempt, for the faults and foibles of mankind. In his chief work, the *Odes*, Horace sometimes informs the reader in polished rhythm that politics should be left to others; that one should enjoy one's blessings, be thankful, and let it go at that. Horace's sensible advice and pious sentiments are often attacked as commonplaces—as they nearly always are. His great gift was that he said everything superlatively well. It is easy to underestimate the depth of Horace's feelings or to overestimate his inner qualities because of his felicitous phrasing.

Ovid

A third important poet of the Augustan period was Ovid (Publius Ovidius Naso, 43 B.C.–A.D. 17). Like Catullus a half century before, Ovid belonged to the younger social set in Rome. The long period of peace and growing wealth and luxury led this group increasingly to depise the old virtues; for them Ovid was spokesperson. Augustus' own daughter, the dissolute Julia, was one of this group. As we have seen, she was eventually banished by the emperor for adultery. Ovid's poem *Ars Amatoria* ("The Art of Love"), basically a handbook on seduction, may have been what brought down Augustus' wrath on the hapless poet. There was also some scandalous affair. The harsh sentence came nine years after publication of the poem; poor Ovid was banished to Tomi, a frontier community on the Black Sea, his personal Siberia. Ovid's most useful work is his *Metamorphoses,* a kind of encyclopedia of mythology, though the artful storyteller often added to the great myths his own details, which on occasion conflict with other narratives. Also quite valuable for the student of Rome is his *Fasti,* a poetic calendar of events at Rome, such as the great festivals. Unfortunately, only the books for the first six months of the year remain.

Livy

Another writer who extolled Rome's glorious destiny was Livy (Titus Livius, 59 B.C.–A.D. 17), greatest of the Latin historians. Though Livy admired Augustus, he nevertheless felt great nostalgia for the republic. Augustus is said to have called him, good-naturedly, "the Pompeian." Not connected with the court in the same fashion of patronage that Vergil and Horace were, Livy was nevertheless close to the family of Augustus and was a sort of tutor to his grandson by adoption, the future Emperor Claudius.

Livy's huge chronicle—which if printed in full today would run to sixteen average-sized volumes—was, like the *Aeneid,* the story of the rise of Rome from humble beginnings to worldwide greatness. Only about one-fourth of its original 142 books are extant, but summaries of the whole still exist. The extant books deal with early Rome and with the period from the outbreak of the Second Punic War to 167 B.C.

The work has its weaknesses: Livy was not sufficiently discriminating in using his sources, did not go to the most basic source materials, and on occasion contradicts himself. Yet his became the standard history of Rome and was never completely redone. Although it is true that he ignored non-Romans, he did state explicitly that his purpose in writing was to perpetuate the achievements of the Romans. His task was great enough without broadening the base of his work. Livy was somehow able to feel himself a part of the past he re-created, and the picture he evoked carries the stamp of authenticity. As a work of art—and history is, in some part, just that—Livy's narrative was never surpassed in antiquity.

Livy's history has been likened to a funeral eulogy delivered over the grave of the republic. The historian typifies for us the attitude of the average upper-class Roman; he mourned the old order but accepted the new. In his heart he knew the republic was dead beyond recovery.

BOOKS FOR FURTHER READING

BOWERSOCK, G. *Augustus and the Greek World*, Oxford, 1965.

CHARLES-PICARD, G. *Augustus and Nero*, New York, 1968.

CHISHOLM, K., and J. FERGUSON. *Rome: The Augustan Age: A Source Book*, Oxford, 1981.

CLARKE, M. *The Roman Mind*, New York, 1968.

D'ARMS, J. *Commerce and Social Standing in Ancient Rome*, Cambridge, Mass., 1981.

DUFF, J. *The Golden Age of Latin Literature*, New York, 1953.

EARL, D. *The Age of Augustus*, New York, 1968.

FINLEY, M. *Slavery in Classical Antiquity; Views and Controversies*, Cambridge, 1960.

GRANT, M. *Roman Literature*, London, 1958.

GRANT, M. *The Twelve Caesars*, New York, 1975.

HAMMOND, M. *The Augustan Principate*, New York, 1968.

LUCE, T. *Livy: The Composition of His History*, Princeton, 1977.

OGILVIE, R. *The Romans and Their Gods in the Age of Augustus*, New York, 1970.

OTIS, B. *Vergil; a Study in Civilized Poetry*, Oxford, 1964.

ROWELL, H. *Rome in the Augustan Age*, Norman, Okla., 1962.

STEVENSON, G. *Roman Provincial Administration*, 2nd ed., Oxford, 1949.

SYME, R. *The Roman Revolution*, Oxford, 1939.

WALSH, P. *Livy: His Historical Aims and Methods*, Cambridge, 1963.

WEBSTER, G. *The Roman Imperial Army*, New York, 1969.

WIEDEMANN, T. *Greek and Roman Slavery*, Baltimore, 1981.

18

THE EMPIRE AFTER AUGUSTUS, TO A.D. 180

A. AUGUSTUS AND A DYNASTIC SUCCESSION: THE JULIO-CLAUDIANS

Augustus had played the role of princeps, the citizen-leader who exercised influence rather than direct power within the modified framework of the traditional state. He had controlled affairs less arbitrarily than either Sulla or Caesar and had behaved somewhat like the dominant figure Cicero had envisioned as the savior of the republic. As we have seen, that indirect influence was really coercive power, and the role was something of a sham, even though Augustus did exercise restraint in many ways.

To attempt to arrange for a continuation of the principate by succession within the family—that is, to establish a dynasty—was an action that did not fit in with the carefully cultivated political image. There was, then, a good bit of awkwardness for Augustus in trying to arrange a succession without specifically stating that that was what he was doing, and eventually there was even more awkwardness and some friction when the chosen successor actually took over the still somewhat disguised reigns of power.

Augustus nevertheless decided, as early as the 20s B.C., to groom one of his relatives to take his place. His first overt action was to obtain for his nephew and his stepsons the privilege of holding important office far in advance of the legal age. By the end of his life it had become clear that he particularly designated a successor by the adoption of the individual and the award of the power of a tribune of the plebs. In spite of the awkwardness, so great was Augustus' popularity and effective power that there was no real difficulty in gaining the acceptance of the general concept of dynastic succession: The problems related mostly to human mortality, for Augustus outlived several of his indicated choices.

Tiberius (A.D. 14–37)

Tiberius was not Augustus' first choice as a successor—nor his second or third. Apparently Augustus found his adopted stepson somehow personally unacceptable as a future princeps. Augustus' first choice was his nephew, Octavia's son Marcellus. His second was Agrippa, his childhood friend, most trusted lieutenant, and son-in-law. The third was Drusus, Tiberius' younger brother. And fourth and fifth came Augustus' grandsons Gaius and Lucius, the sons of Agrippa and the emperor's daughter Julia, who were also called Caesar because Augustus adopted them (as he did Drusus and Tiberius as well). But Augustus outlived them all, and his choice eventually had to fall on Tiberius. He forced Tiberius to divorce Vipsania (the daughter of Agrippa by a first marriage), whom he loved, and to marry his daughter Julia, Agrippa's widow, whom he disliked. This feeling was apparently mutual and perhaps helps to explain Julia's well-known adultery.

Tiberius, nevertheless, had proved himself a competent general and administrator. If he resented the treatment of his stepfather Augustus, it should not be surprising. Yet in some respects Augustus was right: Tiberius was a dour personality; reserved and cold, he was never popular. Even when trying to do something laudable, he tended to be obscure and ungracious. In the beginning, Tiberius attempted to get the Senate to act more independently than it had in recent years, and indeed it did show some independence in debates on minor matters; but mostly his statements only aroused suspicion in the servile senators about his motives. He sat in on their judicial deliberations when it became clear that the senators were not doing their job. As the historian Tacitus said, this was good for justice but bad for freedom. The results tended toward centralization of power, and the fault lay in the system, not the men. The emperor's control was too great to share effectively, and in such a situation true freedom was not possible. Tiberius is a classic example of a man who, quite unwilling, was forced into the mold of a despot.

Tiberius had been required by Augustus to adopt his nephew Germanicus (son of Tiberius' brother Drusus), who was evidently to succeed Tiberius. Germanicus, his uncle felt, had been rash in the German campaign mentioned earlier. Like Augustus, Tiberius thought that the Rhine was the best frontier. In this a major tendency of Tiberius is seen: to continue all the policies of Augustus. He recalled Germanicus from the Rhine area and sent him on a task to the Near East. There, in Asia Minor, Germanicus died—his devoted wife, Agrippina (Augustus' granddaughter), believed from poison—and there were those who suspected the emperor himself of complicity in his sudden death.

Tiberius also had difficulties with his officials at home. Lucius Aelius Sejanus, his praetorian prefect, seems to have set out to succeed Tiberius. (There is, among scholars, vast disagreement about the extent to which Sejanus schemed, was schemed against, or was used by Tiberius.) Convinced that her husband had been murdered, Agrippina became somewhat reckless in her accusations and soon was herself accused of instigating a conspiracy against Tiberius. She was imprisoned, along with two of her sons, who later died while in custody or were murdered. It is possible that Sejanus fabricated the conspiracy as a means of getting rid of some obstacles to his own ambition. Sejanus may also have murdered Tiberius' son Drusus, as Tiberius was told years later by Sejanus' estranged wife—who punctuated her story by her own suicide. The prefect wanted to marry Livia Julia (also called Livilla), sister of Germanicus and widow of Drusus; Tiberius withheld his permission but some time later, it seems, granted it.

Sejanus had wide scope for his intrigues when Tiberius virtually retired, to the island of Capri, for the last eleven years of his reign. From Antonia, the influential and rich daughter of Mark Antony and Octavia, Tiberius eventually heard of Sejanus' machinations, in spite of his isolation from affairs in Rome. The emperor then entrapped and replaced the prefect, who was executed. Agrippina, still alive, nevertheless died in custody; she may have been starved to death. Tiberius had always been of a suspicious nature; now in old age he became embittered as well. In this period scores of persons were tried on charges of treason—as others had been in the days of Sejanus' ascendancy. The emperor himself stopped some trials when he thought the charges unfounded, but he permitted far too many to continue. The proceedings were infamous: Charges were brought by private individuals, informers (*delatores*) who were rewarded from the property of the convicted men. Public prosecutors were unknown. The system itself invited corruption.

Most of the empire enjoyed good government under Tiberius, nevertheless. In spite of Sejanus—and Pontius Pilate—Tiberius generally chose competent officials and governors of provinces. A revolt in North Africa by the elusive Tacfarinas required attention for years, but mostly the frontiers were quiet.

The empire seems also to have been generally prosperous; yet it was impossible for Tiberius through thrifty fiscal policy to amass the tremendous treasury surplus he did (almost 3 billion sesterces) without adversely affecting the economy, particularly in Rome itself. We know of a financial crisis in A.D. 33, during which Tiberius did lend money without interest to those most affected. He did not put on grand festivals and games at home or build lavishly. The financially depressing effects of this policy contributed to his unpopularity there. Tiberius' last years were a dreary time for Romans; for numerous persons in prison or expecting prosecution, it was a terrifying period. When at last the emperor died in A.D. 37 at age seventy-seven, there was rejoicing in the streets.

Gaius (Caligula, A.D. 37–41)

The young man not yet twenty-five who next succeeded to the throne of the Roman Empire had little training for his post, and little to commend him for his task except that he was the son of Germanicus, the most popular member of the dynasty, and through his mother, Agrippina, was the great-grandson of Augustus. Gaius' earliest memories would have included the years in Gaul when his father was campaigning across the Rhine. The boy wore little soldiers' boots (*caligae*), and so was given the nickname "Caligula." The following years brought turmoil to his life, and he lost his father and saw his mother and brothers imprisoned. He lived with his severe great-grandmother, then with his grandmother, and finally with Tiberius on Capri.

Gaius' reign began auspiciously, with cheers, honors, and sacrifices. He paid generous donatives to the praetorian guards and the city plebs, lowered taxes, released men from prison, and put on expensive extravaganzas. Incredible extravagance and personal vagaries, however, soon ended the new ruler's honeymoon, at least insofar as the governing class was concerned. Germanicus, Gaius' father, had implied he might restore the republic. Gaius had no intention at all of following through on this possibility, though it may have been expected of him.

It is possible to sift through ancient sources and conclude that many of the acts of Gaius which are presented as capricious idiocy really had some rational explanation: He was reacting to a conspiracy, rather than killing men without reason; he was training and disciplining his troops, rather than making an elaborate farce of an invasion of Britain which he mobilized for but never carried out; he was aiming at Hellenistic kingship, not merely making sport of the Senate. But to rationalize all the available evidence in this way is to reject much of it. Through it all, Gaius appears as distinctly unbalanced mentally, even if he did have intermittent periods of rational behavior.

Gaius spent huge sums to bridge the Bay of Naples with a causeway of ships, across which he paraded for a couple of days. No matter what the reason, this was a piece of enormously expensive idiocy. Though one may dismiss the stories of his sexual misbehavior even with wives of men invited to imperial parties or of incest with his sisters, there is no doubt that in this respect, too, he was eccentric. He was said to have appointed his favorite horse to a priesthood and declared that he would have it elected consul. He once gave 2 million sesterces (the average Roman could not make as much in a thousand years) to his favorite charioteer.

Gaius deified one of his sisters, Drusilla, after her premature death; the other two he imprisoned for alleged participation in a conspiracy to replace him with another man. He himself did not follow the example of Tiberius, who declined when offered divine honors. Gaius wanted to be addressed as *dominus et deus*, "lord and god". He seems to have wanted to be identified with Jupiter; he built a bridge from his home on the Palatine hill to the Capitol and the Jupiter temple to facilitate his communion with that god. And he somehow extended his palace into the Forum so that the Temple of Castor and Pollux became a kind of entrance foyer. In Judaea, which was now a Roman province, his insistence on placing a statue of himself in the temple at Jerusalem nearly produced a rebellion in A.D. 40. (Yet most of the provinces do not seem to have suffered under Gaius.) These are only a few of the many idiosyncrasies reported.

One great difficulty for those around Gaius was his capriciousness, even in reaction to flattery. The sycophants of the court could never be sure what would please him or what might irritate him. A conspiracy headed by guards officers finally did away with him before he had ruled four years.

Actually, Gaius well illustrates two lessons emphasized and reemphasized in history. First, as has been said, free institutions cannot exist alongside absolutism. (Individual senators did try to end Gaius' reign but could do nothing without troops.) Second, any such system has as its greatest defect the problem of succession: If successors are not chosen by a selection process that in some way relates to the abilities of the various candidates, it is inevitable that at some point a psychopath will end up in control of the government. Of course, one must admit that no governmental structure guarantees that this will not happen.

Claudius (A.D. 41–54)

It is surprising to find that hopes of a restoration of the traditional republic still persisted in Rome among the upper classes, even after the reigns of Tiberius and Gaius had shown how hopeless an aspiration that was. It was perhaps more desperation than hope, born of years of suppression of the position of these classes. The sudden assassination of Gaius brought the Senate into session to consider what sort of government should follow. Such a body was inherently unable to act swiftly, however, and the decision would not go to the tardy.

Imperial guardsmen, roving about and probably looting, apprehensive because Caligula had been murdered by their own officers, by chance encountered Claudius hiding behind a curtain. This fifty-year-old brother of the famed Germanicus, uncle of the dead Gaius, was a logical candidate for the post of emperor. Perhaps, also, they could persuade him to grant amnesty to the guards as a whole. They took Claudius, virtually a prisoner, to the camp. Along the way Claudius encountered a friend, the Jewish prince Herodes Agrippa, who advised him to accept the proffered post.

The question immediately arises, why was Claudius not considered for succession at the death of Augustus or of Tiberius? The answer is that Claudius suffered from a physical disability, some sort of partial paralysis perhaps, which made his head and hands shake at times; he occasionally drooled, and his gait was clumsy. Augustus had not known quite what to do with him. He seemed intelligent enough and could even manage to stand well and make a decent speech in public. But at other times he seemed an embarrassment as a member of the imperial family. He was therefore allowed to hold only minor office and was generally kept out of the public eye. Gaius, though he sometimes made fun of Claudius (he once had him thrown into the Rhine), allowed him to be consul.

Claudius was, nonetheless, given a good education. He studied with the historian Livy and wrote history himself; none of his historical writing remains, but it was not belittled by later writers. He also was much interested in languages: He attempted to add three letters to the Latin alphabet to symbolize sounds not provided for. He wrote of both the history and the language of the Etruscans. Modern scholars would give much to possess these works.

In Claudius' study of history, we may, in fact, find the key to several of his most important policies. He seems to have been much impressed with two theses of Livy. That celebrated historian saw reasons for Rome's greatness in the enlightened treatment of the conquered peoples, Latins and Italians, and in Roman willingness to adopt proven ideas and practices of others. Similarly, Claudius accepted the traditional state, but at the same time, emphasized that change itself was an essential ingredient of it. Claudius seems to have been particularly impressed with the role of Julius Caesar—as well as Augustus—and with Caesar's specific plans.

Following the principles stated by Livy and Caesar's example, Claudius treated the provincials well and interested himself in their problems. He was broadly tolerant in religious matters. Reversing the practice of Augustus, he extended citizenship liberally and even, like Caesar, put some Gauls into the Senate. Caesar had invaded Britain twice and perhaps intended to conquer it; Claudius did conquer it, even joined the expeditionary force himself, and was acclaimed *imperator* a number of times. Caesar intended to build an artificial harbor for Rome at Ostia; Claudius did it, though his engineers attempted to dissuade him because of the enormous expense. Caesar planned to drain Lake Fucinus, around which was valuable farmland that was all but unusable because of the erratic water levels; Claudius did it, again at enormous expense and with only partial success.

Organization of a Bureaucracy

Claudius' detractors in antiquity charged that he was dominated by his freedmen and his women. There is some truth in both charges, yet exaggeration also. Claudius attempted to rationalize the central government he found under his charge. Gifted freedmen were put in control of bureaucratic departments. Most important among the freed Greek slaves were Pallas, his financial officer, and Narcissus, his secretary. Perhaps Claudius chose freedmen to run these important departments because he felt he could trust them. The effect, naturally, was a centralization of control that inevitably ate away at the power of the senatorial officials, and indeed, of the Senate itself. However, senators would not have been willing to take such posts, and if they had, the emperor could hardly have counted on their loyalty to him. After all, the Senate generally had not approved his elevation to the imperial power, and many senators seem to have opposed him as best they could after he was installed. Not surprisingly, numerous senators and other officials were accused of such crimes as treason and executed during his reign.

This apparently well-grounded mistrust of the existing aristocracy may also have bolstered Claudius' view that a healthy state (of the ancestral type, as championed by both Livy and Cicero) required the constant infusion of "new men." Claudius' purging of the Senate lists and introduction of new senators, including

The aqueduct of Claudius in the Campagna. (Art Resource)

Gauls, served not only to bring in new blood but also to remove the threat of dissidents. Claudius in several ways reduced the Senate's power in the provinces, especially in monetary and judicial matters. Yet it is certain that he did not feel he was deliberately destroying the power of the Senate, but rather that he was acting in a traditional and perfectly logical manner.

As for the women in Claudius' life, the charge that they dominated him must have referred primarily to the last two of his four wives, Messalina and Agrippina. Messalina was executed when, it was claimed, she went through with a public "marriage" ceremony with a young patrician named Gaius Silius. Perhaps she did conspire with the latter to get rid of Claudius and take over; but it is just as likely that she lost out to one of Claudius' wily freedmen in a game of power politics. Claudius next married Agrippina the Younger, who was actually his niece, the daughter of Germanicus and the elder Agrippina. There is little doubt that she had a great influence on the aging Emperor; the succession at his death proves this well enough. Claudius had a son of his own, named Britannicus. But it was Agrippina's son by an earlier marriage (to Gnaeus Domitius Ahenobarbus)—Nero—who succeeded to the throne, four years after she had persuaded Claudius to adopt him legally. She had prepared the way through numerous other arrangements that she inveigled Claudius into making, including even the execution of Britannicus' grandmother.

Nero (Art Resource)

Nero (A.D. 54–68)

A complex person, Nero has been much maligned—with some justifica-tion—by Christians and historians. It is important to remember that he was sixteen years old when he came to power and that he was not yet thirty-one when he died. During much of his life he struggled to assert himself over a dominant mother and strong governmental officials. His was the soul of an artist: He sang, not badly, though his voice was somewhat muffled; he wrote passable poetry; he supported (perhaps initiated) important advances in architecture; he wished for Romans, of both upper and lower classes, to choose concerts over gladiatorial contests. It may be legitimately questioned, however, whether the emperor ought to have given free rein to the arts at the expense of politics. He was, after all, the chief of state.

Nero's mother, Agrippina, had obtained the principate for her son, and she expected to serve as a kind of regent, it seems. Here she ran afoul of basic Roman conservatism: Women might indeed be emancipated in a sense, but they were not to hold political office or exercise direct political power. She did succeed in getting rid of some of Claudius' powerful and rich freedmen, although two of Nero's chief ministers, the Stoic philosopher Seneca and the Praetorian Prefect Burrus, contested with Agrippina and gained ascendancy over her son. When Agrippina threatened in veiled fashion to support Claudius' own son, Britannicus, to replace Nero, Nero had Britannicus poisoned at a dinner party that included Agrippina. A few years later, in A.D. 59, Nero had his mother killed also.

The plot to kill Agrippina was an elaborate charade. Both Nero and his mother were at residences on the Bay of Naples. Nero invited her to dinner and, so the sources say, pretended to be reconciled with her. He offered a boat to take her home, across the bay. It had been especially designed to open up suddenly and sink. Unfortunately for the plan, Agrippina escaped, but she was killed by the sword when Nero learned of it. In justification, he put out a story that she had been conspiring against him. In A.D. 62 Nero divorced his wife, Octavia, the daughter of Claudius, and married Poppaea Sabina, previously the wife of his youthful companion Otho, of whom we shall hear more later. A short time after, Octavia was executed on trumped-up charges.

Burrus and especially Seneca—who in most years did not hold office of any sort but exercised his power, presumably, in the *consilium* and in direct persuasion over Nero—are credited with virtually running the entire machinery of government for the first five years of Nero's reign, and they continued to have much influence as advisers for a time after that. Seneca, who was Nero's tutor, had connections with the family that went back some years. Nero eventually decided, however, that he did not want to be dominated by anyone at all. Burrus died in A.D. 62. After a conspiracy headed by the senator Gaius Calpurnius Piso in 65 was exposed, Seneca was implicated and forced to commit suicide, along with the poet Lucan and Piso himself.

Nero had been playing a freer hand since the death of Agrippina, and now he was liberated from all earlier restraint. Much of his time was given over to art and architecture; increasingly, he performed in public, singing and playing the lyre. Finally he decided on a trip to Greece, where he participated in numerous events at the great games, some of which were held out of the usual cycle to honor his visit. He won all the first prizes, of course, hundreds of them. In gratitude he granted Greece an exemption from all taxation.

Rome was devastated by a great fire in A.D. 64, in which approximately half the city burned. About 160 acres of choice property in the burned-out area near the Forum was selected for Nero's greatest architectural project, the construction of his Domus Aurea ("Golden Palace"). It was to be a lavish country villa in the city, complete with a small lake about where the Colosseum now stands. An elaborate dining room somehow was turned by machinery to show on the ceiling, like the dome of a planetarium, the changes of the constellations; perfume and rose petals could, it was said, be sprinkled down on the guests.

Nero came up with plans for his new palace very quickly after the fire, along with general building regulations designed to make the reconstructed areas less like firetraps. There was nothing wrong with the building code; such safety regulations were much needed. And no one should have objected to Nero's building himself a palace; his old one *had* burned. But the speed of the planning and the grand scale of the new palace—which occupied lands formerly used for private residences—led to a report that Nero himself had set the fire. There seems no good reason to believe that he did. But the emperor felt it critically important to find the culprits, and after investigation, decided that a new religious sect, the followers of one Christ ("Chrestus," as the historian Tacitus wrote it), was to blame. There was a brief, agonizing persecution, during which many innocent victims paid the penalty for arson, which was death by burning.

Nero did try to raise the level of popular taste in entertainment, stressing music. His energetic measures to help private persons rebuild the burned-out areas after the great fire were commendable, as was his new building code. One cannot doubt Nero's sincere devotion to the world of art; but he was chief of state, and such a man must be first of all a politician. Moreover, Nero's psyche troubled him from beginning to end. After Piso's conspiracy, he was frightened and permitted the execution of men who surely were guilty of no more than incurring his disapproval. Such a man was the Stoic Thrasea Paetus, whose silent protests (he walked out of the Senate when Nero's story of his mother's "conspiracy" was being told) at length brought on his condemnation. Thrasea's forced suicide in A.D. 66 wrung from Tacitus the protest that tyrannical emperors were a threat not merely to life but even to simple morality—since anyone whose life was wholly moral seemed to reproach the emperor by his very example.

This necessarily brief sketch of Nero's reign might give the impression that the years of Nero's ascendancy were chaotic and that Nero himself was a monster. Yet the first claim is mostly wrong, and Nero was much less a monster than some (the Christians, for example) have judged. The provinces were well governed in Nero's reign; some of those named to important posts were of exceptional caliber. Deprecators of Nero suggest that it was Seneca who made the best selections, but Nero at least approved them. An exception to this generally good picture was Judea, where misrule contributed to the outbreak of violent rebellion in A.D. 66. But the Jews were extraordinarily difficult to govern; the Romans thought their religion mostly atheistic, and the intensity of their devotion to it was beyond the Roman ken.

Two other frontier areas presented major problems. In Britain, operations in the early years of Nero's reign were routine—a gradual extension of Roman control, mostly in north Wales. A problem developed on the east side when a native king died and Rome attempted to add his territory to the province; however, his mistreated widow, Boudicca, raised a rebellion that required three years of serious warfare to put down (A.D. 59–61). Far off to the east in Armenia (now eastern Turkey), another serious conflict arose with the Parthian Empire. Armenia was considered by the Romans as a kind of client state; its location was strategically important. When Parthian kings—neighbors of Armenia to the south—assumed too direct a role in the kingdom, the result was always confrontation with the

Romans. In the early 50s the Parthians intervened in a dynastic quarrel in Armenia and effectively occupied the country. The Romans slowly reacted. Several years of negotiations, military movements, and some actual fighting followed, under Gnaeus Domitius Corbulo, a disciplinarian who was considered perhaps the best general of his day. By the mid-60s, without having fought any really major battle, Corbulo forced a satisfactory compromise: The Parthian candidate for king of Armenia was accepted by Rome, but he had to come to Rome and receive his crown from Nero himself. These two campaigns were almost as expensive as full-scale wars, but in general they were handled competently.

Another major military operation in the East after A.D. 66 was in response to a rebellion of the Jews, which began in Caesarea. It soon became apparent that it could not be controlled locally, and Nero appointed Titus Flavius Vespasianus, a seasoned officer, to a special command. His legions with some difficulty curbed the rebellion, which Vespasian's son Titus brought to an end with the storming of Jerusalem in 70; the temple was burned.

Perhaps Nero's greatest mistake was his neglect of the army. He did not inspect his units on the frontiers, and in the crisis that ultimately came, the soldiers showed no particular loyalty to him. Moreover, the officer class was alarmed when Nero forced Corbulo to commit suicide in A.D. 67, presumably for implication in a conspiracy.

Another of Nero's mistakes was his extravagance. The wars conducted by Corbulo in the East, the rebellion of Queen Boudicca and that in Judea, plus the rebuilding of Rome after the fire were quite costly enough without Nero's grand tour in Greece, the enormously expensive spectacle he put on for the son of the Parthian monarch when he was crowned king of Armenia in Rome, and his lavish expenditure on the Domus Aurea. Nero was forced to depreciate the silver coinage and reduce the weight of the gold; this was the first cheapening of the coinage in nearly three centuries. In many of the executions he ordered, Nero had as a secondary motive the confiscation of the property of those condemned.

The conspiracy that was to cost Nero his throne began while he was still away in Greece. A freedman made a dramatic dash to the East to inform Nero; yet the emperor moved sluggishly, as if not quite sure what to do. Perhaps he did not really believe the threat was great. The first fighting took place in Gaul, where the provincial administrator, Julius Vindex, attempted to head a rebellion that would replace Nero with Servius Sulpicius Galba, governor of one of the Spanish provinces. However, Verginius Rufus, governor of Upper Germany, defeated Vindex's army. Perhaps Nero now thought the threat to his rule was over. But the revolt spread to Africa. Moreover, Galba could not back down, though he had taken little overt action. In Rome Nero found little support where it counted, among the praetorian guards. Promised huge gifts of money by a supporter of Galba, they abandoned Nero, who fled to the countryside near Rome and committed suicide, with the help of a slave. It was June of A.D. 68.

Galba proceeded slowly to Rome, where the Senate accepted him as successor to Nero. The crisis appeared to be over, and with a minimum of fighting.

B. THE YEAR OF THE FOUR EMPERORS (A.D. 69)

Galba had no ties with the Julio-Claudian family but came of the old nobility. He had to act quickly and wisely if he was to retain the throne. From the beginning, several of the army commanders accepted him only with reluctance. Unfortunately for the new emperor, existing conditions made it difficult to please everyone; moreover, the seventy-three-year-old man did not always act with foresight.

Galba found the imperial finances in terrible condition. He therefore did not pay the praetorian guards all that had been promised them. And in attempting to recover money Nero had spent on court favorites, Galba alienated some powerful men who might otherwise have supported him. Attempts to discipline the praetorians and other troops pleased them not at all. Finally, his choice of a second-in-command was extremely important, since he was old—and Galba chose Lucius Calpurnius Piso, an old-line aristocrat but a man who was not widely acceptable.

The legions in Upper and Lower Germany refused to take the regular New Year's oath to Galba in January of A.D. 69. He had been supported by Verginius Rufus after some hesitation; but then Galba had quickly replaced Rufus, to the disgruntlement of his troops. On January 2, the commander of Lower Germany, Aulus Vitellius, was acclaimed emperor by his troops at their encampment near present-day Cologne. (No doubt he engineered the affair, but the attitude of the troops was crucial.) Quickly the legions of Upper Germany fell in line, and soon other troops in the area joined the crowd.

In Rome, meanwhile, Marcus Salvius Otho, who had at first supported Galba, also led a revolt. Otho, husband of Poppaea until Nero decided he wanted her, had hoped to succeed the elderly Galba. The choice of Piso, coupled with the knowledge that Galba's regime was faltering, decided Otho to act decisively in his own interest. He gained the support of the praetorian guard and killed Galba in the Forum on January 15.

Otho was curiously inactive in the early weeks of his reign. He apparently assumed that the German legions wanted only to get rid of Galba and would support him. Eventually he began, too late, to concentrate troops in northern Italy. In a decisive battle at Bedriacum in April, the forces of Vitellius triumphed. Otho fled and then committed suicide, after having "reigned" just one day more than three months.

Vitellius' reign was to be equally short. He seems to have been remembered chiefly for his gluttony. The sources also tell of enormous extravagance and profligacy. Certainly he failed to maintain discipline in his army.

Once the idea took hold that the legions could be kingmakers, the process was not easily halted. Vitellius had not yet reached Rome (he was still in Germany when his supporters beat Otho's troops) before legions in the East and along the Danube decided to get into the act—prodded, of course, by ambitious commanders. Their choice was Titus Flavius Vespasianus, the sixty-year-old commander of the Roman legions besieging Jerusalem against the rebellious Jews.

A legate named Marcus Antonius Primus took the lead in promoting the interests of Vespasian with contingents from the Danubian armies. They marched into northern Italy and, in battles near Cremona, destroyed Vitellius' cause near the same place where it had been won. As Primus moved cautiously on Rome, the Urban Prefect Flavius Sabinus, Vespasian's brother, sought to negotiate with Vitellius for his abdication. But the guardsmen surrounded Sabinus on the Capitol, defeated his forces, killed him, and burned the Temple of Jupiter Optimus Maximus. Primus arrived, however, and quickly took over the city, put down the praetorians, and ended Vitellius' reign. This was on December 21. Mucianus, the governor of Syria who had first encouraged Vespasian to attempt to gain the purple, came to Rome and held it in trust until the new emperor belatedly arrived after some months.

These civil wars had dealt heavy blows to all Italy, especially to the area around Cremona, where several major battles were fought. In such circumstances, troops are never well disciplined, and looting was general; moreover, serious situations cropped up along the frontiers. Mucianus had the luck to pass by with his army as a semibarbarous force attempted to invade from across the Danube, and he put down this threat. In Gaul and Germany a Batavian leader named Julius Civilis, at first pretending to support Vespasian, gathered troops and waged a war of Gallic liberation. The Romans heaved a collective sigh of relief when at last Petillius Cerialis, a relative of Vespasian, succeeded in putting down the revolt of Civilis, and all was peaceful again in the interior of the empire. After facing the chaos which had accompanied this free-for-all race for power, people of all stripes were ready to support Vespasian as the imperial successor, middle-class plebeian though he was. As usual, security was valued above elusive hopes of greater freedom—except by the Jews and the Gauls.

C. THE FLAVIANS

Vespasian (A.D. 69–79)

Before the civil wars Vespasian would have seemed an unlikely candidate for the principate. He was born in Sabine country to an obscure and undistinguished family. He had risen through the ranks in the usual sequence for one of the equestrian order who entered the Senate and was politically successful. He was military tribune, quaestor, aedile, praetor under Gaius, legionary commander in Britain under Claudius, and finally consul. Nero was irritated by Vespasian's habit of going to sleep during the emperor's public performances but still chose to make use of his proven abilities as a general when rebellion broke out in Judea in A.D. 66.

In Judea, Vespasian commanded three legions plus other units, an aggregation of about 60,000 men. When at length he went on to Rome after his accession was assured, he left the army that was besieging Jerusalem under the command of his son Titus. Titus completed the conquest of Jerusalem and the subjugation of the Jews in A.D. 70. The last pocket of resistance was at Masada, near the Dead Sea, where a few hundred Zealots held out until 73. Titus returned to Rome to a triumph. Jewish prisoners were put to work building the Flavian Amphitheater, later known as the Colosseum.

Vespasian carefully paraded his intention to rule in the manner of Augustus, and his powers paralleled those of the earlier sovereign. But he held the consulship almost every year and exercised the censorial powers much more sweepingly than Augustus had. The latter action was perhaps necessary. Civil war and assassination had depleted the senatorial and equestrian orders, and Vespasian had to fill up their ranks. He seems to have chosen well, for many of the leading men in the next several decades were first given important positions by Vespasian, and even the emperors of the second century were descended from men who first reached high position under his rule.

Vespasian needed political control to prevent a continuing chaotic struggle for power, but he also needed money. He announced that he needed 40 billion sesterces (the equivalent perhaps of 5 billion dollars, but such a sum meant much more to the Roman government than it would to ours) to retrieve the economic fortunes of the empire. He therefore had to invent new taxes and to obtain money in every way possible.

Vespasian thus gained a reputation for stinginess. It was claimed that he sometimes squeezed money out of the populace in disreputable ways. He even put a tax on buckets of urine from the toilets, collected for use in whitening fabrics, and the story is told that when his son Titus protested, Vespasian stuck a denarius under his nose and said, "This doesn't stink, does it?" In any case, Vespasian did stabilize the economy and was able to reduce taxes before the end of his reign. All the sources agree that he made wise use of the state's income. Some of the money was spent in the construction of probably the best-known structure ever erected, the vast Colosseum. It was rather pointedly placed on the site of Nero's artificial lake. Vespasian carefully avoided the odium attached to Nero's Domus Aurea, which he left unfinished. Some scholars think he deliberately blackened Nero's memory before the populace to strengthen his own position.

The provinces were perhaps burdened heavily early in Vespasian's reign because of the great need for money, but provincials had mostly escaped the damage inflicted on Italy during the civil wars. Governors were well chosen, and when wise government brought a return to prosperity, taxes presumably were lowered. In Britain, conquest of new areas was begun at this time. Along the frontiers of the upper Rhine and the Danube, new boundaries made for a more defensible line.

The Flavians—especially Vespasian and Domitian—had their troubles with philosophers, just as Nero had. Both Stoics and Cynics criticized Vespasian. They did not feel that the civil strife had turned up the ideal "best man." The imperial biographer Suetonius relates that the emperor took their criticisms in good humor; however, Vespasian finally did exile most of the philosophers. One of the chief Stoics, Helvidius Priscus, was banished and later executed; but Suetonius says Vespasian regretted his decision and sent a messenger to countermand the earlier order—unfortunately, he arrived too late. One wonders about the truth of this affair. It would not be at all astonishing if a *novus homo* like Vespasian was more vulnerable to criticism than Suetonius thought. Suetonius tells also of a time when Vespasian passed a Cynic who railed bitterly at him; the emperor reached down, patted his head, and said, "Good dog." (The Greek word for Cynic derives from the word for dog.) Vespasian, though not an intellectual himself, was not anti-intellectual. He was the first to put professors of Latin and Greek on the state payroll.

Among other stories told of Vespasian's redeeming sense of humor was this one: when he was about to die, he said, "Ah, me, I think I'm about to become a god!" Hereditary succession was Vespasian's definite plan, and his eldest son succeeded him with no difficulty.

Titus (A.D. 79–81)

Titus, handsome and congenial, was less like a plebeian masquerading as a king than his father was, from the aristocratic point of view. He was popular, so his accession was an occasion for joy. But his short reign was bedeviled by three great disasters: A plague worse than any in recent memory carried off many people; there was another great fire in Rome; and Vesuvius, which had emitted preliminary warning shocks for years, erupted with devastating effect. Everyone knows of the resulting burial of the cities of Pompeii and Herculaneum. Several villas and farmhouses also disappeared, and at Naples (Neapolis) volcanic ash lay knee-deep in the streets. It is ironic that this event, for so many a great misfortune, has been a boon for modern students of the ancient world. Archaeological excavations at these sites have turned up rich and graphic remains, some of which will be discussed in another chapter.

Titus was not so thrifty as his father, and perhaps his judgment was not so sound. Perhaps, also, the sources would have praised him less if he had lived longer. His untimely death brought to power his younger brother, Domitian, who probably was no less competent but who was much less attractive personally.

Domitian (A.D. 81–96)

Ancient historians and Christian apologists cast Domitian in the same mold as Gaius and Nero—no doubt with some justification. Domitian, apparently, did intend to rule as an absolute monarch and did, therefore, have relationships with the Senate that fell below the ideal. Perhaps the emperor was marked psychologically as the consequence of a long-standing unfavorable comparison with his more handsome and popular older brother. This may perhaps explain the suspicion, cunning, and cruelty the sources emphasize among his traits.

Yet the sources also make it quite clear that Domitian was intelligent and that he gave meticulous attention to affairs of state, especially in choosing provincial governors and other officials. The researches of modern scholars have generally borne out the truth of this information. Domitian vigorously countered threats to the empire's frontiers and even led his armies personally in campaigns in southern Germany and along the Danube. He permanently strengthened the military units in those areas. In general, the empire enjoyed good government during his reign.

Domitian exalted his own position and liked to be addressed as Dominus et Deus. Like his father, he had trouble with the philosophers and exiled them. He put numerous senators to death for various reasons. Christians seem to have been persecuted because they did not consider themselves Jews—as Domitian regarded them—and therefore did not pay the double-drachma tax Vespasian had imposed on all Jews. At least that is what seems to have initiated the investigation that led to the Christian persecutions, which were spotty and not on an empirewide scale.

In the executions of senators Domitian was not altogether at fault. There is no evidence of such purges in the early years of his rule. In later years he was frightened and angered by conspiracies against his life—fears that were based on real enough threats. Thus it is reasonable to conclude that Domitian was less the cruel egomaniac than a very human individual thrust unexpectedly into power and forced into cunning cruelty by urgent motives: His life depended on it.

The world will doubtless go on remembering Suetonius' story of Domitian sitting alone and engaging in one of his favorite pastimes: catching flies and stabbing them with his stylus, or plotting the death of someone who dared to utter even mild criticism of him. The final conspiracy that did away with the last of the Flavians, murdered in his bedroom, included even Domitian's wife. It was done with little planning for the future, and the result might have been another chaotic clash of arms like that of 68 and 69, except for the wiser and quicker action of the Senate and then of its candidate, Nerva, one of their own.

D. THE "GOOD EMPERORS"

Nerva (A.D. 96–98)

Though he ruled only sixteen months, Nerva deserves his classification as one of the "good emperors," as he and the four who succeeded him were called. His attitude was one of tolerance in peripheral matters and firmness in important ones. He put no senator to death and, indeed, took an oath not to do so except upon vote of the Senate itself. Each of the "good emperors" after him repeated the oath—and they mostly kept it. He treated the ruling classes with respect and consulted the Senate often.

Nerva also started the practice of setting up institutions called *alimenta* for rearing and educating poor children, especially orphan boys. Following a procedure already developed by private benefactors, he used public money to establish trust funds in various towns in Italy. The money, controlled locally, was loaned to area landowners at a low rate of interest, and the income derived from it supported the children. Girls were sometimes supported in this way, too. The purpose was partly simple benevolence and partly a desire to keep Italy populated with young men available to the military. A secondary benefit may have resulted in some instances, when landowners got capital needed for improvements on their land. But since these loans were not repayable and became a permanent obligation on the land, this does not appear to have been a major purpose of the alimenta. Indeed, it is probable that the landowners may sometimes have been required to accept such loans.

In another most important way, Nerva also set the pattern for the "good emperors": He was childless and chose his successor wisely and well. It was important to conciliate the army in the choice and, of course, to choose a capable man. Nerva's choice was Trajan.

Trajan (A.D. 98–117)

Trajan came of an old Roman family that had long since migrated to Spain, where the future emperor was born in A.D. 53, in a colony called Italica. His father, Marcus Ulpius, was the first of the family to reach the consulship, under Vespasian, who also gave the family patrician status. Trajan had long years of army service, in positions ranging from military tribune to commander, and had much administrative experience also. He came well recommended to the imperial office.

It is interesting to compare the power exercised by Trajan with that of Nero or Domitian. Trajan was no less the absolute monarch; in fact, since Nero was so engrossed with his art, it is likely that Trajan supervised the whole structure of the empire more closely. The differences lay in manner and method: Trajan was considerate, diplomatic, tolerant to a point. A number of his letters, preserved for us in the published collection of letters belonging to the younger Pliny, show that he made careful judgments, phrased economically but not bluntly. He put no senators to death—but then, he did not need to. He was called *optimus princeps* by the younger Pliny, and possibly even the philosophers agreed.

Trajan is particularly remembered for his military conquests and for his building achievements. His greatest construction projects were concentrated in Rome and elsewhere in Italy. His new forum, which completed the row of imperial fora begun by Augustus, was the largest, most magnificent, and most useful of all—except perhaps for the oldest, which is always referred to simply as "the Forum." Colonnades, a basilica (for court use), a temple, and two libraries, Latin and Greek, made up his forum proper. Trajan's famous column stood between the libraries. On the side, fronting on outer streets, was a shopping area with stalls on three to four levels. Trajan also built an aqueduct into the city and a magnificent new artificial harbor at Ostia. Other harbor facilities, roads, and bridges improved the communications network of the peninsula. A less ambitious program of construction (aqueducts, public buildings, and the like) was begun in the provinces.

Trajan's wars of conquest were conducted primarily north of the Danube in Dacia (approximately, modern Rumania) and in the Near East. King Decebalus of the Dacians had presented problems on the Danube frontier for some years. In A.D. 90, Domitian had come to an agreement that involved regular subsidy payments to the Dacian ruler by Rome. Perhaps, in return, Decebalus actually performed some service beneficial to Rome. This mutual accord might have continued without war, but Decebalus attacked a Roman ally, and Trajan seems to have ended the arrangement. In two wars, in A.D. 100 to 101 and 105 to 106, he defeated Decebalus and made an imperial province of Dacia. At the beginning of the second campaign, Trajan built a bridge across the Danube, designed by a Syrian architect named Apollodorus, who also designed his forum. Some of its stone pylons remain, though the wooden superstructure was not left in place for long. The spiraling relief sculpture of the Column of Trajan, with its astonishing detail, helps to make up for a deficiency of literary sources, not merely for the Dacian campaigns but also for the whole of Trajan's reign.

A major war in the East against the Parthians (A.D. 114–117) occupied most of Trajan's final years. Here he was again successful and conquered all of Mesopotamia. The Sinai Peninsula had also been occupied and became a province, Arabia Petraea. But Trajan had overextended the empire, and his successor found it necessary to retrench.

Near the end of the emperor's life, a revolt of the Jews of the Diaspora ("Dispersion," that is, outside Palestine) brought new and unexpected problems. The outbreak, in reaction to Jew baiting but also with nationalistic overtones, broke out in Cyrene in 115 B.C. and soon spread to Egypt, Palestine, Cyprus, and even Mesopotamia. As a result of earlier suppression the revolt assumed distinctly anti-Roman overtones. It was extravagantly claimed that a million gentiles were slaughtered. Trajan put a general named Lusius Quietus in command of pacifying forces in Mesopotamia and then Judea, and the inevitable operations that would in turn slaughter Jews began.

Trajan died rather unexpectedly in 117, as he was planning to return to Rome. Oddly, he had not yet named a successor; he was sixty-four and perhaps expected to live longer. It was announced that on his deathbed he had named his kinsman Hadrian his successor. Hadrian was a second cousin, had married Trajan's grandniece, and had been given preferment. Yet Trajan must in some way have mistrusted him, not to have taken formal action. It was rumored that Trajan's wife, Plotina, loved Hadrian, who was about her age, and that she with accomplices fabricated the "adoption." We cannot learn the truth, but in fact there seems to have been no other likely choice.

Hadrian (A.D. 117–138)

Though the new emperor had no real rival and the army supported him, the circumstances surrounding his accession were embarrassing. He had to make tough decisions quickly; there was no time to write courteously to the Senate and wait for a reply before assuming the imperial purple. The Jewish war still blazed, and the Parthian unrest was far from ended. Hadrian therefore took the supreme command and sent an apology to the Senate afterward. There were disturbances in Britain and North Africa and the threat of invasion along the Danube frontier.

Because of the manner of his "adoption" and because of the execution of four senators, Hadrian got off to a bad start in his relationship with the Senate. The praetorian prefect Attianus claimed to have sniffed out a conspiracy against Hadrian on the part of four consulars, including Lusius Quietus. The four accused were executed before Hadrian's arrival in Rome. According to the emperor, this was done without his knowledge and consent, but apparently not all senators believed his story. Hadrian did take an oath not to put senators to death.

Quick action by his subordinates ended the difficulties in the various parts of the empire, and Hadrian made what must have been an unpopular decision: to withdraw from much of the Mesopotamian territories so recently conquered by Trajan. He retained some of these lands, however, enough to control several important trade routes, as well as Arabia Petraea and Dacia. One might say that Trajan had prevented serious trouble in the outposts of the empire by his aggressive campaigning; but probably Hadrian was right in withdrawing from the most ex-

Hadrian's mausoleum; in modern times known as the Castel Sant 'Angelo. Intended not just for Hadrian, but for use as an imperial tomb for many years. (Italian Government Travel Office)

posed, poorly defensible conquests. Trajan had overextended the imperial forces and resources. Elsewhere on the frontiers Hadrian adopted a similarly defensive stance. He built up the fortifications (*limes*) along the line connecting the Rhine and the Danube. In Britain, he built the celebrated wall across the island at a narrow stretch and abandoned the expansionary policies of his predecessor.

Still, it must not be thought that Hadrian was uninterested in military matters. Though he used the army little in actual war, he visited and inspected his legions even on the frontiers, put them through difficult maneuvers, and devised field exercises so effective that they were still standard a century later. His ancient biographer declares that this high state of military preparedness helped Hadrian to preserve peace.

In matters relating to the law and the judiciary, Hadrian brought about several innovations. He added salaried jurisconsults (*jurisprudentes*) to his council (the *consilium principis* initiated under Augustus), which under him became a more precisely organized and useful body. The opinions of the imperial jurisconsults naturally carried more authority than those of even the great lawyers who headed the unofficial schools of law. The praetorian prefect, who for a long time had been more than mere commander of the praetorian guard, was empowered to function more specifically as Hadrian's agent in judicial matters, especially in appeals. Hadrian also devised a more rational organization for the court system in Italy: The peninsula was divided into four judicial districts, each administered by a new official chosen from among the consulars.

This latter change seemed to the senators to reduce their own power, even though the new magistrates were consulars (and hence senators, too), since the emperor's role was thereby enlarged. Importuned by the Senate, Hadrian's successor, Antoninus Pius, rescinded this system, but Marcus Aurelius later restored it. The greater power of the praetorian prefects also meant a reduced role for the Senate. Although this change was doubtless more efficient, because of the careful selection for the prefecture of men who were thoroughly competent in the law, it irritated the Senate as well.

Hadrian's relations with the Senate, therefore, were generally less serene than Trajan's had been. There were the dubious executions early in his reign, but other reasons for the abrasiveness of the relationship are more difficult to establish. Hadrian was a very complex personality, handsome, witty, and urbane; yet one should keep in mind that he, like Trajan, came from Italica in southern Spain. When as quaestor he gave his first speech before the Senate in A.D. 101, he was laughed at for his provincial accent. Perhaps, despite his sophistication, he felt that the capital's aristocrats looked down on him. Certainly he was never very fond of the city of Rome.

It is possible, also, to find some unattractive traits in Hadrian. He was perhaps the first emperor to use the *frumentarii*—army commissaries—as a kind of secret police. He could hold a grudge. He rather overdid the glorification, and indeed deification, of his favorite young man, Antinöus, after the latter drowned in the Nile. Yet the more attractive aspects of his personality seem to outbalance the rest by far.

Perhaps the most traveled of all the emperors to his time, Hadrian spent over half his reign away from the capital. He traveled in most of the provinces, and everywhere he went he inspected troops and military installations and also left practical tokens of his benevolence. Aqueducts, temples, and other public buildings arose quickly in the wake of his visits. Athens especially was the object of his largesse. There he built an entire new city, called Hadrianopolis (the gateway bearing this name still stands), in which he completed the huge Temple of Zeus Olympius, which had been under construction intermittently since the time of Peisistratus (sixth century B.C.). Some of the best-preserved monuments in Rome date from Hadrian's reign. These include his imposing mausoleum (called Castel Sant' Angelo since the Middle Ages), which he constructed because the Mausoleum of Augustus, across the Tiber, was by then full; the Pantheon, originally built by Agrippa (and attributed to him even after its complete reconstruction in this period); and the Temple of Venus and Roma, the remains of which are best seen from high atop the Colosseum. (A Christian church of considerable size now occupies less than half the original temple.)

One of Hadrian's building projects was ill-advised. He attempted to erect a pagan city, called Aelia Capitolina, on the site of ancient Jerusalem, with a temple to Jupiter on the ruins of the Jewish temple. The result was yet another rebellion of the Jews (A.D. 132–135), led by Bar Kochba ("Son of the Star"). Believing to the last that God would deliver them from the overwhelming power of Rome, the Jews suffered exile, a more enduring disaster; Palestine became almost depopulated of Jews. The Christian tradition, on the other hand, holds that under Hadrian all persecution ceased, by order of the enlightened emperor.

Hadrian built almost a complete city as his residence in Tivoli, a few miles east of Rome at the foot of the Alban Hills. The extensive ruins include two theaters, baths, and temples. This was somehow conceived as a showplace, symbolizing the sprawling empire. In one area symbolizing Egypt, for example, were a pool, a temple to Egyptian deities, and statuary representing the Nile. Other areas perhaps symbolized other provinces, and there was a large-scale mosaic map of the entire empire. Perhaps Hadrian's Villa, as this summer residence is called, best epitomizes Hadrian the emperor: He was not, narrowly speaking, a Roman but rather a cosmopolitan; he intended to be not merely a Roman dominating the known world but the unifier of that world. Hence his ambitious travels, his lavish benefices, and also, his bad relations with the more narrowly Roman senators.

Hadrian, too, had no son to name as his heir. He not only adopted his immediate successor but also attempted to make arrangements determining the man who would follow his adopted heir in the next generation as well.

Antoninus Pius (A.D. 138–161)

Hadrian chose his successors well—though Antoninus was his second, not his first, choice. Antoninus Pius seems to have been a paragon of a ruler. The ancient evidence contains no hint of weakness or incapacity, nothing at all unfavorable. Part of the reason for Antoninus' popularity in Rome was his reversal of

Hadrian's pan-imperial policies. This emperor stayed in Rome and showed his love of the city and of Italy in many ways (though his family had for some years lived at Nîmes, in what is today southern France). Moreover, Antoninus often consulted with and deferred to the Senate. Hadrian had, in some significant ways, reduced the functions of that body, such as in the judicial administration of Italy. Antoninus changed back to the older system. Hadrian's continual absences often meant taking important decisions without consulting large numbers of senators. Antoninus still had his consilium of advisers, only part of them senators, but he used the whole body much more frequently than his predecessor had.

Despite this emphasis on the Senate and on Rome itself, there is no indication that under Antoninus the provinces suffered in any way. He chose excellent governors, who served long terms. Existing evidence, partly archaeological and partly literary, indicates general satisfaction with his regime—and implies general prosperity as well—in the provinces. A rhetorician of Greek descent from Asia Minor, Aelius Aristides, delivered an oration in Rome during Antoninus' reign that lauded the governance of the world under the "good emperors." Educated men like him could feel they were part of the governing class, even though they were not of Roman stock.

An outstanding feature of Antoninus' rule was his careful economy in ordinary expenses of government and his quick liberality in crises. He responded as swiftly with funds for earthquake-stricken Rhodes as for Rome when another fire burned down a portion of the city. Following earlier practice, Antoninus assiduously established alimenta for the rearing and education of orphans. To the modern mind, it must seem that no man could be as perfect as Antoninus is reputed to have been; somehow, there must have been feet of clay. Well, perhaps so; but the ancient authors were usually quick to report scandal and weakness. In this instance they did not.

Marcus Aurelius (A.D. 161–180)

It was Hadrian who had made Marcus Aurelius successor to Antoninus, when he insisted that the latter adopt Marcus, along with his cousin Lucius Verus, who ruled jointly with Marcus until Verus' death in A.D. 169. Marcus, who had been preferred by Antoninus and who had married the emperor's daughter Faustina, was clearly the dominant partner from the beginning.

Marcus Aurelius has been acclaimed as the sort of philosopher-king Plato dreamed of. This extraordinary man, born into a consular family long-resident in southern Spain, received the best education that second-century Rome afforded. The finest teachers of law, rhetoric, and philosophy were found to instruct him. Best known among these was the rhetorician Marcus Cornelius Fronto, who remained the young man's close friend and correspondent for many years—even after the emperor-to-be had abandoned rhetoric in favor of Stoicism, which became the dominant intellectual influence of his adult life.

The Stoic who influenced young Marcus most strongly seems to have been

Marcus Aurelius as a rather young ruler; denarius.

the Greek Epictetus, who had begun study as a slave before he was freed by his Roman master, a freedman of Nero. Later he was exiled by Domitian, who like his father, Vespasian, had troubles with an opposition group led by certain philosophers (though probably not including Epictetus). The slave-become-philosopher finished out his life teaching in Epirus. Marcus Aurelius was only twelve or so at the philosopher's death and apparently never met him; but Epictetus' lectures, taken down by disciples and widely disseminated, were available to him. Epictetus emphasized that the individual's happiness lies within his own control; he must not permit anything outside himself, even though it may appear bad, to make him unhappy.

As his *Meditations* clearly show, Marcus Aurelius was a Stoic of the highest level, a high-minded man who wanted only to meet his obligations as an emperor should. His personal ethics were above reproach. Duty, for him, was in Stoic manner almost a religious concept. He was competent both in administration, especially in choosing subordinates, and also in military matters and the law. It has often been said he had only two faults: namely, he arranged for his son to succeed him, and he permitted—even endorsed—a persecution of Christians. To these might be added a third shortcoming: Upon his succession, and occasionally afterward, he distributed too much money to the army, which gradually was becoming the kind of dominant and elitist force that in the not-too-distant future would take over the empire as its right.

It is ironic that Marcus Aurelius, the man of peace, had to fight almost continuous wars. Perhaps Antoninus had given too little attention to diplomacy and the frontiers in the later years of his reign. Trouble with the Parthians began, as usual, over Armenia. In A. D. 162 the situation developed into a major war, and Lucius Verus was sent off to wage it. Victory was eventually achieved, but at considerable cost. Lucius seems to have been much given to luxury and ease, and the victories in the East were chiefly the work of Avidius Cassius, consular governor of Syria. It is generally agreed that when Lucius died in 169, leaving Marcus in sole charge of the empire, the whole Roman world benefited.

Major wars had to be fought in the north along the Danube in the early 170s and again at the end of Marcus' reign. Marcomanni, Sarmatians, Jazyges, and others invaded across the Danube; some reached Aquileia, at the head of the Adriatic, and others penetrated far into Greece. Marcus himself successfully commanded this war. Accompanied by his family, Marcus campaigned far north of the Danube. He apparently intended to create a tier of new provinces as far north as the Baltic. This would have shortened Rome's northern frontiers, and might have affected the later history of the barbarian invasions. There were, besides, Moorish incursions into southern Spain and trouble in Britain. Moreover, in A.D. 175 the Syrian governor, Avidius Cassius, whom Marcus had thought his friend, rebelled—perhaps because of a rumor that Marcus had been killed. Though Avidius controlled much of the eastern empire for a time, his revolt eventually collapsed without any major countermeasures by Marcus, and the would-be emperor was killed, probably by his own subordinates.

Beyond the travail of war and the sadness of Cassius' abortive attempt to claim the throne, Marcus and the empire reeled under a series of natural disasters. In the very first year of his reign terrible floods on the Tiber destroyed property on an unprecedented scale and brought on famine. The army that came back in triumph from the eastern wars brought with it the plague. Epidemic at certain times and places, the disease remained endemic and sporadically destructive of life for several years after. Estimates of the losses in human life run as high as a third of the entire population of the empire. Even though this figure seems too high, there is no doubt that Rome never quite recovered from this grave blow.

Manpower shortages, especially in the military and in the important field of agriculture, were facts of life for every Roman emperor from this time on. As a result, more and more barbarous or semibarbarous units were used in the Roman army. Such groups were often encouraged to settle on vacant land inside the boundaries of the empire; but they did not always settle down peacefully in their assigned spots.

When an earthquake destroyed Smyrna, Marcus helped to rebuild it, at great cost. Continual war and disaster bore down hard on the treasury. Despite the personal thriftiness of the emperor, he was often hard put to keep cash in the state coffers. He even resorted to an auction of some of the prized possessions of the imperial household. The symbolism of this act may have been even more important than the money involved. The coinage seems to show a progressive economic decline—and not just in Marcus' reign. The silver denarius had been gradually cheapened since the time of Nero, until by the end of Marcus' rule its silver content was only about 60 percent of what it had been under Augustus. It is likely, however, that this depreciation in part reflects a rise in the relative price of silver itself.

The persecution of Christians came in two periods, chiefly in the mid-160s and again about ten years later. The first persecution, in which Justin was martyred, reflects the troubled period of the plague; Christians, with their "atheism" (that is, from the prevailing viewpoint), may have been held responsible for the anger of the gods. The second persecution, centered about Lugdunum (Lyons) in Gaul, was the result of local zeal against people marked as criminals merely by their professed religion and was a side effect—no doubt unexpected—of an imperial decree. Marcus, in attempting to take a heavy financial burden off the upper classes in the empire, decreed that criminals might be used in place of trained slaves in the wild-animal baiting in public games. Marcus also seems to have believed the lurid stories of incest and child cannibalism that were widely told of Christians. Again, the great irony: Here was an emperor whose concern for justice made him sit long hours in court and who made some landmark decisions, noted for their humanity. Yet he persecuted Christians without investigating the century-old false charges laid against them.

Marcus died in Vindobona (Vienna) while still on campaign. He had already made the arrangements that put the empire into the hands of his son Commodus. This was perhaps Marcus' worst decision, but he could have made a different one only if he were willing to kill his own son—too great a sacrifice to expect of any fond father.

The empire was to survive the accession of Commodus and would, indeed, endure three centuries more. Most of its citizens in these years would feel that whatever its trials, however agonizing some current distress, the empire remained the one entity for governing their world; no alternative was even conceivable. But the greatest days were over. The Pax Romana, often shattered, no longer provided quite so secure a citadel within which prosperity and optimism could reign serene.

BOOKS FOR FURTHER READING

BALSDON, J. *The Emperor Gaius (Caligula)*, Oxford, 1934.

BIRLEY, A. *Marcus Aurelius*, London, 1966.

CHARLES-PICARD, G. *Augustus and Nero*, New York, 1968.

D'ARMS, J. *Commerce and Social Standing in Ancient Rome*, Cambridge, Mass., 1981.

DUNCAN-JONES, R. *The Economy of the Roman Empire*, Cambridge, 1974.

GRANT, M. *Nero*, New York, 1970.

GRANT, M. *The Twelve Caesars*, New York, 1975.

GRIFFIN, M. *Nero: The End of a Dynasty*, New Haven, 1985.

HAMMOND, M. *The Antonine Monarchy*, Rome, 1959.

HENDERSON, B. *The Life and Principate of the Emperor Hadrian*, London, 1923.

HENDERSON, B. *Five Roman Emperors*, Cambridge, 1927.

JONES, A. *Studies in Roman Government and Law*, New York, 1960.

MACMULLEN, R. *Enemies of the Roman Order*, Cambridge, Mass., 1966.

MILLAR, F. *The Emperor in the Roman World (31 B. C.–A. D. 337)*, Ithaca, N.Y., 1977.

MILLAR, F. *The Roman Empire and Its Neighbours*, New York, 1967.

RICKMAN, G. *The Corn Supply of Ancient Rome*, Oxford, 1980.

SEAGER, R. *Tiberius*, Berkeley, 1972.

STEVENSON, G. *Roman Provincial Administration*, 2nd ed., Oxford, 1949.

WARMINGTON, B. *Nero: Reality and Legend*, New York, 1970.

WATSON, G. *The Roman Soldier*, Ithaca, N.Y., 1969.

WEBSTER, G. *The Roman Imperial Army*, London, 1969.

19

LIFE, LITERATURE, AND CULTURE IN THE HIGH EMPIRE

The Roman Empire in the first two centuries provided amenities of life that the world would not see again until the nineteenth century. The major cities built libraries and other public buildings, constructed finely engineered water-supply and distribution systems, and fashioned at least minimal sanitary facilities. An extensive network of excellent roads made possible convenient travel and rapid communications. Those who were economically able to travel usually could do so without official interference. Authors, lecturers, rhetoricians, and philosophers doubtless felt some restraint, but within limits they could express themselves freely.

A. LIFE

Rome: Facilities

Rome itself, of course, was the queen of cities—with the most cosmopolitan population, the most surging crowds, the most exciting events, and the most marvelous buildings and public squares. By the time of Trajan, there were five forums, boasting numerous temples, basilicas, libraries, and other public buildings, as well as colonnades and open space for socializing. Adjoining the forums were innumerable shops, arranged on as many as five levels.

The population of Rome, by the best estimates, reached nearly a million by the reign of Augustus and was somewhat larger still in the second century A.D.

Panoramic view of the Roman Forum. (Art Resource)

The major streets were paved—though others remained dirt (or mud)—and along the best streets were sidewalks. The city aqueducts, which brought in water from as far away as fifty or sixty miles, had a capacity of more than 300 million gallons per day—though the actual delivery must have been considerably less. The water was distributed all over the city, even to the hilltops, and poured continuously into the many public fountains. The privileged had water brought to their residences by lead pipe and with some pressure. There were valves and other plumbing amenities such as flush toilets.

The concentration of forums and shops produced almost overwhelming crowds and traffic. "Noise pollution" is no modern phenomenon. When shopkeepers and peddlers shouted out their wares or metalworkers and carpenters hammered, all in narrow echoing streets, the noise level was irritatingly high. Nor did this din subside in the evening. Rome's narrow, often steep and twisting streets simply could not accommodate both pedestrian and cart and wagon traffic. From the time of Julius Caesar on, therefore, most carts and wagons were barred from the downtown area during the day. Juvenal relates graphically how impossible it was to sleep at night when the iron tires of heavy wagons ground on the cobbled streets below, the drivers swearing at the tops of their voices at unwilling beasts. Seneca tells what it was like to live above a bathhouse, where one could hear, for weary hours, the slap of the masseur, the grunts of the exercisers, and the shouting of participants in the various games. Many of Rome's thousands lived in *insulae,* or great apartment houses, which sometimes were cheaply constructed and occasionally collapsed. Often they must have lived on streets so narrow that balconies on the floors above shut out much of the natural light.

Despite the *vigiles,* a police force organized by Augustus, travel in the streets at night could be risky business. If muggers didn't assault the lone wayfarer, he or she might suffer the indignity of being drenched with filth thrown from upper-story windows. Streets were supposed to be swept by the property owners every day (again, by decree of Julius Caesar), but this regulation must often have been violated. City codes incorporating rules of this sort were gradually extended throughout the cities of Italy and, eventually, the whole empire. Despite problems in enforcing these rules, there is no doubt that Rome was a more sanitary and healthful place to live in the early empire than many a European city was in early modern times.

Rome was above all the place to be. The center of the Mediterranean world, this was where things happened, and all things naturally gravitated to that center. Most exciting were the great spectacles, officially supported in lavish style. Juvenal said, contemptuously, that the Roman mob cared only for bread and circuses. Food was provided for two or three hundred thousand inhabitants through free grain distribution (the *annona*). The circuses too were free, or almost so. In the mid-second century A.D., about 40 percent of the calendar days were designated as holidays (though it should not be assumed that all Romans were able to cease work on all those days). On about a hundred days each year, public games of one sort or another were provided; these were most often associated with the great festivals, some of which had been celebrated for centuries. Most of these occasions had some religious or semireligious connection. The greatest festivals, which included games and theatrical performances, were those in honor of Jupiter, Apollo, Ceres, Cybele, and Flora.

Perhaps the most exciting events were the horse and chariot races, held in the huge Circus Maximus, seating about 150,000 persons. Including standing room, perhaps a quarter of a million persons could see the races here. Even in its present rather bare, excavated form it remains impressive. There were two or three other outdoor circuses of this type in the city. Anyone who has seen the movie *Ben Hur* can have some impression of the excitement of the race itself, but only the imagination can conjure up the overwhelming effect of the betting, the hawking, the roar of the crowd, and the tremendous competition among the various factions supporting the Blues, the Greens, the Whites, or the Reds. The owners and drivers of the best horses commanded large fees, just as premier athletes and horses do today. There is one story of an official who, feeling the demands of the

The Flavian amphitheater, commonly called the Colosseum, built by Vespasian and Titus.
(Italian Government Travel Office)

chariot crews were unreasonably high, put on dog races instead. Though we have
no information on crowd reaction, it is known that the usual races were quickly
restored.

Just as exciting, and in a more feral way, were the games presented in the
various amphitheaters. Largest of these was the Flavian Amphitheater, later known
as the Colosseum. It derived its familiar name from the Colossus, a statue of Nero
about 125 feet tall, wearing the radiate crown of the sun god and built nearby as
part of his reconstruction of the city after the great fire. The Colosseum was built
in large part with the labor of thousands of Jewish slaves brought to Rome after
the destruction of Jerusalem in A.D. 70. It is perhaps the most impressive of all the
monuments from the ancient Roman past; the remaining portion gives the modern
viewer a feeling for the days of imperial Rome as nothing else can. Built of trav-
ertine that over the centuries has mellowed to a yellowish white, which almost

glows at sunset or by the lights illuminating its arches at night, it was constructed in four tiers of arches in three classic styles (Doric, Ionic, and Corinthian). The capacity of the immense oval structure has been estimated at from about 50,000 to 90,000. From accounts of how the crowds pressed into other similar structures (50,000 persons were once said to have been killed or injured in a much smaller amphitheater in an Italian town), the higher figure is most likely, though spectators would then have been packed into every conceivable space.

In these amphitheaters were held the infamous gladiatorial combats, the contests between men and wild animals, combats of animals (lion versus elephant, for example), animal hunts, and all the various other chilling spectacles that could be devised by the most ingenious minds in show business. There were, indeed, some more civilized treats, such as acrobatics, juggling, and the antics of trained beasts performing much as they might in a modern circus. But the Roman mob demanded blood, and Romans were happiest when shouting *"Jugula"* to a gladiator, mercilessly urging him to slay his fallen adversary.

Both members of a pair of gladiators often survived combat in the arena, but there were deaths in great numbers: Existing accounts of the events mention the total numbers who fought and the number who died. Some of those who fought—hardly professional gladiators—were condemned criminals. The demand for healthy male slaves to make into gladiators must have been tremendous, for it was not Rome alone that thirsted for spilled blood in the arena. The slave system itself was dehumanizing enough; the gory public spectacles can only have contributed to the cheapening of human (and animal) life.

The Social Spectrum in Rome

As in the days of the republic, the governing class was the upper class, and social position for most persons was defined by offices held by members of their family, currently or in the recent past. The senatorial class, as earlier, therefore included almost all the prestigious families. Within this group, the family of the emperor naturally ranked highest, followed closely by families with marital or other close connections with the imperial house. These families lived luxuriously in large houses staffed by scores, sometimes hundreds, of slaves. They had country villas in hills near the city for summertime retreats and others in the resort areas to the south, especially on the Bay of Naples. The greatest excesses of luxury seem to have occurred in the first century. In the second, the Emperors Antoninus Pius and Marcus Aurelius seem deliberately to have introduced an element of restraint.

Upper-class women found their positions defined by their husbands' status. Since the days of the republic such women had enjoyed a considerable freedom. Augustus, strongly conservative in social matters, took no positive move to increase the permitted activities of women, though he did grant independence from a husband's control to women who had at least three children (five in the provinces). Women could move about freely; upper-class women usually used litters. They could attend the races in the circus, the theater, and the amphitheater, though except for the races they sat in separate seats. Some women operated businesses—even sizable ones such as brickyards (respectable enough even for noble ladies) and shipping firms. Yet they could not legally be guardians of even their own children and were required themselves to have male guardians when there was no father or husband. And of course, despite the great power of some women—Livia, Agrippina, the two Faustinas, and later, the Julias of the Severi, for example—no woman ever formally entered politics or held public office. Still, Roman women of all classes enjoyed a degree of freedom not found in other, earlier civilizations.

As for the lower classes in the city, their situation (see the section on Rome preceding) also had not changed markedly from the days of the late republic. By the end of this period they were no longer called together to vote for officials nor to pass laws; yet it was important to the government to keep them pacified, and their needs were not totally ignored. Grain distributions, free entertainment, and low-cost public baths helped to keep them a cut above the lower classes in the less favored cities of the empire—or on the farms. However, the Roman tradition of subsidization of the urban poor did not extend to housing, and most Romans lived crowded in small apartments or single rooms without heat, running water, or garbage removal. They often disposed of their refuse by throwing it out a window. The crowds of Romans probably felt important only when they played their role in festivals, ceremonies, or games—only spectators, to be sure, but in the scheme of things, important enough.

Urban Centers Outside Rome

Towns in the eastern Mediterranean tended to retain their Hellenistic characteristics and the usual structures: an agora, or marketplace, with a council house, temples, and stoas; nearby would be a theater and perhaps an *odeion*, or music hall. In the West, towns tended to mimic Rome. Italian towns had arenas or amphitheaters, circuses, aqueducts, temples, and sometimes basilicas, all much like the mother city. Instead of the Greek-style games, with emphasis on track and field events, Romans and their imitators, as we have seen, preferred bloody and dangerous events. Many of the cities of Gaul, Spain, and North Africa, especially, as can be seen still from the remains, offered their citizens a pleasant existence with amenities that did not quite match those of Rome but far surpassed what was to come after the breakup of the empire.

Ostia, Pompeii, Herculaneum

Volcanic eruption and/or abandonment, disasters for the ancient inhabitants but marvelous for modern scholars—and ordinary tourists—have preserved more or less intact large sections of Ostia, the port for Rome, and two cities on the Bay of Naples, Pompeii and Herculaneum. At these sites, as nowhere else, visitors today can feel that they are actually walking in an ancient city, seeing the

Painting found in a Pompeian house. The figures symbolize the household deities.

same sights and perhaps feeling something like the atmosphere that Romans saw and felt nearly two thousand years ago.

Ostia was abandoned in the early Middle Ages and gradually crumbled into ruin. The durable Roman brick resisted the elements, however; temples, a theater, a public building or two, and many apartment structures have remained well preserved enough to show their form. A local museum houses important objects of art found on the site. Especially impressive to the casual tourist are the apartment houses, which with the addition of electricity and somewhat improved modern plumbing would, if still intact, make attractive and modern-looking quarters acceptable to tenants of discriminating taste even today.

Pompeii was covered with fifteen to twenty feet or more of volcanic ash in the eruption of Vesuvius in A.D. 79, and it is still only about two-thirds excavated. Here, perhaps more than at any other existing site, one can feel oneself transported back into the first century. The huge paving stones of the streets show the grooves carved out by the groaning iron wheels of ancient wagons. The shops lining the major streets seem ready to be filled again with goods and customers. Graffiti,

Pompeii. Street Scene with shops. Note the stepping stones, spaced to permit cartwheels
to pass between them.

perhaps supporting political candidates or making sardonic comments on life, can
still be read on walls. The comfortable, livable houses, attractive inside (though
not so much on the exterior), are typical of Roman life in the seaside resorts of
the Naples area.

In this leisurely setting, disaster came suddenly, and because of this sudden catastrophe much remained in situ for modern rediscovery. We may see the
remains of a loaf of bread, carbonized but still in its original form. Jewelry, cooking
utensils, surgical instruments—so many items of beauty or practical use that they
cannot be listed in full—may be seen in the National Archaeological Museum in
Naples. There are marvelous detached mosaics and frescoes as well as statuary.
There are also the obscenities and pornography that marked the houses of prostitution. Expert excavators learned to pour plaster into the cavities where once
something living had lain. The resulting casts reproduce faithfully such poignant
traces as the chained dog who died in agony and the mother and daughter who
died while fleeing, the mother's arm thrown protectively around her child.

Herculaneum, buried much more deeply under lava and mud, is thus more intact even than Pompeii. It has been excavated more slowly and with greater difficulty, particularly because much of it lay beneath a modern urban site. Some valuable objects were retrieved in antiquity from the ashes of Pompeii, but almost everything at Herculaneum remained for the modern archaeologist. Moreover, archaeologists there, laudably, are attempting to leave more of the frescoes and other objects in their original site for greater realism and appreciation. Unfortunately, the amount of money available for such projects from the Italian government is insufficient—to such an extent that some of these valuable sites are actually imperiled.

The total impression gained from these graphic remains is of pleasant living in well-planned, clean, and prosperous towns. Ostia prospered because of trade; Pompeii and Herculaneum were favored by location in a resort area. Thus they cannot be entirely typical, and one should remember that most Italians—like most residents of the empire elsewhere—must have lived in far less satisfactory conditions. But it is equally certain that most inhabitants of the empire at its height were better housed and lived in better circumstances than people in the same areas were to enjoy again for many centuries after.

Society: The Empire

The gradual extension of citizenship and the integration of the upper classes everywhere into the governmental structure created a privileged class in the provinces that strongly supported the empire. The Christian apostle Paul, who was a Roman citizen, certainly felt the unity of the empire; his writings reflect admiration for the universal state. In the second century, Aelius Aristides of Smyrna in Asia Minor could feel that Rome in a sense belonged to him as well as to the native Romans. Some few upper-class men from the provinces, especially from Hellenized areas, even made their way into the highest imperial offices.

Italian and provincial citizens of Rome enjoyed favored status. In Italy, the exemption from taxation plus the reflected prosperity and prestige of the capital made for a level of well-being above that of noncitizens and provincials. Of the citizens in the provinces, the most favored were likely to be veterans or their descendants, for veteran colonies had been sent out regularly since the time of Caesar. These communities usually had the same privileges as those within Italy; that is, they paid neither land nor head tax. Some other provincial towns were immune from one of these taxes. Also, in the courts provincial governors would see to it that citizens got speedy if not favorable treatment.

The lot of noncitizens of lower class throughout the empire was surely less happy. The demands of the state for manpower, the natural heavy labor of agriculture, and wages that never rose much above subsistence level, in part because of slavery, all tended to depress the conditions of lower-class life. The plague during Marcus Aurelius' reign, of course, much accentuated the manpower shortages. Only a dramatic rise in general productivity through improved agricultural practices and changes in other forms of production could have saved the situation for the lower classes—and, ultimately, for the empire. These increases and improvements, generally speaking, never came.

An upper class with too much privilege and money, a lower class kept at subsistence level, and lack of innovation in agricultural and other production meant, inevitably, that the empire never developed a middle class of any size. Although there were the merchants and traders to produce and ship the pottery and other goods the society required, not enough of the small business owners and entrepreneurs prospered to make any real impact on the social and economic fiber of the state. Rome remained more a *two*-class than a *three*-class society. This division shows up in a tendency in law during the second century and after: Litigants in court were increasingly classified as *honestiores* and *humiliores* (actually, though not literally, upper class and lower class), with differing legal principles and penalties applying to each group.

B. LITERATURE AFTER AUGUSTUS: THE SILVER AGE

As the name implies, the so-called silver age of Latin literature produced authors whose work failed to measure up to that of the greatest writers of the Augustan period. In style, these writers of the first and second centuries A.D. evidenced, first, a revulsion against the ample, flowing Latin of Cicero, Vergil, and Livy, and then an imitation of it. Next came a determined effort to be different, which all too often only emphasized the mediocrity of the writer.

Seneca

Stoicism motivated several of the silver age writers, including Seneca (Lucius Annaeus Seneca; c. 4 B.C.–A.D. 65), tutor and for several years a sort of prime minister to Nero. Seneca was born in Spain, where his family was then resident. He was brought to Rome as a child and educated there. His dignified tragedies are written in a peculiar one-dimensional style, evidently intended not to be acted out onstage but to be declaimed. These plays seem dull and draggy today, but they contain occasional brilliant lines, and Seneca's tragedy was long a significant literary influence, especially during the Renaissance. Seneca's *Moral Essays* and *Letters* display moral teaching of the highest caliber, though their author does not seem always to have conformed to his own lofty idealism. During his time at the imperial court he became enormously rich. The last three years of his life, devoted to literary activity, were spent in retirement from public life. Then, accused of complicity in a plot on Nero's life, Seneca was forced to commit suicide.

Lucan

The idealistic morality of Stoicism also is seen in a passage from *Pharsalia*, a long, sometimes tiresome epic by Seneca's nephew Lucan (Marcus Annaeus Lucanus; A.D. 39–65), written in praise of Pompey's cause. When asked to consult the oracle of Jupiter Hammon, Cato the Younger, a leader of the hard-pressed opponents of Caesar and a professed Stoic, replied,[1]

> *What, Labienus, would'st thou have me ask?*
> *Whether 'tis better to die free in arms*
> *Than live to see a tyranny? If life*
> *Is nothing worth, however long? If age*
> *Doth profit? Whether any force can harm*
> *The good? If Fortune threatens virtue vainly?*
> *If 'tis enough to will what merits praise,*
> *And right ne'er needs the crown of good success?*

Lucan's poem, filled with republican sentiment, naturally aroused Nero's anger, and Lucan was forbidden to give public readings of his works in the salons of the day. The resentful poet joined Piso's conspiracy against the emperor and was forced to commit suicide at a tragically early age—less than half that of his philosopher uncle, implicated in the same conspiracy.

Columella

The first century A.D. saw several writers who combined literature and scholarship in the manner that Cicero had so well exemplified. Their works range widely, from Columella's *De Re Rustica* (*On Agriculture*; c. A.D. 65) to Quintilian's work on rhetorical training. Columella, like Seneca, came from Spain; their ages, too, were similar. Columella was concerned rather more with practical than with literary matters. Despite certain advice that to us may seem ridiculous or even fantastic, it is apparent from his writings that the educated Roman farmer had a good knowledge of such important farm practices as fertilization and crop rotation. Absentee landlordism and slavery, it is equally apparent, were still the bane of agricultural well-being.

Quintilian

Quintilian (Marcus Fabius Quintilianus; c. A.D. 30–95), also from Roman Spain, was an outstanding educator and had his own rather exclusive academy. His *Principles of Oratory* commend a broad educational program designed to produce a polished orator and cultured gentleman. More important to the modern scholar are his judgments of literature and sketches of authors he considered important; for example, he greatly admired Cicero. Interestingly, he advised that parents first teach their children Greek; Latin they could easily pick up later.

---

[1]A. N. Bryan-Brown, trans., in *The Mind of Rome*, ed. C. Bailey (Oxford, 1926), p. 57.

Pliny The Elder

Another first-century work of scholarship is the encyclopedic *Natural History* of Pliny the Elder (A.D. 23–79), which covers a broad field, from zoology and botany to mining and metallurgy, anthropology, and medicine. Not valued highly today either as literature or as science, it nevertheless does have valuable elements of each. Pliny, who knew a good story and could tell it well, included much trivial information of interest: Augustus' favorite wine and the color of Tiberius' eyes, for example. The scholar, who did not have the modern zeal for experimentation and careful method, also included much information that now seems patently incredible. During his lifetime Pliny held both military and provincial administrative posts. He was asphyxiated near Mount Vesuvius during the celebrated eruption that caused the obliteration of Pompeii, where he had gone while others were fleeing. As commander of the imperial fleet at Misenum, he probably wished to give aid as well as to make careful empiric observation. The typical bookish scholar, Pliny read constantly, slept little, and kept several secretaries busy.

Petronius

One of the most interesting works of antiquity is the bawdy, picaresque *Satyricon* of Gaius Petronius (d. A.D. 65), which approaches the modern novel in form, although there does not appear to be a connected plot. Of the extant fragments, one of the most vivid and amusing deals with a lavish banquet given by one Trimalchio, a newly rich "climber." Anxious to flaunt his culture, he makes many ludicrous errors: for example, saying that Corinthian bronze is the metal that resulted when, at the fall of Troy, *Hannibal* put all the metal loot in a huge pile and burned it.

Tacitus wrote of Petronius (probably, but not certainly, the same man) that he was a kind of professional debauchee. Closely associated with Nero, Petronius became his official judge of elegance and taste and even bore the surname "Arbiter." Charged with treason by a jealous rival, he ended his life by opening his veins. Written in the pithy, vulgar, and sometimes indecent language of the common man, perhaps the *Satyricon* was created purely for the hilarity and pleasure of the imperial court. Some modern scholars, however, detect an undertone of criticism of the corrupt Roman world of which its author was a part. Whatever his real attitude, the originality of the work seems unquestionable.

Apuleius

The next century—actually beyond the limits of the silver age proper—saw the production of still another work somewhat resembling a novel. The *Metamorphoses* (best known as *The Golden Ass*) of Lucius Apuleius (c. A.D. 123–185) combines a series of tales, often hilarious and sometimes risqué, into a loosely connected narrative. The story relates the adventures of a man temporarily turned, through magic that backfired, into an ass. In the fourteenth century Boccaccio made use of these stories, many of which probably were not original with Apuleius. This work is interesting because of its anti-Christian bias. Its author was an initiate into the mysteries of Isis, and later a priest of Isis, Osiris, and Aesculapius. Some other, rather florid rhetorical works by him also survive. Apuleius' distinctive language perhaps relates to his background; he was a North African educated in Carthage and Athens.

Satire: Martial and Juvenal

Good-humored satire of the type found also in Horace may be seen in the work of Petronius. But quite a different form, biting and sarcastic, is found in other silver age authors. Seneca lampooned the emperor Claudius in a short work (*Apocolocyntosis*) relating the events in heaven immediately after Claudius' death. When it is proposed that Claudius be made a god, as Caesar and Augustus were supposed to have been, there is much objection to the idea, and finally Gaius, who had often tyrannized over his uncle in life, asserts his authority and has Claudius made clerk to a freedman.

Satire is cutting and merciless in the *Epigrams* of Martial (Marcus Valerius Martialis; c. A.D. 40–104), another notable Latin writer born in Spain. Martial's work is an unconscionable mixture of good and bad, mingling condemnation of hypocrisy with condonation of every moral indecency. Since Martial named names in these lampoons, it is astonishing he was not strangled by some victim of his cruel wit in a dark alley, instead of dying a peaceful death after having retired to the Spanish countryside.

Somewhat similar are the poetic works of the last of the great Roman satirists, Juvenal (Decimus Junius Juvenalis; c. A.D. 55–133). Writing in the first third of the second century, Juvenal was driven by indignation, relieved with occasional flashes of a serious-minded humor. He ridiculed the faults and affectations of Romans, especially women, whom he hated with an unrelieved pessimism. He detested the "sewage" of foreign influence and condemned vice, which he nevertheless described in vivid detail. Stoic influence is evident in the Tenth Satire, where the poet advises that peace of mind can be attained through virtue and counsels that one should pray for "a sound mind in a sound body" (*mens sana in corpore sano*). Despite his obvious exaggeration, Juvenal's somber and sordid picture of a gross, decadent Rome has too often been totally accepted and written indiscriminately into our histories of this era.

Historians: Tacitus, Suetonius, and Others

This same picture of deteriorating moral fiber is the chief impression derived from study of the two important historians of the silver age: Cornelius Tacitus (c. A.D. 5–115) and Gaius Suetonius (about A.D. 69–130).

Tacitus' chief works are his books of history, the *Annals* and the *Histories,* which together cover the period between the death of Augustus (A.D. 14) and the assassination of Domitian (A.D. 96). The surviving books recount nothing later than the civil wars of A.D. 69, and there are earlier gaps as well, notably for Nero's last years. Tacitus writes of almost unrelieved tyranny, rife with vice and depravity at the top. Many critics call him the greatest of Roman historians, but he falls short of this rank. Though he claimed he wrote without prejudice, prejudice warps his whole work. To the Emperor Tiberius, for example, against whom Tacitus had a special animus, the historian confidently, on very flimsy evidence, ascribes the basest motives—motives the author could not possibly have known. That is, Tacitus claimed to know what Tiberius *thought.* Similarly, his *Germania* is less an attempt to present a factual account of Germanic life and tribal institutions than an expression of an ideal of discipline and simplicity to which Tacitus felt Rome must return. His biography of his father-in-law, *Agricola,* also has the obvious purpose of recommending a return to austere older standards of military discipline and imperial aggressiveness.

Nevertheless, Tacitus used his sources more carefully than any other Roman historian and did not deliberately falsify facts. This keen discrimination; his terse, forceful prose style; and the acute perception evident in numerous startlingly lucid generalizations have justly earned for him a high reputation. For Tacitus, history was much more than an accurate presentation of past events of significance; it was a powerful tool with which he might influence the direction of events.

As a historian Suetonius does not rank with Tacitus, for his *Lives of the Caesars* (covering twelve emperors, from Julius Caesar to Domitian) is a motley collection of fact and scandalous fiction. Nevertheless, it is fascinating and even convincing to read. Some of his stories are of that type which, if not true, ought to be, because they seem to illustrate the character of the subject so well. Moreover, Suetonius did use some excellent sources and thereby has preserved for us some of this worthwhile basic material; for example, he quotes from Augustus' letters. If the reader discounts the colorful scandal Suetonius could not bring himself to leave out, the anecdotal *Lives* becomes a valuable work for today's historians.

A different segment of Roman society from that so bleakly described by Juvenal and Tacitus is revealed in the letters of Pliny the Younger (A.D. 61/62–c. 113), nephew of Pliny the Elder. In his voluminous letters—cultured, civilized, and sensible—may be discerned something of that more responsible class of Romans upon whom fell the tasks of empire. One of the best-known of his letters, written to Trajan about A.D. 111 from Bithynia, where Pliny was serving as governor, asks for advice on methods of dealing with Christians, whose "depraved, excessive superstition" had spread extensively in that area. His own procedure, he said, was to execute only those accused who refused to curse Christ and sacrifice to the emperor. Trajan's answer was that he was doing quite right: No general rule could be laid down; Pliny was not to engage in active persecution nor to accept anonymous accusations, but if a Christian was denounced before him and persisted in refusing to adore the gods, he must of course be punished.

Not a Roman but very important to Roman history is the famous Plutarch (A.D. c. 46–120), whose *Parallel Lives* of celebrated Greeks and Romans has inspired leaders of many generations. Eminently readable and studded with illustrative anecdotes, Plutarch's *Lives* gave Shakespeare most of the information used in his plays set in antiquity and provided, in quite another way, serious reading for the young Napoleon Bonaparte. In his distinctive biographical scheme Plutarch paired Alexander the Great with Caesar, Demosthenes with Cicero. The Roman *Lives* are mostly those of great figures from the last two centuries of the republic.

During the second century and after, Latin literature skidded rapidly from good to mediocre, and from mediocre to worse. A current-day scholar has written about this period and termed it the "Silver-Plated Age."[2] Some writings of this era notably in law, were important, but the best of Roman literature was produced during the two middle centuries of Roman history, which encompassed both the golden and silver ages.

C. PHILOSOPHY AND RELIGION

Prosperous and pragmatic, the Romans obviously did not provide the most fertile soil for widespread growth of any philosophical system; yet the major philosophical schools were in evidence—Epicureans, Cynics, Skeptics, and Pythagoreans. Recently uncovered evidence indicates that in the first two centuries of the empire the last-named group was more numerous and influential than previously was thought. The philosophy that took deep root and acquired distinctively Roman characteristics, however, was Stoicism.

Stoicism

As we have seen, it was Panaetius, a Greek Stoic teacher who lived at the home of Scipio Aemilianus in the second century B.C., who first popularized Stoicism in Italy. This philosophy, mostly stripped of its cosmogony and stressing self-sufficiency, virtue, and public service, strongly appealed to important Romans during the next three centuries of Roman history. Mucius Scaevola, the great jurist of the first century B.C., analyzed and organized the law in accordance with Stoic principles. Cicero, though he proclaimed himself a skeptical Academic, often reflected Stoic influence. Cato the Younger was a professed Stoic. Seneca, Nero's great tutor and minister, wrote essays and letters explicitly elaborating his Stoic convictions. Such men strove for moral reform and moral integrity, rather than for a commitment to abstruse logic or subtle philosophical principle.

---

[2]T. B. Jones, *The Silver-Plated Age* (Sandoval, N.M., 1962).

Some Stoics and other philosophers felt compelled to oppose certain of the Roman emperors and formed a core of opposition the rulers found difficult to deal with. One such adversary was Thrasea Paetus. He was far from being an activist, however; he once expressed his disapproval of Nero's actions merely by walking out of the Senate. Yet, after Piso's conspiracy, Thrasea was condemned and forced to commit suicide. His son-in-law Helvidius Priscus attacked the Flavian regime; Vespasian exiled and finally executed him. Later Domitian put to death his son. These philosophers apparently felt that only the "best man" somehow was fit to rule—and the prevailing system was not turning up such men.

One of the most notable Stoic teachers of the age was Epictetus, an ex-slave, mentioned previously in connection with Marcus Aurelius. He did not involve himself in political criticism, though his teacher Musonius Rufus, a contemporary of Seneca, had been banished by both Nero and Vespasian. Epictetus nonetheless was caught up in a general expulsion of philosophers by Domitian and lived out most of his life in Epirus. His best efforts were directed to the common man rather than to the educated elite. A commonly reproduced prayer of our own times—"Oh, Lord, help me to accept what I cannot change, to change for the better what can be changed, and to have the wisdom to distinguish between the two"—could have been the prayer of Epictetus, for these words convey the central impact of his teaching.

With the advent of the "good emperors," philosophical opposition to the government tended to subside. Hadrian was especially interested in philosophy; and of course, Marcus Aurelius made a personal profession of Stoicism in his *Meditations*.

Oriental Influences in Roman Religion

From earliest times, the most important influences for religious change came to Rome from Greece and the East. During the late republic, Rome was infiltrated by devotees of several new exotic religions. Most of these were mystery religions; that is, each jealously preserved some secret lore promising special benefit to the initiate, usually involving a hope of life after death. The new religions were brought in mostly by immigrants—slaves, traders, and others. The worship of Cybele (Magna Mater) had been brought in under the sponsorship of the ruling classes during the Second Punic War, but most of these new religions arrived unofficially.

The new cults were the products of Hellenistic religious syncretism. This process, operative especially in the centuries after Alexander, had transformed both deity and religion, giving a universal aspect to all important gods. From Egypt, for example, came the worship of Isis and Osiris, once Nile gods but now deities whose power and influence were felt to be all-pervasive. A prayer to Isis found in Apuleius' *Golden Ass* indicates a concept of a beneficent, omnipresent, omnipotent deity—or almost that. Shrines to Isis were torn down in Rome during the republic, in the anti-Egyptian reaction that accompanied the last phase of the civil war. Only

Mithraic cultic group; painting. Mithra is killing the sacred bull, from which all things will be created. Flanking figures are torch bearers (one torch upright, the other inverted); surrounding scenes showing the deeds of Mithra for mankind. Upper right, sun god (Mithra?) (Art Resource)

in the reign of Emperor Gaius was a temple dedicated to the Egyptian goddess permitted within Rome's sacred boundaries.

One of the more important of the newer oriental religions was Mithraism, which gained numerous adherents and became one of the most powerful competitors of Christianity. Roman troops who served in Asia in the first century B.C. brought back this form of worship. Mithra was a chief lieutenant of Ahura-Mazda in the Zoroastrian religion, and therefore of Persian origin, and was closely identified with the sun. Many characteristics of Zoroastrianism carried over into this later sect: an emphasis on light versus darkness, purity of life, strong connections with the sun, and a Persian mythology.

Mithra was conceived as a creator-benefactor of humankind. In the Mithraic creation myth he was said to have pursued and killed the sacred bull, from the blood and parts of which all things were made. The cult statue that was the focal feature of the Mithraeum, the half-buried structure where the initiates met, shows Mithra astride the bull, in the act of pulling its head back by the nostrils and stabbing it with his dagger. Pictured below are several creatures—zodiacal figures, for the most part—whose role is not always clear. Fine examples of these cult statues may be seen in the world's great museums, the best of them being in the Louvre and the British Museum.

Mithraism was a man's religion (women were not admitted into its mysteries) and so had a special appeal to soldiers. The religion first spread among the camps marking the Danube and Rhine frontiers. Numerous Mithraea have been found in Roman cities—Rome and Ostia, for example. There were several degrees of progression for the initiates. In some oriental cults, the ceremony of the tau-robolium was practiced: A bull was sacrificed above a grate, while the initiates below allowed themselves to be bathed in its dripping blood. Christian writers ridiculed this ceremony, though its symbolism certainly was not alien to them.

Mithraics worshiped the sun on the first day of the week (Sunday), ob-served the birthday of the sun about December 25, made use of ceremonial wash-ings for purification, and held ceremonial meals. The several parallels with Christianity are obvious, but it is not always certain who borrowed from whom, or indeed whether either borrowed directly from the other. Christians probably set December 25 as the birthdate of Christ to offset the Mithraic and other pagan celebrations, such as the Roman Saturnalia. But Christian baptism derived from an old Jewish practice, and the tradition of the Lord's Supper seems to bear little relation to Mithraic practice.

Christianity

Though Christianity is often presented as just another of the oriental mys-tery religions that arrived in Rome from the East, it was much more than that, of course. This religion, like its parent Judaism, had its roots in history. Moses, the prophets, Jesus—all are real figures set in real history, even if they have acquired an admixture of myth. The influence of Jesus rests less, perhaps, on the claims that his followers made for his divinity than on the record of his teaching. This was in many ways similar to the ethical pronouncements of the Jewish scriptures or of the greatest of the Greek philosophers. Probably the Greek Orphics and the Mithraics also taught a code of lofty ethics. But in its simplicity and depth of feeling, its probing and enlightening impact, Jesus' teaching was unique.

The similarities between Christianity and certain pagan cults sometimes appall modern Christians, who, ignorant of the world of the past, imagine that Christianity burst upon history totally unique, completely different from other contemporary cults. Actually these very correspondences made it easier for Chris-tianity to spread. For example, a man who was attracted by the high ethical pro-nouncements of the Stoics but repelled by their stern, almost inhuman *apatheia* (determination to be unmoved by emotions, even the gentler ones) would quite probably have been ripe for Christian conversion.

As everyone knows, Christianity began as a sect of Judaism in Palestine. After a period of success in Jerusalem, adherents of the new group were scattered by persecution. Thereafter the movement flourished among the more Hellenized Jews outside Palestine. One of these, Paul, became the most influential of the "apostles" (personal messengers) of Christ in propagating the new religion and soon was converting gentiles as well as Jews, so that after a time gentiles predom-inated. By the time of Trajan, as we learn from Pliny's letters, Christianity seemed to threaten paganism in Asia Minor.

We have already noted the deadly flareup of persecution under Nero. This wave of persecution was brief and not widespread. However, at this time or soon after, it became firm policy that Christians, by their profession of the religion, upon admission that they were, in fact, Christians, were automatically branded enemies of the state, subject to the death penalty. It was this policy that Tertullian, in the late second century, so strongly protested. Arguing that Christians were basically good citizens, he said that it was unreasonable to condemn them except for a specific crime. Sporadic persecution did not halt the growth of the new movement, and may indeed have helped. One did not profess this new religion lightly, and those who did so were dedicated. The problems that were later to beset the church—heresies and questions of church-state relations, of the internal government of the church itself, or of the nature of Christ—all these concerns were of secondary importance in an era when persecution and martyrdom seemed always near.

The reasons for the phenomenal growth of these new religions are not easy to discern. The world was mostly at peace and mostly prosperous, yet people by the thousands felt the need for something more, a deeper dimension to their lives. They were asking important questions, seeking spiritual sustenance. The new cults appealed mostly, it is true, to the middle and lower classes. Their ethical and spiritual emphasis contrasted strongly with the world portrayed by Suetonius, Juvenal, and Martial. They thought the world was going to pieces, morally; obviously, it was not. The decline the next chapter must deal with cannot have resulted principally from a deteriorating moral fiber in society—as many have so often mistakenly claimed.

D. ROMAN LAW

Growth of the Law

The mid-second century A.D., which saw the decline of Latin literature, witnessed great strides in the study of law and its codification. From the Twelve Tables of the fifth century B.C.—the first written Roman code—the law had developed as Rome evolved into empire. Applied to many peoples, backward and advanced, it developed equitably and effectively but also became complex, sometimes jumbled and confused. Now began a great period of juridical compilation, classification, and clarification. Through legal opinions and publications, a series of great jurists of the second and the early third centuries, the period termed the classical age of Roman law, drew from centuries of accumulated experience the great legal principles still taught in law schools everywhere in the Western world. Perhaps the greatest of these jurists were Gaius, Paul, Papinian, and Ulpian.

Romans had been forced at an early date to distinguish between civil or domestic law and the more or less international law they encountered when away from their home city. The edicts of the urban praetors, formulas developed by them to instruct judges in specific cases, decisions actually rendered, and the opinions of jurists (jurisconsults) all contributed much to the formulation of the civil law, which applied to Roman citizens.

As Rome acquired provinces, the praetors, proconsuls, or propraetors who administered them were given wide latitude in establishing fundamental law in their territories. Each governor published his edict, setting forth the law for the area under his jurisdiction. These edicts were not, of course, newly formulated each time a new governor arrived. Some, such as that of Mucius Scaevola, a distinguished jurisconsult who was governor of the province of Asia in 94 B.C., became models that were used again and again, with necessary modification.

Centralization and Elaboration Under the Empire

The imperial system brought gradual centralization of the sources of law and a more unified administration of it. The popular assemblies gradually lost their legislative power, and even the decrees of the Senate mostly reflected the will of the princeps. Decisions of the emperors had virtually the force of law, and indeed this became an explicit principle toward the end of the second century. The spectacular jury trials that had made the reputations of such men as Cicero under the republic were finally eliminated, and pleading took place before judges only, except for cases in the Senate or personally heard by the emperor. At least in the early empire, the Roman citizen enjoyed an appeals system that could go straight to the emperor himself. The Christian Apostle Paul could gain a hearing before the highest officer of the empire by saying simply, "I appeal to Caesar."

During the early years of the empire, the concept of *jus gentium*—law of nations—evolved, both philosophically and legally. From the idea of common custom, it had come to mean a kind of universal law. Combined with this was the concept of *jus naturalis,* or natural law, often connected with Stoicism. Its basic provisions or, rather, ideals were conceived of as embodying natural rights. It seems ironic that the late second and early third centuries, an age which saw growing autocracy in Roman government, should also have been the age known as the classical period of Roman law, during which the great jurists were elaborating important principles of human rights. The concept of equality before the law was based, ultimately, on the idea that all men are born equal—a principle specifically stated by Ulpian, praetorian prefect under Alexander Severus in the 220s. Yet during the same period, as we have seen, citizens were divided into honestiores and humiliores (roughly, the rich and the poor), and to each group were applied differing procedures and penalties.

The great jurists strove to bring order out of chaos, to classify, simplify, and point up clearly the philosophical concepts inherent in the law. The first effective condensations were unofficial works designed for use as textbooks in the private schools of law. After the work of generations of jurisconsults showed that their interpretations of the law were in many instances as important as the law itself, the emperors decreed that the opinions of certain of them were to be followed by the courts. Eventually, official classified condensations, or codifications, were produced for judicial guidance.

BOOKS FOR FURTHER READING

ARNOLD, E. *Roman Stoicism,* London, 1911.

BAINTON, R. *History of Christianity,* 2 vols., Middlesex, Eng., 1967.

BALSDON, J. *Romans and Aliens,* Chapel Hill, 1979.

BALSDON, J. *Roman Women,* New York, 1963.

BRION, M. *Pompeii and Herculaneum: The Glory and the Grief,* tr. J. Rosenberg, New York, 1961.

BRUCE, F. *The Spreading Flame,* Exeter, Eng., 1958.

BURFORD, A. *Craftsmen in Greek and Roman Society,* London, 1972.

CARCOPINO, J. *Daily Life in Ancient Rome,* New Haven, 1940.

CASSON, L. *Travel in the Ancient World,* Toronto, 1974.

CLARKE, M. L. *The Roman Mind,* New York, 1968.

DILL, S. *Roman Society from Nero to Marcus Aurelius,* New York, 1956.

DOREY, T., ed. *Empire and Aftermath: Silver Latin II,* London, 1975.

DUDLEY, E., ed. *Neronians and Flavians: Silver Latin I,* London, 1972.

DUFF, J. *Silver Age of Latin Literature,* London, 1927.

GLOVER, T. R. *The Conflict of Religion in the Early Roman Empire,* London, 1920.

GWYNN, A. *Roman Education from Cicero to Quintilian,* Oxford, 1926.

MacMULLEN, R. *Christianizing the Roman Empire,* A.D. 100–400, New Haven, 1984.

MacMULLEN, R. *Paganism in the Roman Empire,* New Haven, 1981.

MATTINGLY, H. *The Man on the Roman Street,* New York, 1966.

MEEKER, W. *The First Urban Christians: The Social World of the Apostle Paul,* New Haven, 1983.

ROSE, H. *Ancient Roman Religion,* New York, 1948.

STARR, C. *Civilization and the Caesars,* Ithaca, N.Y., 1954.

WARDMAN, A. *Religion and Statecraft Among the Romans,* Baltimore, 1982.

WATSON, A. *The Law of the Ancient Romans,* Dallas, 1970.

WOLFF, H. *Roman Law: An Historical Introduction,* Norman, Okla., 1951.

20

FROM PRINCIPATE TO MILITARY AUTHORITARIANISM

Despite the idiosyncrasies of some emperors, occasional deliberate (as well as incidental) injustice, and a series of disasters, the Roman Empire in the first two centuries must be accounted a resounding success. Most of the *principes* followed the Augustan model, choosing to share power to some degree with the senatorial aristocracy and providing for participation in affairs by many persons of middle rank (*equites*) as well, through the second-level career structure and through the army. These principes were really emperors, of course, whose power dominated the state. But most used their power humanely, with consideration both for the historical position of the traditional ruling class and for the dignity and sensibilities of its members.

The inhabitants of the empire in this high period, as in the first century, for the most part lived out their lives in relative peace, with a fair degree of prosperity and with little interference from the central government. It is true that the general emphasis was on security rather than freedom, but the system provided some of each.

A. PORTENTS OF DECLINE

Local Government

The cities that were centers of trade and culture in the eastern half of the empire served as building blocks in the imperial structure; it is often said that the empire was a collection of city-states. In the West—especially in Spain, France, and North Africa—similar urban-centered units developed, and the earlier tribal organization continued only in the rural areas. In general these basic, local centers flourished with the Pax Romana and remained effective. The Roman practice of giving citizenship to the local *decurions* (elected councilors) gave prestige to local officeholding and made for vigorous government at these levels. But Rome required the decurions to assist in the recruitment of soldiers and in the collection of taxes. As long as the army provided attractive careers for young men, recruitment was not a difficult problem, nor was the collection of taxes during general prosperity. In future years, however, when all those eligible for local office would be already citizens, when civil wars and invasions would demand larger armies with difficult conditions of service, when trade would decline and taxes rise, the burdens of local political office would outweigh any possible benefit.

Even in the first two centuries the tendencies that eventually would lead to the debilitation of local government can be discerned. There was a kind of inevitability about the gradual centralization: Difficult problems were referred to the emperors, and the result was increasing uniformity; or the central government was asked to intervene in the immediate best interest of some city or area, say, because of financial difficulties; greater control by the imperial bureaucracy followed in either instance. The special mission of the younger Pliny to Bithynia under Trajan, as mentioned earlier, is a case in point: He was sent in place of the usual senatorial appointee because a number of cities in the province had vastly overextended themselves in public works construction projects. Trajan also sent persons called *correctors* on similar missions to other provinces. Such actions ensured greater efficiency at the expense of local initiative.

Provincial government during these years probably was better than in the late republic. Governors, whether legates of the emperor or senatorial proconsuls, were more carefully chosen; they served longer terms, were more closely supervised from Rome, and were salaried, so that they were much less likely to attempt to squeeze a fortune out of the provincials in a quick two-year tour of duty. Hesitant to act on their own authority, however, they referred many local questions to the emperor, and thus important policy decisions were made at Rome; even matters of detail often were decided by the princeps or by his staff.

Imperial Administration

The growth of an imperial staff at Rome deserves comment. Augustus had made use of his own household staff in the manner of any great noble of the republic. Every Roman commander had a headquarters council, and so did Augustus; it included senators, and it was probably here that proposed actions in the Senate were given preliminary screening. This body, a sort of cabinet, in later years (possibly from the beginning) was called the *consilium principis*, the Council of the Princeps. The Emperor Claudius gave great authority to four of his freedmen, putting them in charge of formally organized departments, most important of which were treasury and correspondence. These represent the beginnings of a bureaucracy or civil service. Almost a century later, Hadrian appointed equestrian officials to head the departments; by his time, obviously, the posts were seen as important enough to be held by persons of this status. The size of the departments and their volume of work continually expanded. To some degree this civil service provided continuity in administration and organization along rational lines, even during changes at the top of the political structure, but it is not likely that the element of continuity was important except in the lower offices. Any comparison with this feature of modern civil service bureaucracies would be misleading. The busy emperors exercised a great deal of personal supervision over a plethora of important matters.

The Economy

The long period of internal peace and security made the first two centuries of the empire a relatively prosperous age. Standards of living could not rise continuously as we have come to expect in modern times, however, for there were no regular increases in productivity through improved methods, new sources of power, or better machines—even though the Romans and provincials, especially the Gauls, were inventive and produced such machines as water wheels for grinding grain.

It is easy to find portents of economic problems to come. The lack of a substantial and growing middle class is one. Another is seen in the coinage: Nero both lightened and debased the silver; afterward there were fluctuations, but the tendency was toward continuing, gradual debasement. By the end of the reign of Marcus Aurelius the standard silver denarius contained no more than about 60 percent of the silver by weight of a similar coin of Augustus. To some extent this may only reflect a rise in the market price of silver because of shortages (owing to a combination of reduced output of mines, greater monetary demand, and the export of silver to pay for imported luxuries); nevertheless, the cheapened coinage seems to reflect a serious financial problem. Another indication of economic weakness involves the land: As early as the time of Hadrian, we hear of agricultural land being abandoned by farmers oppressed by absentee landlordism and excessive taxation. The Emperors Antoninus Pius and Marcus Aurelius both rather strictly restrained public spending, and though it may have been partly a gesture in public relations, the latter even auctioned off some imperial treasures to support his military campaigns in the north.

The wars on the frontiers and especially those of Marcus Aurelius, combined as they were with a devastating plague, bore heavily on both manpower and the economy. The military establishment, in fact, even in times of peace was enormously expensive. The army seems to us to have been small, both in relation to needs and by comparison with modern capabilities, but an essentially rural economy could not support much more. Even in the time of Augustus, when three legions were lost in Germany in the battle with Arminius, they were not replaced. The future would, nevertheless, bring a gradual increase in the size of the army and, inexorably, lower living standards for most people of the empire.

Measured in terms of production, the weakening economic situation was marked in the central core of the empire, Italy itself. In large part the reason was commercial competition from the newer and richer provincial territories. Italy, which during the early empire had shipped pottery (especially the famed red Arretine ware) all over the West, along with fine glassware and various metal items, gradually lost out to the increased provincial competition, particularly from Spain and Gaul. Imitations of Italian products soon began to be imported even into Italy itself. Commodities imported on a massive scale included not only grain, which had been imported in sizeable quantity for centuries, but also oil, wine, pungent fish sauce, and other foodstuffs. Italy held up financially, to some degree, because it was the center of government, and taxes and other moneys tended to flow toward the center. It has been said that imperial Rome exported government and imported everything else. Although this exaggerates the case, it was decidedly not a healthy situation economically.

This gradual economic decline was masked during the second century by the careful, thrifty policies of the "good emperors." Ideally, a long period of peace coupled with rule by a continued succession of wise emperors might have retrieved this worsening situation; but neither peace nor wise leadership lay in Rome's future.

B. THE MILITARY MONARCHY

Commodus

Lucius Commodus (A.D. 180–192), only nineteen when his father Marcus Aurelius died, quickly made peace in the north. He soon dismissed the advisers bequeathed him along with the empire and, with bad judgment that was truly exceptional, appointed new ones. General misgovernment brought on a conspiracy, which was detected in time; but thereafter Commodus was frightened. As a result, he executed large numbers of persons and listened willingly to new tales of treason. He began not to trust even his own ministers, who tended to be deposed and executed with marked regularity. At one point his praetorian prefect (by now the most important person in Rome after the emperor) was a freedman whose venality set new records.

Commodus was a simpleminded man who gave himself over to personal pleasure and the games. Tall and strong, he himself wrestled, hunted wild beasts, and played the role of gladiator—sometimes in public, it seems. He commissioned statues of himself carrying the club and wearing the lionskin that were the accouterments of Hercules, with whom he identified.

In the last years of Commodus' reign, some of the more prominent persons who were condemned, it was said, were guilty only of owning property to be confiscated for replenishing the depleted imperial coffers. Inevitably a new conspiracy was hatched that at length did away with Commodus. He was first poisoned, then strangled by his wrestling partner.

Relying on the precedent set at the assassination of Domitian, the Senate attempted to seize the initiative and named a distinguished older man, Pertinax, to replace Commodus. This action did not please the praetorian guard, however, which as the historian Dio Cassius says, had gotten used to "delicate" living. There was not enough money in the treasury to buy the praetorians' acquiescence, although the attempt was made. Less than three months after his reluctant acceptance of power, a group of praetorians murdered Pertinax. Then they conducted a kind of auction for the succession at their camp between the father-in-law of Pertinax and Didius Julianus, who finally made the highest bid (that is, agreed to pay them the most for their support) and was acclaimed emperor. This spectacle was too much even for the city populace, and more repugnant still to the legions, who were not about to allow the praetorians to name emperors in such fashion.

Such a turbulent situation roused the ambitions of every charismatic general, and soon there were three serious candidates for the imperial post: Clodius Albinus, governor of Britain; Pescennius Niger, governor of Syria; and Lucius Septimius Severus, governor of Pannonia. Didius Julianus was executed only a little more than two months after assuming power. Severus made an ally of Albinus while he struggled to defeat Niger, and then he turned on Albinus. Victory against him in A.D. 197 made Septimius Severus the sole ruler of the empire he had largely commanded since being acclaimed by the provincial legions in 193.

The Severan Dynasty: Lucius Septimius Severus
(A.D. 193–211)

The principate, with its appearance of partnership between the emperor and the Senate—important even if it was in part only an elaborate facade—was now dead. Septimius Severus was a military monarch. Although he in several ways ruled well and managed to stabilize and unify the empire, in some ways he also symbolizes all that was wrong with the imperial system. He was first a general, only secondarily a civilian administrator of empire. This is seen in the advice he is reported to have given his sons at his death—that they should live in concord, enrich the army, and despise everyone else. The army was now the sole basis of power, and Septimius never forgot it. He was rather vindictive, even against persons who had been forced to support one of the other early candidates for the throne. Born in North Africa, he spoke Latin with an accent. He was by no means uneducated but had little feeling for long-established tradition.

Septimius was superstitious and, even more than some of his predecessors, depended on the horoscopes cast by his astrologers. It was said that when he married for the second time (he was already an important administrator who had reached the consulship and governed two or three provinces) he looked for a woman whose horoscope predicted great things for her husband. This search led him to Julia Domna, who came of a Syrian noble family that included several remarkable women—about whom more later.

Septimius successfully fought wars in Britain and Parthia; in the latter, he even captured the enemy capital, Ctesiphon, in A.D. 198. It is ironic that Roman campaigns against their perennial foe Parthia only weakened that kingdom, so that it eventually fell before the Sassanid Persians, who fought the Romans as fiercely as the Parthians had.

As emperor, Septimius found it necessary to enlarge the army, which now comprised several legions more than in the days of Augustus, and to raise the pay. The praetorian guard, which had deteriorated especially under Commodus, was simply disbanded by Septimius, who then reconstituted it immediately, in effect, but with troops drawn from the loyal legions. For a time, at least, their position as elite, privileged guards was reduced.

Septimius also militarized the government, by making extensive use of generals in positions of power. In a sense, of course, important officials had always been generals also. But now the situation was reversed: The officials in question came from a lower rank—the equestrian order rather than the senatorial—and they proved themselves in the army rather than through the usual sequence of promotion in civilian positions. It was not merely the fact of the emperor as effective commanding general that induces historians to designate the Roman state of the century following Septimius Severus' accession a "military monarchy."

Septimius conducted internal affairs with great efficiency—especially the collection of taxes and tribute. He was able to pay the higher salaries of soldiers, give them special donatives, and still leave his successor a treasury far from empty. The city of Rome itself he also nurtured with care; at his death he left, it was said, enough grain and oil to feed the city for several years. He spent huge sums on building programs, particularly in adding massively to the complex of imperial palaces on the Palatine in Rome. In his native North Africa he virtually rebuilt whole cities, as the remains of his birthplace Leptis Magna demonstrate to present-day tourists.

Caracalla (A.D. 211–217)

Septimius left his power jointly to his two sons: Caracalla, the elder, and Geta. Julia Domna, their dynamic mother, was doubtless expected to play an important role in preserving harmony between them. She failed in this, however, and Geta was soon killed in an attack in Julia's own presence; she herself was wounded. Before the end of Caracalla's reign, nevertheless, she reasserted herself; she received official petitions, answered official correspondence, and was named jointly with Caracalla on imperial dispatches.

Caracalla is remembered chiefly for two things. In A.D. 212 he made citizens of almost all free persons in the empire. The citizenship had gradually been extended, so that perhaps a majority of free persons were already citizens; yet this

Caracalla, son of Septimius, remembered for making citizens of almost all free persons in Europe and for the public bath in Rome. (The Metropolitan Museum of Art, Samuel D. Lee, Fund, 1940)

was a notable move. Some of his contemporaries were unkind enough to suggest that since citizens paid an accession tax, Caracalla's main intention was to make a bigger tax haul. In any case, the move did not mean equality for all, since other distinctions were as marked as ever: for example, that between those termed *humiliores* and those called *honestiores* in law and the courts. Humiliores could be beaten or subjected to other corporal punishment; upper-class honestiores could not. The other notable accomplishment for which Caracalla is remembered is his huge public baths in Rome. Even in ruins, their brick-and-concrete core (which now houses one of the largest outdoor opera theaters in the world) is still impressive and of staggering scale to the modern viewer.

Caracalla liked to see himself in the image of Alexander the Great. He even had an army unit called the Macedonians. Perhaps it was chiefly this personal fantasy which led him to prepare an expedition to intervene in the affairs of the divided and decadent Parthian kingdom in the East. Caracalla, however, had few of Alexander's finer qualities. He made many enemies and was killed in the sixth year of his reign, during the Eastern campaign, at Edessa. Julia perhaps considered seizing power in her own name, but was prevented by the Praetorian Prefect Macrinus, who himself laid hold on the empire for a little more than a year. Julia was already sick with the cancer that would soon carry her off.

Other equally competent women of her family, however, continued to fashion positions of power for themselves. Her sister Julia Maesa had two daughters, Soaemias and Mamaea. All were important in the intrigues of state. Julia Maesa persuaded the soldiers to rise against Macrinus; she and Soaemias actually joined the ensuing battle and rallied the troops at a critical point. Macrinus was killed, and Maesa was able to arrange the accession first of one, then of the other of her grandsons, Elagabalus and Alexander Severus.

Elagabalus (A.D. 218–222)

The eldest of Julia Maesa's grandsons was Varius Avitus, better known as Elagabalus. At the time when the army gave him its support he was almost fifteen years old. His chief interests were exotic religion and sex. Fortunately for the empire, his mother and grandmother actually administered public affairs. He introduced the Eastern solar deity after whom he was named to Rome (symbolized in a black stone) and celebrated a marriage to another sun god in some sort of syncretic emphasis on worship of the sun as the chief god of the empire. He himself, perhaps in the guise of a deity, married a vestal virgin.

Probably under his grandmother's guidance, Elagabalus set up a Senate of Women, who concerned themselves primarily with making rules on the behavior and dress of women. When in his extraordinary behavior the emperor made himself look more like a woman than a man, he numbered his days, for the army would not long support such a monarch. Julia Maesa persuaded him to adopt his cousin Alexander in A.D. 221, so that when he was predictably murdered (along with his mother) by the praetorian guards, this boy succeeded to the throne.

Alexander Severus (A.D. 222–235)

Since Alexander was not yet fourteen years old when he was acclaimed emperor, some sort of regency was inevitable. His mother and his grandmother, Mamaea and Maesa, acting somewhat more circumspectly than the dead Soaemias had, saw to affairs. Maesa was so nearly empress that when she died she was officially designated a goddess. Mamaea also played the role of coruler, not merely the mother of the emperor; she presided at important meetings and called herself "Mother of the Army and of the Senate." Our sources indicate that as Alexander grew up, he acquired the finer virtues of dedication and equity. It is interesting that he displayed a surprising religious eclecticism; in his private shrine, besides deified former emperors, he kept busts of Orpheus; the neopythagorean mystic, Apollonius of Tyana; Abraham; and Christ. There is a Christian tradition that his mother, Mamaea, became a Christian.

Alexander did not have a forceful character, despite his virtues. Unhappily he chose as praetorian prefect the great jurist Ulpian, highly competent in the law but unpopular with the soldiers of the guard who soon killed him. When emergency demonstrated Alexander's incompetence as general, the legions also became disaffected.

The crises that exposed the military incapacity of Alexander, and of course of his mother as well, occurred on the empire's eastern and northern frontiers. In the East, the dynast of the rising Sassanid Persian kingdom invaded Roman territory. The Persians at length were fended off, but the Roman troops did not behave well in battle, nor did their commanders, including Alexander. A similar threat arose in the North with an invasion of Germans across the Rhine. Alexander and Mamaea arrived in the area to do their best, only to be murdered by mutinous Roman troops. Perhaps the disgruntled troops blamed female government for the empire's military problems—which seem to have included some attempt by the slain emperor to curtail the political sway of the army.

C. BARRACK-ROOM EMPERORS; ADMINISTRATIVE CHAOS

In the half century after the death of Alexander Severus, Rome was racked by civil war, barbarian and Persian invasions, and the plague. There were scores of claimants to the throne, at least twenty-five or thirty of whom must be classified as serious contenders. For instance, in a single nine-year-period, one emperor (Gallienus) fought off eighteen challengers. All civilian concerns had to be subordinated to the overriding problems of defense, against both invaders and would-be emperors. The foreign invasions probably should be regarded as the most serious problem: From the North, Franks, Alamanni, Goths, and other Germanic peoples poured by the hundred thousand into the empire. Repeatedly they penetrated Asia Minor, Greece, the Danubian and Gallic provinces, Spain, and even Italy itself. Only by the greatest efforts, the fortunate competence of several of the emperors, and sheer luck did the empire survive. In the following paragraphs we shall mention only a few of the more important rulers during this troubled age.

Maximinus to Decius (A.D. 235–251)

It seems somehow symbolic that Gaius Julius Maximinus was a Thracian of Germanic parentage who was noted more for his great physical stature than for anything else. Proclaimed emperor by his soldiers in A.D. 235, he ignored the Roman Senate (which still functioned, but with much-reduced power and status), fought numerous opponents unsuccessfully, and was killed by his own men within three years. Succeeding emperors were named by the Senate or, more often, seized power from positions of strength. One of these latter was known as "Philip the Arab" (Marcus Julius Philippus), who celebrated the one-thousandth anniversary of the city of Rome (753 B.C.–A.D. 248; note that in our reckoning there is no year zero)—but it looked as if there would never be a future jubilee for any emperor to celebrate. Philip was killed by Gaius Decius, an Illyrian who gained power with the help of his troops.

Decius reigned less than three years (249–251), and during this time the plague struck, along with the fierce Goths. He died in battle against the invaders—something a bit unique, for most emperors of this era were killed by their own men or fell in battle against challengers to their power.

Decius is remembered by Christians as a great persecutor. Philip was said to have favored the Christians, and perhaps Decius was in part reacting to the policy of his slain enemy; however, he probably believed that Christian disregard for the state gods had brought on the empire the twin disasters of invasion and plague. This was the first empire-wide persecution, a real effort to suppress Christianity completely; yet it is certain that local officials did not always cooperate in the suppression. Decius' decree required all citizens to appear before the local authorities and take an oath to the emperor—such an oath as Christians could not swear. Everyone was to carry on his or her person notarized proof of having sworn the oath. Many Christians yielded, and others yielded through the ruse of sending paid surrogates to appear and take the oath in their names. They argued bitterly among themselves about the ethics of this latter practice. Certainly they rejoiced at the death of Decius, as the first systematic persecutor on a broad scale.

Valerian, Gallienus, and Aurelian (A.D. 253–275)

Valerian and Gallienus, a father-and-son team, were not at all incompetent, and in fact—unusual in these years—were not uncultivated men. As emperor, Valerian (Publius Valerianus, 253–260) occupied himself chiefly with a Persian invasion, which achieved even the capture of Antioch. This war, too, was accompanied by the recurrent plague. Valerian won an initial battle and then penetrated into Mesopotamia, where he was defeated. When he attempted to negotiate with

An Antoninianus (= two denarii?) of Trajan Decius (249–251 A.D.). Note the radiate crown. Decius first mounted an empire-wide persecution of Christians.

the Persian monarch Sapor I, Valerian was treacherously taken prisoner and ultimately died in captivity. The world was treated to the spectacle (memorialized on a Persian coin of the time) of a captive Roman emperor on his knees in humiliation before King Sapor.

Publius Gallienus (260–268), meanwhile, with little better success attempted to stem the migration of hordes of Franks, Alamanni, and Goths, who were near to overwhelming the Rhine and Danube defenses. The Goths overran Dacia, and one small group penetrated as far as the walls of Athens. Only by vigorous action did Gallienus salvage the central segment of the empire. To make matters worse, a Roman general named Postumus seized Britain, Gaul, and Spain and carved out an independent state. Gallienus, hampered by a continuous succession of Roman challengers to his power, could not regain the lost provinces. His successor, Claudius II (268–270), was eventually able to roll back the invading Gothic hordes, and thus earned the surname "Gothicus."

In the East, a bit of luck saved the situation: Odenathus, king of the rich trading city of Palmyra in Syria, chose to make an alliance with the Romans and inflicted a serious defeat on the Persians. But soon Odenathus himself, and after his assassination in A.D. 267 his beautiful widow, Zenobia, seized a large chunk of Roman territory and ruled as independent monarchs. The empire had effectively broken up into three parts.

Aurelian (Lucius Domitius Aurelianus, A.D. 270–275), son of a small farmer in the Danube Valley, performed heroically in restoring the unity of the empire—though he was forced to abandon Dacia, held by Rome since Trajan's time. He twice defeated Palmyra; the second time he destroyed it. Its ruins are among the most imposing in the ancient Roman world. Queen Zenobia was led in Aurelian's triumph in Rome but was afterward permitted to live out her life in a villa near Tivoli.

A threat to Italy caused Aurelian to begin building a great wall around the city of Rome, the first such fortification since Hannibal's menace. It is this wall, with medieval additions, that is admired by tourists at various places within the present city.

Aurelian restored order along the Danube and at last reconquered the Gallic kingdom, now ruled by Gaius Tetricus from his capital at Treverorum (Trèves). The emperor was justly hailed as *restitutor orbis* ("restorer of the world"), a title Hadrian had once enjoyed for quite different accomplishments. Ironically, Aurelian was killed by some of his own officers who believed the false story, circulated by a clerk who knew he was being investigated for irregularities, that they were about to be executed.

When the truth of this affair came out, Aurelian's generals were so chagrined that they did not name a successor; instead, they actually asked the Senate at Rome to do so. After some understandable hesitation—did the generals really mean it?—the Senate, so long accustomed to being ignored, named an elderly senator called Marcus Tacitus. No return to civilian direction of affairs was to be hoped for, however, and in a few months some soldiers killed Tacitus. The fatal pattern of barrack-room intrigue continued. Rome had to suffer nearly another decade, until at last Diocletian was able to restore a measure of stability.

D. ECONOMIC AND SOCIAL COLLAPSE

No state could withstand such buffeting as Rome endured in the third century without serious damage. Indeed, most other states could not have survived. The most serious damage, ultimately, came not to the army nor to the top-level administration but to the economy and to society at the lower levels.

Economic Chaos

The economic decline, catastrophic and complete, hardly needs to be documented. The cost of maintaining huge standing armies for continual civil wars and foreign invasion would alone have bankrupted the empire. But in addition, trade of all sorts shrank; plague contributed to the chronic manpower shortage; and the production of farms and the typical small industry declined ruinously. Except for landowners whose farms adjoined the frontiers, those who owned farms along the great military roads suffered most. When troops have no money, they still must eat; if the legionaries did not simply seize what they needed, they requisitioned it, and for the produce taken they gave paper which, though legal, often was worthless.

The coinage portrays graphically to modern eyes the deterioration of the monetary system along with the economy. Rampant inflation brought cheapening of the coins: Gold disappeared; the silver was adulterated with base metals so that, finally, "silver" coins had only the thinnest coating of precious metal. Remaining specimens sometimes show only flecks of silver over the bronze core. The standard silver coin at the beginning of this period was the denarius. Even then, under the Severi, this was worth only about half the value of the denarius prior to Nero. Soon it was all but abandoned in favor of another coin, larger but with a smaller percentage of silver—the *antoninianus*, apparently valued at double the denarius. Within a few decades this coin, too, was debased, until it became almost worthless. Those who possessed valuable coins hoarded them. In some places, barter replaced a money economy.

Damage to Social Classes

The aristocracy naturally suffered; in Rome the senators lost power as well as wealth and influence. Perhaps it would be more accurate to say that the generals were now the aristocrats, for success could make an equestrian commander an instant noble—if not an instant emperor. The middle class of traders, bankers, and moneylenders suffered most of all. This class, which had always been too small for the good of the empire, now all but disappeared.

As for the lower classes, especially the rural small farmers, they too suffered. Chaotic politics, wars, and uncertain markets hurt their living standard, but perhaps the manpower drain of the draft hurt them most of all. As soldiers the peasants might be well cared for; the soldiers were probably the best treated of any social group. But the overall health of the state demanded that they be in the business of production, not of destruction.

Restoration of society and the economy would require herculean labor. Perhaps it is not too pessimistic to say that a complete restoration was impossible, but it did prove possible to shore up the foundations.

E. RETURN TO ORDER: DIOCLETIAN AND CONSTANTINE

What had happened during a half century of civil war, foreign invasion, and economic and social dislocation was something akin to revolution. Power now resided in new hands; the class structures had been altered, and militarily talented men of all ranks could rise to the top. Traditions of all sorts had been swept away. The results were chaotic; but at least if a strong figure rose, he would find less organized resistance to his efforts at reconstruction. The man who was to begin such a process was Diocletian.

Diocletian and the Tetrarchy (A.D. 285–305)

Like several of his predecessors, Gaius Aurelius Diocletianus came of Illyrian peasant stock. He rose through a combination of military and administrative skill, the latter quality being the more notable. The man had a certain charisma; he chose strong men as subordinates and retained their loyalty. More than anything else, it was his ability to control the generals that made possible a break in the long series of civil wars in which most emperors had been overthrown by their own lieutenants. Thus Diocletian could devote himself primarily to the tasks of administration. His subordinates, especially Maximian, did most of the work of restoring peace on the frontiers. It should be remembered, too, that in the tasks of unifying and protecting the empire, Diocletian was much aided by the work of his immediate predecessors, among them Aurelian.

What Diocletian created is often referred to as an oriental despotism. Those who use such terms refer in part to the manner in which, from this time on, the emperors made themselves inaccessible and surrounded themselves with the trappings, even the dress, of oriental monarchs. But the powers of the emperor also had become more nakedly absolute.

Diocletian, as a general himself, could hardly be expected to attempt to reestablish the sort of partnership between emperor and Senate that had characterized the first two centuries of empire. Moreover such a course would have been impossible. The problems he faced were acute and required drastic solutions. The army had to be maintained at a high level, and the emperor must command it directly, at least at times. He could not share his power with the Senate; nor could he stay in Rome for constant consultation with that body. The Senate, though retaining some of its ancient prestige, was by now little more than a city council for the capital. Even this claim is not quite accurate, for Rome, though it retained its mystique as the Eternal City, was no longer a real capital: Diocletian usually resided at Nicomedia, in Asia Minor near the Bosporus, and his chief lieutenant, Maximian, usually governed from Milan.

Diocletian's greatest achievement was to bring an end to the internal competition for office. This was absolutely necessary before he could improve the chaotic economic situation. Doubtless the most important ingredient in this achievement was the quality of the emperor himself; but there was new administrative machinery, too. Almost at once, Diocletian made Maximian a caesar, subordinate to himself as augustus. Then, when Maximian's troops hailed him as augustus after he crushed some invading Germanic tribesmen, Diocletian accepted that. The two commanders thus became theoretically equal, though Diocletian, in true military style, maintained his seniority in rank. After a few years, each of the Augusti took a caesar as his chief lieutenant: For Diocletian, it was Galerius; for Maximian, Constantius Chlorus.

The empire was restructured, basically divided in half (shades of the future), with Diocletian ruling the East and Maximian the West. The halves were further subdivided into quarters, with the caesars each controlling one segment. Any of the four rulers could, in time of crisis, lend help to his nearest comrade in the chain of command. Thus, when Constantius campaigned against a Gallic usurper, Carausius, in northwest Gaul and Britain, Maximian moved up from his headquarters in Milan to look out for the Rhine frontier. The death of any of the four rulers would not have precipitated a crisis, since one of the others would have stepped in to keep order and a successor would have been quickly named.

Diocletian's army was larger but divided into smaller and more mobile units, stationed along the frontiers. Reserve detachments were positioned some distance back from the frontiers for defense in depth and greater flexibility. Adding to its mobility was an emphasis on cavalry.

The civilian government also was reorganized. Although the four rulers gave their chief attention to military matters, four praetorian prefects governed civilian affairs. The number of administrative provinces was increased to more than a hundred; perhaps the intent was to prevent rebellion on the part of a powerful provincial governor. The provinces were grouped into twelve *dioceses*, headed by officials called *vicars*. The provincial governors now were often termed *duces*.

Constantine the Great (A.D. 306–337)

Diocletian decided to abdicate, effective in A.D. 305. This was a rather astonishing and unprecedented move. He persuaded—perhaps coerced—Maximian to retire at the same time. As expected, the younger caesars became augusti, and two new caesars were appointed. Though Constantius technically outranked Galerius, Diocletian permitted Galerius to make the new designations.

Notably left out of the new tetrarchy by Galerius were Constantine, the son of Constantius, and Maxentius, the son of Maximian. At the death of Constantius the next year, Constantine was hailed augustus in his place. At this, Maxentius seized Rome and declared himself augustus as well. Maximian came out of retirement to help his son and resumed his title of augustus. After a series of events that included some actual fighting, six persons all now claimed the title of augustus! At one point Diocletian came out of retirement and made new arrangements in an effort to perpetuate his system, but soon the struggle resumed.

Galerius died of a wasting disease in 311. By then, Maximian had been killed. This left four rulers: Constantine in the extreme west, Maxentius in Italy and Africa, Licinius on the Danube, and Maximin Daia in Asia. Constantine and Maxentius prepared for a confrontation. Constantine seemingly claimed right to the whole empire by saying he was descended from an earlier emperor, Claudius Gothicus; he emphasized this relationship by adopting as his chief god Sol Invictus, the "Unconquered Sun," in the manner of Claudius and several other emperors from Aurelian on. In this, perhaps, Constantine was wooing the large number of Roman soldiers who also worshiped the sun in the Mithraic religion.

In 312 Constantine mounted an expedition and marched on Maxentius in Italy. He could manage only 40,000 men; Maxentius had two or three times as many available. The adventure seemed foolhardy and has been explained in religious terms; perhaps Constantine was already influenced by the Christian views he later accepted. At any rate, it was later written by his biographers that one evening on the march he saw a cross in the sky with the writing, in Greek, "In this sign, conquer." This, it was said, was confirmed by a vision that night, which told him to put the monogram for Christ in Greek, the Chi-Rho (**XP**), on the armor of his troops.

Whatever the truth, Constantine dared a great deal. He gained some preliminary victories in northern Italy, but his great triumph came at the Milvian Bridge, just north of Rome. Constantine won that battle, and with it control of all the West. Superior tactics had forced Maxentius to fight at a disadvantage, but of course, Christians attributed the victory to the intervention of God. The Roman Senate named Constantine senior augustus, and almost immediately the emperor attempted to use his power to stop all persecution of Christians in the East. Licinius, who had become augustus of the East, joined with Constantine in this act and, together with him, signed the Edict of Milan in 313, proclaiming toleration of Christianity throughout the empire.

The strife among and attrition of the augusti continued until only two remained: Constantine in the West and Licinius in the East. This arrangement lasted until 324, when the two came to war. Ambition was the most likely reason for their clash, but there was also a difference in religious policy: Licinius had begun to attack the Christians, in an attempt to destroy the higher levels of organization in the Church, whereas Constantine was attempting to take over the Church hierarchy. Constantine won out, and the whole empire was again ruled by one man.

Religious Policy Under Diocletian and Constantine

There was a kind of inevitability about the struggle between Christianity and the pagan state of Rome. Jesus' own position was not intransigent ("Render unto Caesar the things that are Caesar's and unto God the things that are God's"), and the Apostle Paul was essentially loyal to the Roman state ("The powers that exist are appointed by God"). Yet Rome's pagan religiosity was so completely intertwined with the state itself that any attack on its religion must immediately be an attack on the state as well.

The Jews' and Christians' exclusiveness not only precluded them from practicing anything pagan in nature but also led them to deny the existence of gods other than the One. They were thus labeled atheists. Judaism had at least the advantage of being a legally recognized religion, but Christianity was long denied that status. Moreover, after the elimination of the Jewish state during the wars of Vespasian and Hadrian, the Jews no longer seemed a real threat to the secular state. Christianity, however, seemed the more dangerous as it grew apace; its hierarchical organization grew also, and to emperors such as Decius and Aurelian it seemed a state within a state, essentially unpatriotic and sapping the foundations of Roman society and government. They therefore tried to stamp it out.

Diocletian had severely persecuted Christians. Perhaps this was a result of the influence of his caesar, Galerius; most Christian writers thought so. The worst persecution occurred toward the end of Diocletian's reign. Galerius continued the harsh attacks until he was afflicted with a terrible disease and had second thoughts. Then, in 311 he reversed himself and issued an edict of toleration, but the change did not stay the progress of his disease. After him, Maximin Daia again began persecuting the Church, and eventually, as we have seen, so did Licinius. In the West, even in Diocletian's time, the persecutions were always less severe and less extensive than elsewhere, and after Constantine gained power they of course ceased.

Constantine is accounted the first Christian emperor. Exactly when and in what way he was converted, it is difficult to say. He may have been much influenced by the painful fate of the arch-persecutor Galerius. One cannot reject out of hand the reports that he saw a vision and had a dream before the battle of the Milvian Bridge. Some sort of personal conviction must have been there, since Christians were hardly strong enough to have made it politically advantageous to favor them. The emperor continued to be *pontifex maximus*, to use pagan themes— even the radiate crown of the sun god—on his coinage, and was not baptized until the very end of his life. Yet he embraced the Church, to a degree dominated it, and even coerced bishops when he felt it necessary.

Above all, under him Christianity was recognized as an officially acceptable religion, a status dating from the Edict of Milan.

Economic Policy Under Diocletian and Constantine

The disastrous economic collapse in the third century had been caused largely by invasions and civil wars, with all their attendant evils: ravaging of cities and fields (not always by non-Roman armies), heavy tax burdens, the military draft, and the decline of trade and small industry. Inflation and debasement of the coinage were results rather than causes, but were painful nonetheless. Obviously the most important single blessing for the stricken economy was the restoration of order, both along the frontiers and internally. Equally important was a restored discipline in the army, for the undisciplined soldier could manage a good deal of depredation on his own. These positive changes Diocletian and Constantine in large part accomplished, with beneficial economic effect.

Improvement was not always immediate. We hear of productive lands that lay idle for lack of tenants. Inflation also, which so often becomes a psychological phenomenon as well as one based on economic necessity, was not easily stemmed. Diocletian thus found it necessary to issue his famous price edict in 301, setting maximum prices for commodities and labor all over the empire. The prices established seem a bit high for antiquity, yet they are surely much below those which were then being extorted. One tends to doubt how successfully this measure— extreme and characteristic of absolutist thinking—curbed prices in the marketplace. It seems, in any case, to have been applied only in the East.

Diocletian and Constantine reformed the coinage and issued a new gold coin, the *solidus*, somewhat lighter than the old *aureus*, which had disappeared during the preceding half century. New and finer silver coins were also introduced. In the time of Constantine the solidus appears to have been minted in sufficient quantity to form the basis of the monetary system; in Diocletian's reign these coins were probably not available in sufficient numbers. It is notable that Diocletian, in reforming the tax system, arranged for the collection of taxes in kind, that is, in produce, and much of the government's disbursements were also made in produce; this hardly implies total success on the monetary front.

Many of the changes of the catastrophic third century proved irreversible. The ruined middle class could not be re-created. On the level of local government, a large segment of the governing classes—those which furnished the members of the city councils, the *decuriones*—had been ruined. These classes did reestablish themselves to a degree in the more secure times, but never to their old levels in numbers and prosperity. The decuriones were saddled by law with compulsory and heavy financial burdens. Eventually laws were added to force well-to-do persons to serve as decurions. The effect of all this was stifling.

One notable and permanent change in this era saw many tenant farmers converted virtually into serfs; no longer free to leave their tenant contracts, they were thus bound to the soil. Whether these *coloni* derived from slaves made into tenants, barbarian prisoners converted into tenants, or free men who under pressure of an age of disorder had slipped into this half-free status is not known. Their condition, which developed gradually over many decades, was firmly established by the time of Constantine. This tendency to bind people to their occupations was not limited to agrarian activities. Before the end of this period, edicts of the central government attempted to tie people of all sorts to their occupations. Their work became a hereditary obligation to the state.

The degree to which the Roman state now attempted to control the lives of all its citizens was unprecedented; compelled by the turmoil of the times, its effects were ultimately deadly.

From Rome to Constantinople

Under Diocletian, Rome was no longer the administrative center of the empire, only the symbolic capital; it was an age when military concerns controlled imperial decisions. Constantine's choices of sites for administration reduced further the political position of Rome. From the beginning of his rule in the West he had made Augusta Treverorum (later called Trèves; modern Trier), in what is today northeastern France, his capital, and even after the defeat of Maxentius and his march into Rome, he preferred to be in Trèves or in Sirmium on the Save near the Danube—almost anywhere other than Rome, it seems. The reason was that Rome lay too far from the frontiers, but also the venerable city almost suffocated with traditions, all of which had some sort of pagan associations. Constantine's refusal more than once to sacrifice to Jupiter on the Capitol at the usual times caused riots; in other ways he irritated the nobility there and at the same time felt himself unnecessarily constrained by the old city.

Constantine's building programs indicate well his own priorities and preferences. His construction projects tended toward the grandiose and, indeed, were grander than the imperial treasury could afford. At Trèves he built an extensive palace complex with a summer villa a few miles away. The baths there were the largest of those in any province. Later a spacious cathedral was constructed, and a magnificent basilica still stands. Extensive projects were also carried out at Sirmium, at Cirta in North Africa, and in other places—such as, quite naturally, at Jerusalem and Bethlehem—where churches were put up. It is possibly owing to Constantine's penchant for large structures that from this time forward, the term *churches* usually refers to buildings rather than to groups of communicants.

Despite his personal ambivalence about Rome, Constantine also spent tremendous sums on buildings there. He completed a huge basilica on the edge of the Forum, begun by Maxentius; a single side aisle survives, mute evidence of its one-time grandeur. Mostly, however, he built churches, and mostly outside the city proper. These include three of the major churches today (though all have been rebuilt, one twice): San Giovanni in Laterano, which is within the walls; St. Peter's on the Vatican; and St. Paul's Outside the Walls; there were others also. Another

Arch of Constantine (Art Resource)

Constantinian landmark familiar to tourists is an arch, both large and impressive, which stands near the Colosseum. Many of its relief sculptures were taken from other structures.

Most significant for the future of the empire was the largest of Constantine's construction projects, the building up of Byzantium—renamed Constantinople—as essentially a second capital city. The work began in 330. Located on the Bosporus in today's European Turkey, the new city presaged the coming division of the empire. Constantinople was an imitation of Rome in several ways; under a son of Constantine, it even included a Senate and officials like those of the old capital. One reason for the new city and for its location was defensibility: In the high period of the empire this would have been thought unimportant. The city was placed on high ground rising sharply from the sea on a triangular-shaped peninsula; fortified and properly defended, it made an almost impregnable, secure center of government. On the north, a protected bay, the Golden Horn, affords a fine harbor even for modern ships. Septimius Severus had also favored the site and erected important structures there; in some instances Constantine simply enlarged and embellished the earlier works. He laid out a magnificent forum, put up a large palace with an equally impressive hippodrome nearby (as in Rome); he built several churches and constructed a roomy basilica as a Senate house. The walls enclosed about two-thirds of the peninsula. Future emperors would continue the building program. A new outer wall embracing the whole peninsula was erected by Thedosius the Great; it was actually a triple wall, with a moat that could be flooded, the final element of strength that would make it possible for Constantinople to survive the invasions that would overwhelm Rome and the West, and to endure for yet another thousand years.

BOOKS FOR FURTHER READING

BARNES, T. *The New Empire of Diocletian and Constantine*, Cambridge, Mass., 1982.

BIRLEY, A. *Septimius Severus: The African Emperor*, New York, 1972.

DÖRRIES, H. *Constantine the Great*, New York, 1972.

GRANT, M. *The Climax of Rome*, New York, 1970.

GRANT, R. *Augustus to Constantine: The Thrust of the Christian Movement into the World*, New York, 1970.

GUTERMAN, S. *Religious Toleration and Persecution in Ancient Rome*, London, 1951.

HYDE, W. *Paganism to Christianity in the Roman Empire*, Philadelphia, 1946.

JONES, A. *Constantine and the Conversion of Europe*, London, 1948.

MACMULLEN, R. *Constantine*, 1969.

MACMULLEN, R. *The Roman Government's Response to Crisis*, New Haven, 1976.

MILLAR, F. *The Emperor and the Roman World*, New York, 1977.

PARKER, H. *The Roman Legions*, Oxford, 1928.

ROSTOVTZEFF, M. *Social and Economic History of the Roman Empire*, 2nd Eng. ed., Oxford, 1957.

TURTON, G. *The Syrian Princesses: The Women Who Ruled Rome*, A.D. 193–235, London, 1974.

21

ROME (A.D. 337–476) FROM CONSTANTINE TO ROMULUS AUGUSTULUS

The Roman Empire survived the civil wars, economic disruption, foreign challenges, and barbarian invasions of the third century, remaining almost intact, territorially; Dacia had been abandoned by Aurelian and some eastern segments had been taken by the Sassanid Persian monarchs, but the very survival of the empire is itself testimony to the remarkable resilience of the structure. Perhaps it shows even more clearly the fact that people all over the civilized world could conceive of no viable alternative to eternal Rome, the empire that had unified the entire Mediterranean world and brought generally sound administration and a better system of justice for all. In the far reaches of the empire, people who had never seen the city of Rome—and never would—yet thought of themselves as Romans. Not until the overwhelming invasions of the fifth century did any leader really scheme to destroy and replace rather than simply to take over the enduring framework that had so successfully brought the civilized world together.

The changeover from pagan to Christian Rome, which in retrospect seems so momentous to anyone oriented to a Christianized Western civilization, did not really change political conditions in Rome after Constantine (though it changed much else). Many Christians in early years did indeed bitterly hope for the extinction of "eternal Rome"—a term that in itself seemed blasphemously arrogant to Christians—but they changed their minds once they gained control of the political structure; after this they felt that the health of the Church was closely linked to the continued good health of the empire.

The emperors after Constantine could not restore the political, economic, and social well-being of the state to the standards of the high empire. The centralization of power, for example, could not be reversed: The local government in the city-states that formed the building blocks of the earlier empire had been seriously impaired and could not be entirely reconstituted. Though a trading class again grew up with the recovery under Diocletian, it was never so strong as in the days of Marcus Aurelius. Nor was there ever, in the late empire, the degree of freedom from the threat of outside invasion that existed after Augustus in the first century and after Trajan in the second. Although there were periods of relative peace when inhabitants of the empire—as in North Africa—felt as secure as ever, the continuing barbarian incursions reached such a scale in the fifth century that the western empire was overrun and partitioned into the semicivilized units that we call the "successor states."

In the fourth century, however, the reconstituted political and military structures remained strong. At the center—his power restrained no longer by constitutional tradition but only by practical necessity and the likelihood of overthrow if he was incompetent—ruled the emperor with his advisory body of generals and civil officials, called his *consistory* (so named because these officials now stood always in the presence of the divine one, the emperor). His aristocratic supporters who held high office came from families unheard of in the Rome of the late republic or earlier empire; most had risen through military, not civil, office. Chief officials and other leaders of society were senators, but few of them actually resided in Rome and attended sessions of the Senate there. The position carried with it the title *clarissimus*; a primary benefit was immunity from local obligations in areas where they owned land. The four praetorian prefects governed the four prefectures and looked after civil and judicial matters, supervising provincial administration; each prefect had the help of vicars, who oversaw groups of provinces called *dioceses*. The governors of the numerous provinces in turn saw to it that the councilors of the local government units, called *decuriones* or *curiales*, did their work—especially collecting taxes. Sometimes forced to serve in this local post and held personally responsible for taxes not collected, curiales all too often in this age were seen as local tyrants; they had become primarily instruments of the central government.

The army of course still had the emperor as commander-in-chief; directly under him were several masters: one or more masters of the horse, as in the days of the republic, under a dictator then, plus master(s) of foot soldiers and others. Cavalry now made up much of the army; elite units were called *comrades (comitatenses*; originally members of the personal escort troop of the emperor, the *comitatus*) and were led by commanders called *counts (comes)*. The legions, once the proud core of the army, were now much smaller and made up of second-class troops; their commanders, in charge of segments of the frontiers, were *dukes (duces)*. Various other types of units existed, some of hired tribesmen from beyond the frontiers. Especially in the western half of the empire, more and more army units were actually resident Germans, armed in their own fashion and fighting in their own tactical style. The reasons for the use of such troops included the apparent general shortage of manpower, the reluctance of citizens to serve in the armies, and perhaps most important, costs: The Germans were paid much less, and citizens not serving in the army paid more taxes. As compared to earlier days, then, the army was much more mobile, since there was more cavalry and the infantry was less heavily armored. Possibly the quality was down somewhat, but for several decades after Constantine the army did a relatively good job of guarding the frontiers.

Only one institution flourished and proliferated in the century and a half now under consideration, and that was the Church. Its organization expanded in conformity with the political structure; its wealth grew as emperors and other individuals made gifts that never had to be dispersed through inheritance; and the power and influence of prelates increased, especially in the West, when at last the battered civil authority began to decline. That power would survive the breakup of the western empire and endure within the successor states. Christianity strongly influenced the social and cultural development of the late empire (even if not the political structure), and the survival of the Church provided a degree of cultural unity among the successor states that otherwise might have been totally lost.

A. THE EMPIRE IN THE FOURTH CENTURY UNDER THE DYNASTY OF CONSTANTINE

Though Diocletian's tetrarchy had dissolved in a struggle for power soon after his retirement, and Constantine had ultimately controlled the entire empire, the concept that a college of rulers was needed did not fall with his system. Constantine made use of his sons during the latter years of his reign after he had disposed of Licinius, and when he died the empire was divided among the three of them; in future years the principle of dynastic succession in general continued. This did not mean the end of civil war—Constantine's sons fought each other—but never again did succession problems degenerate into complete chaos as in the third century. A period of relative peace, with monetary and other reforms, left the empire in a fairly strong situation.

The absolute character of the regime must be stressed. One of the best observers of the century was the excellent historian Ammianus Marcellinus; he makes it quite clear that if an emperor—such as Constantius II—was suspicious and not overly concerned with justice, or if—like Valentinian—the emperor's temper had a short fuse, innocent persons or those guilty of only minor offenses could suffer torture, execution, or exile. It was a brutal age in which all those in high command were totally inured to killing; Christianity did not seem to change that for the better.

Constantine II, Constans, and Constantius II
(A.D. 337–360)

Constantine the Great had disposed of his oldest son, along with the son's mother, on charges of adultery; three sons remained, and it was apparently Constantine's intention to leave the empire under their joint control, along with a son of one of his three half brothers. Soon after Constantine's death, however, Constantius II aroused troops at Constantinople against all the relatives of his father, and the half brothers, along with their sons, were all killed, except for two boys aged about six and nine, Julian and Gallus. The empire was then divided among the three brothers, with the youngest, Constans, in a subordinate role. Constantine II took the western regions; Constans as his lieutenant controlled Africa, Italy, and Illyricum. Constantius II took the eastern half of the empire. Constantine II had problems with barbarian invaders and also with Constans, who did not appreciate his secondary role. In 340 the two brothers fought a civil war, in which Constans was victorious and thereafter ruled alone in the West. He himself fell victim to a conspiracy led by one of his generals ten years later. When Constantius II by 353 had defeated this usurper, he controlled the entire empire.

Following the collegiate principle, Constantius II chose to associate others with him in command, and despite recent experience, he thought it safest to choose kinsmen; he first picked his cousin Gallus, who somehow didn't turn out well: He was executed in a short time. His next choice was the last of his cousins, Gallus' half brother Julian, who was married to his own daughter, Helena. Sent by Constantius to Gaul, where a Frankish rebellion and invasions by Germans—Alamanni and others—demanded attention, Julian soon demonstrated his competence and restored order within two or three years.

Constantius, it seems, never entirely trusted Julian and kept spies among his staff. The event that brought the two to the brink of civil war was Constantius' demand that half or more of Julian's army be sent east, where, he said, they were needed in a war against Persia. The request itself was unexceptionable; however, most of Julian's troops were Gauls, and he had earlier promised them that they would not be required to leave their families to serve elsewhere in the empire. Julian apparently felt threatened; he therefore arranged for his troops to "demand" that he be elevated to the post of augustus, and after a suitable period of hesitation he accepted. Thereafter civil war would inevitably have occurred except for the sudden death of Constantius in 360. Although some resistance to his elevation continued for a few months, Julian now controlled the whole empire.

Julian, The "Apostate" (A.D. 360–363)

One of the most intriguing figures of antiquity, Julian is, after Constantine, perhaps the person best known to us from this century. As is so often the case, the wealth of information does not make it possible entirely to understand the subject, only to recognize the complexity and indeed the contradictions that enter into human character and motivation. The psychological trauma that went with the killing of his father and brothers as well as the ensuing virtual imprisonment for him and Gallus, his brother—not to mention the latter's execution— must surely have filled him with resentment, even hatred. This treatment at the hands of his Christian (though Arian) cousin Constantius may also have tilted him away from Christianity, back toward a sort of idealistic paganism that he professed openly only after his elevation to augustus. He was also rather ascetic, somewhat puritan, in his outlook, even a bit monkish; when Helena died in childbirth, Julian never remarried. He was repelled by the opulent ease and corruption that he found in both Constantinople and Antioch. Julian embraced Hellenic culture entire, especially the old religion, which he held to be an essential element. Neoplatonism, it seemed to him, provided a more satisfactory explanation for all that exists than the Christian world view.

Julian made it clear that his intent was to restore the traditional religion, with emphasis on Hellenic deities, but he did not persecute Christianity; he wanted to achieve his goals through education. Yet his officials did engage in some persecution, which he did not punish; for example, a few Christian soldiers who refused to carry out pagan rites as ordered by their commanders were executed. If he had wanted, however, Julian could not have made this sort of repression into standard policy: Probably half or more of his soldiers were Christian. He restored the temples to the old gods and in general deplored the "atheism" of the "Galilaeans." He attempted to organize paganism into a formal structure analogous to that of Christianity. Christians were of course appalled by their emperor's lapse—hence the epithet "the Apostate"—but curiously, Julian's policy brought out no general protest or specific conspiracy. Still, his reign was brief; if he had lived, he might have provoked some such violent reaction.

As caesar in Gaul, Julian had carried through reforms and had succeeded in drastically reducing taxes. Now, as augustus, he tried to reestablish Hellenism in the eastern empire. He attempted to restore the health of local government by reducing the burdens of the local councilors or curiales, and he increased their numbers for the same reason. The new eligibles protested, for as we have seen, local office had become a heavy burden. He attempted also to revive the vitality of Hellenic studies, and to this end prohibited Christians from teaching in the traditional schools on the ground of their lack of sympathy with Greco-Roman literature and learning. Not only did he greatly reduce the palace staff and hangers-on in Constantinople, he also tried to impose his puritan lifestyle everywhere. He was much disappointed at the reaction. In Antioch, pagan elements were still strong and temples frequented; still Julian found not only distaste but also resistance, and finally even dislike, because he decried the Antiochines' luxurious way of life, their lack of dedication to the sterner ideals of antiquity. Probably what frustrated him most was the realization that his efforts were doomed to fail.

A Persian attack on the empire in the reign of Constantius had remained unpunished. Julian now organized a massive campaign against that foe. He was probably influenced in part by his great admiration for Alexander the Great, who had daringly invaded Persia on an epoch-making campaign almost seven centuries earlier, when he was about the same age as Julian. The would-be Alexander got together a huge army and successfully penetrated to the Euphrates; after that, however, the campaign went badly. The competent Julian might have retrieved the situation, but he was killed by the chance cast of a lance; one rumor had it that it belonged to one of his own Christian soldiers. So ended the dynasty established by Constantine the Great. The year was A.D. 363.

B. THE EMPIRE IN THE LATER FOURTH CENTURY

Julian left no obvious heir, and it was the army that decided the succession at his untimely death. After some maneuvering, one of Julian's officers, Jovian, was elevated to the purple. He was, incidentally, Christian (it did not seem to matter much to the army what his religion was); he made peace with the Persians on the best terms he could get. Jovian lived only a few more months; he is remembered primarily for his reversal of Julian's anti-Christian policy, though he continued the practice of general religious tolerance. After his death, civil and military officers in Constantinople named his successor, a leading general named Valentinian (364–375), who soon raised his brother, Valens (364–378), to the rank of augustus also; the latter ruled the eastern half of the empire and Valentinian the western half. On his death, Valentinian was succeeded by his son, Gratian (367–383), with his brother, Valentinian II (375–392), who was for some years actually too young to rule. In the East, the ruler following the death of Valens in battle in 378 was Theodosius, eventually called "The Great" (d. 395), who after a time gained control of the whole empire.

Almost all the information for this period relates to barbarian invasions, internal struggles for power, or matters involving the Christian Church. We shall not attempt to survey even the most serious of the events that wracked the Roman world in these decades, but we shall focus on one short period, emphasizing those actions and happenings that seem, from the perspective of the twentieth century, most portentous for the future.

Christian Church and State After Julian

As we have seen, general religious toleration (the policy of Julian in spite of some restrictions on Christians), continued when the Christian line of rulers resumed. Just as in the period after Constantine's proclaimed toleration for Christianity, the Church was again free to give attention to its organization, public stance, rites, schools, and the like. Internal problems, especially of doctrine, could again take center stage, however, and we hear much of serious quarrelling among Church leaders. The most important controversy involved Arianism, by now accounted heresy. Arius had argued for a subordinate position for Jesus in relation to God, with implications for the nature of the godhead, of course, but also for humans as well. The Nicene Creed, formulated at the Council of Nicaea under Constantine (A.D. 325), basically rejected the Arian view but had not settled the controversy; indeed there were a dozen councils and synods by the time of Julian—

the pagan historian Ammianus said that Christian bishops were always galloping about—which made opposing pronouncements and ousted rival church leaders.

The most indefatigable opponent of Arianism was Athanasius, bishop of Alexandria, who was several times forced to leave his city and was more than once proclaimed deposed. However, his position was accepted in Rome and the West in general and finally declared orthodox. Constantius II and some later emperors were Arian, and it was not until the time of Theodosius that Arianism was banned throughout the whole empire. One complication was that many of the Germanic peoples had been converted to the Arian form of Christianity. The best-known missionary to the Goths was Ulfilas, who was able to preach to them in their own language and translated the Bible into Gothic. Most of the Germanic peoples remained Arian until the sixth century.

The organization of the Church became increasingly formalized. The presbyters and deacons of the villages gave place to the clergy—especially the bishops—of the nearest cities; these in turn were subordinate to the bishops of the large cities, sometimes called *metropolitans*. Bishops of the greatest cities were naturally most important and influential of all. In the West the bishop of Rome exercised a broad influence; only somewhat less important was the bishop of Milan, one of the administrative capitals of the empire. In the East, the bishops of Constantinople, Antioch, Jerusalem, and Alexandria were preeminent.

The Church retained close ties with the civil government. Since Constantine the emperors had been appealed to by Church leaders for one reason and another, and they usually responded. Civil authority enforced the banishments of both Athanasius and of Arians at various times. The responses of the emperors, however, were not always immediate or vigorous. Some bishops long inveighed against the presentation of games on Sundays, and indeed Constantine had placed some restrictions on activities on that day; but not until 392, near the end of Theodosius' reign, was the scheduling of games such as horse racing on "the Lord's Day" forbidden. Even then the edict was not carefully enforced: After all, some of the rank-and-file Christians liked a good horse race also.

The Christian emperors, moreover, avoided arousing the ire of pagans, for many of them were quite important persons; so they often continued in practices that some Church leaders found reprehensible. For example, the first six such emperors retained the title *pontifex maximus*, despite all its pagan connotations. Gratian, son of Valentinian, was the first to renounce that title, which later devolved on the bishop of Rome. Gratian also took other steps that appalled his pagan subjects. He had the Altar to Victory removed from the Senate house in Rome, for example, in the year 382. For perhaps a thousand years, sessions of the Senate had begun with an offering before that altar, and most senators bitterly opposed the change.

Gratian went further: He issued an edict that same year ending state funding for pagan rites and for institutions such as the college of the Vestal Virgins. He even took away their private funding through foundations established over the centuries, confiscating the funds for the state treasury. Later, Gratian was to waver in this policy, but the eminent bishop of Milan, Ambrose, demanded and received from the emperor his promise not to alter it. This degree of suppression was not enough for some churchmen, who urged upon the emperors the extirpation of paganism root and branch.

Theodosius, whom Christians called "The Great," came near to attempting just that. The Catholic church was established as the official religion of the empire. Many temples were closed, even destroyed. In Alexandria, the Christian bishop, with the support of the civil authorities, caused bloody riots when he demolished the magnificent Sarapaeum. Sacrifices were forbidden, along with such pagan activities as soothsaying. The emperor also moved against Christian heretics: In 380 he issued his edict "On the Catholic Faith"; it threatened penalties for those who did not accept the Nicene Creed. The Arian bishop of Constantinople was deposed and replaced, and dissident clerics elsewhere were driven from the cities. For a time there was trouble in the West, where a usurper, after the assassination of Valentinian in 392, defended the old Roman religion. Theodosius soon defeated him, however, and afterward not only ruled the entire empire but established his policies everywhere.

The position of the emperor did not change much with the establishment of the Christian religion and the suppression of the old ways. The emperor could no longer be termed a god, but his person was still in some sense sacred and his role even in relation to religion was not greatly diminished. Yet the influence of the Christian clergy did on occasion impinge somewhat on the emperor's prerogatives. The bishop of Milan in this period, Ambrose, an extremely competent person of aristocratic background, not only had political influence over Gratian but also both influenced Theodosius and successfully clashed with him. In one instance, surprisingly, Theodosius appears more just than Ambrose: A bishop of a city in Mesopotamia had instigated the burning, not of a pagan temple, but of a Jewish synagogue. The emperor ordered the rebuilding of the synagogue at Christian expense, but Ambrose persuaded him to reverse his decision. In another, better-known incident, Theodosius was certainly at fault. As the result of a trivial uprising in Macedonia, the emperor slaughtered a great many of the residents of Thessalonica. Ambrose confronted the emperor before the Church and refused access to communion until he had confessed and made amends. As for the role of the Church (meaning the clergy) within the state, Ambrose made a classic statement that the Church would strive to make into standard policy in future centuries: "In questions affecting the faith, it is the Bishops who are the judges of Christian Emperors, and not the Emperors who are the judges of the Bishops."[1] The future conflict of Church and state is thus foreshadowed in this time.

---

[1] *Ep. xxi.* 4; translation by P. de Labriolle, *The History and Literature of Christianity*, London, 1924, p. 275.

Goths and Huns: Danube Frontier Out of Control;
Disaster at Adrianople (A.D. 378)

North of the Danube, the Visigoths, under the great tribal leaders Athan-aric and Fritigern, had achieved a relatively stable situation in the fourth century and mostly maintained satisfactory relations with the empire. Further north and east was the Ostrogothic kingdom—if an organization defined by tribal districts rather than by distinct boundaries may be called that—ruled by the competent Ermanaric. His territory stretched from the Baltic coasts down and across the Ukraine to the Sea of Azov. Beyond that lived the Alans, enemies of the Goths, and still further east, the Huns. Beginning probably in the 360s the Huns moved west and attacked the Goths, possibly with the cooperation of at least some of the Alans, setting off a chain reaction that led to an all but irretrievable disaster for the Roman Empire.

During the next several decades, the Huns, the most feared of all the bar-barians, forced numberless Goths across the Roman frontiers at the lower Danube and themselves pierced the Roman borders on the central Danube and some years later at the Rhine. Primarily nomadic horsemen inured to long hours and days astride their sturdy mounts, the speed and irrepressible ferocity of their attacks sent shock waves of consternation throughout the empire. The great Christian leader Jerome (about whom more later) saw them as the horsemen of the Apoc-alypse, heralding the end of the world. Popular accounts depicted them as sub-human, capable of unimaginable horrors.

By 376 the Huns had defeated Ermanaric, and soon after, almost without a fight, they reduced the Visigoths to abject panic through swift maneuvering. Driven west and south, Visigoths, Ostrogoths, and others streamed across the Dan-ube as refugees, with or without the permission of Roman authorities. The Ro-mans at first saw them as potential soldiers to use to protect the frontiers—the army was predominantly made up of Germanic troops already—but the over-whelming volume of immigrants, 200,000 or more, brought apprehension. The Roman policy changed to one of containment, even of deliberate starvation of the unwelcome horde, and this inevitably meant war. The emperor in the East, Valens, appealed for help to his brother Gratian, who commanded the West, and the latter led an army down the Danube.

The fateful battle of Adrianople in Thrace (378) broke out before Gratian could arrive to help; the Visigoths with their superior cavalry destroyed the Roman army and killed the Roman Emperor Valens. The history of Ammianus includes a description of the battle, terming it the greatest Roman disaster since Cannae, six centuries earlier. A Christian bishop, Gregory of Nazianzen, wrote, "The cities are devastated, myriads of people are killed, the earth is soaked with blood, and a foreign people is running through the land as if it were theirs."[2] Theodosius later

---

[2]As translated in J. O. Maenchen-Helfen, *The World of the Huns*, Berkeley, 1973, p. 34.

defeated the Goths and eventually permitted them to stay in regions along the Danube as hired protectors of the frontier; they retained their tribal identity and so were not absorbed in the manner of earlier immigrants. In retrospect, Adrianople appears to have been crucial; after that debacle a chain of events led inexorably to the end of the Roman Empire in the West.

C. THE FIFTH CENTURY TO THE END OF THE EMPIRE IN THE WEST

After Theodosius died in 395, the empire was never again united. He divided the rule between his two sons: Arcadius, aged eighteen, got the East, and Honorius, only eleven, the West. As regent Theodosius had chosen Stilicho, his senior general, the greatest of the age, a Vandal but certainly no barbarian. As long as he lived, Stilicho held the Visigoths away from Rome and soundly defeated Alans and others who also penetrated into the peninsula.

Honorius, who lived until 423, had to face a usurper who controlled Britain plus some of Gaul and Spain, as well as another overwhelming irruption of migrating barbarians who forced the Rhine defenses, and in the same period, a siege of Rome itself. His only contribution was to make Ravenna into a place of refuge and administration in place of Milan. Aetius, the chief general, exercised great power during the latter part of the reign. Honorius' successor was Valentinian III (423–455).

In the West during this troubled century the emperors after Valentinian III were inconsequential, sometimes merely puppets of others—such as Ricimer, a Suevan commander who made and broke emperors; he was even given the title of Patrician by the eastern emperor, a term that in this period belonged only to the highest officials. This series of ephemeral emperors mostly just tried to survive, looking out for their own political interests and hiring German generals and troops to try to stem the flood of half-civilized peoples that continued to pour across the frontiers. The last of these "Roman" emperors, Romulus Augustulus (475–476), was replaced by a Gothic ruler.

In the East, Arcadius, son of Theodosius, died in 408 and was succeeded by his son, Theodosius II (408–450); since the latter was an infant, the government was run by a praetorian prefect, although Pulcheria, Theodosius' older sister, given the title of augusta, played an influential role—as, later, did Eudocia, Theodosius' wife. Like other eastern emperors in this age, Theodosius intervened in the West— for example, to secure the succession of Valentinian III, the son of Galla Placidia— but on the whole neither he nor his successors were able even to delay the deterioration and fall of Roman dominion there. Theodosius, much preoccupied with religious matters, perhaps is most noted for his promulgation in 438 of a code of law named for him that was important also in its influence on the successor states in the West. He also greatly strengthened the fortifications of Constantinople and added sea walls.

Of the emperors in the eastern empire in the last half of the fifth century, only Zeno (474–491) will be mentioned here. His crowning achievement was the deliverance of his dominions from the Ostrogothic threat by cleverly shuttling them off to Italy.

D. BARBARIANS OVERWHELM THE WEST: ROME SACKED BY VISIGOTHS AND VANDALS

Hunnish pressures, as we have seen, forced Visigoths and others across the Danube in such numbers in the 370s that the eastern emperor, Valens, felt they must be controlled by battle; the result was disaster for Rome at Adrianople in 378. As already noted, Theodosius retrieved the situation and made an agreement with the Visigoths, who afterward gradually shifted toward the West until, under their leader Alaric, they controlled one or two of the provinces along the Danube—including Noricum—and then turned their attention to Italy.

Stilicho, the Vandal general who early in the fifth century would confront Alaric in Italy, had married a niece of Theodosius; he had helped that emperor cope with both the Visigoths and a pagan pretender, Eugenius. Theodosius seems to have intended Stilicho to be regent for both his sons, but high officials in the East foiled his efforts to gain effective control there. Indeed, one of them, a praetorian prefect named Eutropius, used Visigothic leader Alaric to help keep Stilicho away, even naming Alaric master of soldiers in Illyricum. When Alaric and the Visigoths, along with some Alans, invaded Italy in 401, Stilicho drove them out, and he stopped an abortive second invasion two years later. But he spared Alaric when he could have killed him; when he recommended a large payment in gold to the Visigothic leader to gain his help in connection with other serious invasions after 405, he came to be mistrusted and was killed in 408. At the end he could have resisted, probably with success; but he was loyal to Honorius, son of Theodosius, and chose to submit. The West would not again have so competent a leader.

The situation in the West now became desperate: In 405 and after, Vandals, Alans, Suevi, and other barbarians, probably driven by the Huns, streamed across the Rhine. At the same time, a usurper named Constantine seized much of Britain, Gaul, and Spain. Then came another invasion of Italy itself by the Visigoths under Alaric, who really wanted only some agreement with Honorius concerning the position of the Goths and, doubtless, some regular subsidy. The anti-German stance of the court at the time prevented any agreement, and Alaric, after moving about in Italy for a year or more, besieged Rome and took it, in 410. The city was despoiled but not seriously damaged by the Visigoths; most of the Germans were after all Christians, though Arian, and had a sincere respect both for the city and the Church.

Rome had last fallen to the Gauls, eight centuries earlier. This most recent rape of the Eternal City alarmed everyone throughout the civilized world. St. Jerome, from his relatively safe location in Bethlehem, declared that if Rome fell all was lost. Three years after the sack of Rome, he declared himself still "paralyzed by my grief" and added, somewhat exaggeratedly, "the world is falling in ruins . . . the glorious city that was the head of the Roman Empire has been engulfed in one terrific blaze."[3]

The migration of peoples within the western regions continued; Vandals moved into southern Spain and across into Roman Africa, which they subdued and made into a kingdom of their own. The Visigoths in Spain and southwestern Gaul (Aquitaine) were for many years federated allies of the empire, but eventually they did the same.

One of the minor incidents of the Visigothic incursion was to have long-term effects: Galla Placidia Augusta, daughter of Theodosius, half sister of Honorius, was carried off by Alaric into Spain, where the Visigoths migrated. Alaric died in 411 and was succeeded by his brother, Athaulf, who at first viewed Placidia as a bargaining chip in negotiations with the government; somewhat later, however, he took her as his bride. Athaulf came to be pro-Roman, ruling much of Spain as an ally of Rome with official sanction from Honorius. Many Christians, such as the historian Orosius, saw Placidia as the instrument of God in a time of troubles, and they credited her with making her husband into a supporter of the idea of the empire and the rule of law. Their child was called Theodosius; if he had lived he might well one day have been one of the rulers of the West, but he died early and Athaulf was assassinated. Then Placidia was traded back to Honorius. In Ravenna she was now married to a high court official and became the mother of Valentinian III, who, as we have seen, succeeded Honorius; she was virtually the regent for her five-year-old son-emperor, and for about twelve years, really governed the western empire. She continued to have much influence even later, after the general Aetius gained the ascendancy. Always pious and orthodox, Placidia constructed churches in several places, especially at Ravenna. The mausoleum there bearing her name may not be hers, for she was, as she intended, buried in Rome.

Atilla and His Empire

Attila, son of the previous king of the Huns, took over the somewhat loosely organized empire about 434 and from his headquarters in Hungary fashioned it into a more tightly knit unit. Short in stature but impressive in appearance and vain, he was totally intransigent in negotiations: He made outrageous demands as pretexts, and war came on the heels of a refusal to meet them. He reportedly said that he intended to conquer the whole world. Often he threatened and almost as often attacked the eastern empire, which bought him off with tremendous sums of gold. For years he extorted an annual subsidy paid in gold.

In 451 Attila crossed the Rhine with his horde and laid siege to Orleans. Valentinian's general, Aetius, organized the counterstroke. He knew the Huns well: He had been with them for some years as a hostage, and indeed earlier he was a

---

[3]*Epistles* 128: 5; translation of F. A. Wright in the Loeb Classical Library.

friend of Attila. He persuaded the Visigoths, the Franks, and others to join him, and in a celebrated victory at Chalons, forced the Huns out of Gaul. They now invaded Italy and ravaged the Po Valley before withdrawing because of famine and disease—and also because of a Roman embassy led by Pope Leo I. Attila died in 453, and the Hunnish threat was ended.

The Romans had little time to congratulate themselves on their victory. Political intrigue and violence brought the deaths of both Aetius and Valentinian; and then, in 455, the Vandals invaded Italy by sea from North Africa. Their king was Gaiseric, who ruled them for about a half century; it was he who in 429 had led the Vandals in an invasion of Africa because of its wealth and food supply. By 439 he had seized Carthage; he then built a fleet and in pirate fashion roved the sea and scourged the coasts of Sicily. When the Vandals landed in Italy, appeared suddenly before Rome, and seized the city, it was Pope Leo who was again able to influence a barbarian leader: Gaiseric spared the city itself; however, the Vandals thoroughly sacked Rome of its movable wealth before returning to Africa. The "eternal" city by now seemed thoroughly mortal.

The Successor States in the West

In 476, the date conventionally used for the end of the Roman Empire in the West, the last "Roman" emperor, Romulus Augustulus, was replaced by a German, Odoacer. The latter was certainly more competent than the last several ephemeral rulers, and the people of Italy may well have been better off under his control. But the eastern emperor, Zeno, fearing Odoacer's ambitions, took action to eliminate him. In fact, Zeno was able to get rid of two troublesome barbarian kings at once. After the fall of the Hunnish empire, the Ostrogoths had settled in Pannonia on the middle Danube and established a kingdom under Theoderic. The king encroached on the eastern dominions and in general was a thorn in Zeno's side. Zeno now offered to back him in an invasion of Italy and to recognize him as the western emperor if he were successful. Theoderic did indeed take over much of Italy, kill Odoacer, and set up a new kingdom there.

By about A.D. 500, then, the major successor kingdoms in the West were the Ostrogothic Kingdom in Italy (extending to the north), a Saxon Kingdom in Britain, kingdoms of Franks and Burgundians in Gaul, a Visigothic Kingdom in Spain (spilling over into southern Gaul), and the Vandal Kingdom in Africa. Though the fiction of official sovereignty deriving from the sanction of the eastern emperors was long maintained, the fact was that the Roman Empire in the West had disappeared.

The Eastern Roman Empire:
Another Thousand Years

The line of "Roman" emperors in the East did not come to an end in this fateful age as in the West, and the eastern half of the empire continued for another millennium. Historians call it the Late Roman or Eastern Roman Empire, and later

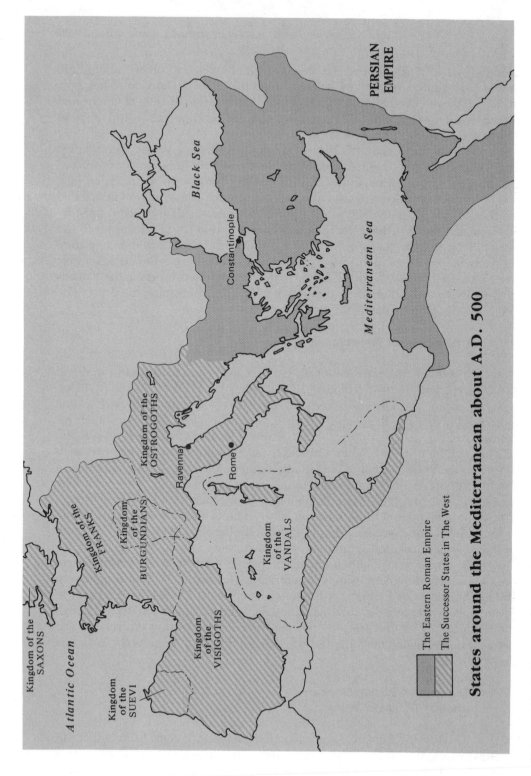

States around the Mediterranean about A.D. 500

States around the Mediterranean about A.D. 500.

the Byzantine Empire (after the Greek name for Constantinople, Byzantium). The term *Roman* may seem anomalous, but in spite of the Greek character of the regime, including the use of Greek as the official language, the citizens called themselves Romans, so strong was the concept of Rome as a symbol of universal rule and of effective government and order. From Constantinople efforts continued even after 500 to regain control over the whole. Most successful was Justinian (527–565); with the help of effective generals, including the romantically interesting Belisarius and the less interesting but very competent eunuch Narses, Justinian reconquered most of Ostrogothic Italy, the Vandal Kingdom in North Africa, and part of Visigothic Spain. Ultimately, however, the effort was too much, and those areas were soon lost to the eastern empire. From the point of view of later history Justinian's most significant achievement was his law code, the *corpus iuris civilis*. Promulgated in 534, it was the most influential code ever put together, the basis for many a modern code as for many of the fundamental principles that underlie even the common law used in Britain and the United States.

Great Christian Figures of the Late Empire

The pagan, highly educated, extremely competent historian of the late fourth century, Ammianus Marcellinus, has perhaps been mentioned in enough detail to indicate the flavor of his work. Almost all other literature important enough for mention in a history survey was by Christian writers. Ambrose (c. 340–397), bishop of Milan, also has appeared in several different contexts; he was more important for his oratory and personal influence than for his writings, but he did write a great deal and much is extant. Most interesting, as may be expected, is his correspondence; most important may be his work *On the Offices*; his exegetical and other works concern only scholars.

Augustine (354–430) is the most influential of all the church fathers. Born in North Africa of a Christian mother, Monica, and a pagan father, Augustine was educated, among other places, at Rome and Milan. He pained his pious mother by living a rather loose life—he even took a concubine—and by toying with Manichaeism, a sort of part-Zoroastrian, part-Gnostic religion with some Christian elements. At Milan, however, he came into contact with Ambrose, who converted him, almost in spite of himself. He returned to North Africa, eventually to become the bishop of Hippo. Most interesting of his many works is his *Confessions*, which tells of his early life. Most significant, surely, is his *City of God*, written near the end of his life. On one level it is a defense of Christianity against the charge that its neglect of the traditional Roman deities caused the decline of the empire; on another, it is Augustine's explication of the way in which God works in history; on still another level it is a synthesis of Christian theology. It was to be strongly influential for centuries, affecting such diverse personalities as Charlemagne and Luther.

Jerome (c. 347–419), too, has been mentioned, primarily for his reaction to disaster in the empire. One of those who strongly influenced him was at one point the bishop of Constantinople, Gregory of Nazianzus, a noted theologian (also mentioned earlier). Born in Dalmatia, Jerome was educated at Rome, and like Augustine he was much attracted by the great pagan literature that he studied as a youth. But as he traveled to Jerusalem a vision came to him at Antioch that caused him to renounce worldly things for a near hermitic existence for three years. He moved to Rome in 382, perhaps at the invitation of Pope Damasus; here he wrote a series of biographies of monks and one of the Apostle Paul; here also he became a kind of spiritual adviser to a group of women, some of whom accompanied him when he removed to Bethlehem for the last decades of his life and gave financial support to his projects, such as hostels for pilgrims. His most important work was his translation of the Bible into the Latin of the common people—the Vulgate, which became the official Bible of the Catholic church.

Orosius, the Christian historian, has also been mentioned. The contemporary of Augustine and his disciple, Orosius wrote *Seven Books of History Against the Pagans,* a tendentious work depending much on Livy in its early books; it was designed to attack paganism and defend Christianity by showing that the troubles of the age were predicted by the prophets. The work is of a much lower quality than that of Ammianus, and it seems to symbolize the decline of literature—and of the age as well.

BOOKS FOR FURTHER READING

ARNHEIM, M. *The Senatorial Aristocracy in the Later Roman Empire,* Oxford, 1972.

BOWERSOCK, G. *Julian the Apostate,* London, 1978.

BROWN, P. *Augustine of Hippo,* Berkeley, 1967.

BROWN, P. *The World of Late Antiquity: A.D. 150–750,* London, 1971.

BURNS, T. *A History of the Ostrogoths,* Bloomington, Ind., 1984.

DOWNEY, G. *The Late Roman Empire,* New York, 1969.

DREW, K. *The Barbarian Invasions,* New York, 1970.

FREND, W. *The Rise of Christianity,* Philadelphia, 1984.

HAYWOOD, R. *The Myth of Rome's Fall,* New York, 1958.

JONES, A. *The Later Roman Empire,* 2 vols., Norman, Okla., 1964.

JONES, T. *In the Twilight of Antiquity,* Minneapolis, 1978.

KELLEY, J. *Jerome: His Life, Writings, and Controversies,* London, 1975.

LAISTNER, M. *Christianity and Pagan Culture in the Later Empire,* Ithaca, N.Y., 1951.

LAISTNER, M. *The Conflict Between Pagan and Christian in the Fourth Century,* Oxford, 1963.

MACMULLEN, R. *Soldier and Civilian in the Later Roman Empire,* Cambridge, Mass., 1963.

MAENCHEN-HELFEN, J. *The World of the Huns,* Berkeley, 1973.

OOST, S. *Galla Placidia Augusta,* Chicago, 1968.

RANDERS-PEHRSON, J. *Barbarians and Romans: The Birth Struggle of Europe, 400–700,* Norman, Okla., 1983.

THOMPSON, E. *Romans and Barbarians: The Decline of the Western Empire,* Madison, 1982.

VOGT, J. *The Decline of Rome,* Eng. trans., New York, 1967.

22

OUR HERITAGE FROM ANTIQUITY:

the essential substructures of modern civilization

A. THE HERITAGE FROM THE ANCIENT NEAR EAST

The Most Basic Foundations

The first tender plants of civilization were nourished in the Near East—and nurtured to maturity. Among those tender plants was the capacity to produce food, and the development of that capacity led to population growth. The greater density of population in turn created problems, each of which when solved produced new social institutions and, ultimately, political institutions as well. Problem solving in one area thus led to the earliest legal systems, as we have seen.

A systematic agriculture with an increasing variety of tools was absolutely essential to the genesis of this early civilization. The economy of all the ancient world rested on agriculture. Indeed, even the economy of the modern world rests on agriculture to a degree that is often unsuspected. The ability of twentieth century industrial nations to import needed foodstuffs sometimes causes leaders to overemphasize industry and neglect agriculture. But the readers of this book may see the day when a highly industrialized state may no longer count confidently on the easy availability of foodstuffs from other regions of the world.

The intellectual basis for civilization, too, was laid in the Near East, where the accumulation of information was made possible by systems of writing. The alphabet is the gift of the Near East. The first seeds of literature, philosophy, medicine, surgery, pharmacology—all the fruits of the mind of humankind that may be recorded in writing and preserved for the future—were sown in the ancient Near East.

A Religious Outlook on Life

It may sometimes seem that modern humanity's god is Materialism and that Scientists are the prophets. Yet it is nonetheless true that religion remains a vital ingredient in the lives of many—perhaps most—peoples of the world, Americans among them. The threads of our beliefs go back to the ancient Near East. The unique contributions of the Hebrews and Persians are well known, but religion was a fundamental element in all civilizations of the Near East from the very beginning.

At its worst, religion has served as a tool—all the more effective when those who use it also believe in it—used by the upper classes to help them control those beneath them. At its best, religion has called forth the most spiritual thought and the most altruistic actions of which humans are capable. Some of both the best and the worst can be found in the heritage of the Near East.

As is usual with historians of Western civilization, we have passed in this book from the ancient Near East to Greece and Rome with only an occasional look back to the cradle of civilization. It would be a mistake to assume, however, that in these later phases of history the Near East—and at intervals the Far East—had no impact on the direction of events or the development of occidental culture. The great philosophical systems of the West were drawn up by men who felt the influence of the older and more mature Near East. The Roman Empire, in both structure and ideal, gradually acquired an orientalized form. And at last an oriental religion—Christianity—suffused all of Western civilization and changed all it touched.

B. THE HERITAGE OF GREECE

The Rational Approach to Life

Since the days of the Renaissance, modern people in the Western world have attempted, none too successfully, to combine the religious approach to life characteristic of the Orient (especially the Judeo-Christian view of God and humankind) with the rational approach first worked out by Greek thinkers. Reason made possible the separation of superstition from real religion and tended to relegate religion to its proper sphere. Reason brought the beginnings of science and with it the first systematic approach to an understanding of the nature of the physical world. Reason caused people to take fresh looks at all their institutions, with some various and interesting results. Reason developed philosophical systems that brought a free-ranging reevaluation of humanity's position in the universe, its ethical values. In all these things Greeks were pioneers of the mind.

Literature

Several categories of literature were either created by the Greeks or given form and style by them. Homer may have had the advantage of an epic tradition that went back to the Sumerian's saga of Gilgamesh. Yet he created the world's greatest epic. Herodotus knew of works of a basic historical nature that were ancient when he was born, yet to a considerable degree he created history as a discipline; and Thucydides has been the most-imitated historian who ever lived. The myriad forms and styles of Greek poetry have served as models for every generation of poets since the days of Sappho—which is not to say, of course, that nothing new developed after the Greeks.

Theater and Art

The theater was purely a Greek invention. Of the world's greatest playwrights, whether tragic or comic, several were Greek. No more influential way than the theater has yet been devised for transmitting and disseminating thought and feeling, though to be sure, modern television and movie screens make possible a wider viewing of dramatic productions.

In architecture and sculpture the Greek influence has been as tremendous as it has been enduring. Though today's architects no longer place Greek-style columns and porticoes on their buildings, their ideas of line and function show that they still drink from Greek springs. It is, in short, impossible to imagine a world in which the ancient Greeks will not continue to have an enormous intellectual impact.

C. THE HERITAGE OF ROME

In many ways Rome served as a transmitter of ideas, not a creator. Yet to many things Rome imparted its own peculiar stamp, and in some ways the Romans did make original contributions.

Government: Idea and Structure

A most important idea passed on by Rome was that of the unity of the civilized world. The idea was transmitted by Rome not so much on the basis of theory as on the basis of political achievement. The idea itself derived in part from the ephemeral achievement of Alexander the Great and from the great oriental empires that preceded him, in particular the Persian with its concept of one world. Kings of the European states in the centuries after the fall of Rome often aspired to a Roman—that is to say, a universal—state. Hence the medieval use of the term *Holy Roman Empire*, which, despite its name, never approached the ideal. Leaders, not only of the Roman Empire's immediate successor states in the West, but also those of states existing into recent times, looked to Rome also for ideas about specific structures. In the French revolutionary period there were consuls, tribunes, tribunates, and other bodies named after Roman structures, though they were hardly Roman in reality. And in the New World, it was no accident that the upper house of the United States Congress was given the name *Senate*.

Much of a society's governmental structure is expressed in law, and here, it must be reemphasized, is one of Rome's greatest achievements. Again the influence was perhaps stronger a century and a half ago—the Code Napoleon, for example, was specifically based on Roman law—but all the codes and procedures used in Western countries today still owe much to Rome.

Language and Literature

Several of the major languages of the Western world are termed *Romance* because they derive directly from Rome, from dialects of the Latin. Several other of the major tongues of the world have been affected by the Latin vocabulary and Latin grammar. The grammatical influence has not always been beneficial: Attempts to impose the Latin forms on German and English, for example, have not always yielded happy results.

Latin literature must rank second to Greek. It was not, however, merely imitative; on the contrary, Latin prose and poetry have real distinction. The influence of Latin literature was great in early modern times, partly because Latin was more easily read by Western scholars than Greek. Yet thousands of those who could read both have preferred, say, Cicero's congenial style to the heavier language of Thucydides or the more difficult dialectics of Plato. Satire, history, and biography are among the strengths often noted in Latin literature.

D. ANCIENT INFLUENCE TODAY: DISPARATE VIEWS

That the minds of those knowledgeable about the heritage of the ancient world should be impressed with such disparate views regarding that heritage is rather amusing. On the one hand, some, remembering the wealth of ideas and practices that still persist and feeling that the basic changes in modern times are fundamentally inconsequential and technological, think that everything of importance in the modern world owes much to the ancient. On the other hand, others, feeling perhaps overwhelmed in a world of change, a world that seems to have lost its awareness of its traditions, and with that its stability, feel that the ancient world's influence has shrunk to nothingness. Doubtless the truth lies somewhere in between. Wherever it lies, no educated person in today's Western world can doubt that the wellsprings of one's civilization have their sources deep in ancient soil.

INDEX

For major entries, see also Table of Contents and Charts